AUTHENTIC TRANSCRIPTIONS WITH NOTES AND TABLATURE

The Best of Melissa Etheridge

CONTENTS

Music transcriptions by Pete Billmann, Jeff Jacobson, David Stocker and Jeff Story

ISBN 978-0-634-04579-0

7777 W. Bluemound Rd. P.O. Box 13819 Milwaukee, WI 53213

from *Yes I Am*

All American Girl

Words and Music by Melissa Etheridge

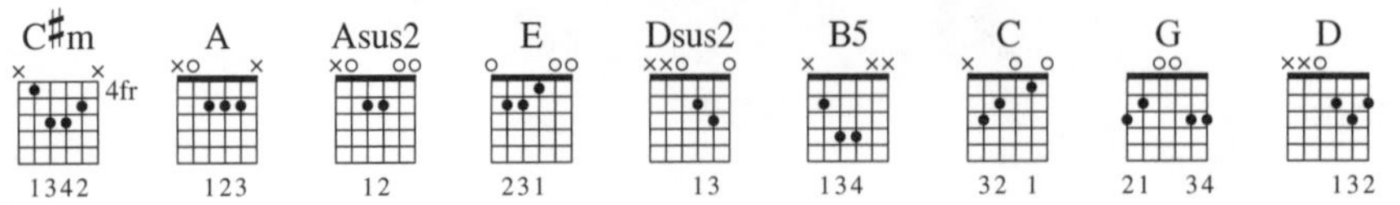

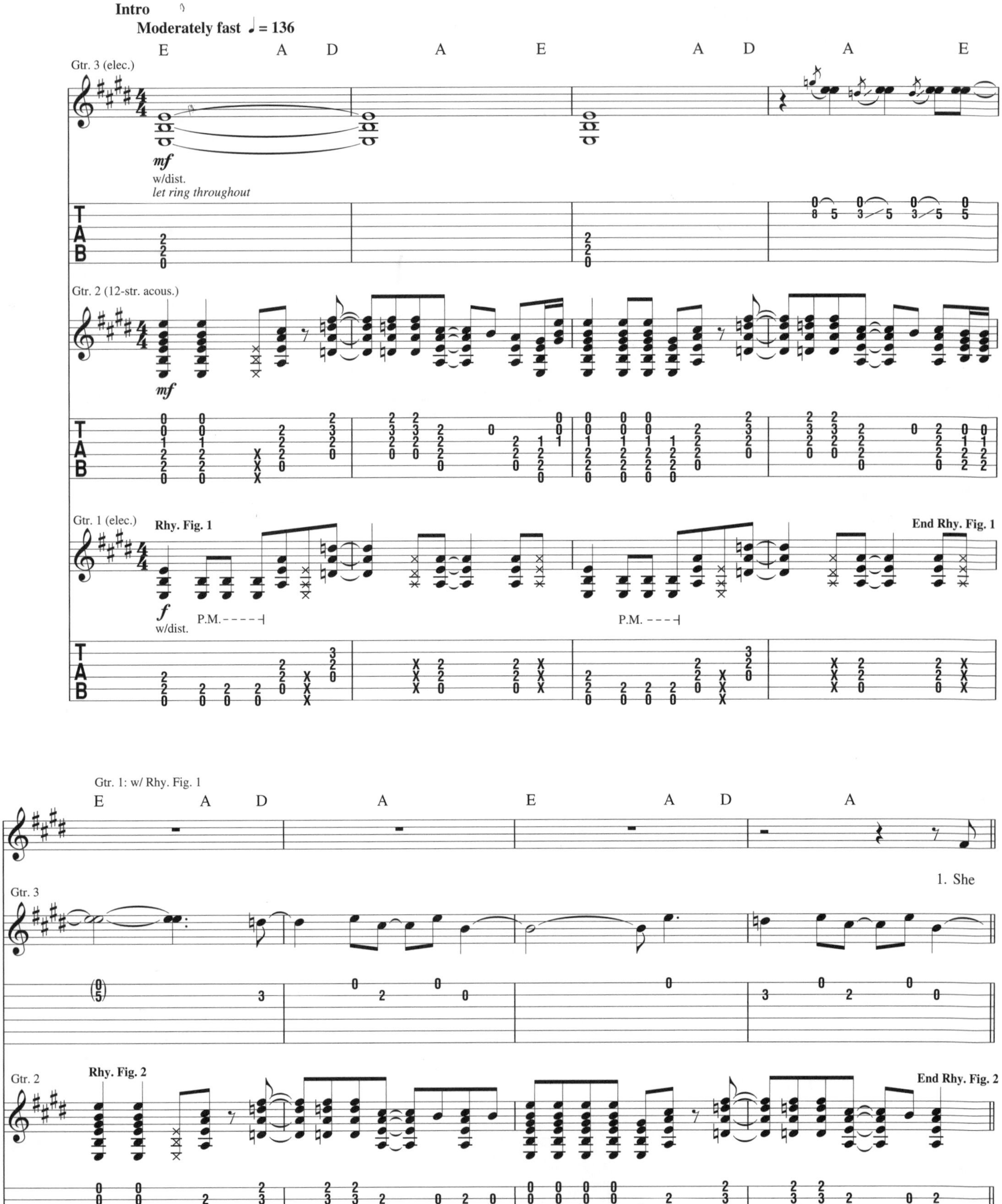

C♯m
A
Asus2
E
Dsus2
B5
C
G
D
4fr

Intro
Moderately fast ♩ = 136
E A D A E A D A E
Gtr. 3 (elec.)
mf
w/dist.
let ring throughout
Gtr. 2 (12-str. acous.)
mf
Gtr. 1 (elec.)
Rhy. Fig. 1
End Rhy. Fig. 1
f
w/dist.
P.M.
Gtr. 1: w/ Rhy. Fig. 1
E A D A E A D A
1. She
Gtr. 3
Gtr. 2
Rhy. Fig. 2
End Rhy. Fig. 2

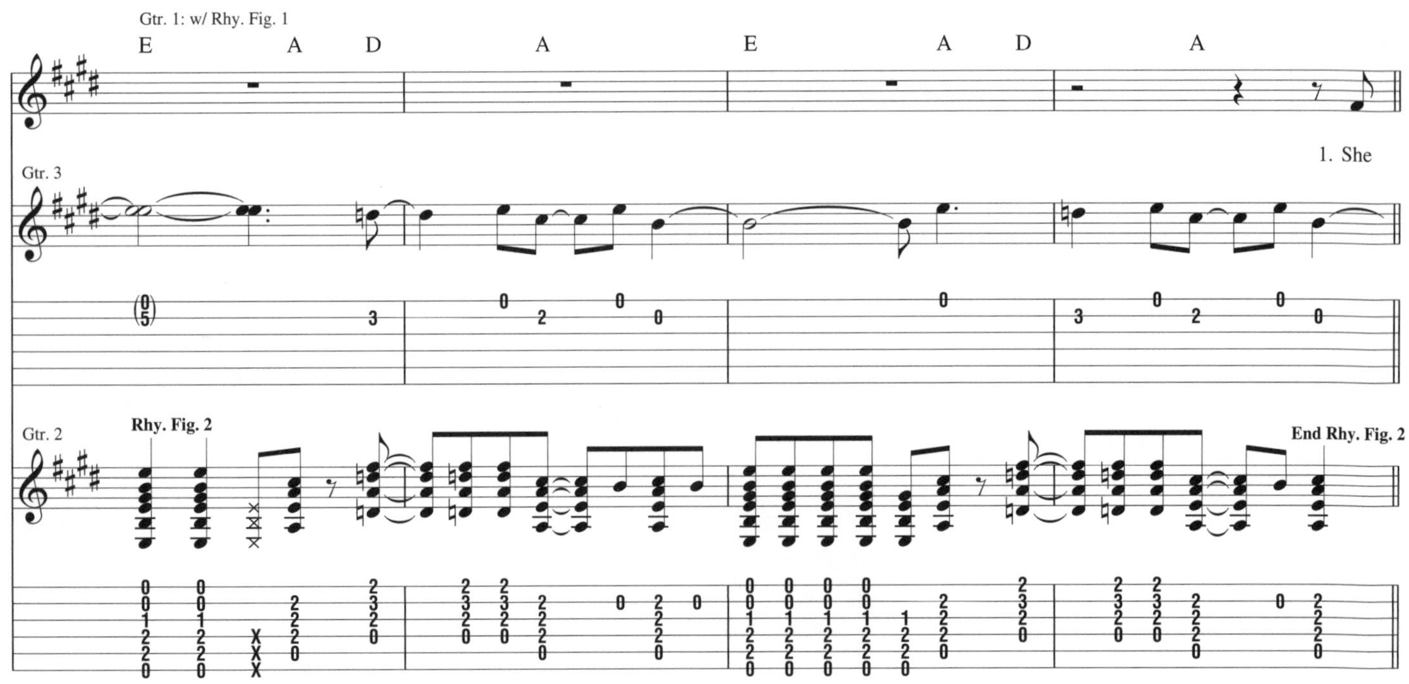

Verse
Gtr. 3 tacet
B5
A5
E
A
D
A
wakes up in the morn - ing
with a pain in her jet ___ black
head. ___
Gtr. 3
Gtr. 2
Gtr. 2
divisi
Rhy. Fig. 3A
End Rhy. Fig. 3A
P.M.
Gtr. 1
Rhy. Fig. 3
End Rhy. Fig. 3
P.M.
P.M.
P.M.

Gtrs. 1 & 2: w/ Rhy. Figs. 3 & 3A
B5
A5
E
A
D
A
De - caf cof - fee in her hand ___
and a Marl - bor - o red. ___
She drives ___

Bridge
C♯m
A
Asus2
E
Rhy. Fig. 4A
Gtr. 2
___ down to the of - fice
in her Jap - a - nese ___ car ___
with the ra - di - o ___ blast - ing. She dreams of
Gtr. 1
Rhy. Fig. 4

Dsus2
Gtr. 2
tak - in' it too far (But) to - day she'll pay the bills. She won't
Gtr. 3
mf
Gtr. 1
A
Asus2
B5
End Rhy. Fig. 4A
think a - bout the thrills that pass a - way. She's an
End Rhy. Fig. 4
P.M.
Chorus
Gtr. 1: w/ Rhy. Fig. 1 (2 times)
Gtr. 2: w/ Rhy. Fig. 2 (2 times)
E A D A E A D
all A - mer - i - can girl,
Gtr. 3
Rhy. Fig. 5
P.M.
P.M.

A E A D A E A D
an all A - mer - i - can girl.
Gtr. 3
P.M.
Gtr. 3 tacet
A A Asus2 A Asus2 B5
Gtr. 2
She will live and die in this man's world, an
End Rhy. Fig. 5
Gtr. 1
P.M.
To Coda
Gtr. 1: w/ Rhy. Fig. 1
Gtr. 2: w/ Rhy. Fig. 2
N.C. E A D A E A D A
all A - mer - i - can girl.
2. Her eyes
Verse
Gtrs. 1 & 2: w/ Rhy. Figs. 3 & 3A (2 times)
B5 A5 E A D A
are black as leath-er, and her hair is kill-er red.
How
Gtr. 3
Rhy. Fig. 6
End Rhy. Fig. 6
P.M.

Gtr. 3: w/ Rhy. Fig. 6
B5
A5
E
A D
A
could she keep the ba - by
when she could bare - ly keep her head?
She don't

Bridge

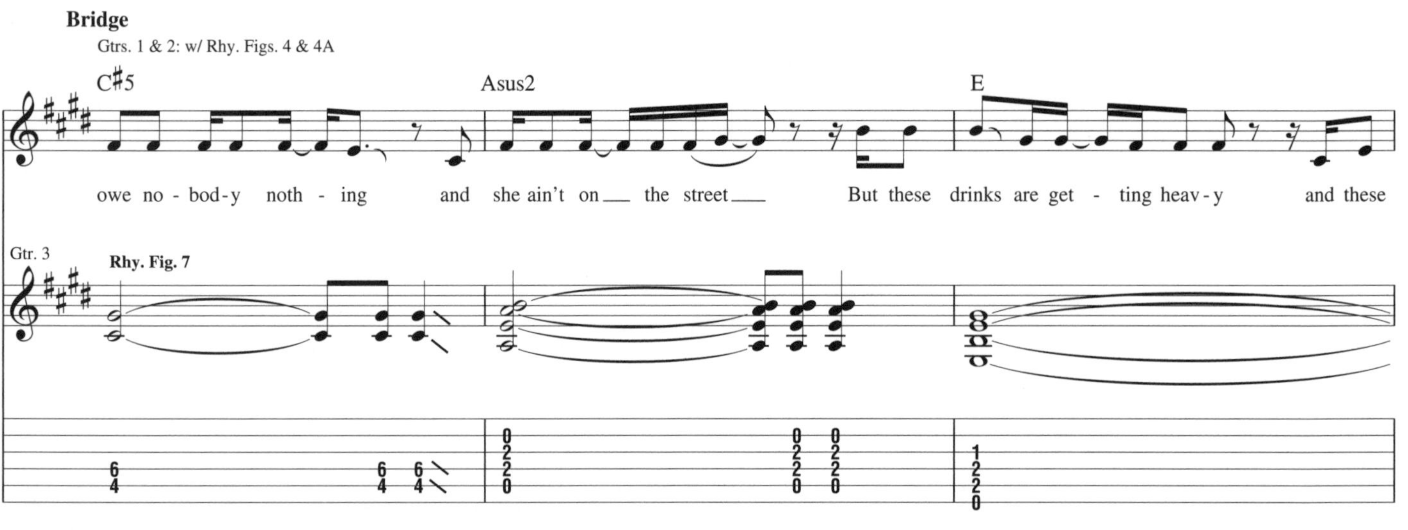
Gtrs. 1 & 2: w/ Rhy. Figs. 4 & 4A
C♯5
Asus2
E
owe no - bod - y noth - ing
and she ain't on the street
But these drinks are get - ting heav - y and these
Gtr. 3
Rhy. Fig. 7

Esus4
E
Dsus2
tips are get - ting weak.
And she don't un - der - stand
why she can't

D.S. al Coda
A
Asus2
B5
climb out of the sand
and break a - way.
She's an
End Rhy. Fig. 7

Coda
Half-time feel
C
G
Gtr. 2
girl.
Gtr. 1
hold bend
Gtr. 3
End half-time feel
D
A
dim.
Gtr. 2: w/ Rhy. Fig. 2 (2 times)
E
A
D
A
E
A
D
A
Spoken: All right.
Oh, yeah.
Come on.
Oh.
Gtr. 1
Gtr. 3
divisi

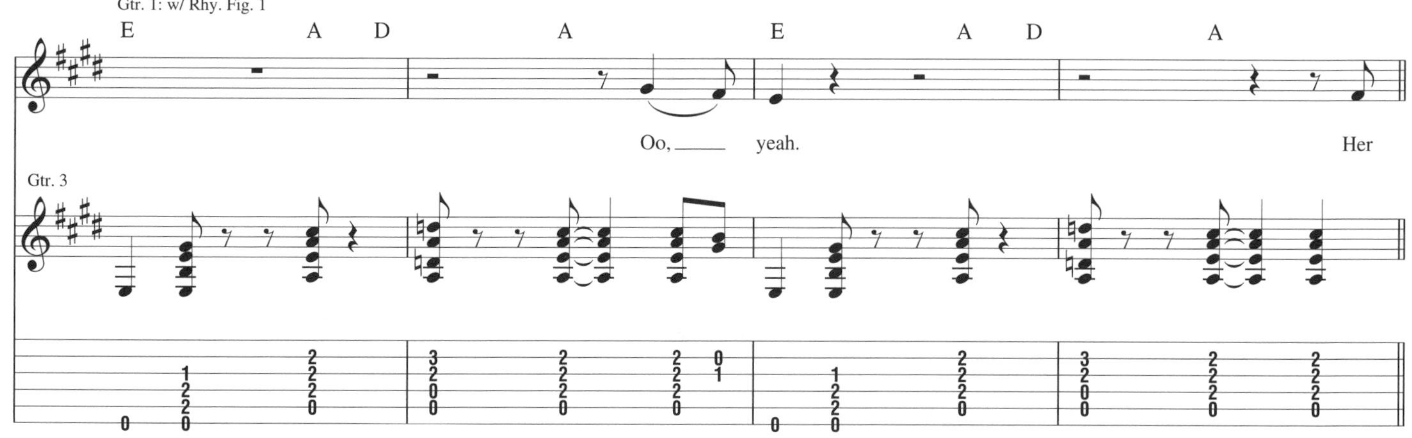

Gtr. 1: w/ Rhy. Fig. 1
E A D A E A D A
Oo, yeah. Her
Gtr. 3

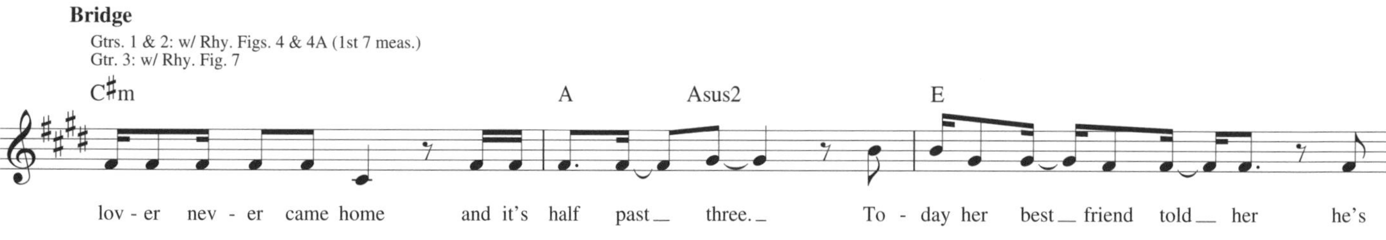

Bridge
Gtrs. 1 & 2: w/ Rhy. Figs. 4 & 4A (1st 7 meas.)
Gtr. 3: w/ Rhy. Fig. 7
C♯m A Asus2 E
lov - er nev - er came home and it's half past three. To - day her best friend told her he's

Esus4 E Dsus2 A Asus2
H. I. V. Some - thing's got - ta give some - where. Forc-ing cir - cles in - to squares,

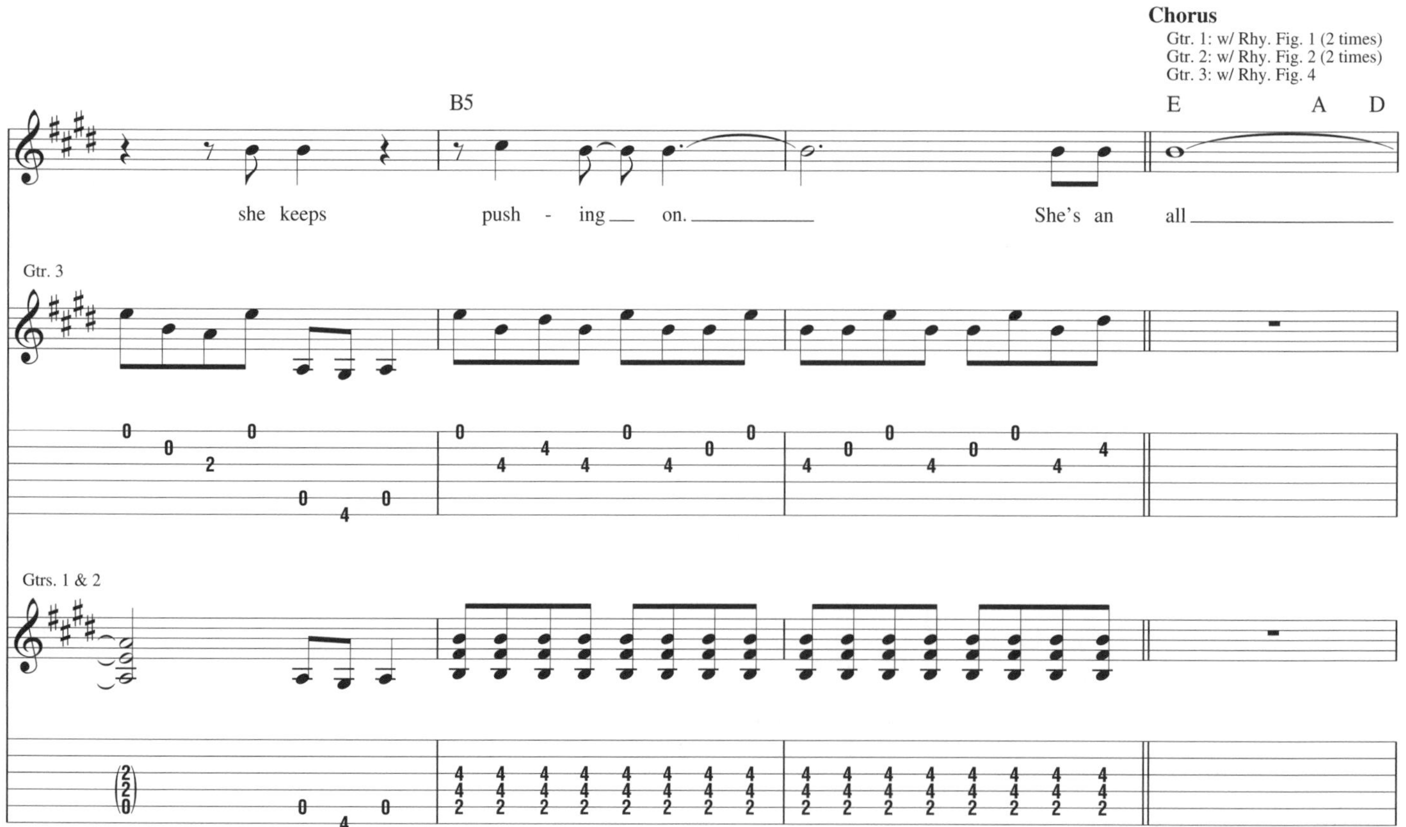

Chorus
Gtr. 1: w/ Rhy. Fig. 1 (2 times)
Gtr. 2: w/ Rhy. Fig. 2 (2 times)
Gtr. 3: w/ Rhy. Fig. 4
B5 E A D
she keeps push - ing on. She's an all
Gtr. 3
Gtrs. 1 & 2

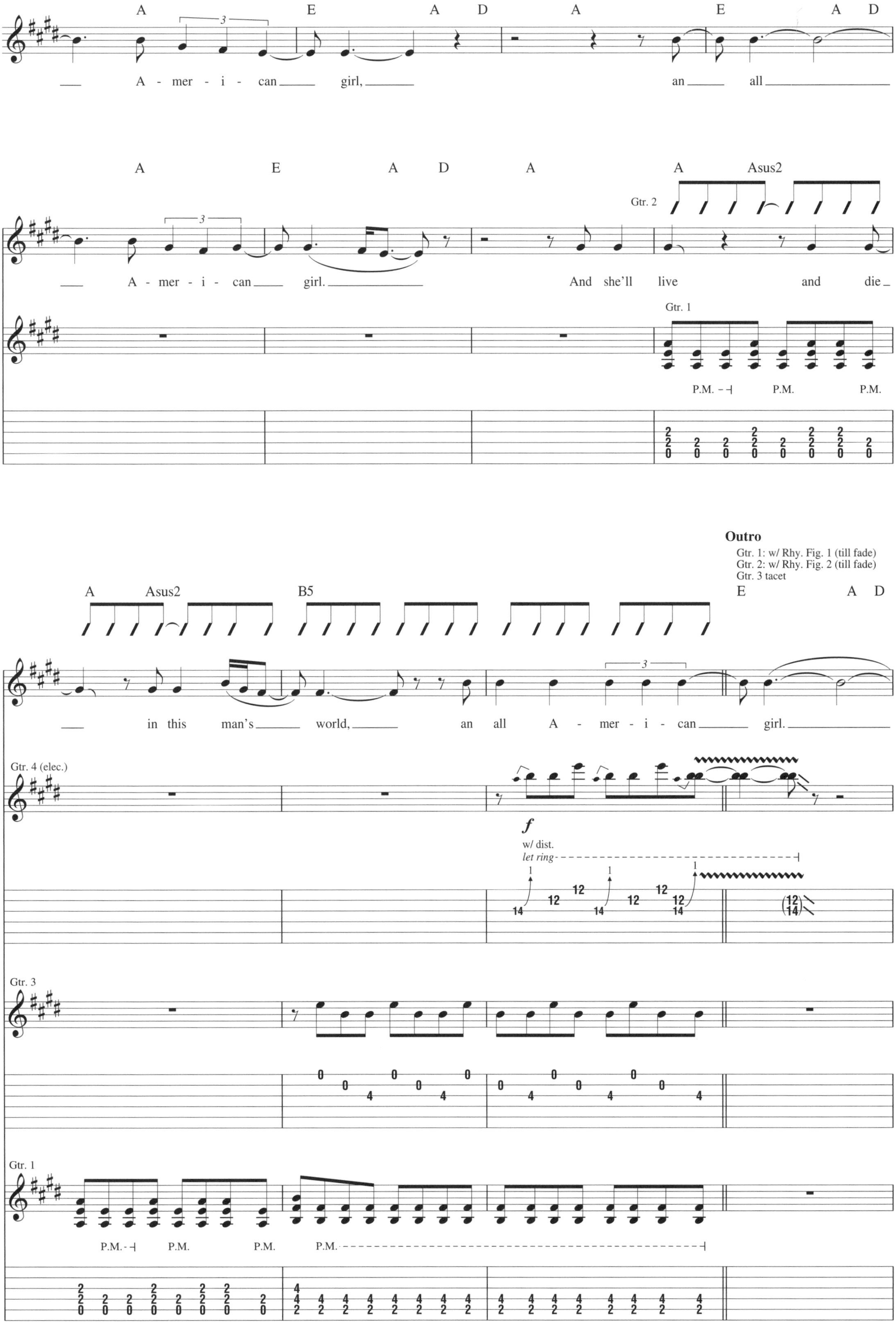

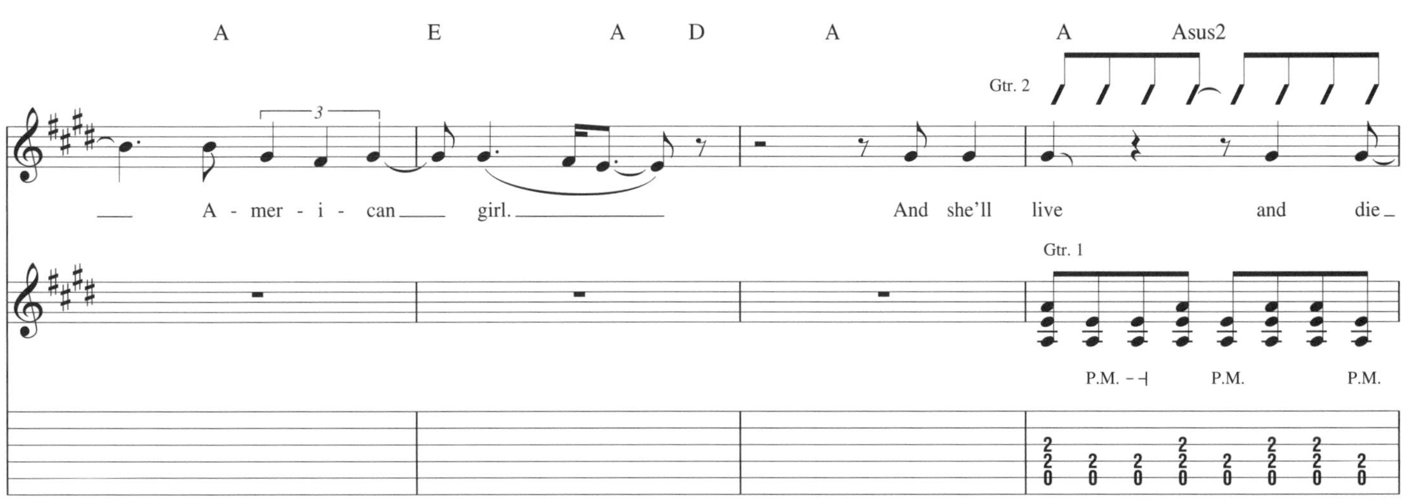

Outro

Gtr. 1: w/ Rhy. Fig. 1 (till fade)
Gtr. 2: w/ Rhy. Fig. 2 (till fade)
Gtr. 3 tacet

A Asus2 B5 E A D

in this man's world, an all A - mer - i - can girl.

Gtr. 4 (elec.)

f

w/ dist.

let ring

Gtr. 3

Gtr. 1

P.M. P.M. P.M. P.M.

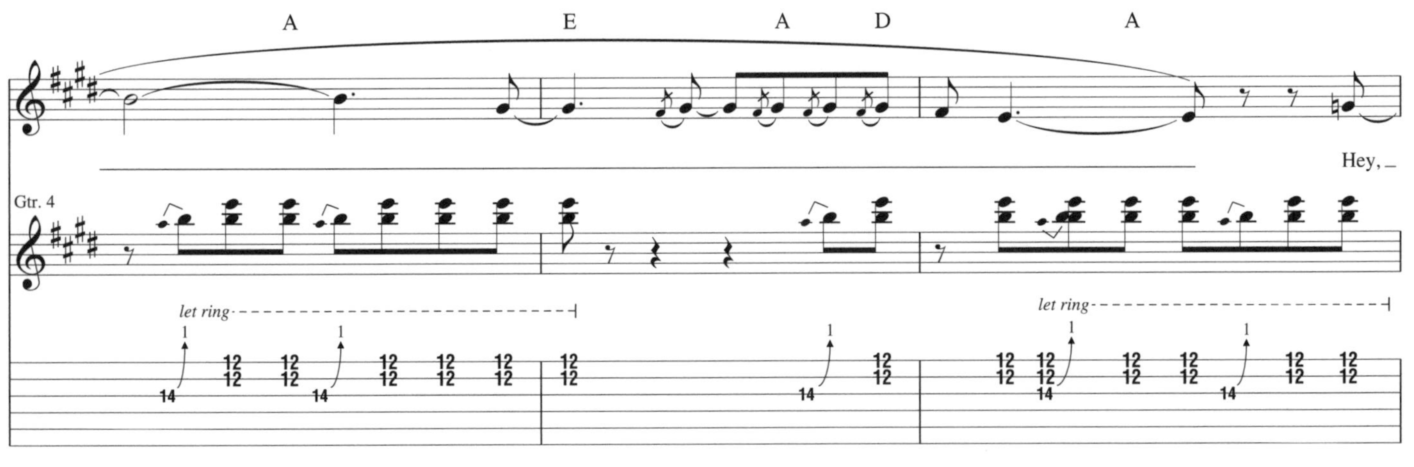
A E A D A
Hey,
Gtr. 4
let ring
let ring

E A D A E A D
she's all A - mer - i - can, yeah.
*Both strings are bent with ring finger.

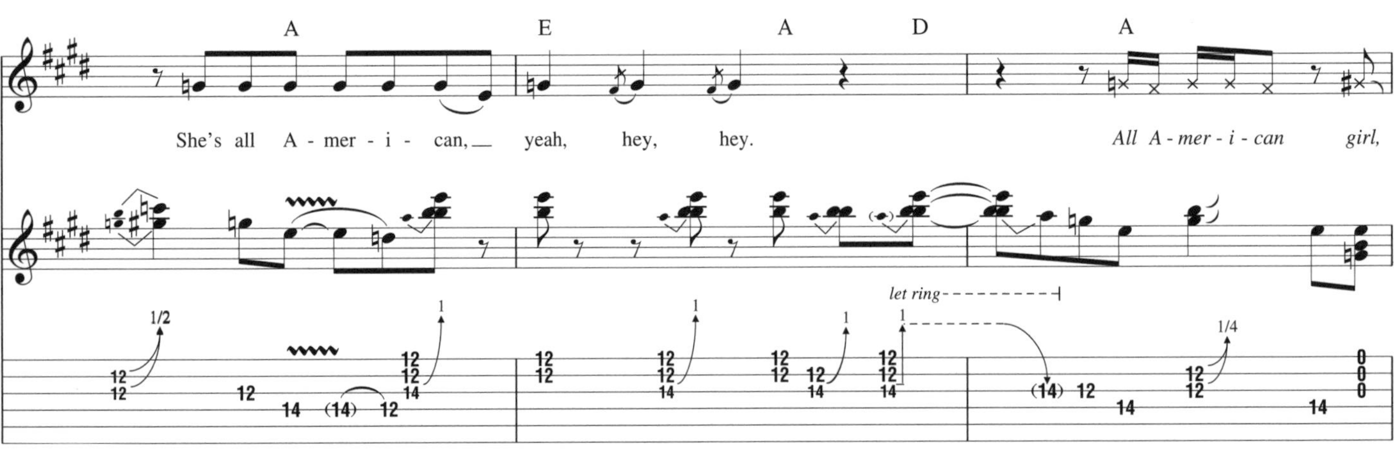
A E A D A
She's all A - mer - i - can, yeah, hey, hey. All A - mer - i - can girl,
let ring

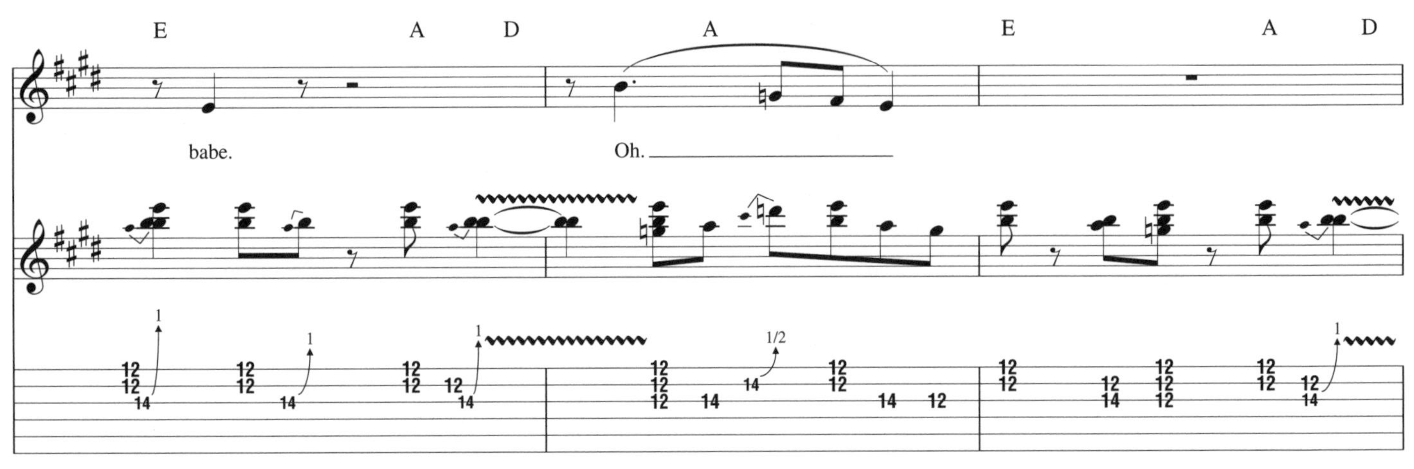
E A D A E A D
babe. Oh.

A E A D A
She's all A - mer - i - can, yeah, hey. An all A - mer - i - can girl.
E A D A E A D
Begin fade
A E A D A E A D
Hey. Oh. Oh. Oh.
A E A D A E A D
Fade out
Yeah. Yeah. Yeah.

from *Melissa Etheridge*

Bring Me Some Water

Words and Music by Melissa Etheridge

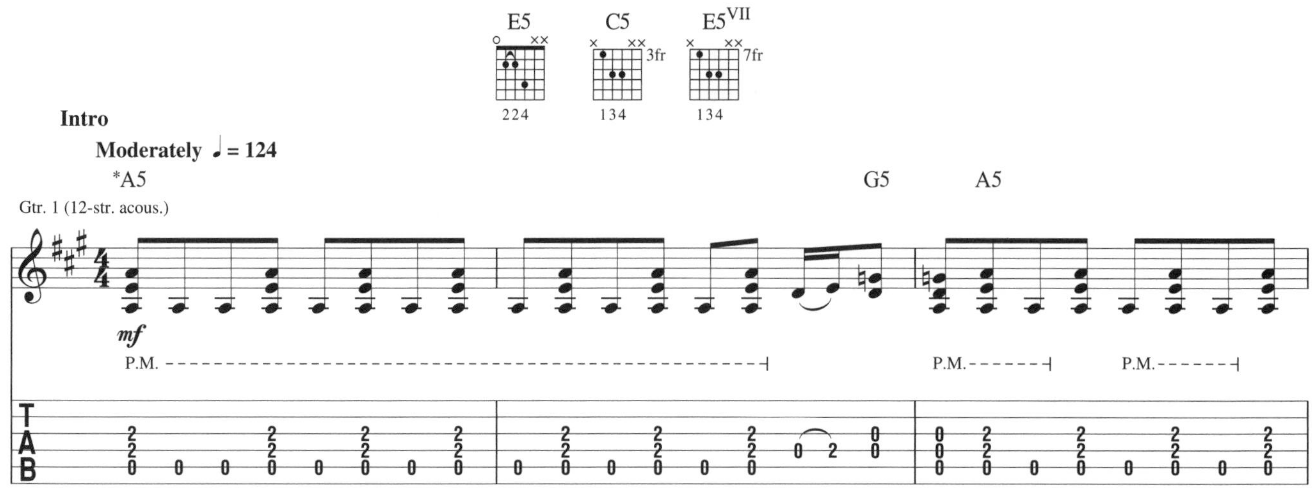

* Chord symbols reflect overall harmony.

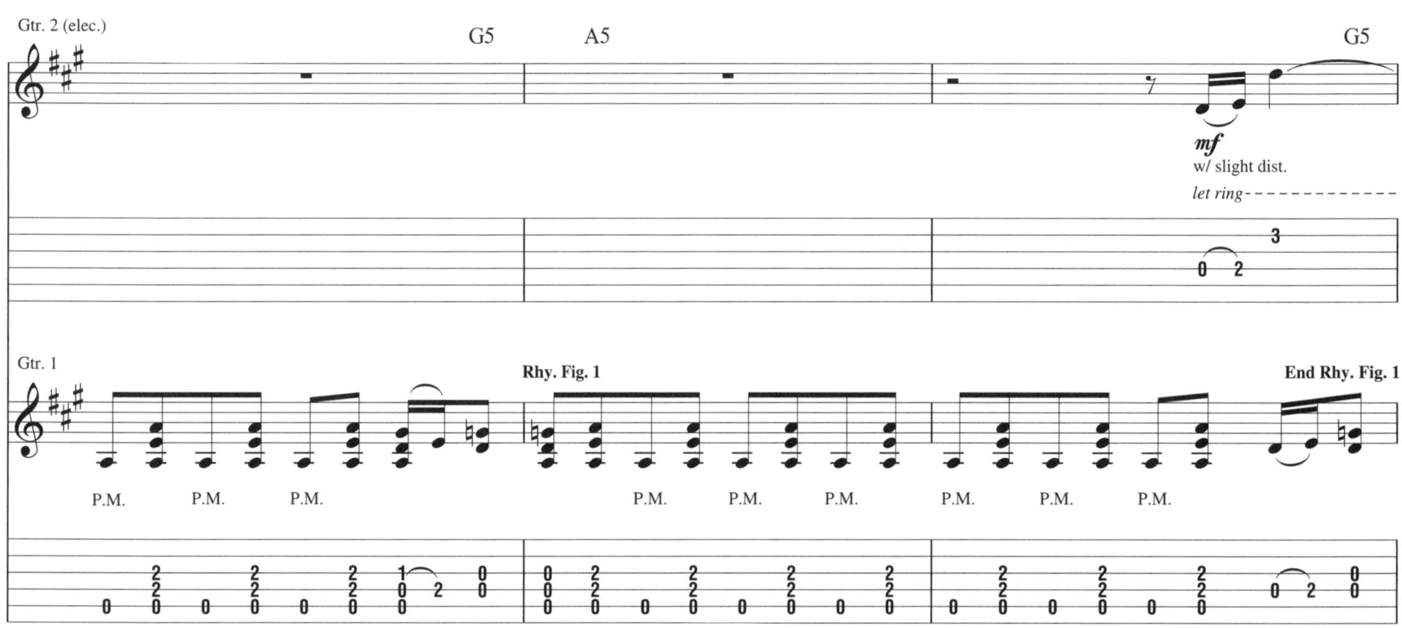

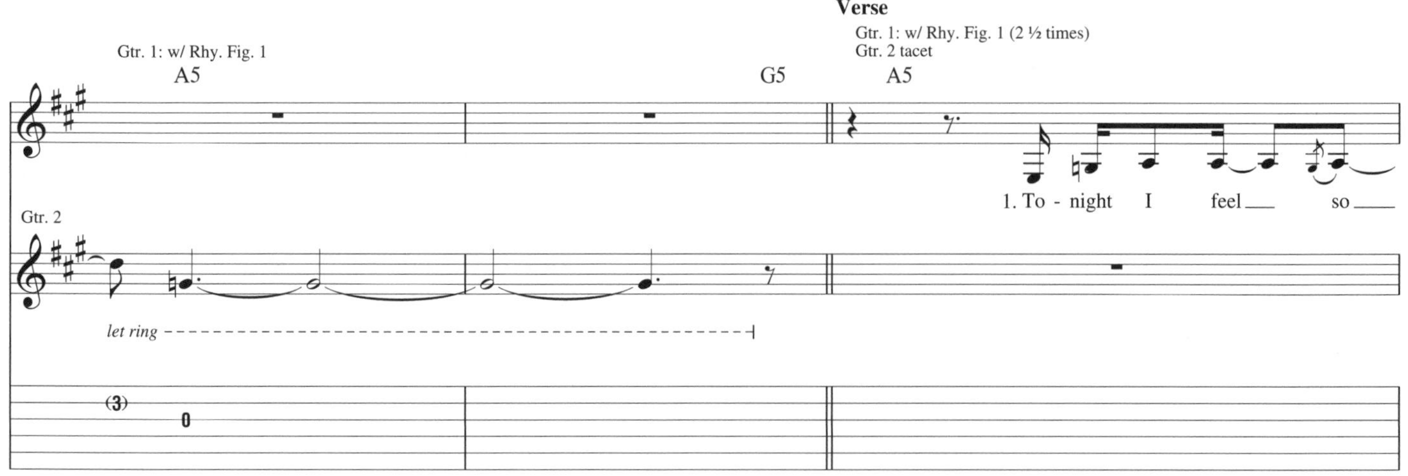

G5
A5
G5
weak,
but all in love is fair.
Gtr. 2
let ring

A5
A7
N.C.
I turn the oth - er cheek,
and I feel the slap and the sting of the
Gtr. 2
let ring
Gtr. 1
P.M.
P.M.
P.M.

D7
D5
D7
D5
D7
D5
foul night air. And I know you're on - ly hu - man. And I
let ring
Rhy. Fig. 2
P.M.
P.M.
P.M.
P.M.
P.M.

G5 A5
G5 A5
D7 D5
D7
have - n't got talk - in' room.
But, to - night while I'm mak - ing ex -
let ring
P.M.

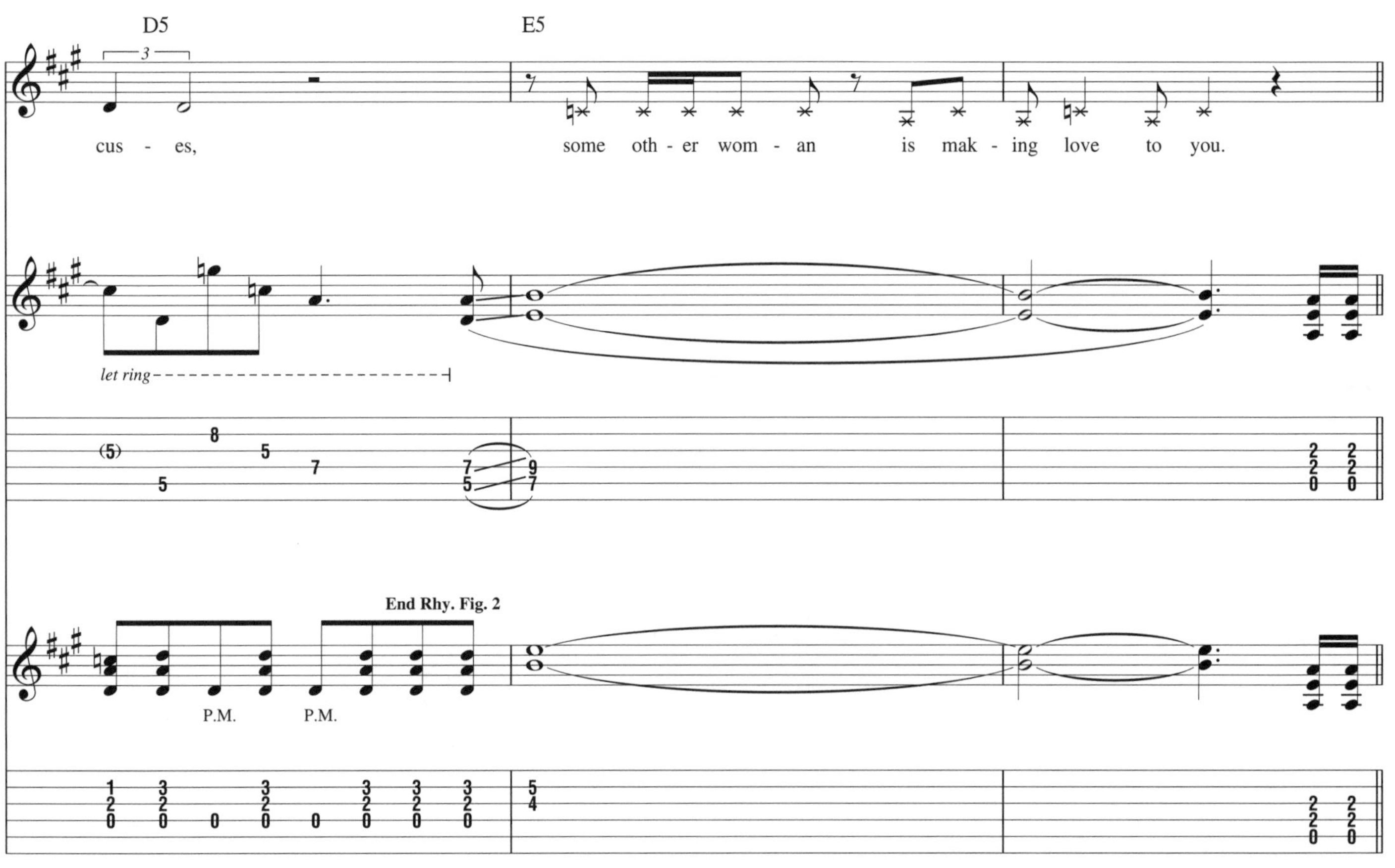
D5
E5
cus - es,
some oth - er wom - an is mak - ing love to you.
let ring
End Rhy. Fig. 2
P.M.

Chorus
Gtr. 1: w/ Rhy. Fig. 3 (6 times)
A5
G5
Dsus2
A5
G5
Some - bod - y bring me some wa - ter.
Can't you see I'm burn - in' a - live.
Gtr. 2
let ring
Gtr. 1
Rhy. Fig. 3
End Rhy. Fig. 3
let ring

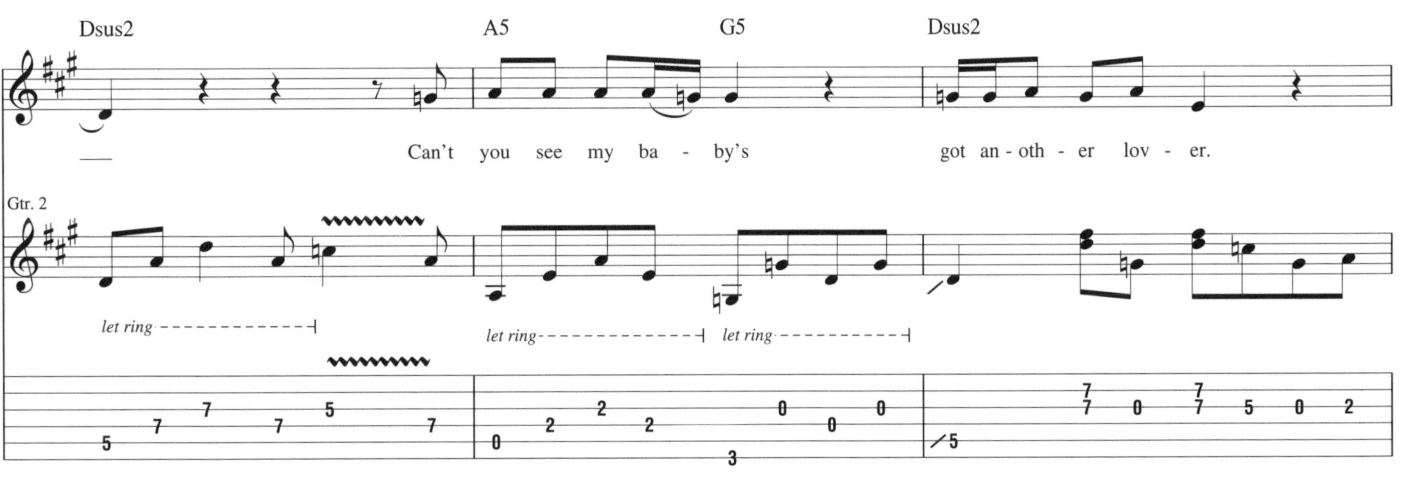
Dsus2
A5
G5
Dsus2
Can't you see my ba - by's got an - oth - er lov - er.
Gtr. 2
let ring

A5
G5
Dsus2
A5
G5
I don't know how I'm gon - na sur - vive.
Some - bod - y bring me some wa -
let ring
1/4

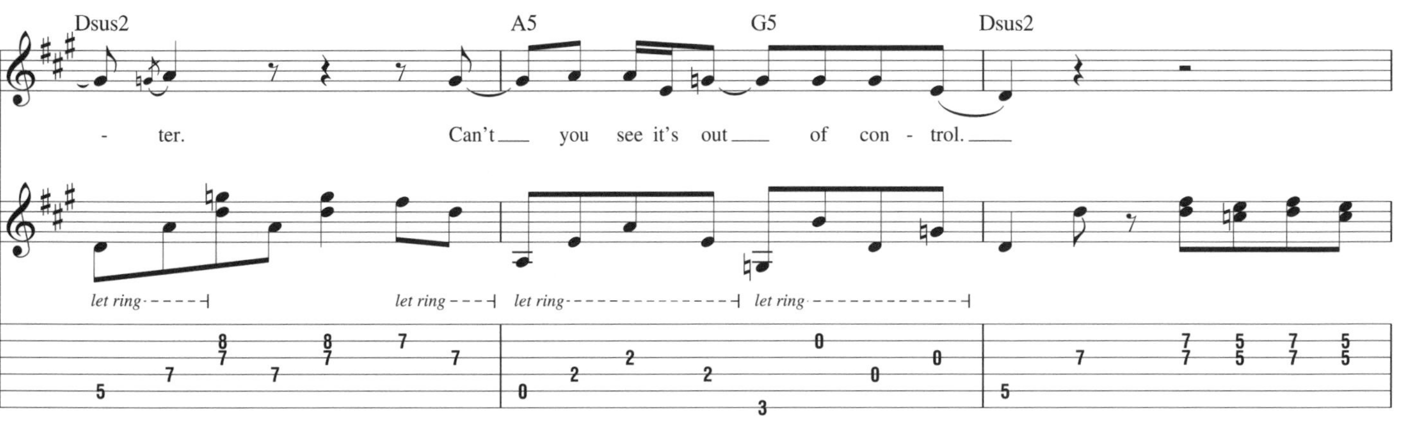
Dsus2
A5
G5
Dsus2
- ter.
Can't you see it's out of con - trol.
let ring
let ring
let ring
let ring

A5
G5
Dsus2
E5
Ba - by's got my heart, and my ba-by's got my mind. But to - night the sweet dev - il, the
Gtr. 2
let ring
let ring
let ring
Gtr. 1

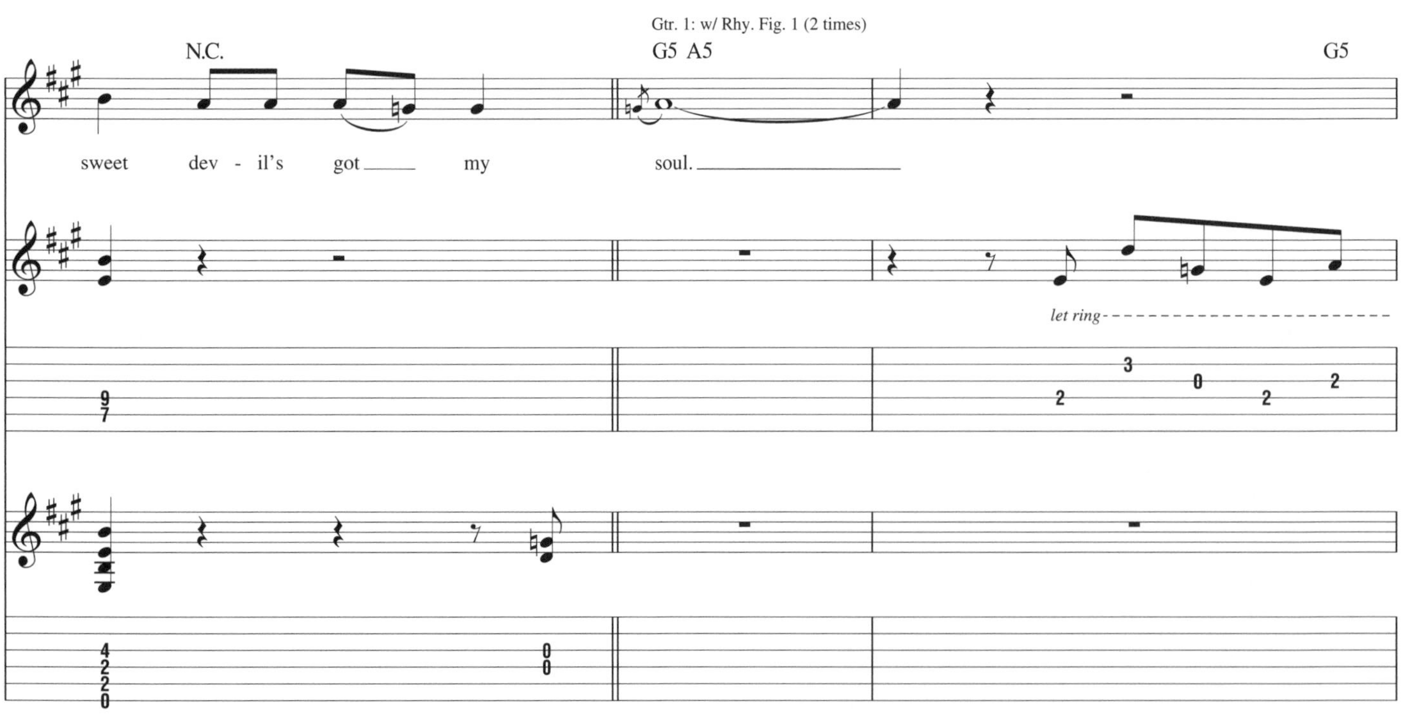
Gtr. 1: w/ Rhy. Fig. 1 (2 times)
N.C.
G5 A5
G5
sweet dev - il's got my soul.
let ring

Verse

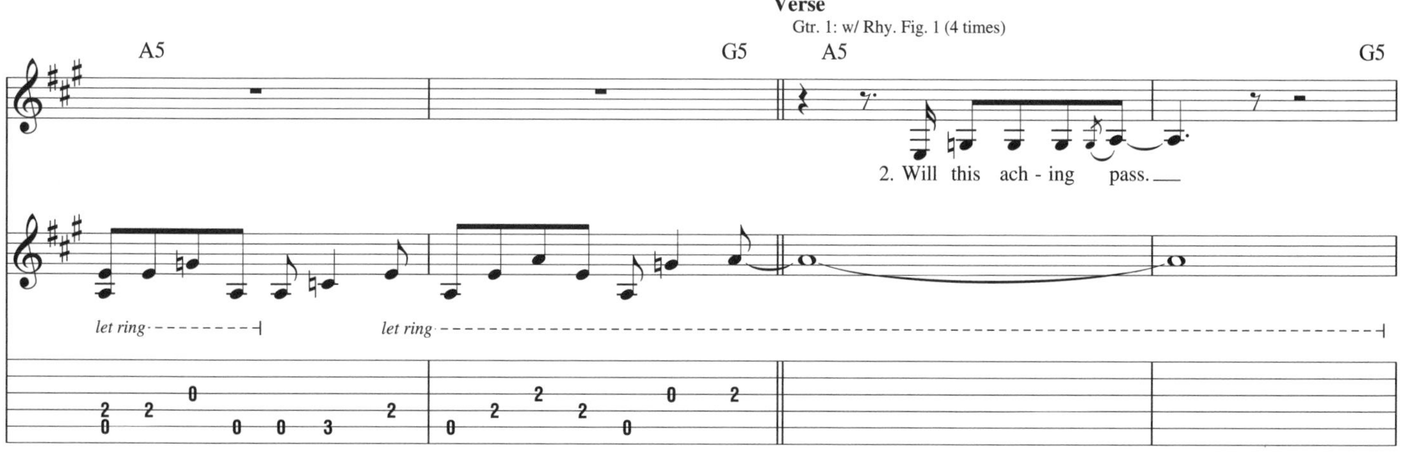
Verse
Gtr. 1: w/ Rhy. Fig. 1 (4 times)
A5
G5
A5
G5
2. Will this ach - ing pass.
let ring
let ring

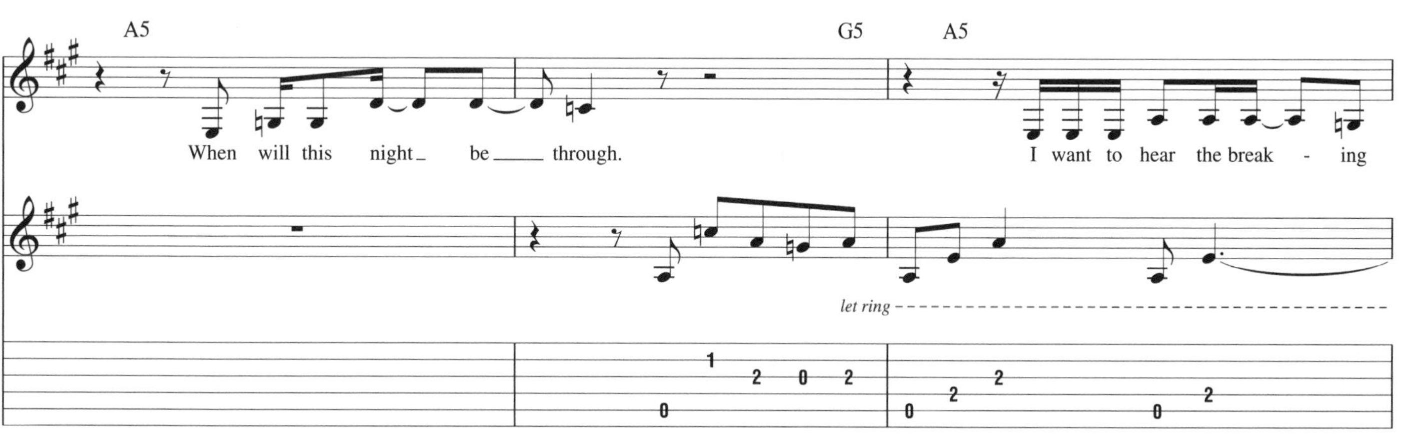
A5
G5
A5
When will this night be through.
I want to hear the break - ing
let ring

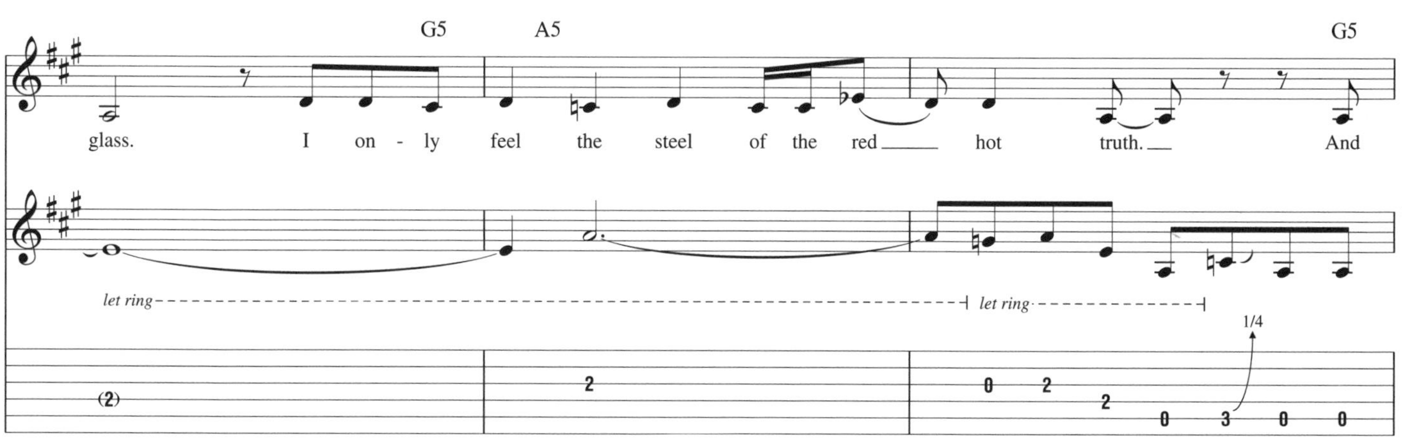
G5
A5
G5
glass. I on - ly feel the steel of the red hot truth. And
let ring
let ring
1/4

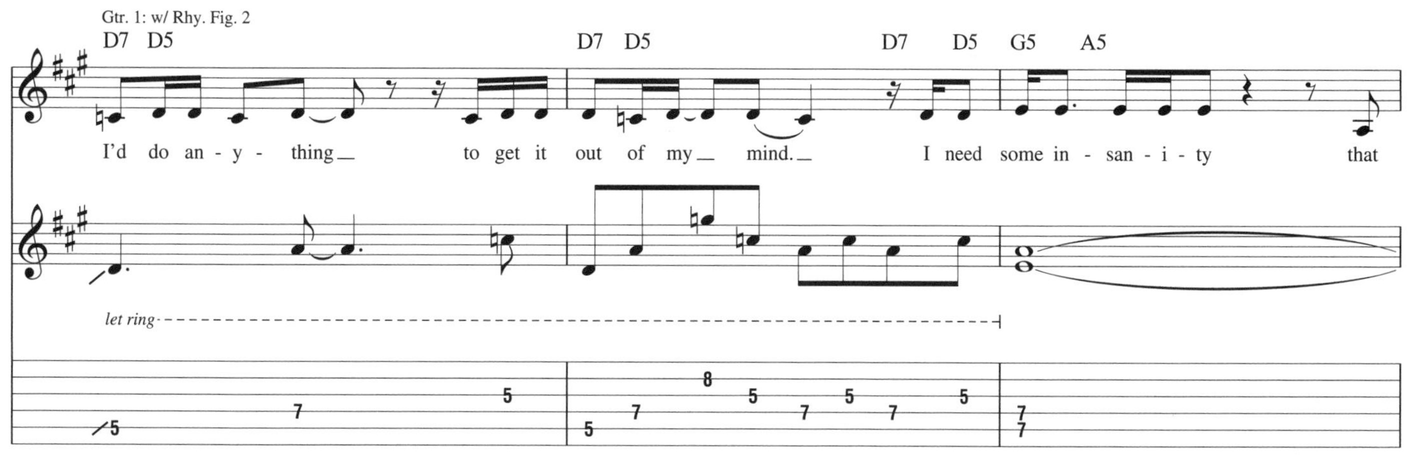
Gtr. 1: w/ Rhy. Fig. 2
D7 D5
D7 D5
D7 D5 G5 A5
I'd do an - y - thing to get it out of my mind. I need some in - san - i - ty that
let ring

G5
A5
D7
D5
D7
D5
tem - po - rar - y kind.
Tell me how will I ev - er be the same, when I
let ring
let ring

E5
know that that wom - an is whis - per - ing your name.
Gtr. 2
Gtr. 1

Chorus

Gtr. 1: w/ Rhy. Fig. 3 (3 times)
A
G
D
A
G
Some - bod - y bring me some wa - ter.
Can't you see I'm burn - in' a - live.
Gtr. 2
let ring
let ring
let ring
let ring

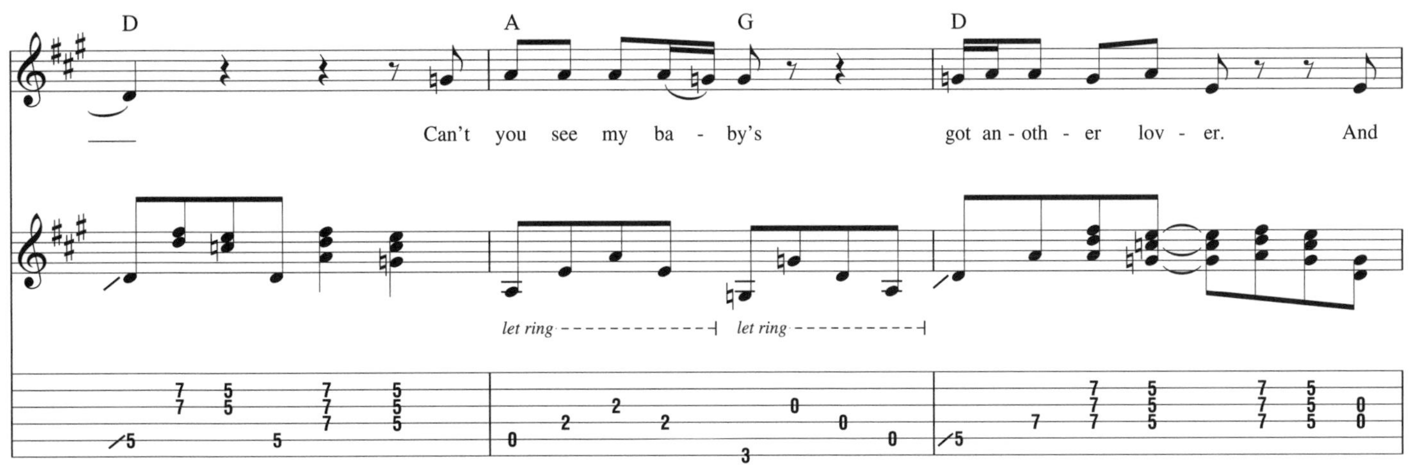
D
A
G
D
Can't you see my ba - by's got an - oth - er lov - er. And
let ring
let ring

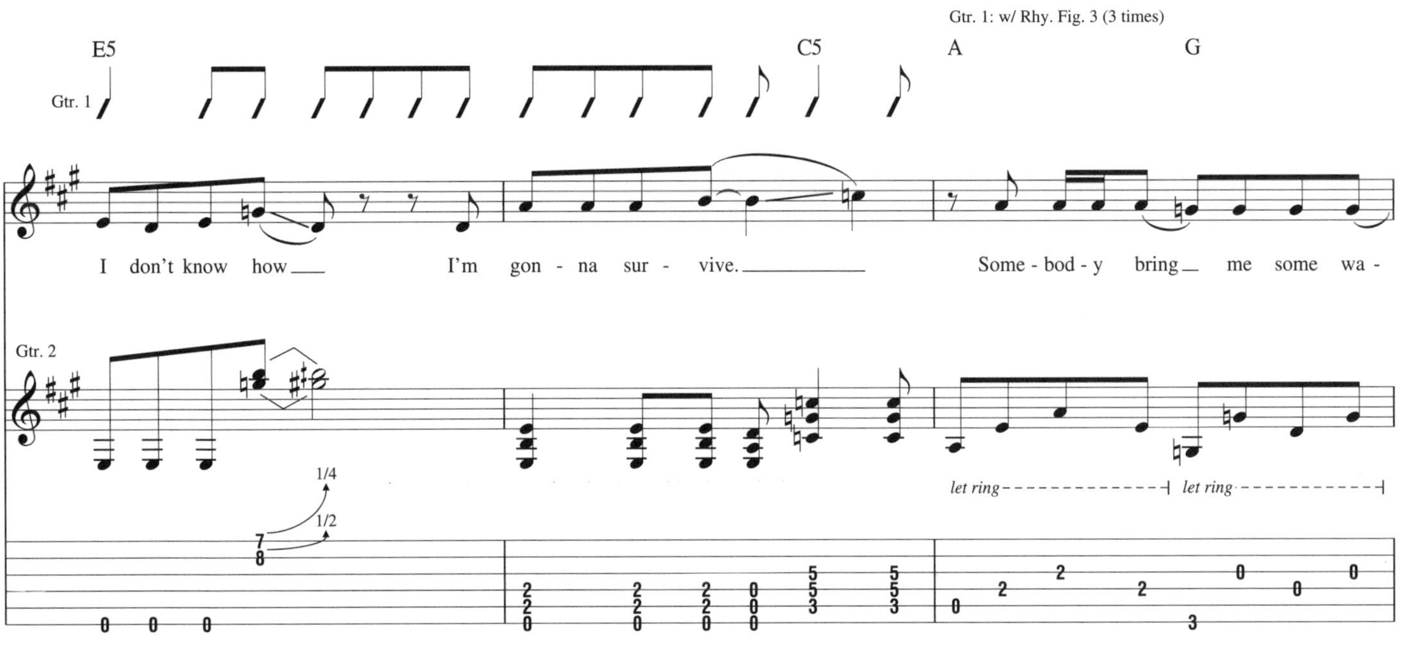
Gtr. 1: w/ Rhy. Fig. 3 (3 times)
E5
C5
A
G
Gtr. 1
I don't know how I'm gon - na sur - vive. Some - bod - y bring me some wa -
Gtr. 2
1/4
1/2
let ring
let ring

D
A
G
D
ter. Can't you see it's out of con - trol.
1/2
1
let ring

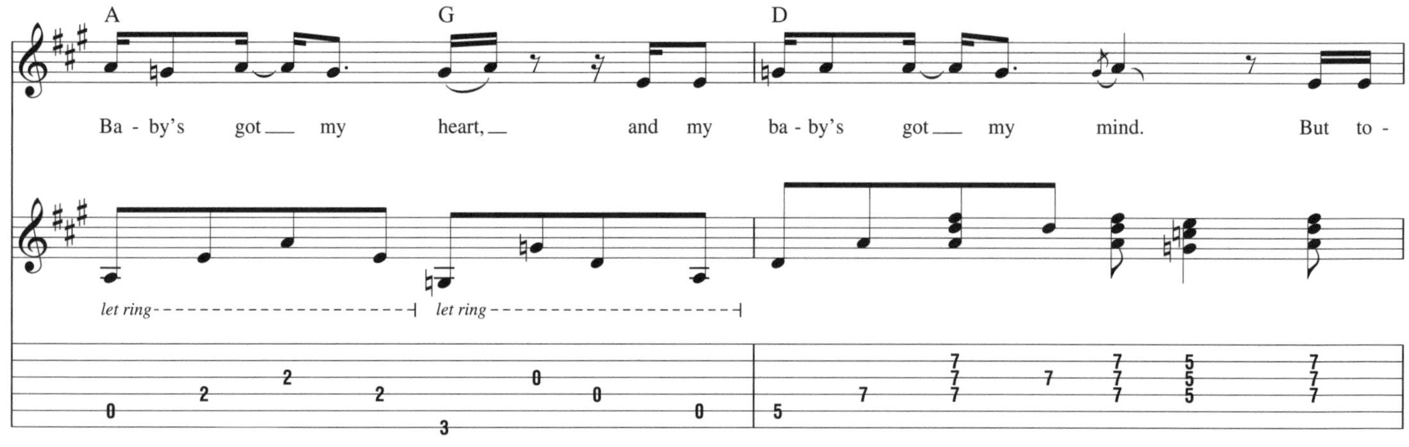

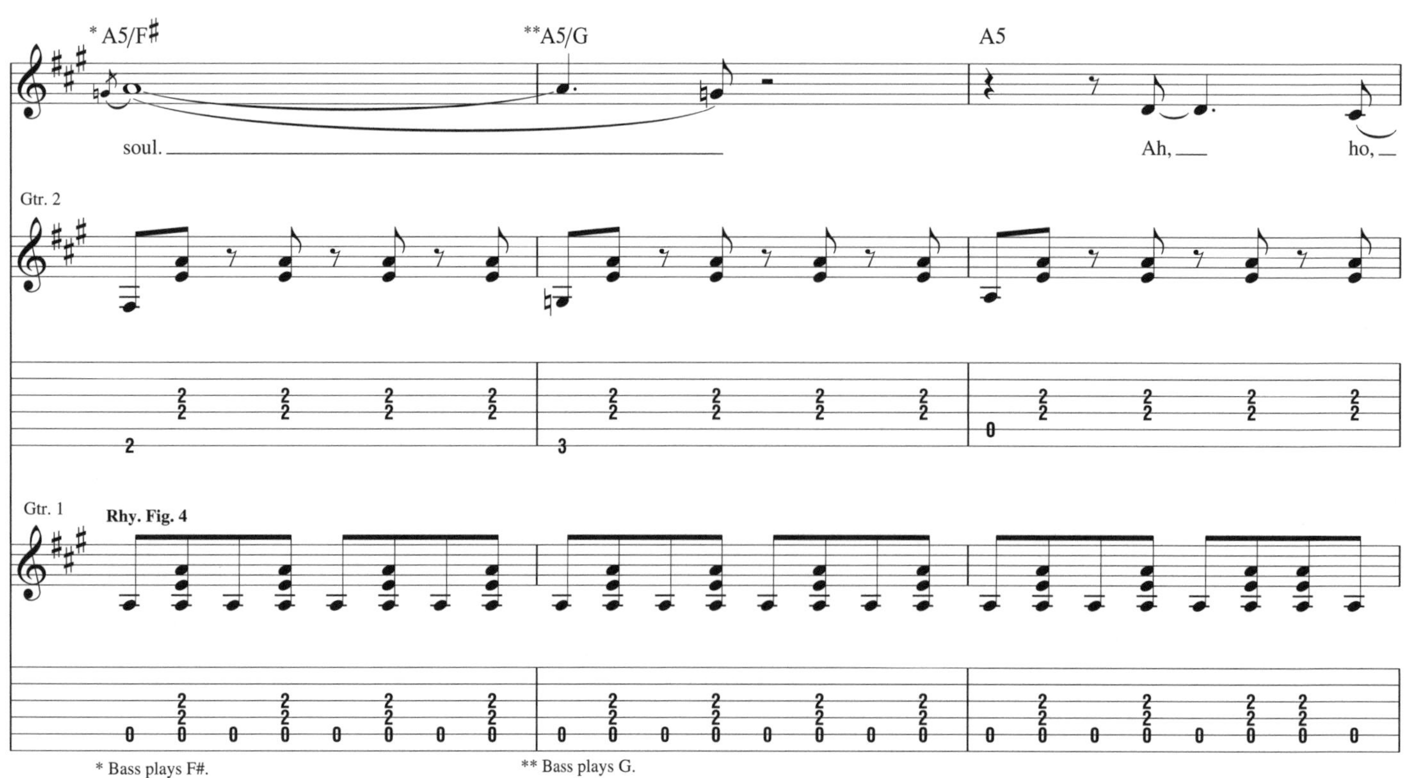

* Bass plays F#.

** Bass plays G.

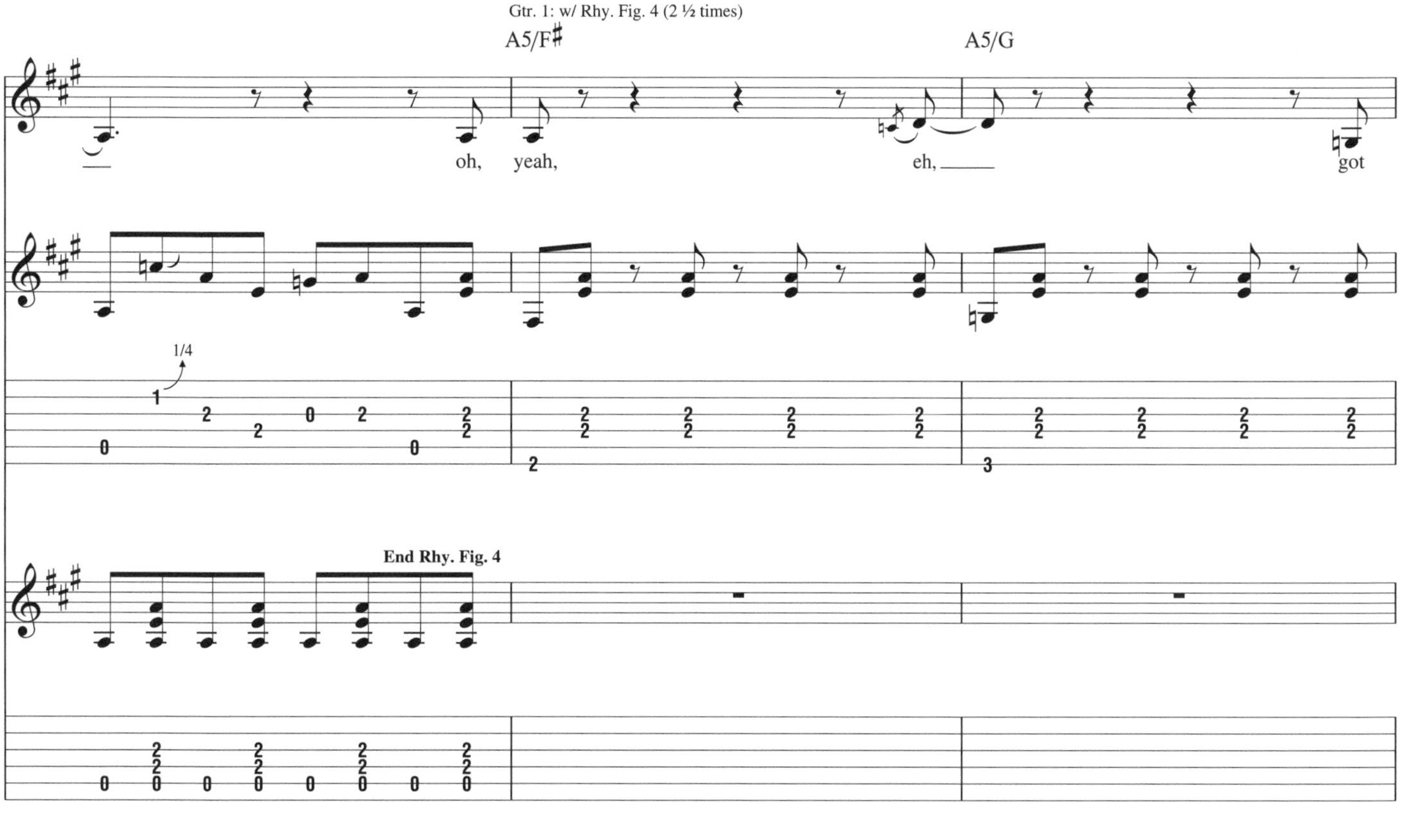
Gtr. 1: w/ Rhy. Fig. 4 (2 ½ times)
A5/F♯
A5/G
oh, yeah,
eh,
got
1/4
End Rhy. Fig. 4

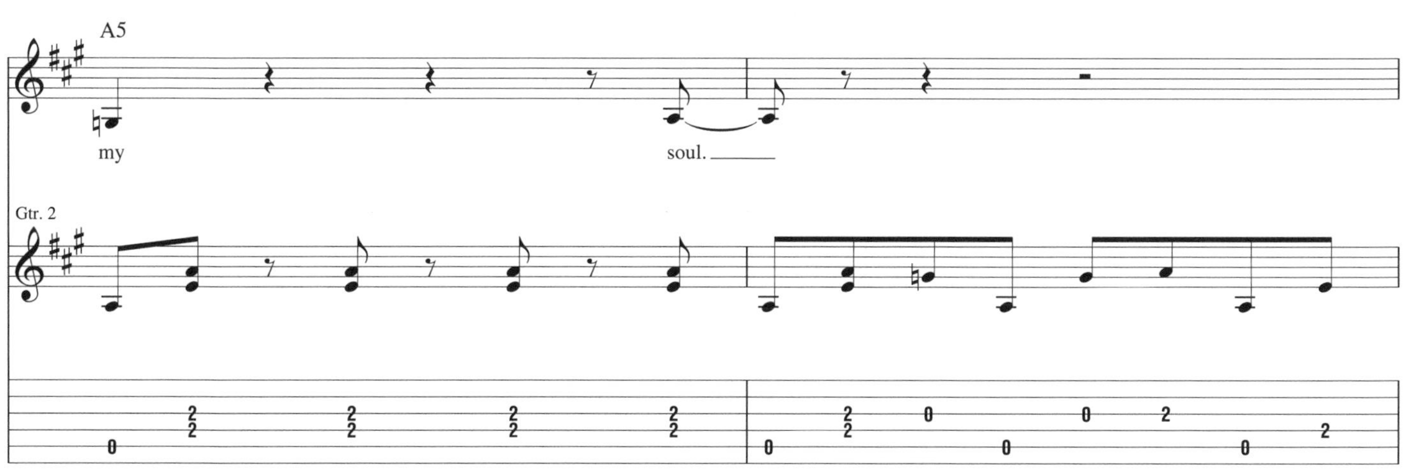
A5
my
soul.
Gtr. 2

A5/F♯
A5/G
A5
Ah,
ha,
ha,
ah,
ha.

*A5/B
Oo,
P.M..
1/4
* Bass plays B.

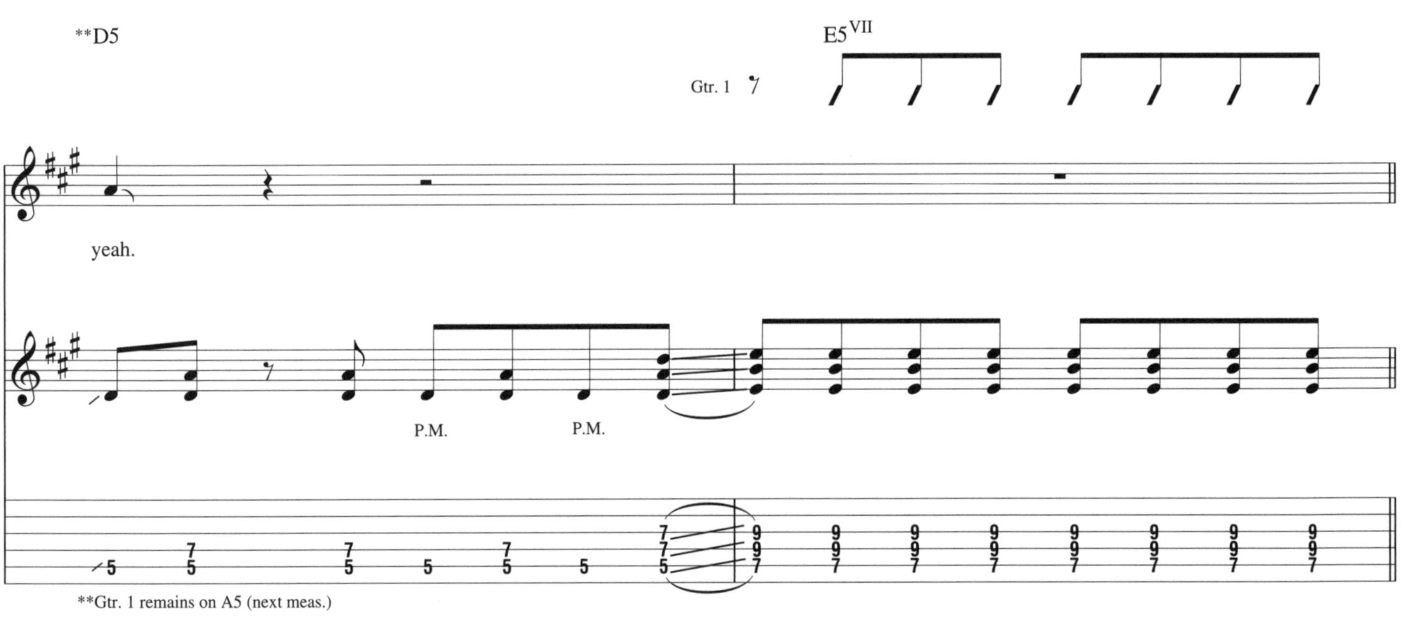
**D5
E5VII
Gtr. 1
yeah.
P.M.
P.M.
**Gtr. 1 remains on A5 (next meas.)

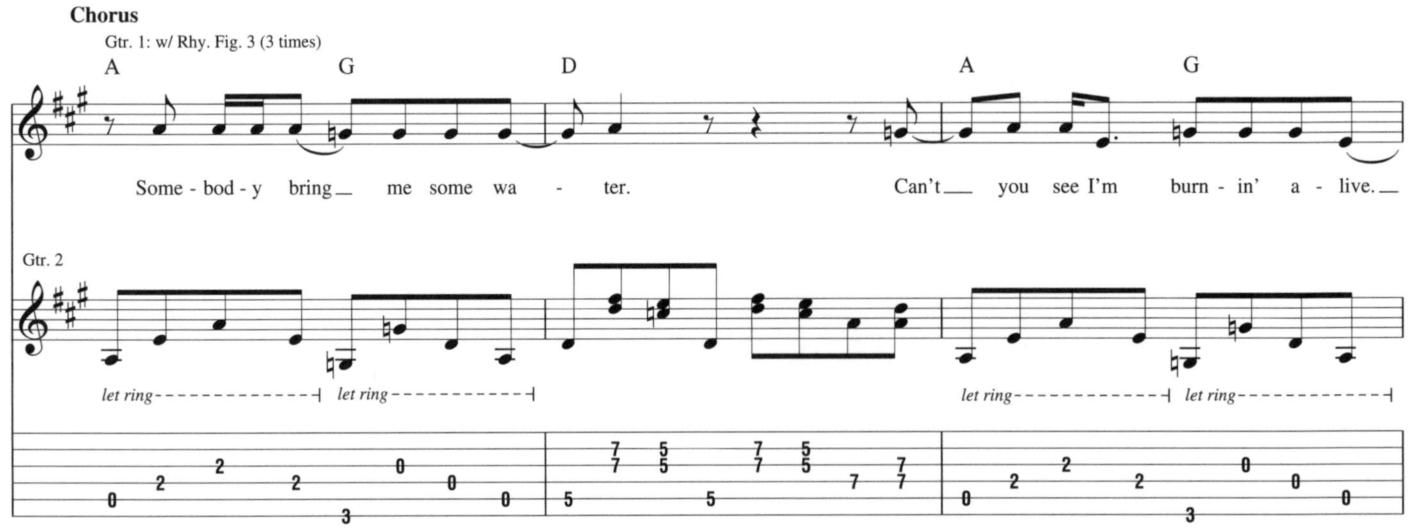
Chorus
Gtr. 1: w/ Rhy. Fig. 3 (3 times)
A
G
D
A
G
Some - bod - y bring me some wa - ter.
Can't you see I'm burn - in' a - live.
Gtr. 2
let ring
let ring
let ring
let ring

D
A
G
D
Can't you see my ba - by's got an - oth - er lov - er. And
let ring
let ring
1/2
1

E5VII
C5
Gtr. 1
I don't know how I'm gon - na sur - vive.
Gtr. 2
1/4
1/2

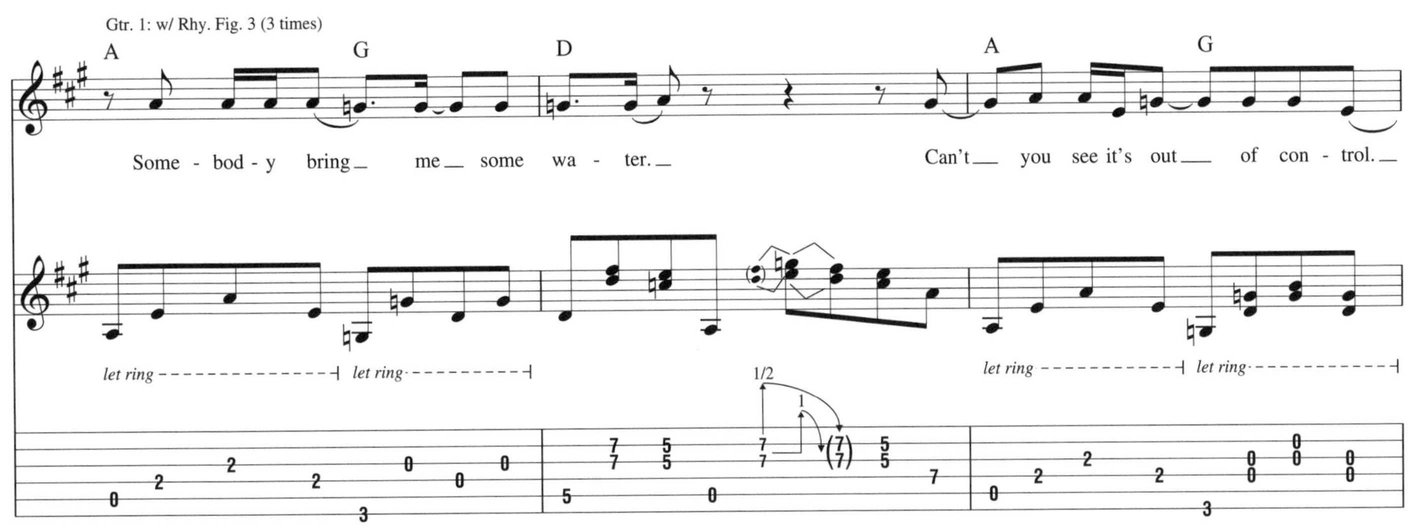
Gtr. 1: w/ Rhy. Fig. 3 (3 times)
A
G
D
A
G
Some - bod - y bring me some wa - ter. Can't you see it's out of con - trol.
let ring
let ring
let ring
let ring
1/2
1

D
A
G
Ba - by's got my heart, and my
let ring
let ring

D
E5VII
Gtr. 1
(cont. in notation)
ba - by's got my mind. But to - night the sweet dev - il,

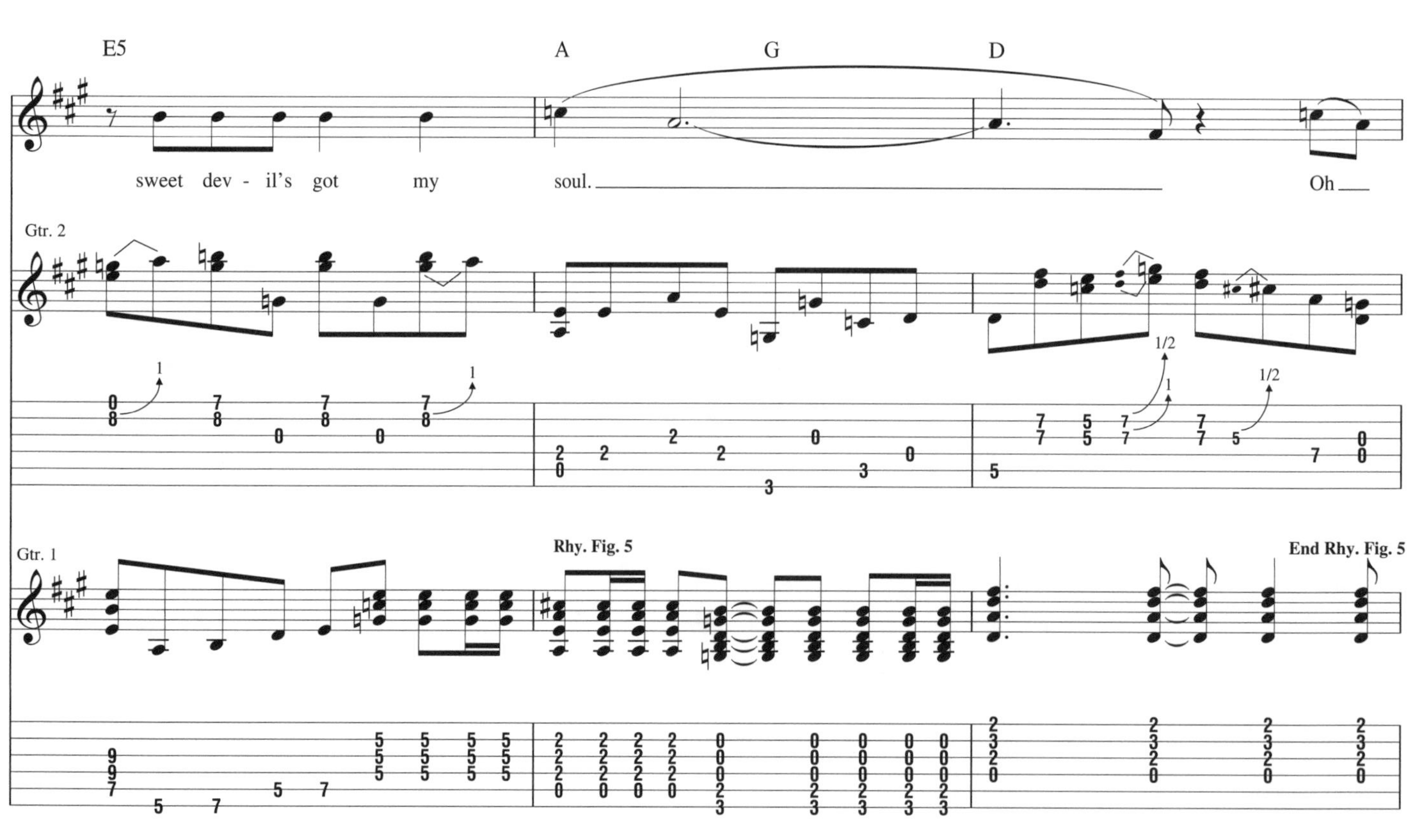
E5
A
G
D
sweet dev - il's got my soul. Oh
Gtr. 2
Gtr. 1
Rhy. Fig. 5
End Rhy. Fig. 5

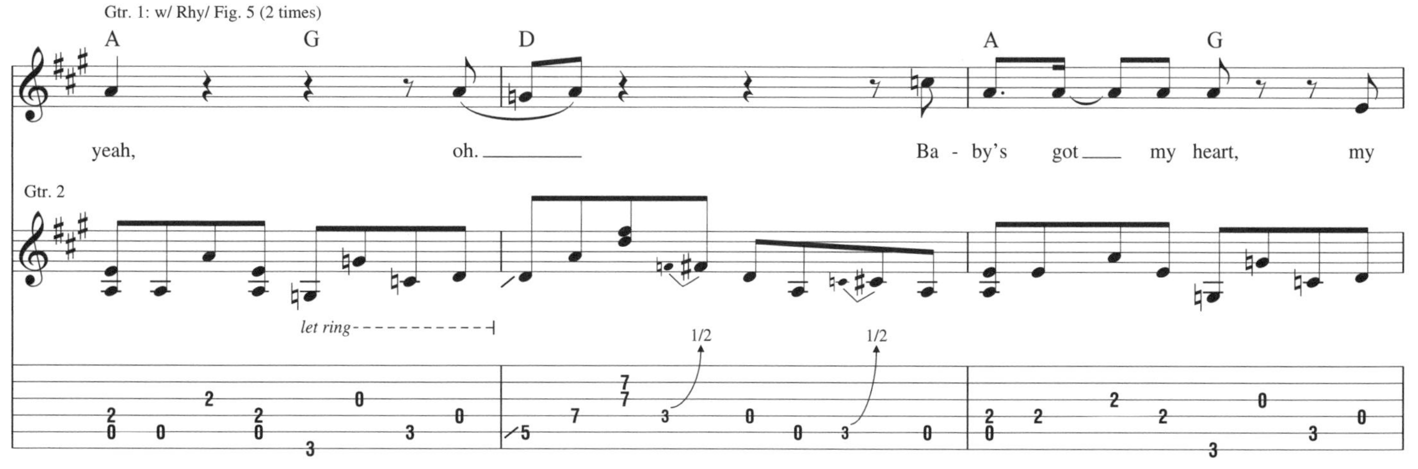
Gtr. 1: w/ Rhy/ Fig. 5 (2 times)
A
G
D
A
G
yeah, oh.
Ba - by's got my heart, my
Gtr. 2
let ring
1/2
1/2

D
E
E5VII
E
E5VII
E
open
open
open
Gtr. 1
ba - by's got my mind. But to - night the sweet dev - il, the
1/4
1/4
1/4
1/4
1/2
1/2
1/2
1/2

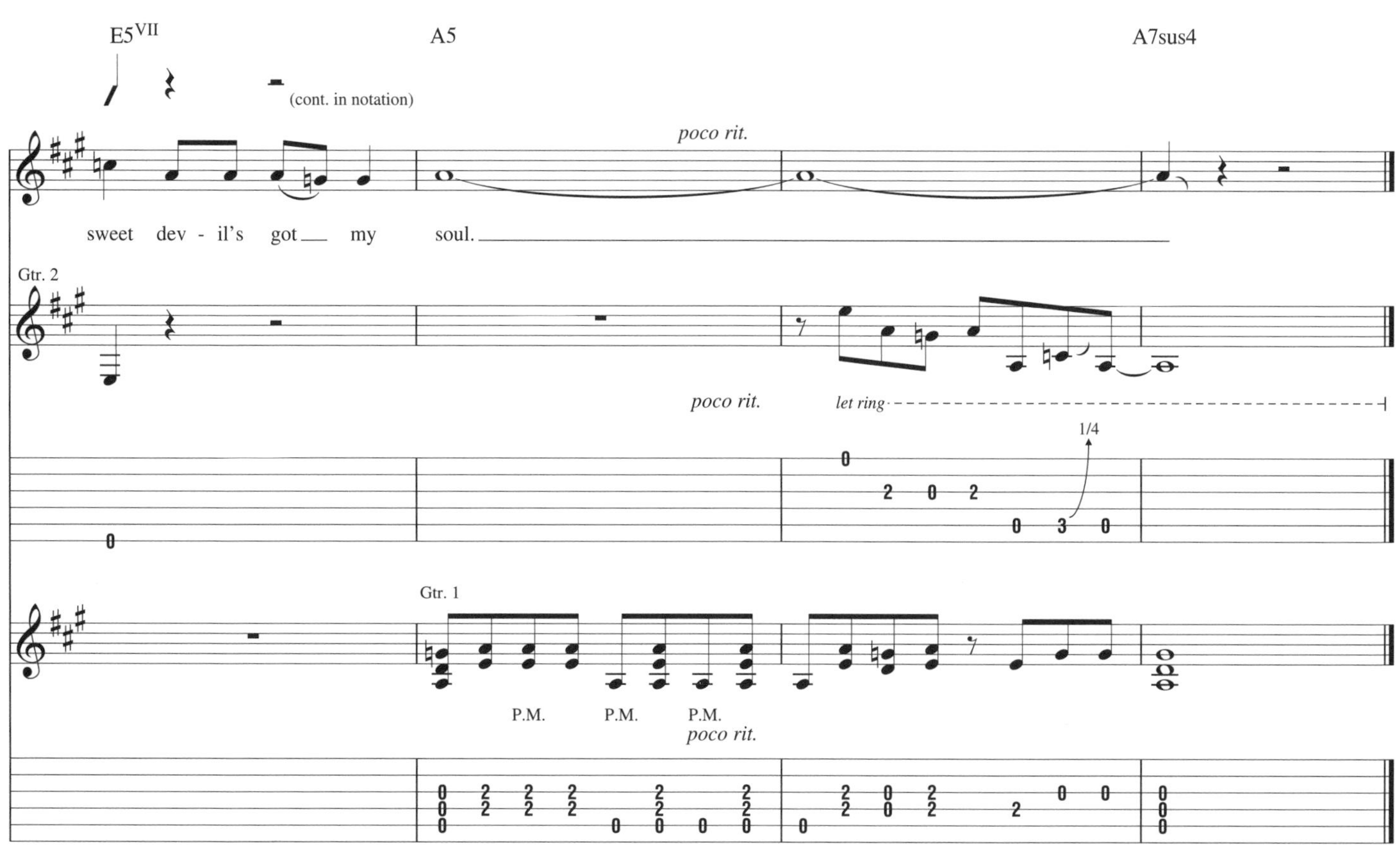
E5VII
A5
A7sus4
(cont. in notation)
poco rit.
sweet dev - il's got my soul.
Gtr. 2
poco rit.
let ring
1/4
Gtr. 1
P.M.
P.M.
P.M.
poco rit.

from *Yes I Am*

Come to My Window

Words and Music by Melissa Etheridge

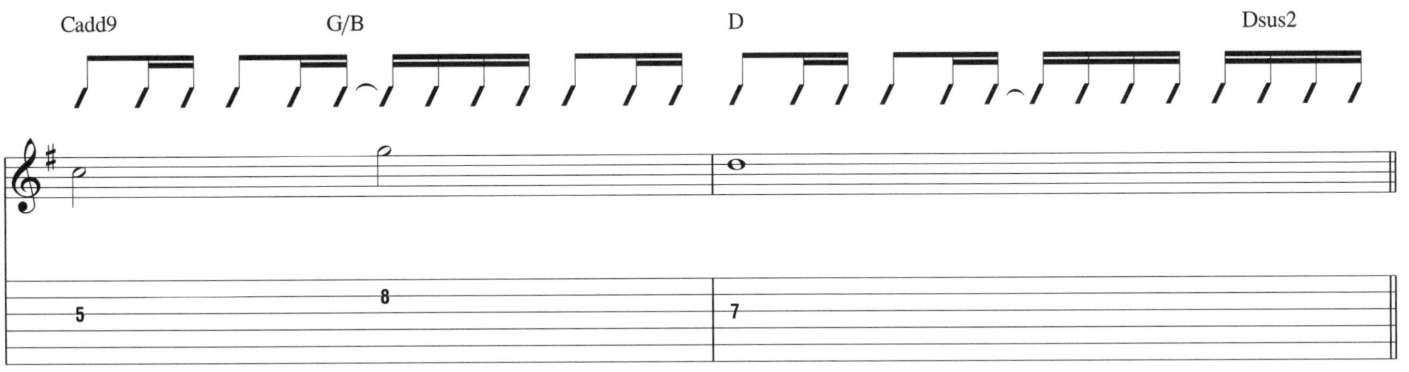
Cadd9
G/B
D
Dsus2
5
8
7

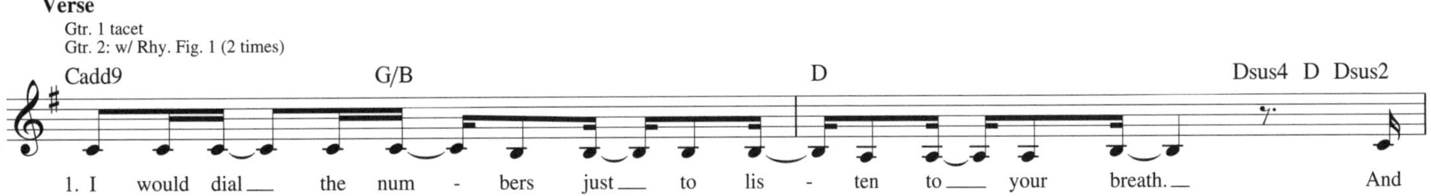
Verse
Gtr. 1 tacet
Gtr. 2: w/ Rhy. Fig. 1 (2 times)
Cadd9
G/B
D
Dsus4 D Dsus2
1. I would dial the num - bers just to lis - ten to your breath. And

Cadd9
G/B
D
Dsus2
D Dsus2
I would stand in - side my hell and hold the hand of death.

Cadd9
G/B
D
Dsus4 D Dsus2
You don't know how far I'd go to ease this pre - cious ache. And

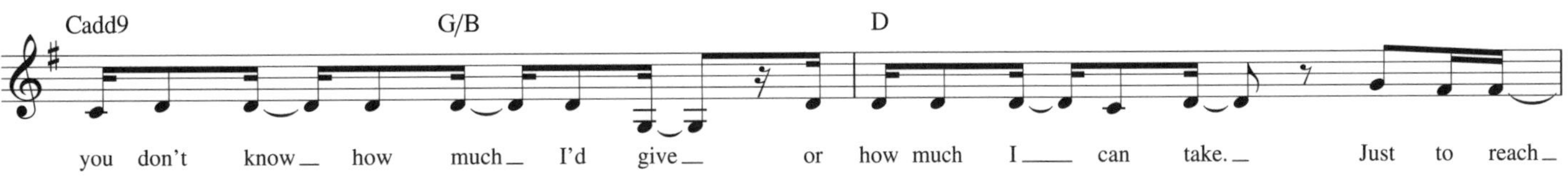
Cadd9
G/B
D
you don't know how much I'd give or how much I can take. Just to reach

Em
Cadd9
D
Dsus4
D
Gtr. 2
you. Just to reach you. Oh, to
Gtr. 1
4
X
2
5
X
3
7
X
5

Em
Cadd9
D
Dsus2
reach you, oh.
Chorus
Gtr. 1 tacet
G
A7sus4
Rhy. Fig. 2
Gtr. 2
Come to my win - dow.
Riff A
Gtr. 3
(12-str. elec.)
w/ clean tone
let ring throughout
Crawl in - side, wait by the light of the moon.
End Rhy. Fig. 2
End Riff A
Gtr. 2: w/ Rhy. Fig. 2
Gtr. 3: w/ Riff A
To Coda
Come to my win - dow, I'll be home soon.

Verse
Gtr. 2: w/ Rhy. Fig. 1 (2 times)
Cadd9
G/B
Dsus4
Dsus2
D
Dsus4
D
Dsus2
2. Keep-ing my eyes o - pen I can - not af - ford to sleep.
Cadd9
G/B
D
Dsus4
D
Dsus2
Giv - ing a - way prom - is - es I know that I can't keep.
Gtr. 1
Cadd9
G/B
Dsus2
D
Dsus2
Dsus4
D
Dsus2
Noth - ing fills the black - ness that has seeped in - to my chest. I
D.S. al Coda
Cadd9
G/B
D
Dsus4
D
Dsus4
D
need you in my blood I am for - sak - ing all the rest. Just to reach
Coda
A7sus4
D
Bridge
Em
Gtr. 2
I don't care what they think.
Gtr. 1

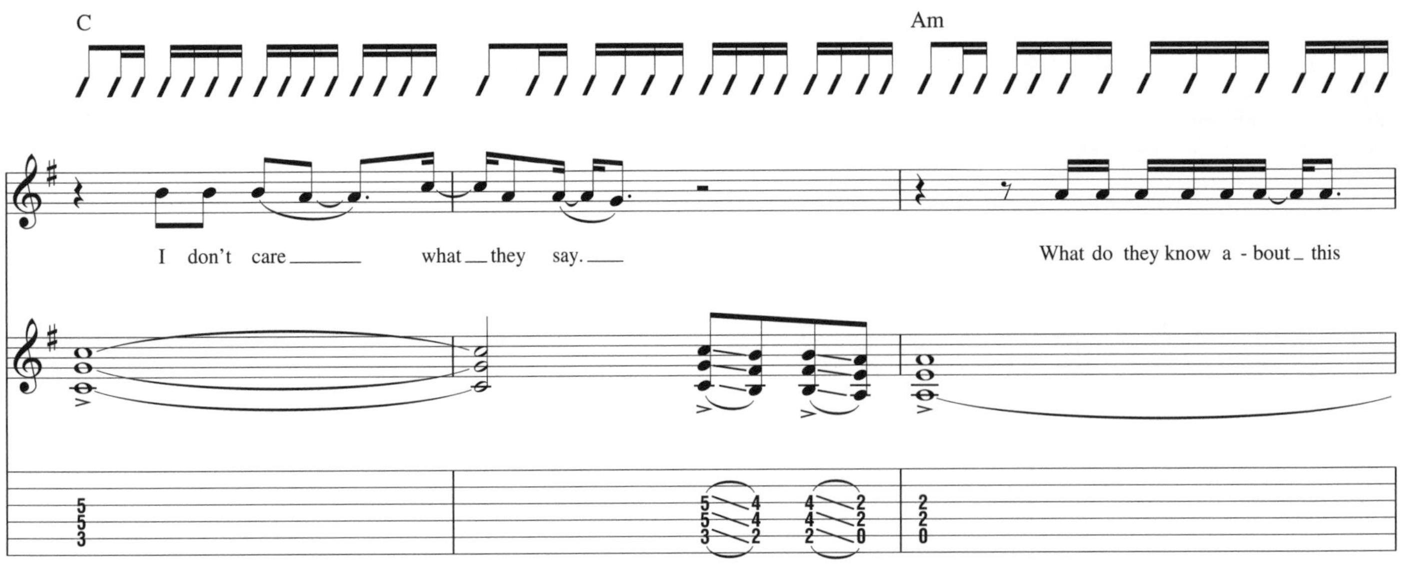
C
Am
I don't care what they say.
What do they know a - bout this

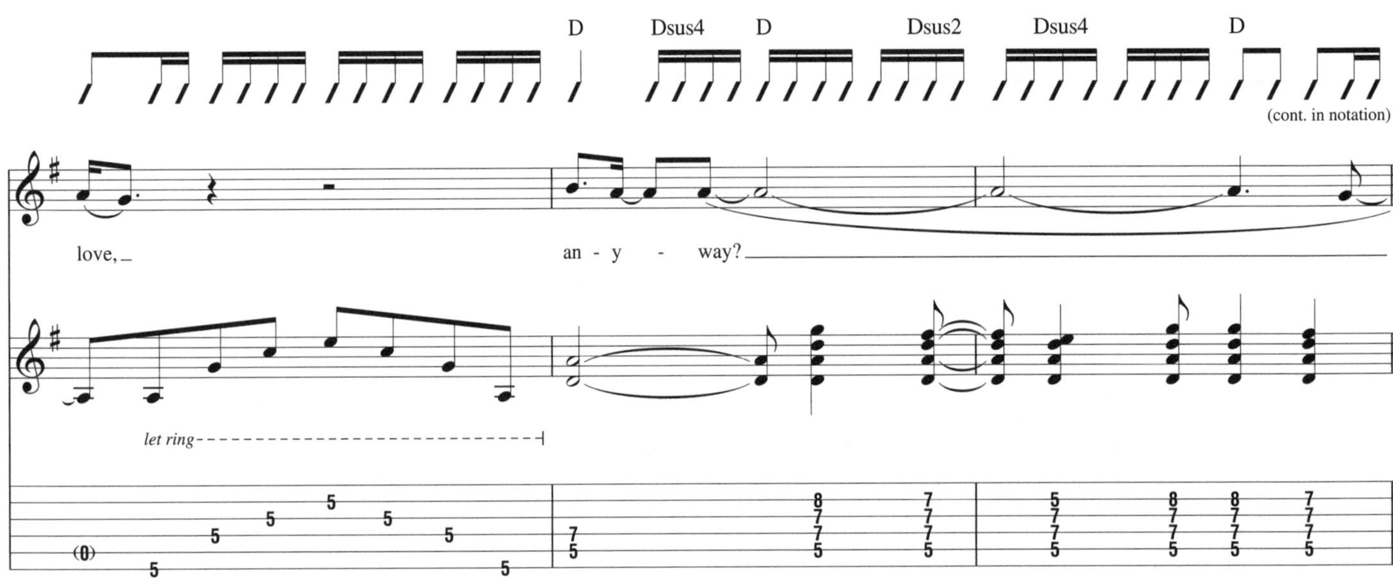
D
Dsus4
D
Dsus2
Dsus4
D
(cont. in notation)
love,
an - y - way?
let ring

Interlude

Gtr. 1 tacet
G
Cadd9
A7sus4
Dsus4
D
Dsus2
D Dsus2
Gtr. 2
let ring

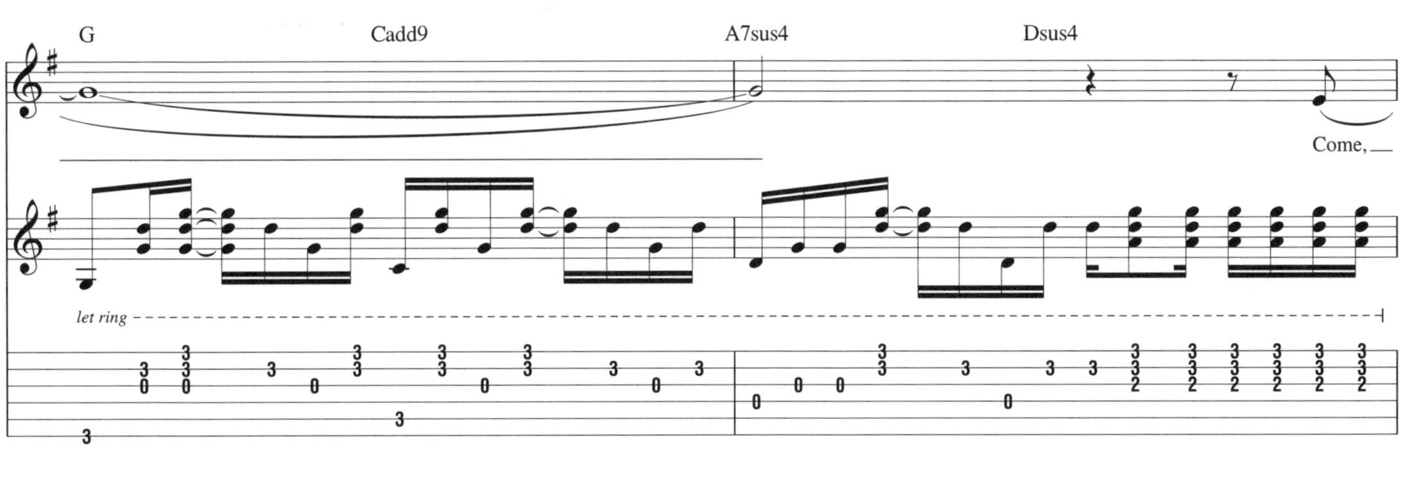
G
Cadd9
A7sus4
Dsus4
Come,
let ring

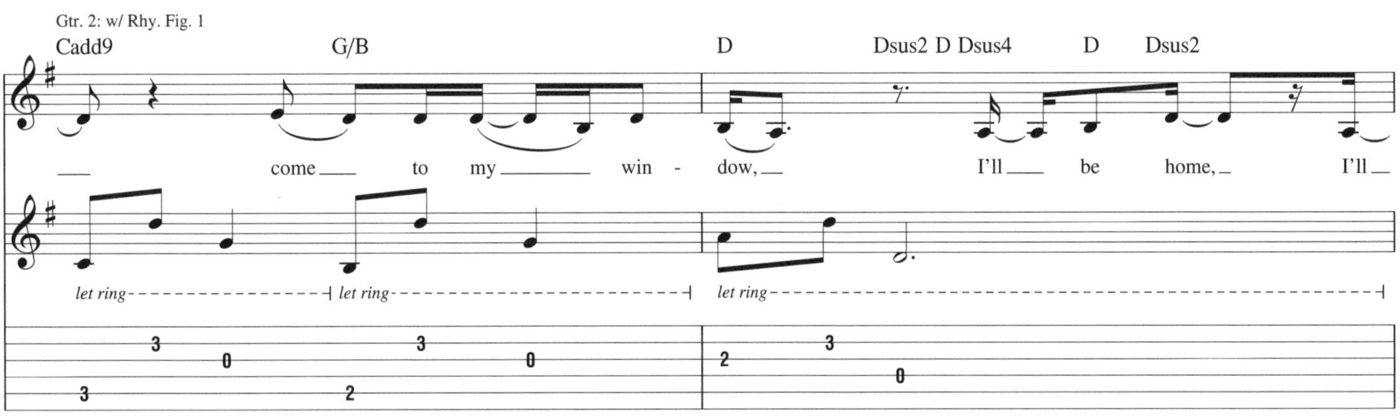
Gtr. 2: w/ Rhy. Fig. 1
Cadd9
G/B
D
Dsus2 D Dsus4
D
Dsus2
come to my win - dow, I'll be home, I'll
let ring
let ring
let ring

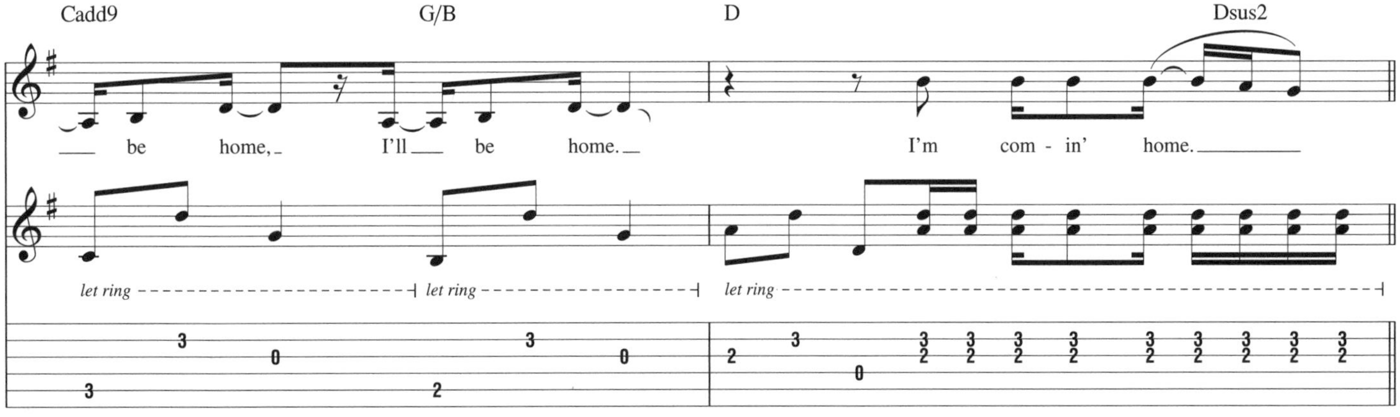
Cadd9
G/B
D
Dsus2
be home, I'll be home. I'm com - in' home.
let ring
let ring
let ring

Chorus
Gtr. 2: w/ Rhy. Fig. 2 (2 times)
Gtr. 3: w/ Riff A (2 times)
G
Cadd9
A7sus4
D
Dsus2
D
G
Cadd9
A7sus4
D
Dsus2
D
Come to my win - dow. Oh, crawl in - side, wait by the light of the moon.

2nd time, Begin fade
G
Cadd9
A7sus4
D
Dsus2
G
Cadd9
Come to my win - dow, I'll be home soon, I'll be home, I'll

Outro
Gtr. 2: w/ Rhy. Fig. 2
Gtr. 3: w/ Riff A
Repeat and Fade
A7sus4
D
Dsus2
G
Cadd9
A7sus4
D
Dsus2
be home, I'm com - in' home.

from *Never Enough*

Dance Without Sleeping

Words and Music by Melissa Etheridge, Mauricio Fritz Lewak and Kevin McCormick

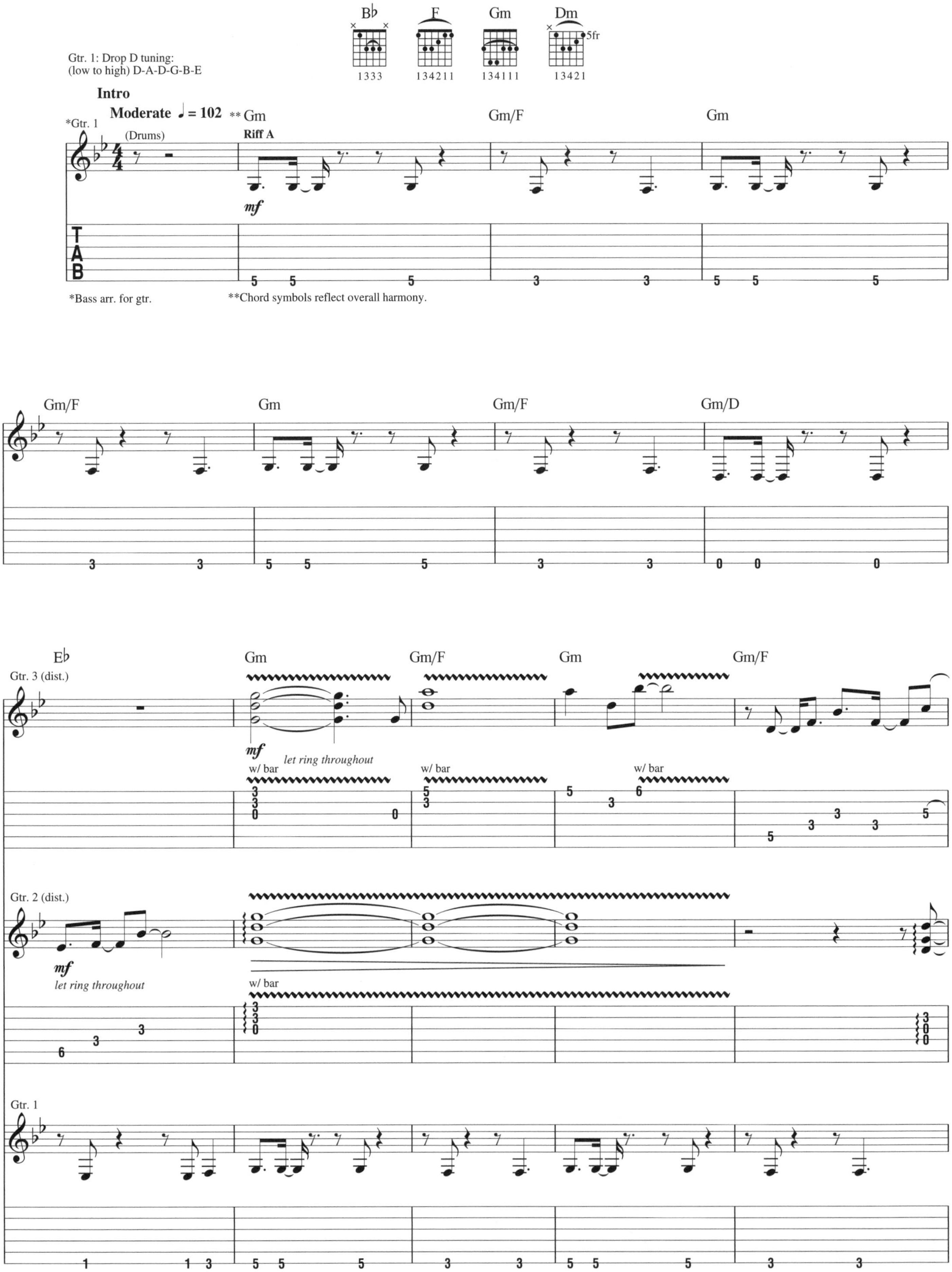

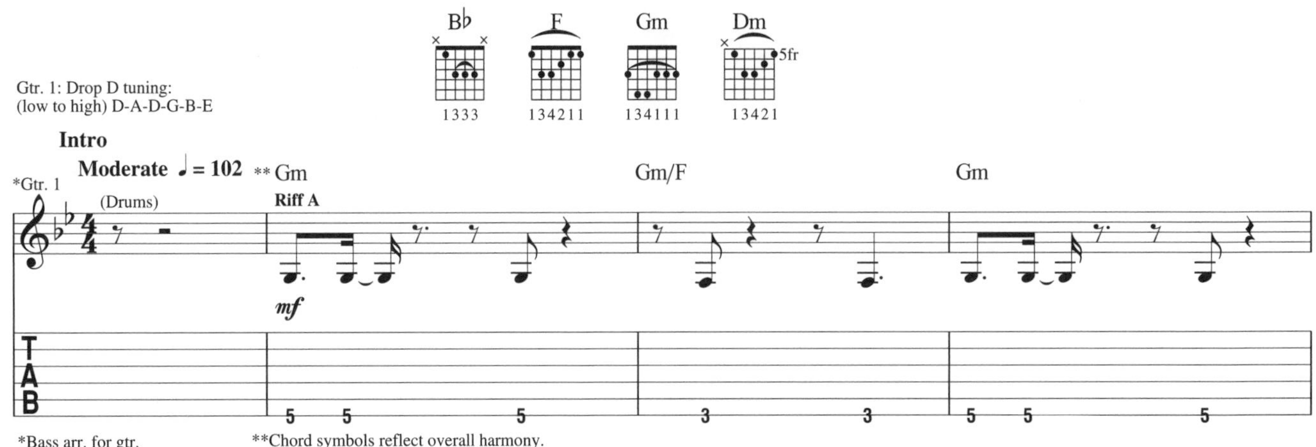

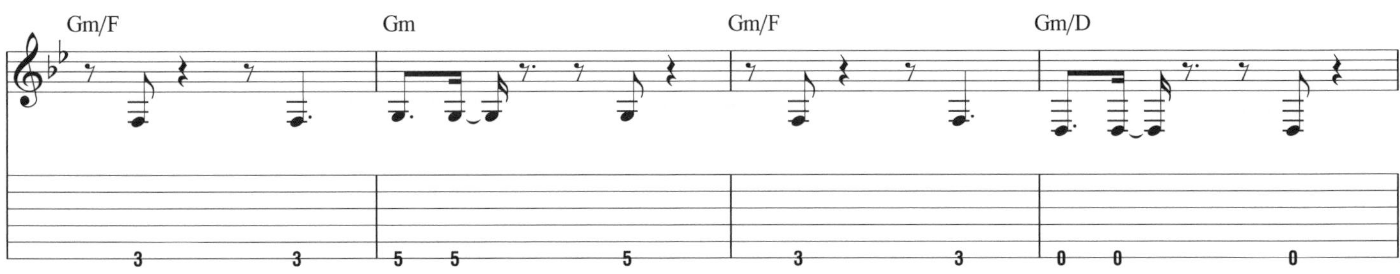

Eb Gm Gm/F Gm Gm/F

Gtr. 3 (dist.)

mf *let ring throughout*

w/ bar w/ bar w/ bar

Gtr. 2 (dist.)

mf *let ring throughout*

w/ bar

Gtr. 1

Gm
Gsus2
Gm
Gm/D
E♭
w/ bar
w/ bar
w/ bar
End Riff A
Verse
Gtr 1: w/ Riff A
Gm
Gm/F
Gtrs. 2 & 3 tacet
Gm
1. I don't want to talk about it.
I've done e-nough, I think.
Gtr. 3
Gtr. 2
divisi
Gm/F
Gm
Gsus2
Gm
Don't want to spend more mon-ey.
Gm/D
E♭
Gm
Don't want an-oth-er drink.
I would scratch out all
Gtr. 3
w/ bar
w/ bar

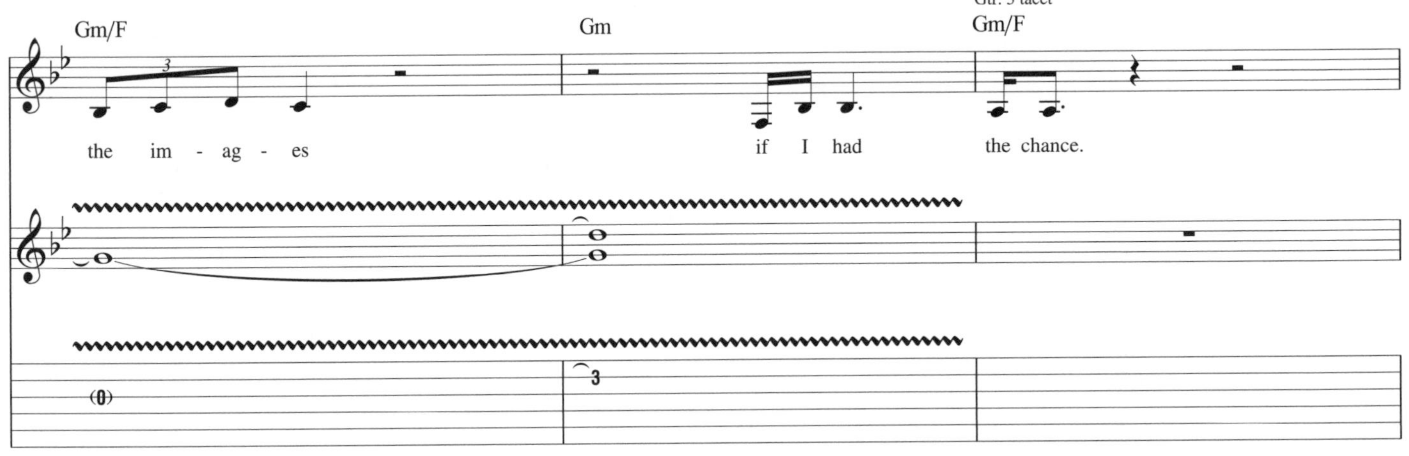
Gtr. 3 tacet
Gm/F
Gm
Gm/F
the im - ag - es
if I had
the chance.

Gm
Gsus2
Gm
Gm/D
Don't ask me what I'm think - ing.
Can't you see I
Gtr. 2

Chorus
E♭
B♭
F
Rhy. Fig. 1
Gtr. 2
on - ly want to
dance with - out sleep - ing, I'll
dance with - out fear.
Rhy. Fig. 1A
Gtr. 3
Gtr. 2
divisi
(Gtr. 2, cont. in slashes)
w/ bar
Riff B
Gtr. 1

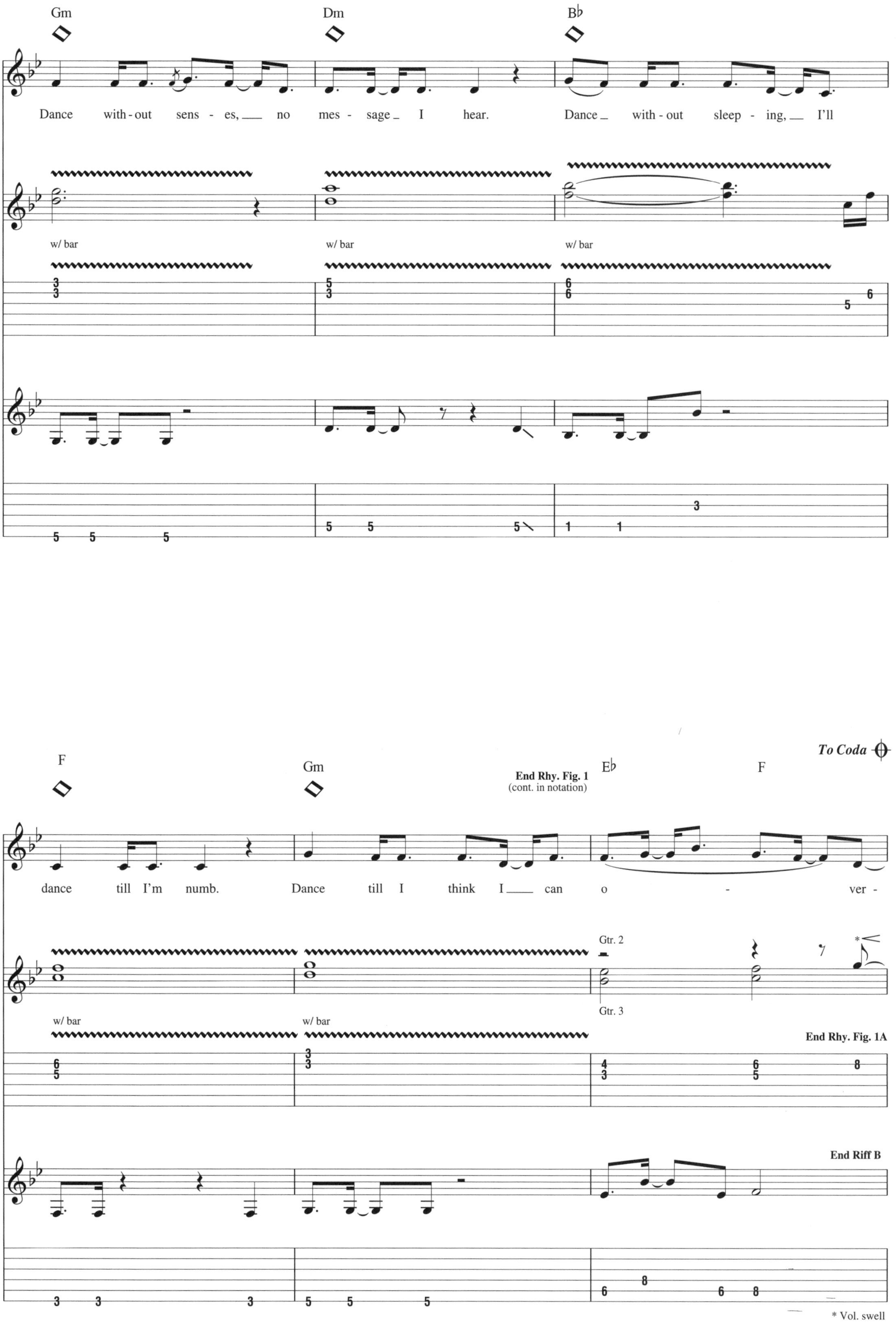

To Coda

F Gm E♭ F

End Rhy. Fig. 1
(cont. in notation)

dance till I'm numb. Dance till I think I can o - ver -

Gr. 2

Gr. 3

w/ bar w/ bar

End Rhy. Fig. 1A

End Riff B

* Vol. swell

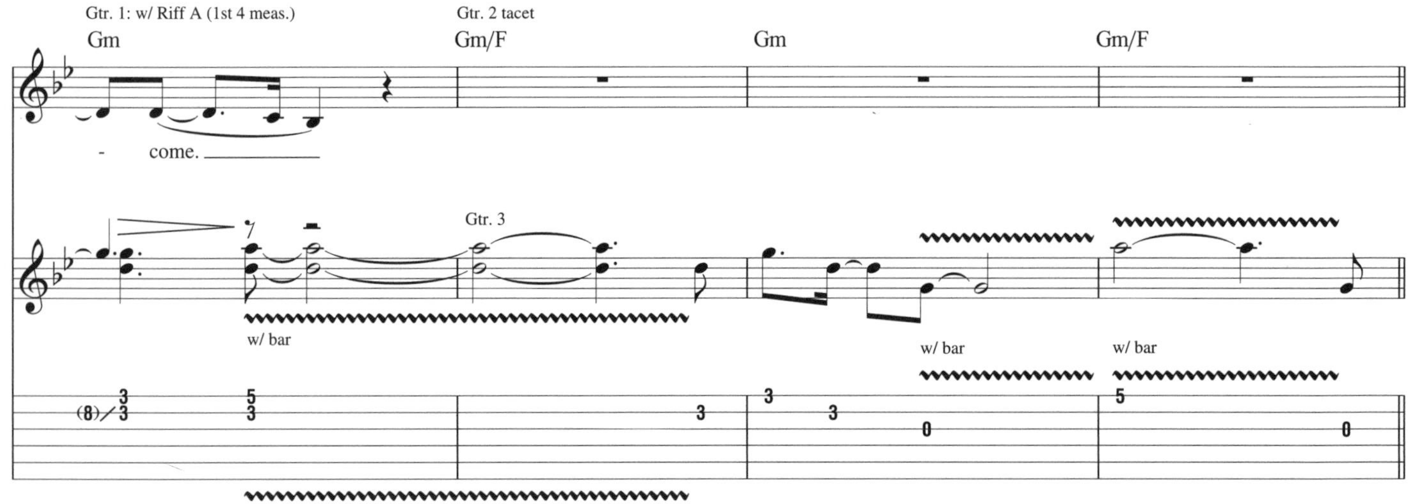
Gtr. 1: w/ Riff A (1st 4 meas.)
Gtr. 2 tacet
Gm
Gm/F
Gm
Gm/F
- come.
Gtr. 3
w/ bar
w/ bar
w/ bar

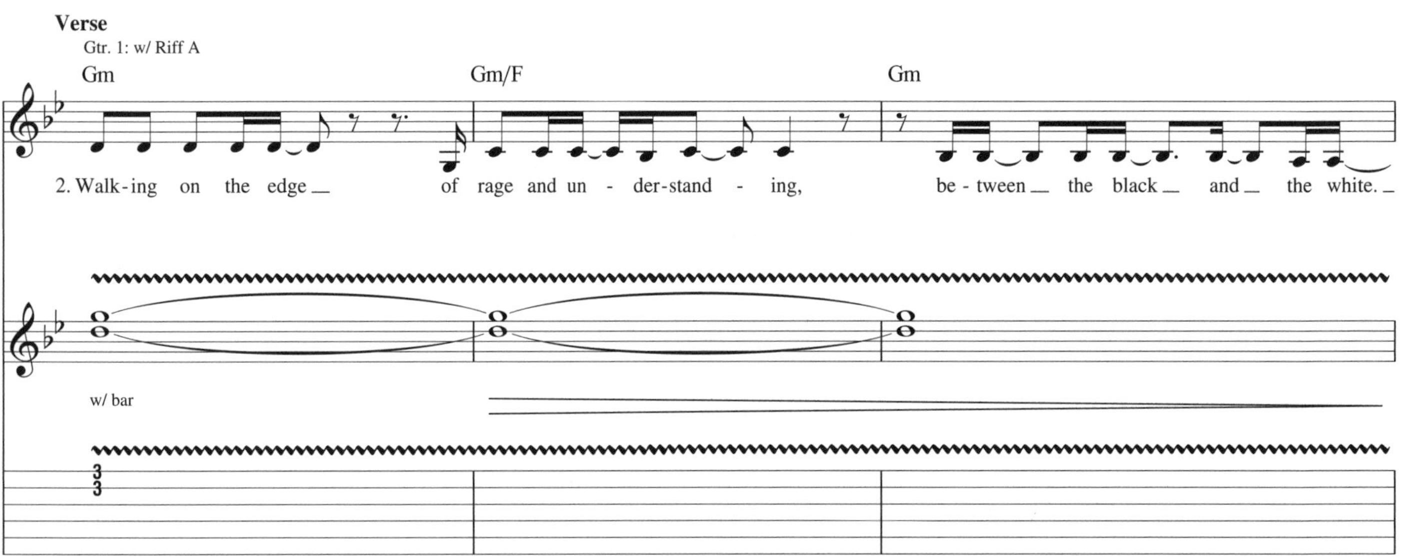
Verse
Gtr. 1: w/ Riff A
Gm
Gm/F
Gm
2. Walk-ing on the edge of rage and un - der-stand - ing, be - tween the black and the white.
w/ bar

Gm/F
Gm
Gm/F
Gm/D
This child is so an - gry, a - lone here
Gtr. 3
Gtr. 2

E♭
Gm
Gm/F
to - night.
A - larm - ing des - per - a - tion
w/ bar
w/ bar
Gm
Gm/F
Gm
leads me to be - lieve,
with all my shields and
w/ bar
w/ bar
w/ bar
w/ bar
D.S. al Coda
Gsus2
Gm
Gm/D
E♭
pro - tec - tion,
it's on - ly me I de - ceive.
w/ bar
w/ bar

Coda

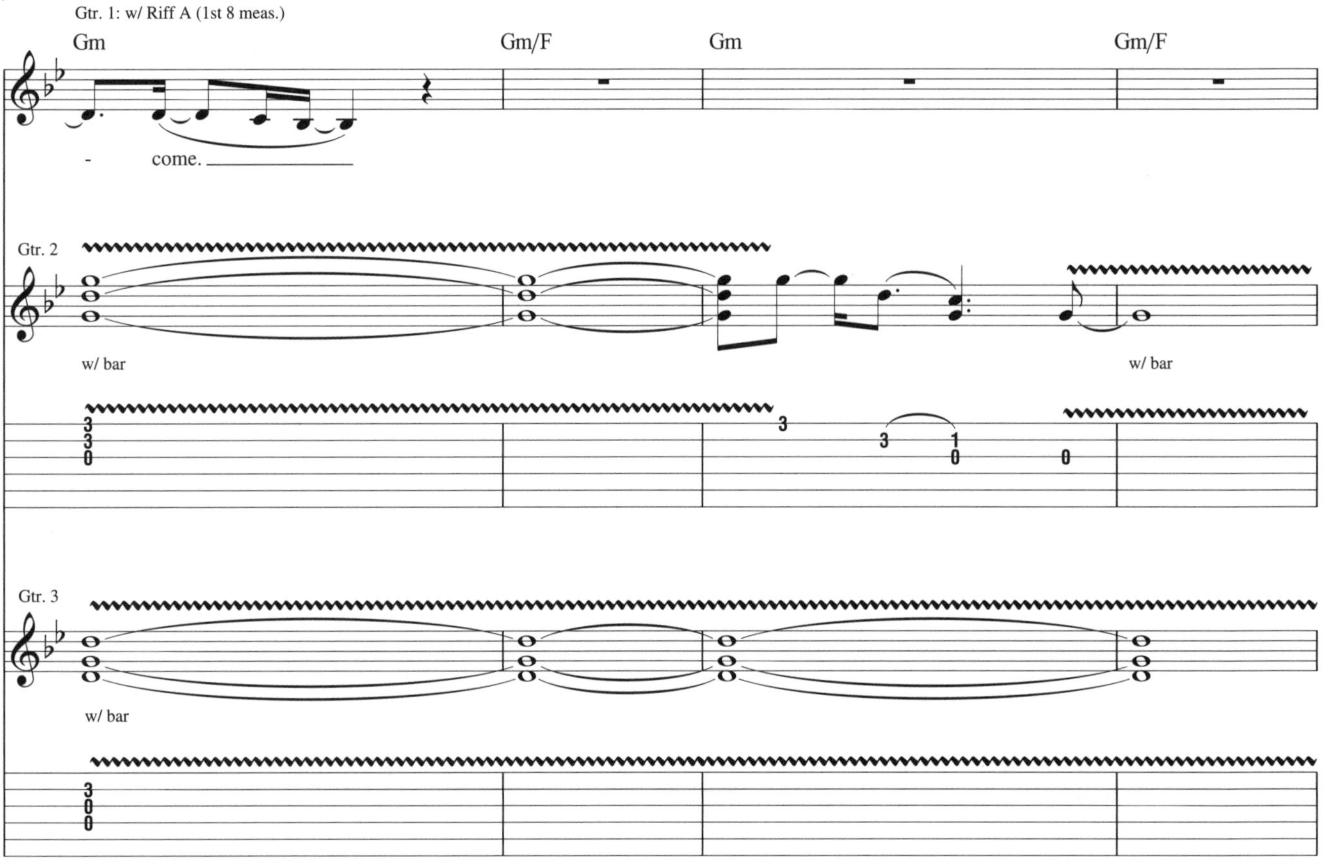
Gtr. 1: w/ Riff A (1st 8 meas.)
Gm
Gm/F
Gm
Gm/F
- come.
Gtr. 2
w/ bar
w/ bar
Gtr. 3
w/ bar

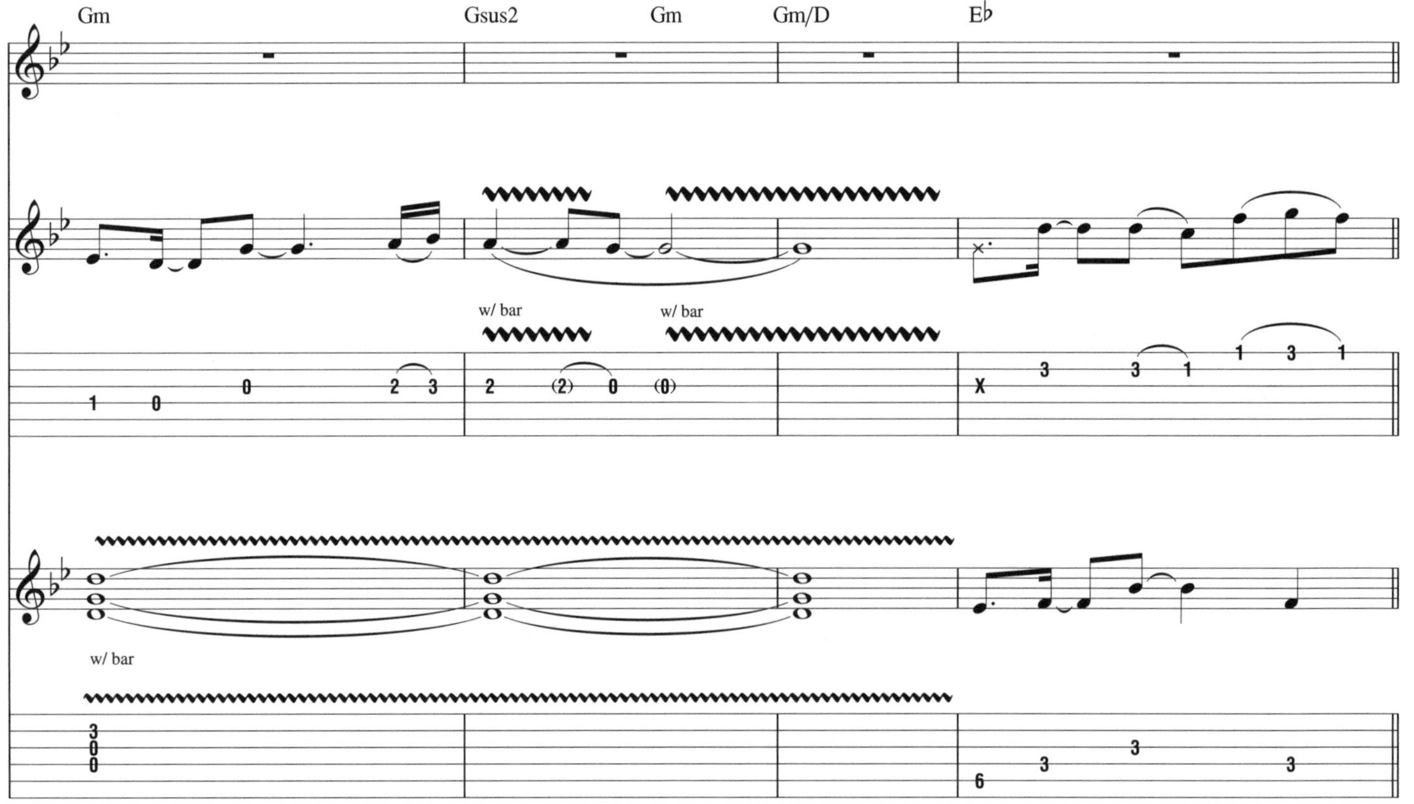
Gm
Gsus2
Gm
Gm/D
E♭
w/ bar
w/ bar
w/ bar

Verse
Gm
Gtr. 2 tacet
E♭
Gm
E♭
3. The eyes on a mag - a-zine, the voice on the ra - di-o,
Gtr. 2
Gtr. 3
Gtr. 3
divisi
w/ bar
w/ bar
Gtr. 1
Riff C
Gm
Gsus2
Gm
Gm/D
E♭
the kiss on the mov - ie screen: this is the sto - ry I know.
w/ bar
Gtr. 3
Gtr. 2
divisi
End Riff C
Gtr. 1: w/ Riff C
Gm
E♭
Fa - thers hold on and they nev - er go.
Gtr. 2
w/ bar
Gtr. 3

Gm
E♭
Gm
Moth - ers hold on and they nev - er go.
Lov - ers hold on and they
w/ bar

Gsus2
Gm
Gm/D
E♭
nev - er go.
Lov - ers, they come and they nev - er go.

Chorus
Gtr. 1: w/ Riff B (2 times)
Gtr. 2: w/ Rhy. Fig. 1
Gtr. 3: w/ Rhy. Fig. 1A (2 times)
B♭
F
Gm
Dance with-out sleep-ing, I'll dance with-out fear.
Dance with-out sens-es, no
Dm
B♭
F
mes-sage I hear.
Dance with-out sleep-ing, I'll dance till I'm numb.
Gm
E♭
F
B♭
Dance till I think I can o-ver-come.
Dance with-out sleep-ing, I'll
Gtr. 2
F
Gm
Dm
dance with-out fear.
Dance with-out sens-es, no mes-sage I hear.
B♭
F
Gm
E♭
F
Dance with-out sleep-ing, I'll dance till I'm numb.
Dance till I think I can o-ver-

Outro

Gtr. 1: w/ Riff A (2 times)
Gtr. 2 tacet

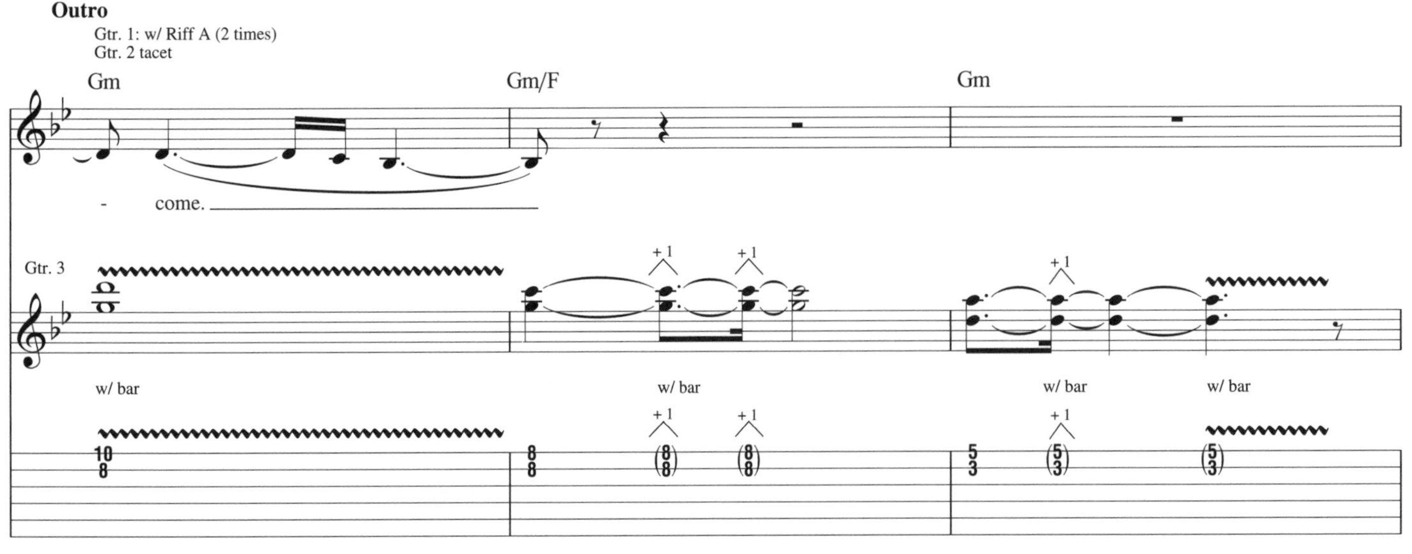

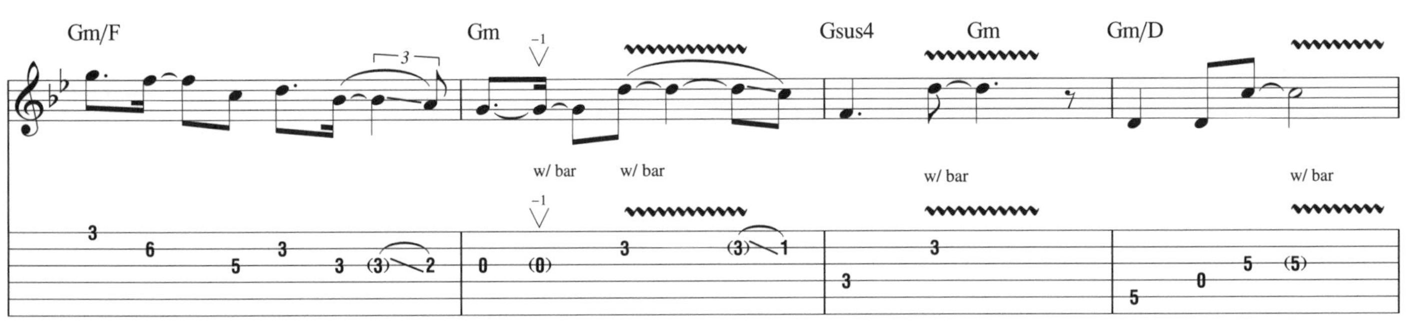

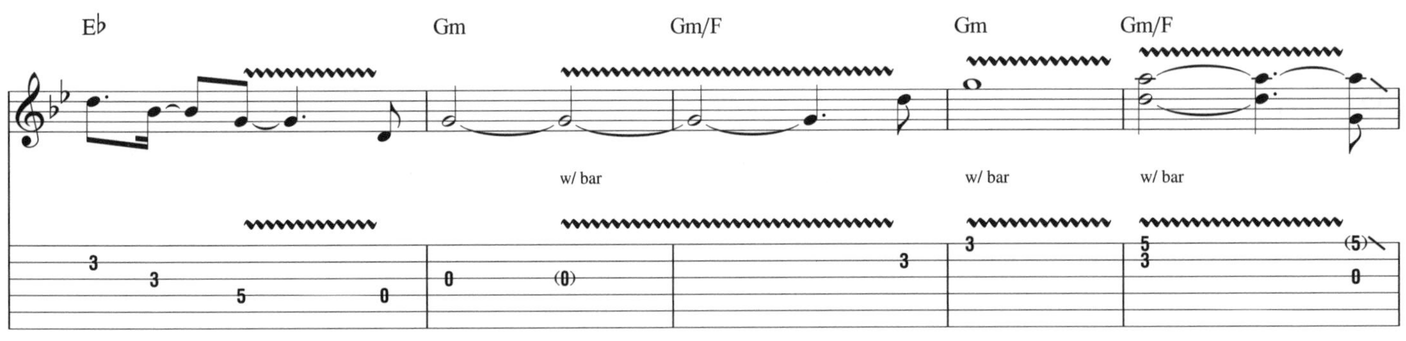

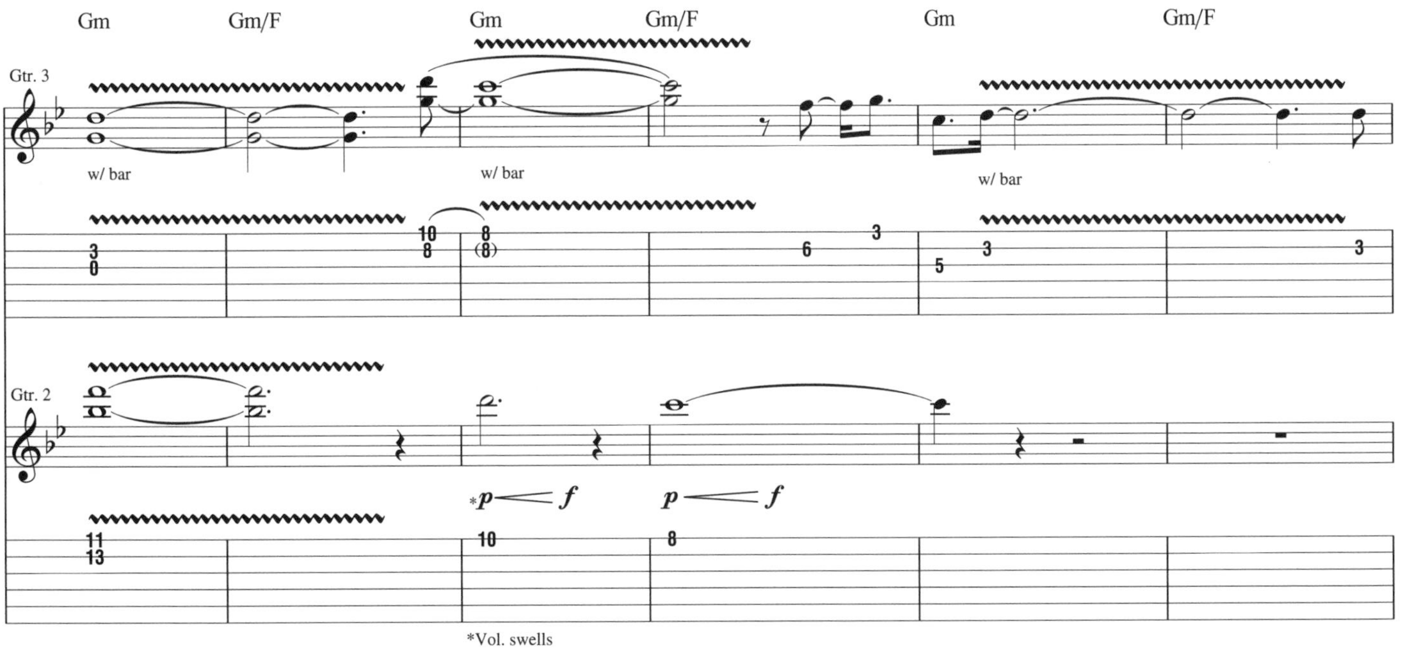
Gm
Gm/F
Gm
Gm/F
Gm
Gm/F
Gtr. 3
w/ bar
w/ bar
w/ bar
Gtr. 2
*p
f
p
f
*Vol. swells

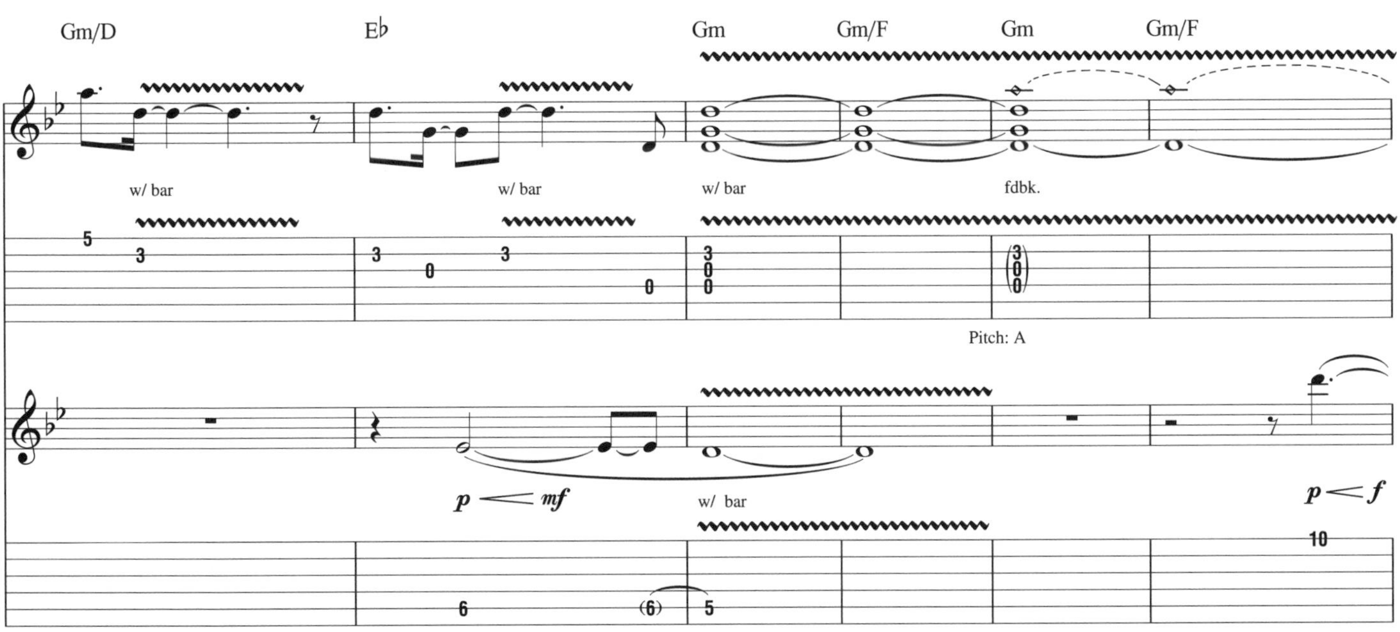
Gm/D
E♭
Gm
Gm/F
Gm
Gm/F
w/ bar
w/ bar
w/ bar
fdbk.
Pitch: A
p
mf
w/ bar
p
f

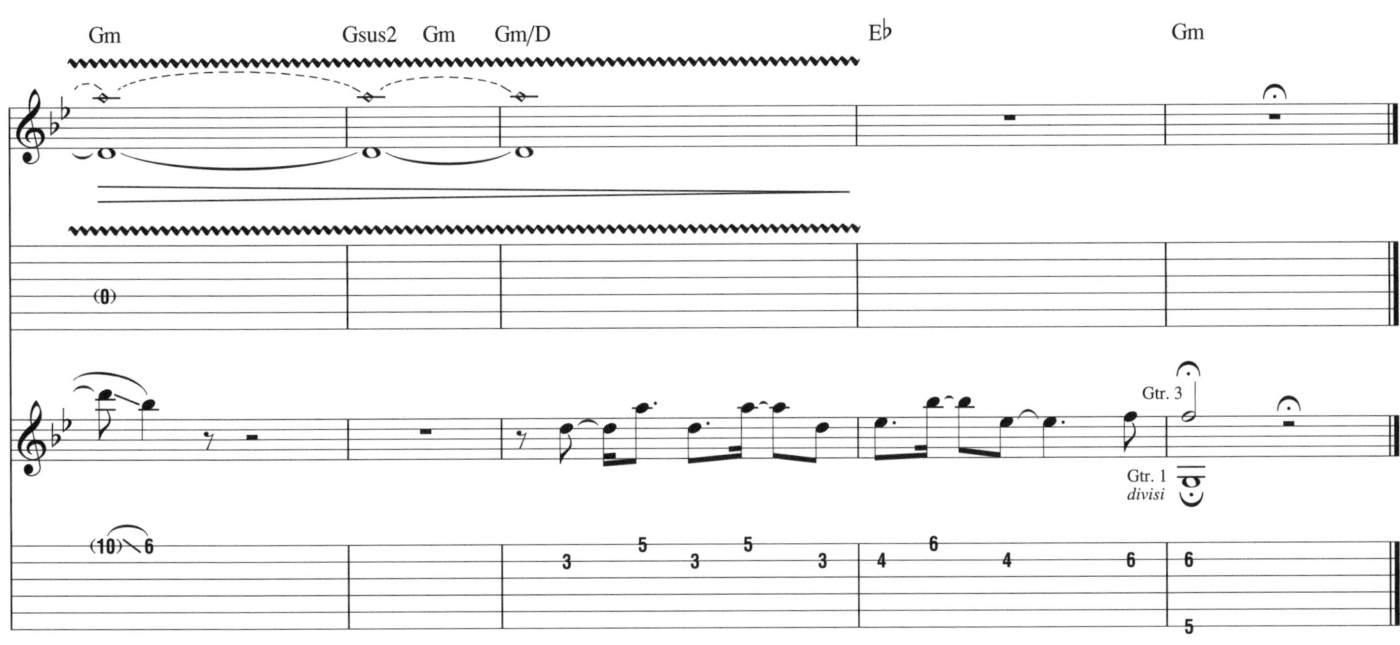
Gm
Gsus2
Gm
Gm/D
E♭
Gm
Gtr. 3
Gtr. 1
divisi

from *Breakdown*

Enough of Me

Words and Music by Melissa Etheridge

G5
D/A
Dsus4
Csus2
2 34
132
134
2 34

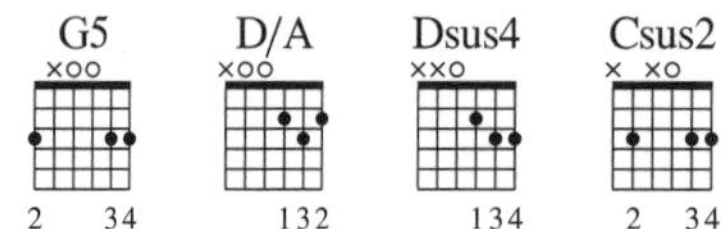

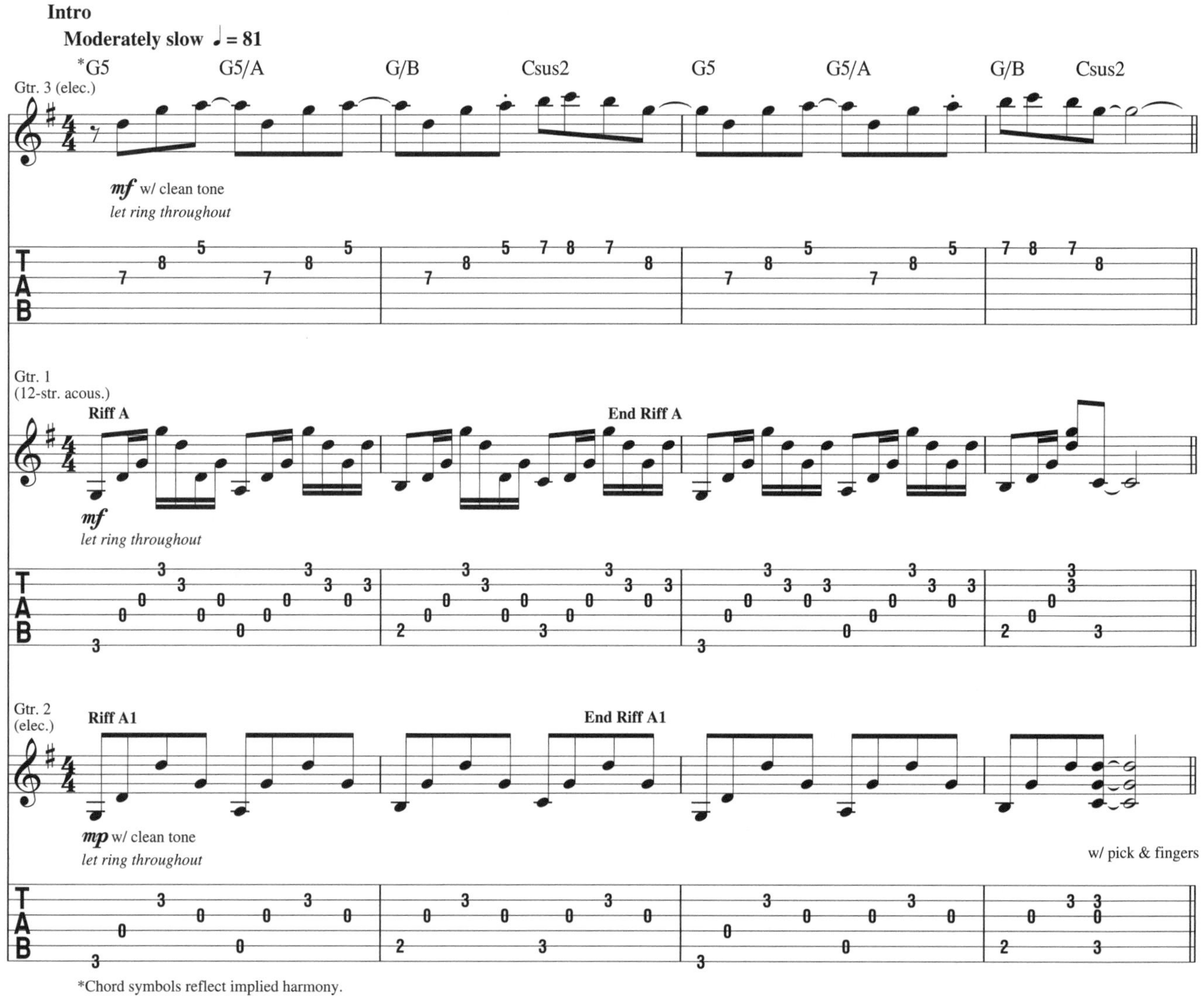

Intro
Moderately slow ♩ = 81
*G5
G5/A
G/B
Csus2
G5
G5/A
G/B
Csus2
Gtr. 3 (elec.)
mf w/ clean tone
let ring throughout
Gtr. 1
(12-str. acous.)
Riff A
End Riff A
mf
let ring throughout
Gtr. 2
(elec.)
Riff A1
End Riff A1
mp w/ clean tone
let ring throughout
w/ pick & fingers
*Chord symbols reflect implied harmony.

Verse
Gtrs. 1 & 2: w/ Riffs A & A1 (3 1/2 times)
Gtr. 3 tacet
G5
G5/A
G/B
Csus2
1. We were all wound - ed in some do - mes - tic war.
2. I was so sure one and one gave you one.
Gtr. 3
pp
(8)

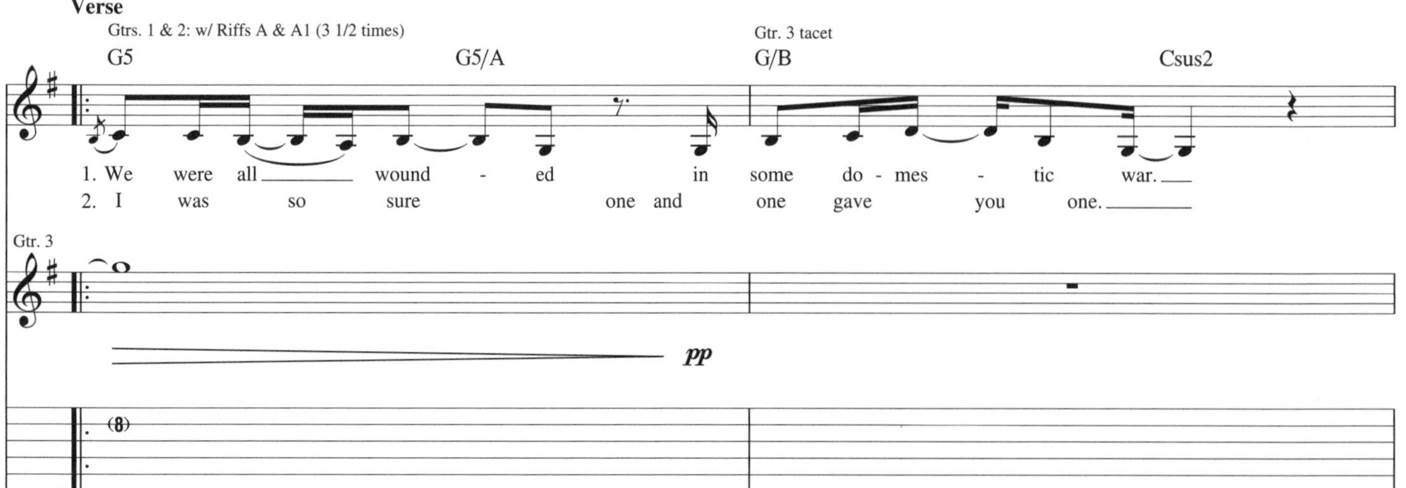

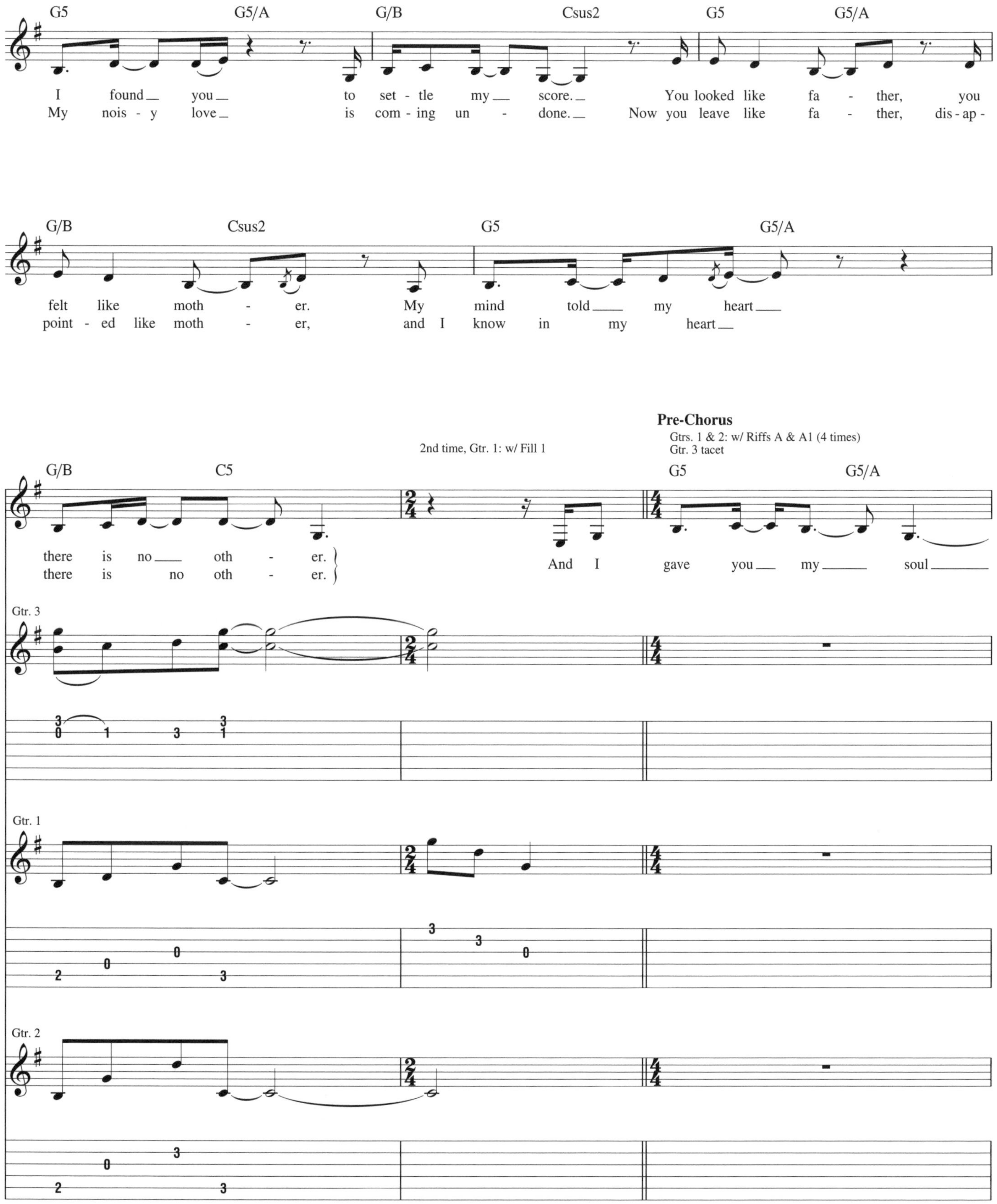

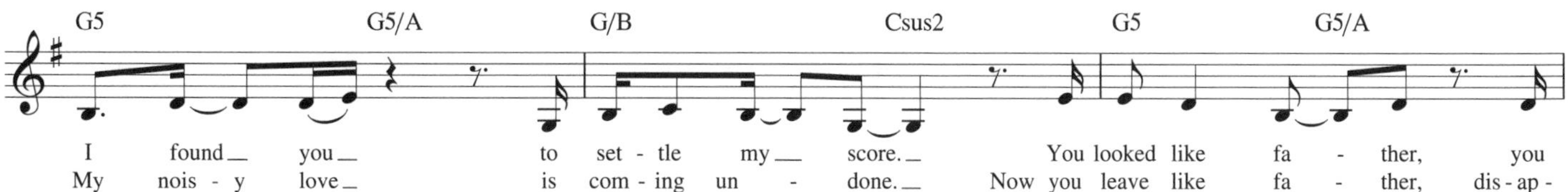

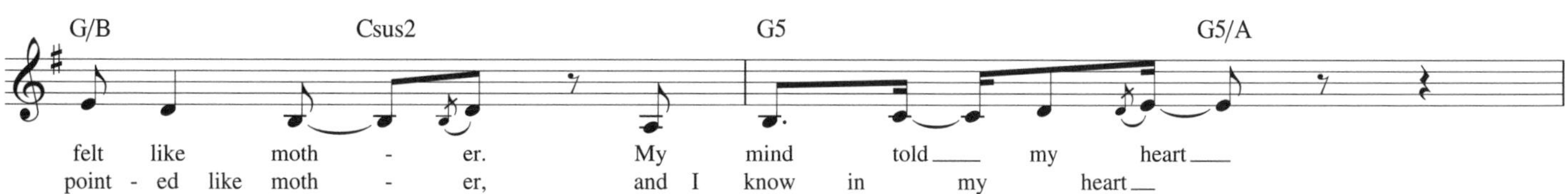

G5 G5/A G/B Csus2 G5 G5/A
I found you to set - tle my score. You looked like fa - ther, you
My nois - y love is com - ing un - done. Now you leave like fa - ther, dis - ap -
G/B Csus2 G5 G5/A
felt like moth - er. My mind told my heart
point - ed like moth - er, and I know in my heart
2nd time, Gtr. 1: w/ Fill 1
Pre-Chorus
Gtrs. 1 & 2: w/ Riffs A & A1 (4 times)
Gtr. 3 tacet
G/B C5 G5 G5/A
there is no oth - er.
there is no oth - er.
And I gave you my soul
Gtr. 3
Gtr. 1
Gtr. 2

Fill 1
Gtr. 1

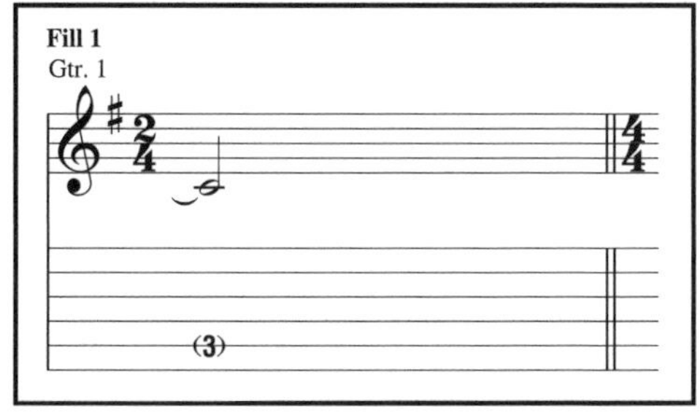

G/B Csus2 G5 G5/A G/B Csus2
and ev - 'ry ounce of con - trol. And I
2nd time, Gtr. 3: w/ Fill 2
G5 G5/A G/B Csus2 G5 G5/A
gave you my skin and my o - rig - i - nal sin. And I gave you my pride and my side.
gave you my shame and my e - ter - nal flame. And I gave you my need and my seed.
G/B Csus2
Chorus
G5 D/A Dsus4 Csus2 G5
Rhy. Fig. 1
Gtr. 5 (12-str. elec.)
w/ clean tone
let ring throughout
(cont. in notation)
Oh, my pride. Oh, my need. Ain't that e - nough. I turned your dreams in - to light - ning. Ain't that e - nough.
Gtr. 4 (elec.)
w/ slight dist.
let ring throughout
To Coda
D/A Dsus4 Csus2 G5 D/A Dsus4 Csus2
I held the world back for you. Ain't that e - nough. I loved you past the point of dy - ing. Ain't that e - nough
Gtr. 4
Gtr. 5
End Rhy. Fig. 1
Fill 2
Gtr. 3
pp
f

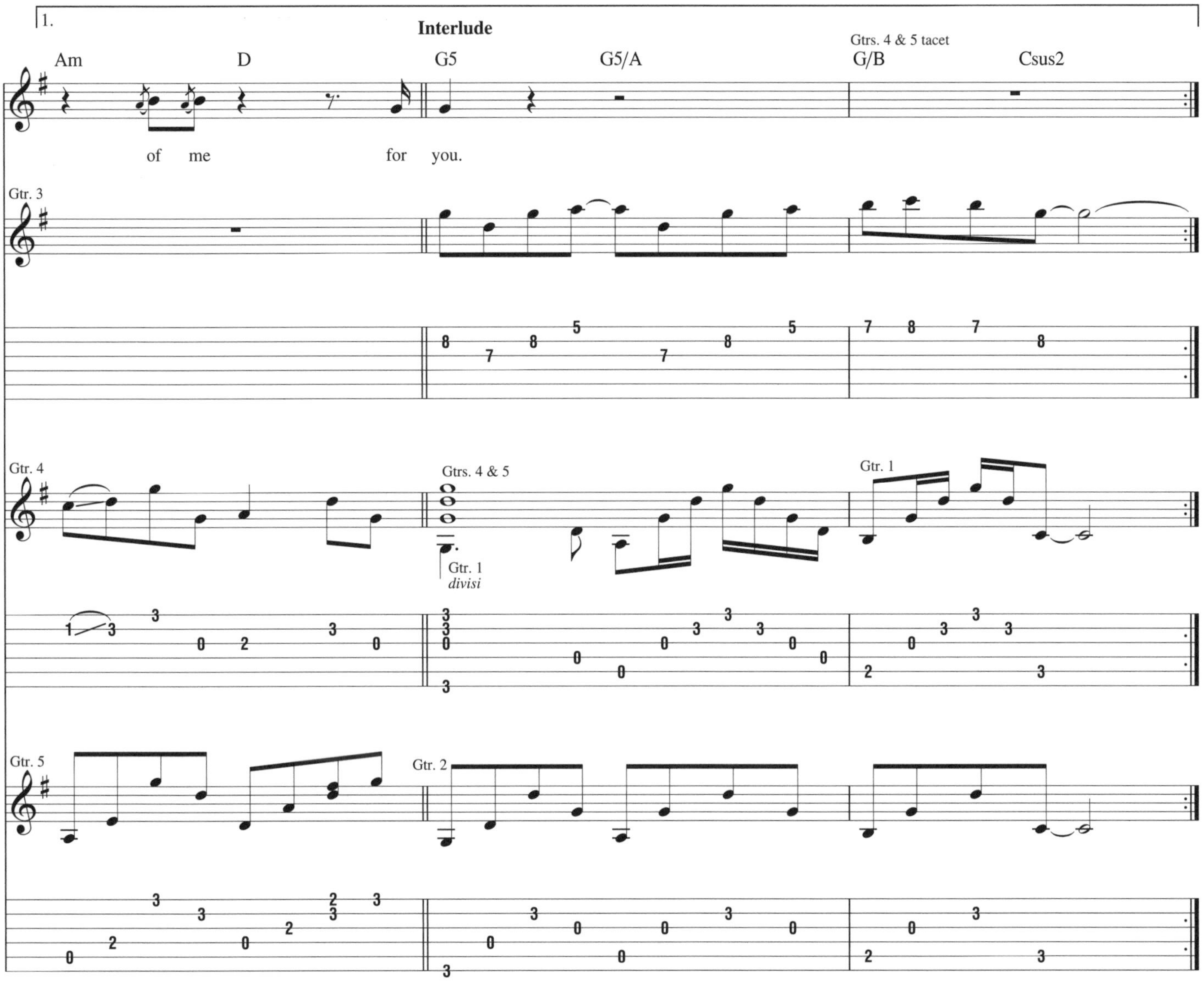

1.
Interlude
Am
D
G5
G5/A
Gtrs. 4 & 5 tacet
G/B
Csus2
of me
for you.
Gtr. 3
Gtr. 4
Gtrs. 4 & 5
Gtr. 1
divisi
Gtr. 1
Gtr. 5
Gtr. 2

2.
Bridge
Am7
D
C
G/B
Am
of me
for
you.
Gtr. 4
Gtr. 5

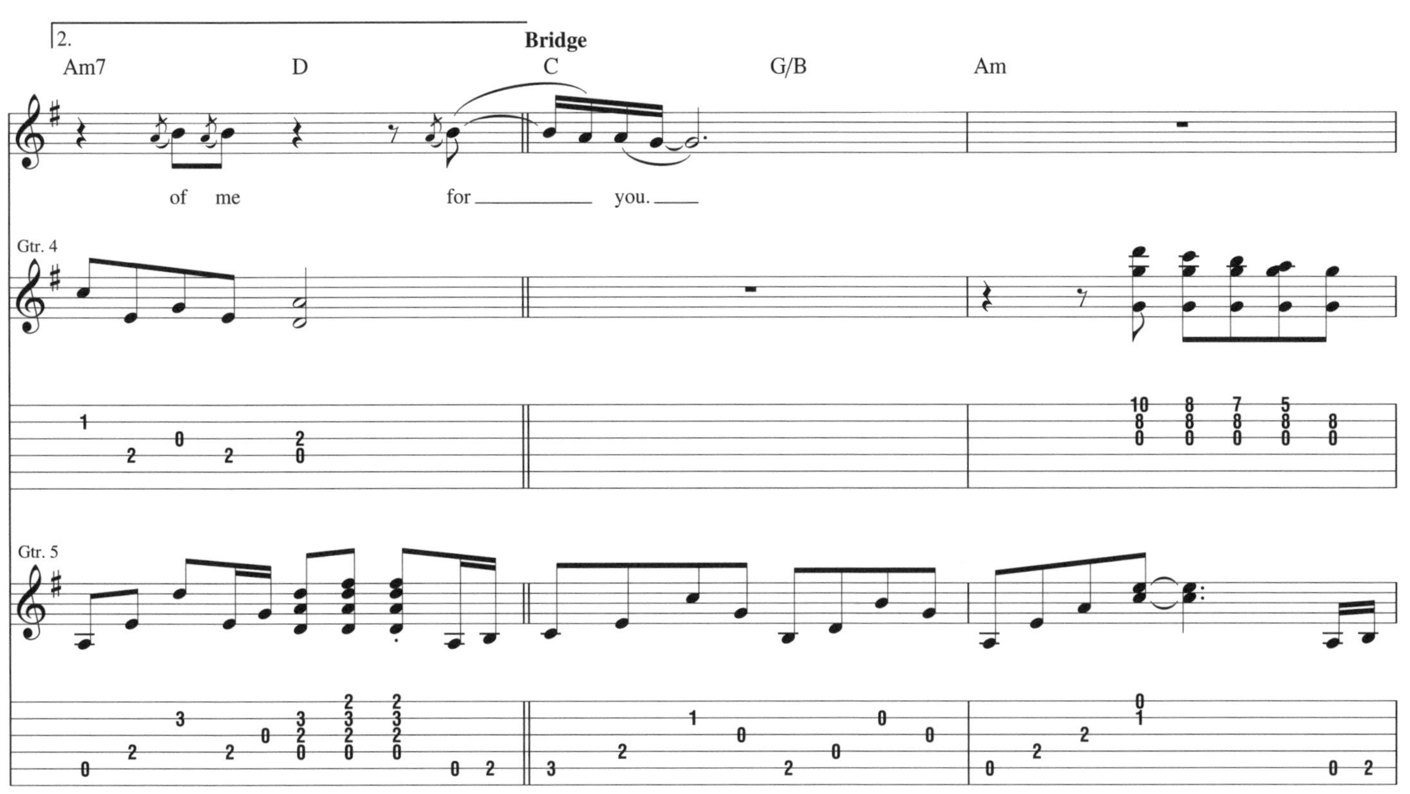

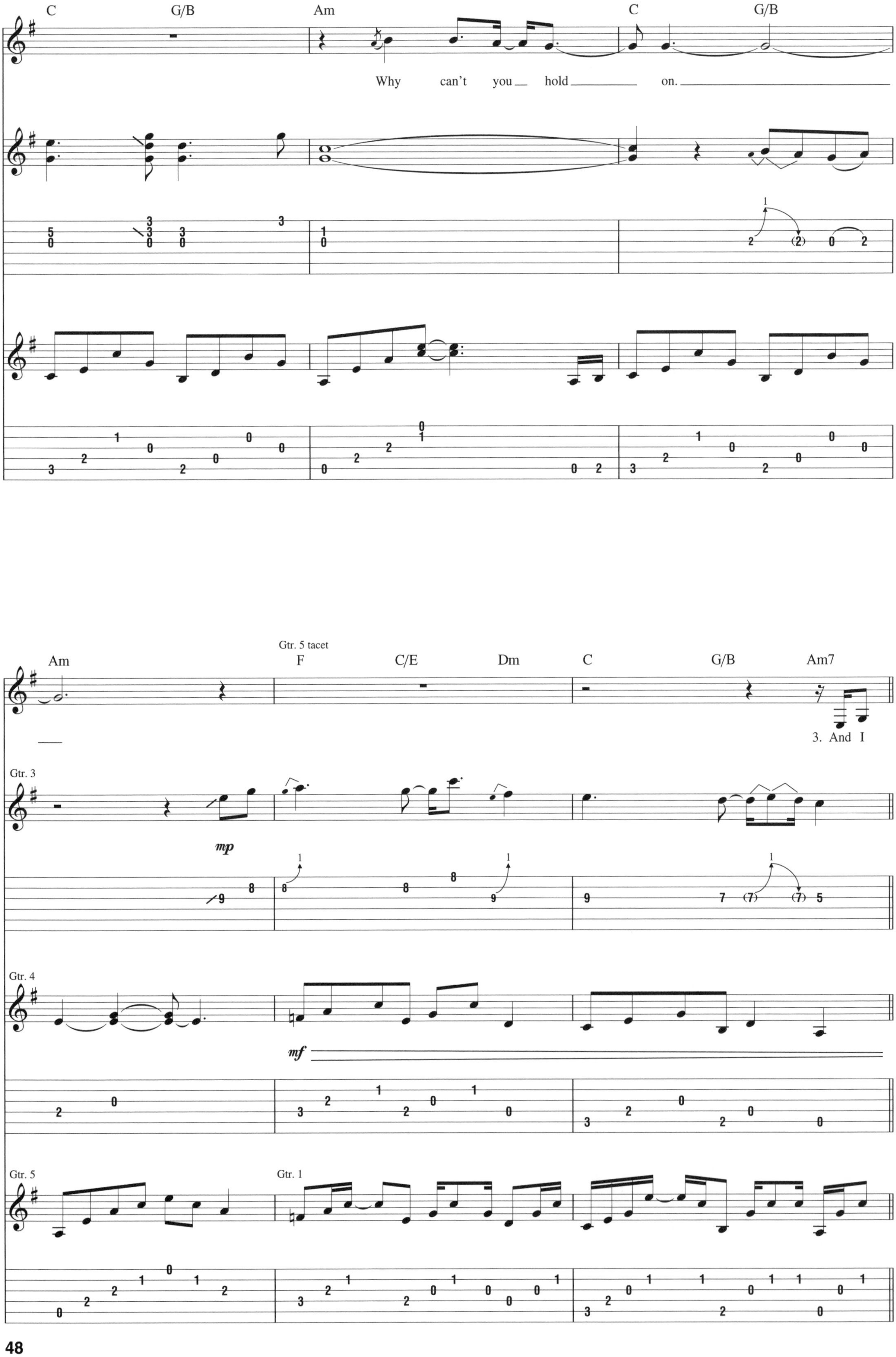

Gtr. 5 tacet

Am F C/E Dm C G/B Am7

3. And I

Gtr. 3

mp

Gtr. 4

mf

Gtr. 5

Gtr. 1

Verse
Gtr. 1: w/ Riff A (5 times)
Gtr. 3 tacet
Gtr. 4 tacet
G5 G5/A G/B Csus2 G5 G5/A
gave you my soul and ev - 'ry ounce of con - trol.
Gtr. 4
pp
G/B Csus2 G5 G5/B
And I gave you my skin and my o -
Gtr. 2: w/ Riff A1 (3 times)
G/B Csus2 G5 G5/A G/B Csus2
rig - i - nal sin. And I gave you my shame and my e - ter - nal flame. And I
Gtr. 3
pp cresc.
D.S. al Coda
G5 G5/A G/B Csus2 G5 G5/A G/B Csus2
gave you my pride and I gave you my side. And I gave you my need and my seed. Oh, my need. Ain't that e - nough.
Gtr. 3
Gtr. 1

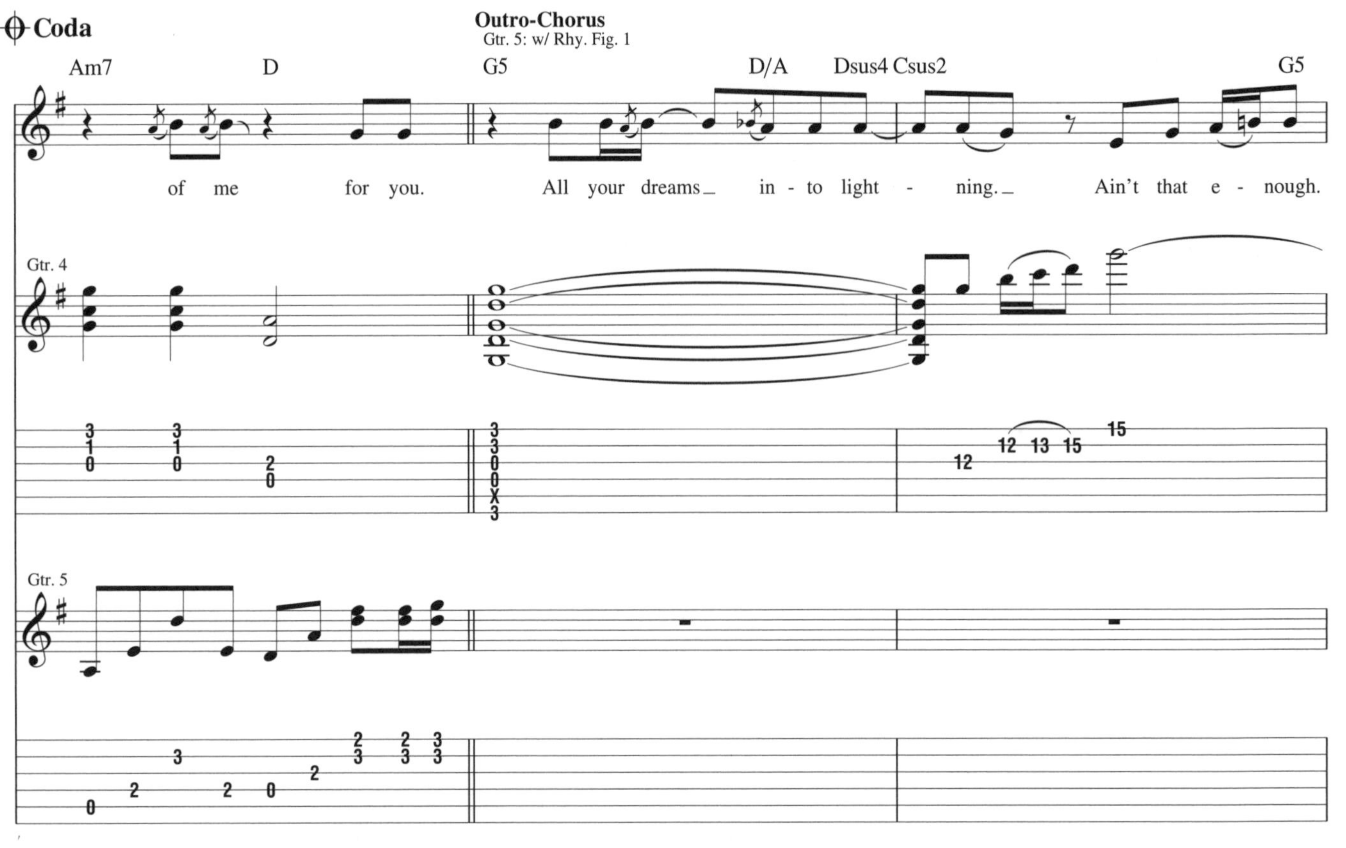
Coda
Outro-Chorus
Gtr. 5: w/ Rhy. Fig. 1
Am7
D
G5
D/A
Dsus4 Csus2
G5
of me for you. All your dreams_ in - to light - ning._ Ain't that e - nough.
Gtr. 4
Gtr. 5

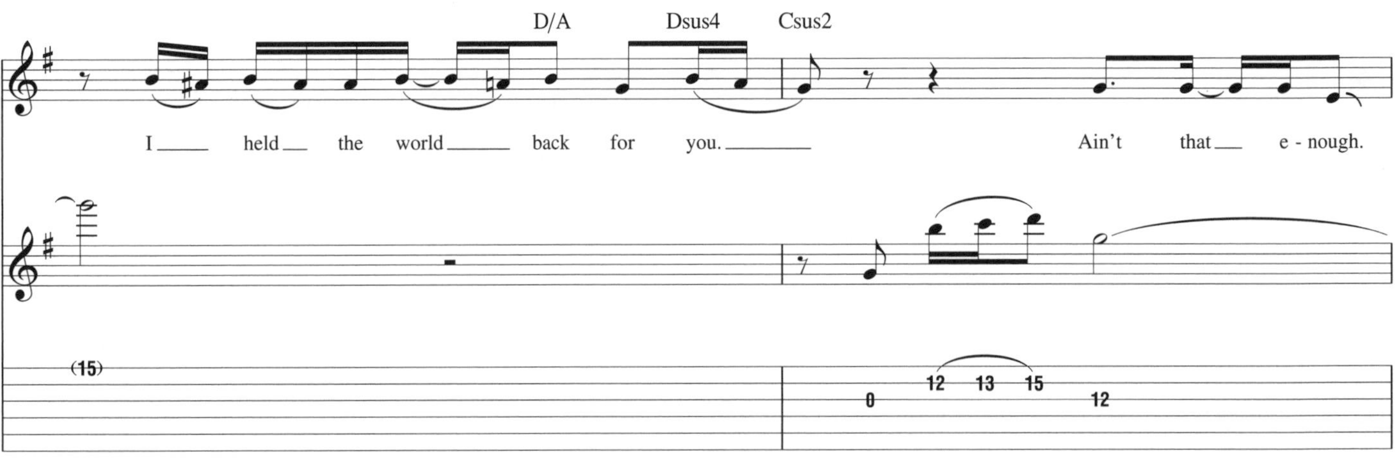
D/A
Dsus4
Csus2
I_ held_ the world_ back for you._ Ain't that_ e - nough.

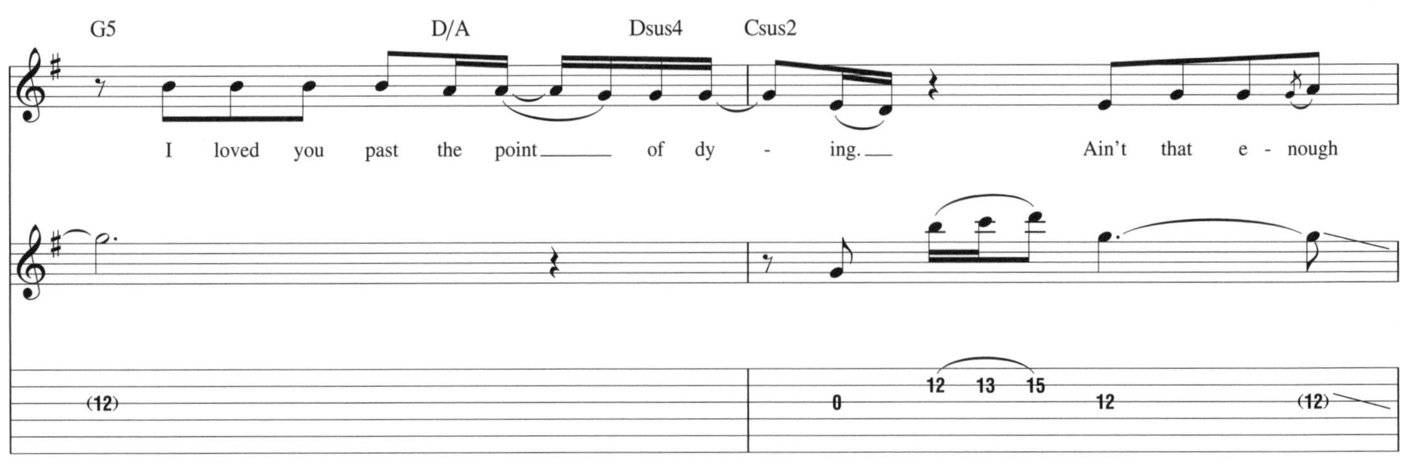
G5
D/A
Dsus4
Csus2
I loved you past the point_ of dy - ing._ Ain't that e - nough

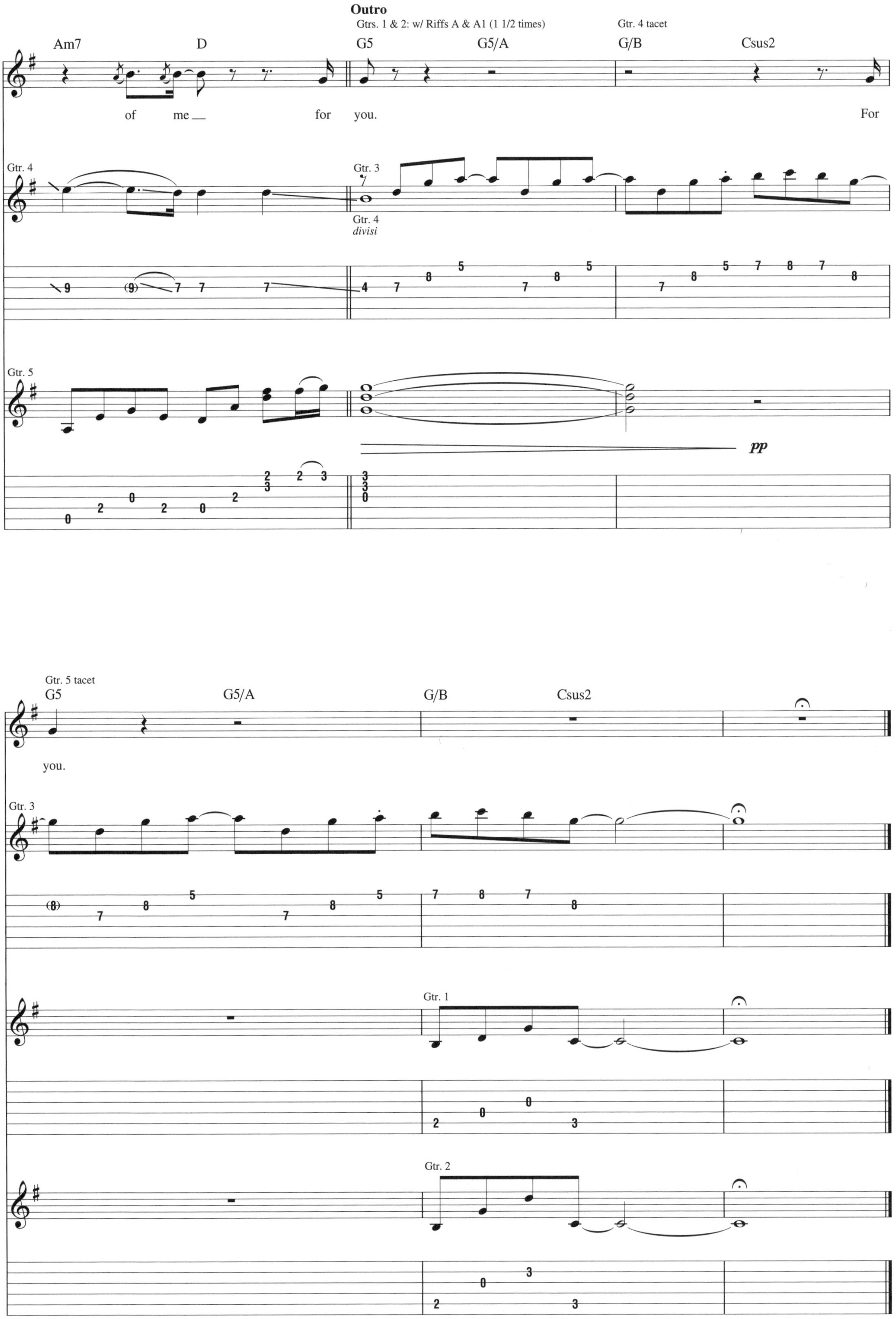

Outro

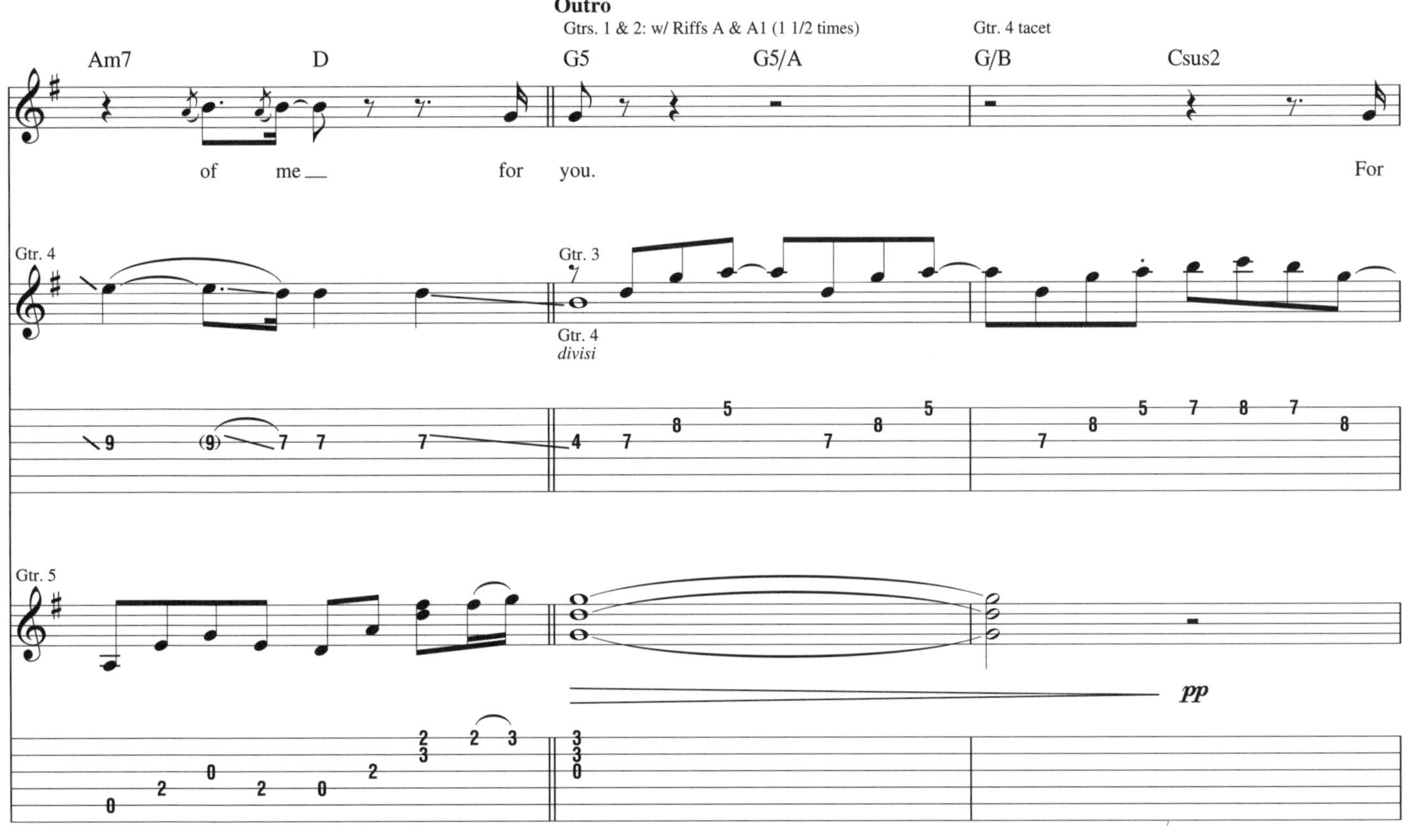

Gtr. 5 tacet

G5 G5/A G/B Csus2

you.

Gtr. 3

Gtr. 1

Gtr. 2

from *Skin*

I Want to Be in Love

Words and Music by Melissa Etheridge

A | Asus2 | Dmaj7sus2 | D^6_9(no3rd) | Bm | $Bsus^2_4$ | Bsus4

Dsus2 | F♯5 | Esus4 | E | D | A type 2 | Bm type 2

Intro

Moderately ♩ = 120

A Asus2 | A Asus2 | Dmaj7sus2 D^6_9(no3rd)

* Gtr. 1 (acous.)

mf

let ring throughout

Dmaj7sus2 D^6_9(no3rd) | Bm $Bsus^2_4$ Bsus4 | Dsus2 Dmaj7sus2 D^6_9(no3rd)

Oo, ______ yeah.

A Asus2 | A Asus2

1. I have

Verse

Bm

climbed the high-est moun-tain, I have

Rhy. Fig. 1

Dsus2 Dmaj7sus2 D^6_9(no3rd) | A Asus2

sailed a - cross the sea, I have wres-tled with my de - mons and woke up

A
Asus2
Bm
Bsus 2/4
Bsus4
with only me. I have been a-round the block three
Dsus2
Dmaj7sus2
D6/9(no3rd)
F#5
times, may-be four and I think I de-
A
Esus4
E
serve, just a lit-tle more. In
End Rhy. Fig. 1
(cont. in slashes)
Chorus
Rhy. Fig. 2
Gtr. 1
front of to-tal strang-ers, won't you kiss me.
Whispered: Won't you kiss me.
* Gtr. 2
mf
* Piano arr. for gtr.

Dsus2
Flow - ers for no rea - son, but you miss me.
But you miss me.
4 6 7

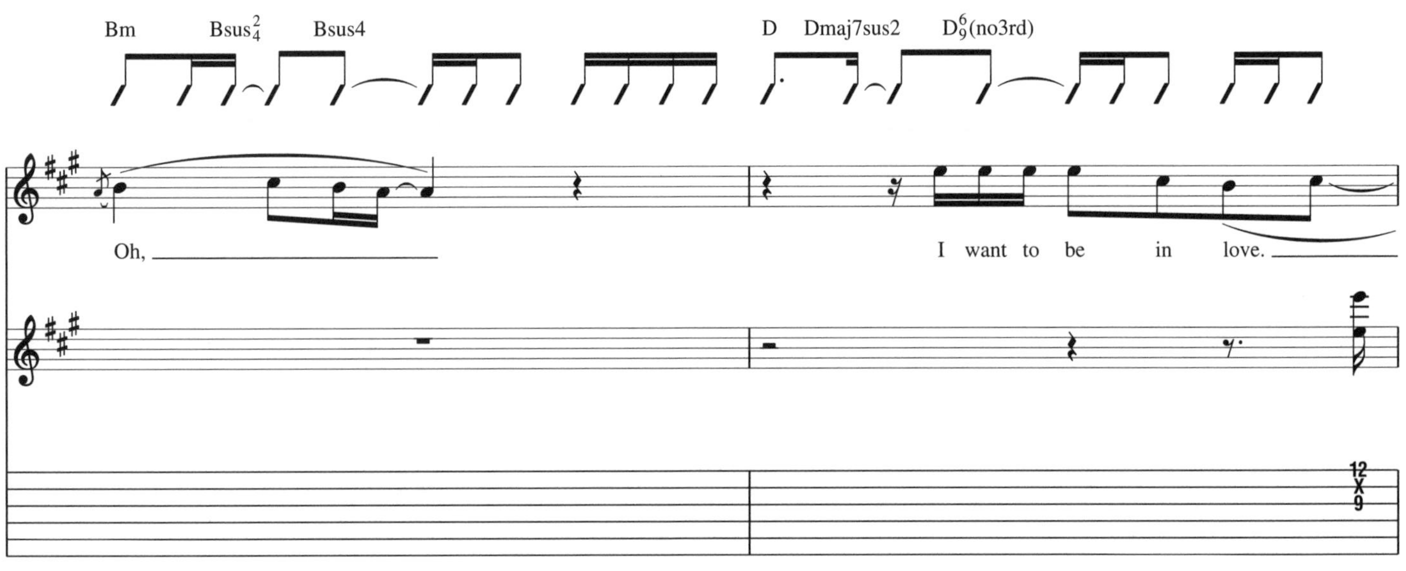
Bm Bsus$^{2}_{4}$ Bsus4
D Dmaj7sus2 D$^{6}_{9}$(no3rd)
Oh,
I want to be in love.
12
X
9

A Asus2 A
End Rhy. Fig. 2
(I want to be in love, be in love.)
You're
12
X
9

Gtr. 1: w/ Rhy. Fig. 2
A
Asus2
A
Asus2
stand - ing on ___ the door - step in the rain ___
'cause you
Riff A
6 7 5

Dsus2
Bm Bsus$^{2}_{4}$ Bsus4
could-n't wait to see me once a - gain. ______
Oh, ________________
4 6 7

D Dmaj7sus2 D$^{6}_{9}$(no3rd)
A
Asus2
A
I want to be in love. ________
2. I have
(I want to be in love, ______ be in love.)
End Riff A
12 X 9
12 X 9
4 6 7

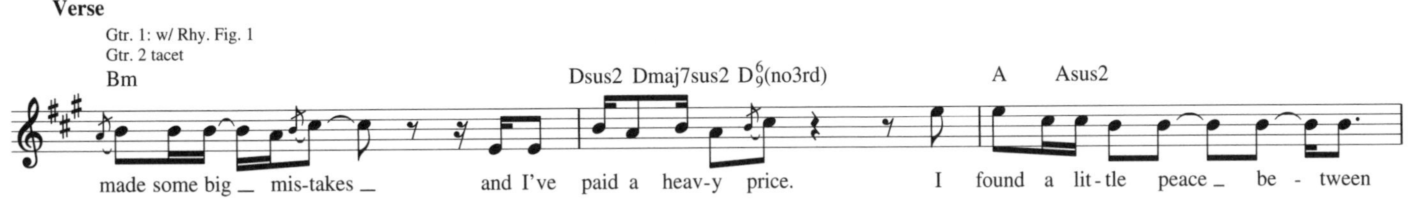
Verse
Gtr. 1: w/ Rhy. Fig. 1
Gtr. 2 tacet
Bm
Dsus2 Dmaj7sus2 D$^{6}_{9}$(no3rd)
A
Asus2
made some big __ mis-takes __
and I've paid a heav-y price.
I found a lit-tle peace __ be - tween

A
Asus2
Bm
Bsus2/4
Bsus4
will and sac - ri - fice. I have watched as all my dreams went

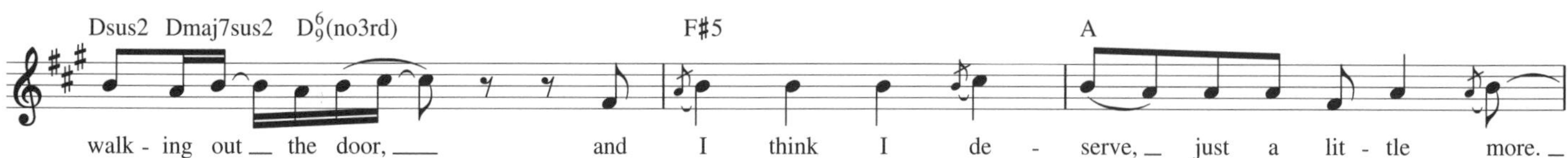
Dsus2
Dmaj7sus2
D6/9(no3rd)
F#5
A
walk - ing out the door, and I think I de - serve, just a lit - tle more.

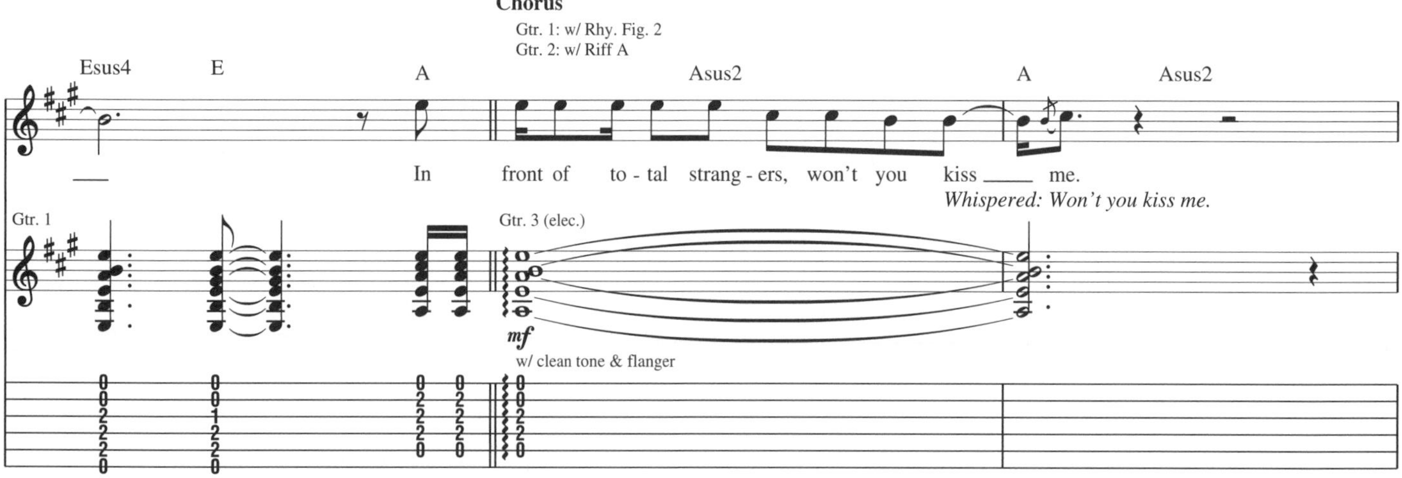
Chorus
Gtr. 1: w/ Rhy. Fig. 2
Gtr. 2: w/ Riff A
Esus4
E
A
Asus2
A
Asus2
In front of to - tal strang - ers, won't you kiss me.
Whispered: Won't you kiss me.
Gtr. 1
Gtr. 3 (elec.)
mf
w/ clean tone & flanger

Dsus2
Bm
Bsus2/4
Bsus4
Flow - ers for no rea - son, but you miss me.
But you miss me.
Oh,

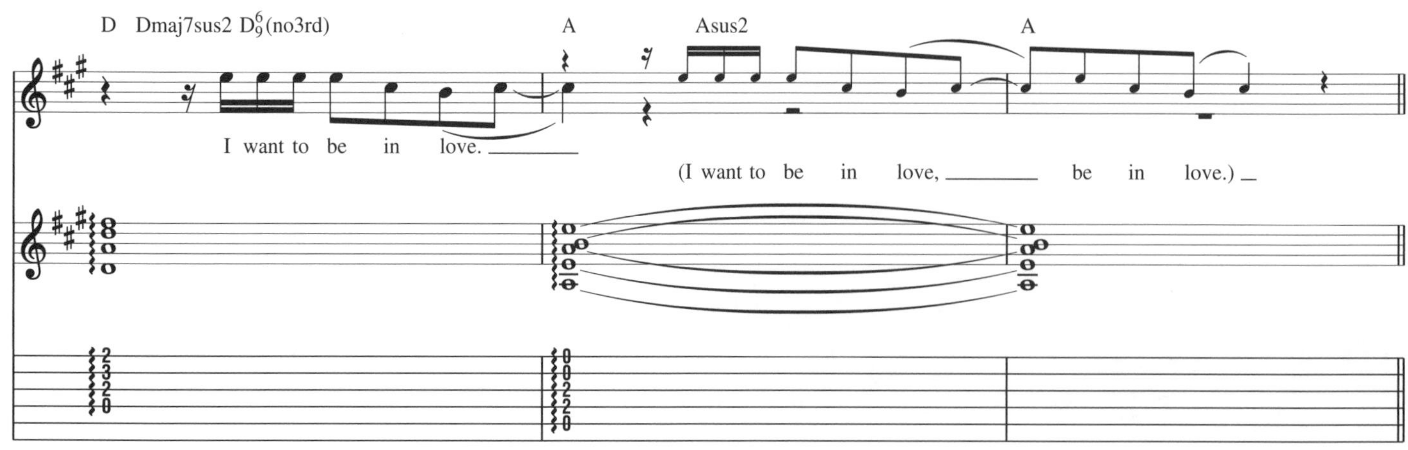
D
Dmaj7sus2
D6/9(no3rd)
A
Asus2
A
I want to be in love.
(I want to be in love, be in love.)

Bridge

F#5 | A type2

Gtr. 1

sim.

I'm ___ look-ing for ___ a heart ___ of gold. ___ I'm ___ look-ing for

Gtr. 3

Gtr. 4 (elec.)

mf w/ clean tone

P.M.

Bm type2 | D

a hand ___ to hold. ___ A hap-py end, ___ strong ___ and kind, ___

let ring

let ring

P.M.

let ring

let ring

F♯m
A
Esus4
E
E
Asus2
some - where to rest my troub-led mind.
In
let ring
P.M.
P.M.
P.M.
let ring
Chorus
Gtr. 4 tacet
Asus2
Gtr. 1
D$^6_9$(no3rd)
front of to-tal strang-ers, won't you kiss me.
Whispered: Won't you kiss me.
Flow-ers for no rea - son, but you miss
Gtr. 3
Bm
Bsus$^2_4$
Bsus4
Dsus2
Dmaj7sus2
D$^6_9$(no3rd)
A
me.
Oh,
I want to be in love.

Gtr. 1: w/ Rhy. Fig. 2 (2 times)
Gtr. 2: w/ Riff A (1st 4 meas. only)
Asus2
A
Asus2
On Tues - day light the can - dles, bring me wine.
Riff B
let ring throughout
A
Asus2
Dsus2
Wednes - day morn - ing I won't get to work on
time.
Bm
Bsus$^2_4$
Bsus4
Oh,
D
Dmaj7sus2
D$^6_9$(no3rd)
A
Asus2
A
I want to be in love.
(I want to be in love, be in love.)
Yeah, sur -
End Riff B

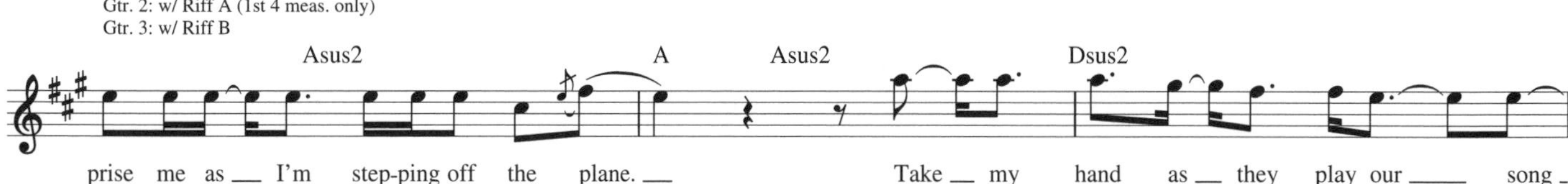
Gtr. 2: w/ Riff A (1st 4 meas. only)
Gtr. 3: w/ Riff B
Asus2
A
Asus2
Dsus2
prise me as I'm step-ping off the plane.
Take my hand as they play our song

Bm Bsus$^2_4$ Bsus4
D Dmaj7sus2 D$^6_9$(no3rd)
a - gain.
Oh,
whoa,
I want to be in love.

Outro-Chorus
Gtr. 1: w/ Rhy. Fig. 2 (till fade)
Gtr. 2: w/ Riff A (1st 4 meas. only)
Gtr. 3: w/ Riff B (till fade)
A
Asus2
A
A
Asus2
I
want to be
in
front of to - tal strang - ers

A
Asus2
Dsus2
when you kiss me.
Flow - ers for no rea - son, but you miss me.

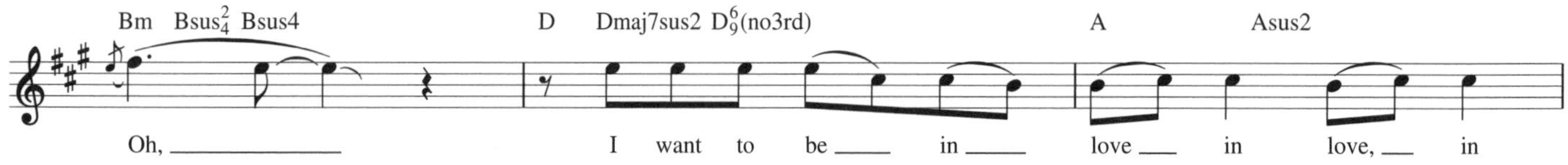
Bm Bsus$^2_4$ Bsus4
D Dmaj7sus2 D$^6_9$(no3rd)
A
Asus2
Oh,
I want to be in
love in love, in

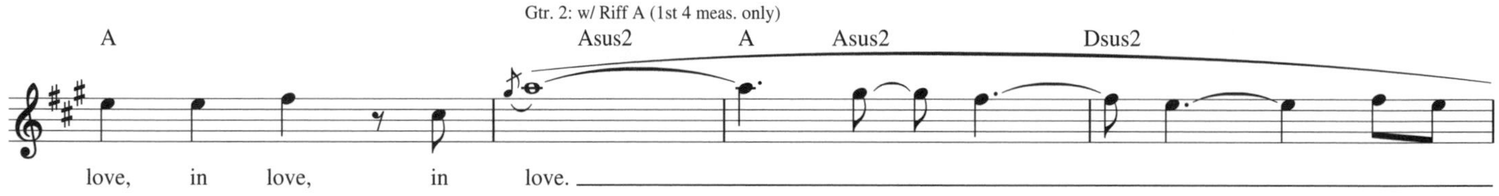
A
Gtr. 2: w/ Riff A (1st 4 meas. only)
Asus2
A
Asus2
Dsus2
love, in love, in
love.

Begin fade
Bm Bsus$^2_4$ Bsus4
D Dmaj7sus2 D$^6_9$(no3rd)
Oh,
(I want to be in love,

Fade out
A
Asus2
A
Gtr. 2: w/ Riff A (1st 4 meas. only)
Asus2
A Asus2
Dsus2
be in love,
I want to be in love.)

from *Your Little Secret*

I Want to Come Over

Words and Music by Melissa Etheridge

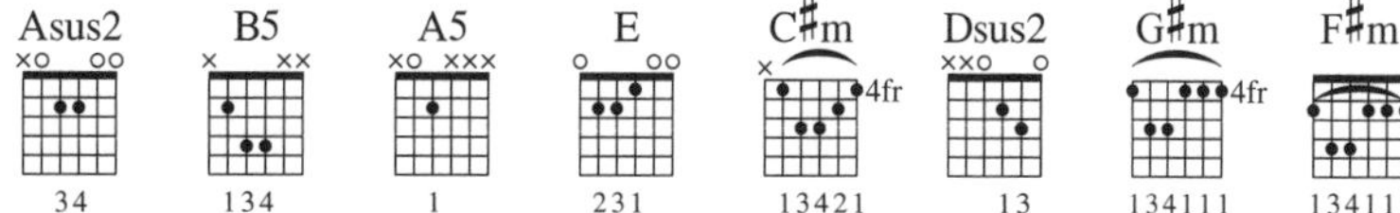

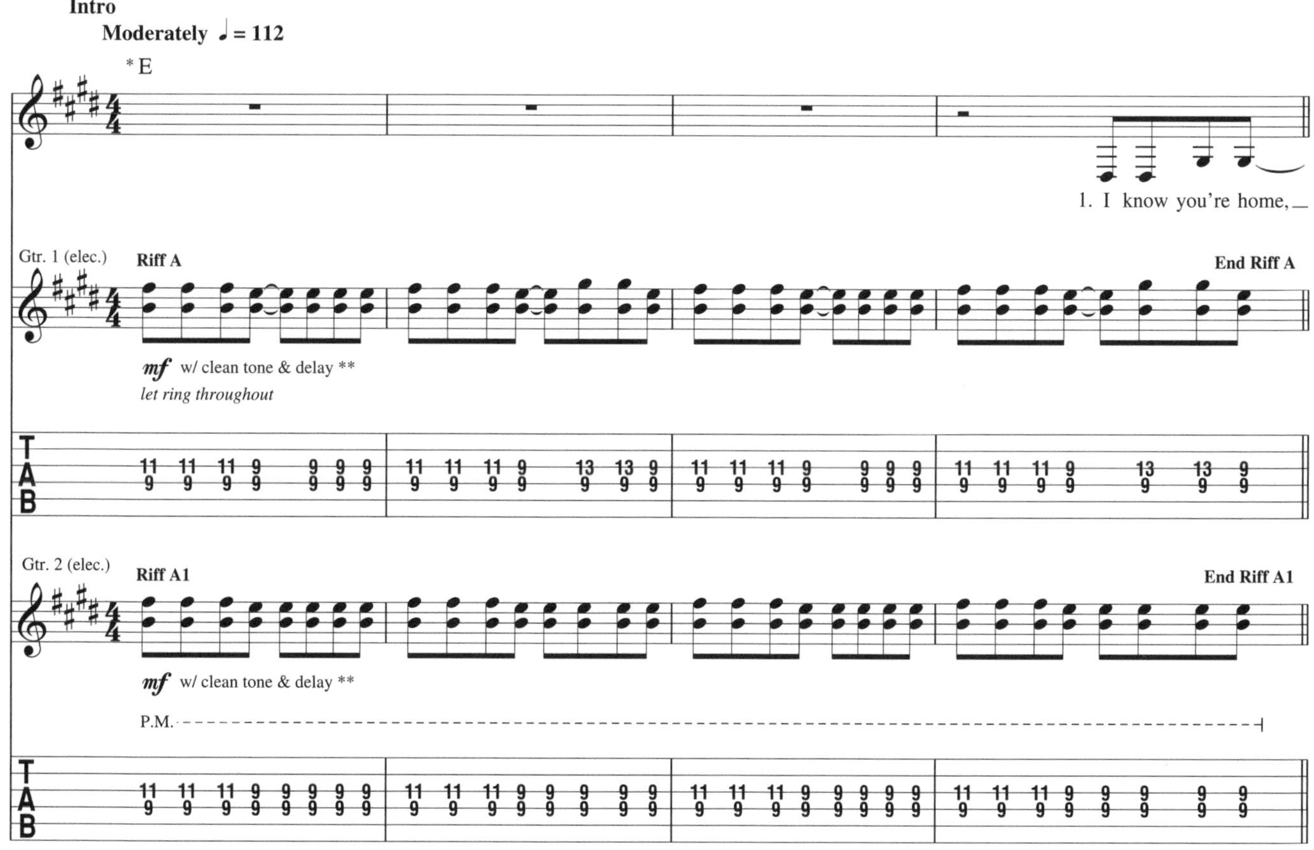

*Chord symbols reflect overall harmony.

**Delay set for dotted eighth note regeneration w/ 2 repeats.

D
A
E
the night is thin.
I know you're a - lone,

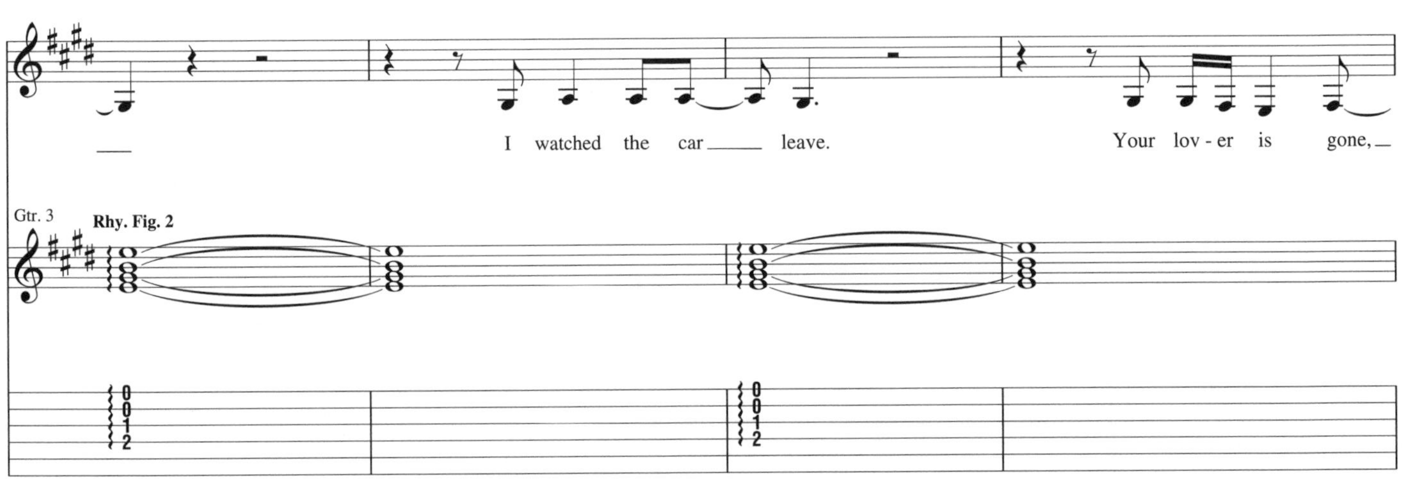
I watched the car leave.
Your lov - er is gone,
Gtr. 3
Rhy. Fig. 2

Dsus2
A5
E
let me in.
Gtr. 3
End Rhy. Fig. 2
Gtr. 4 (elec.)
mf w/ clean tone
let ring throughout
(cont. in slashes)

Pre-Chorus
Asus2
Gtr. 4
B5
O - pen your back door, I just need to touch you once
Gtrs. 3, 5 (12-str. acous.)
& *6 (elec.)
mf w/ slight dist.
let ring throughout
*Gtr. 6, two gtrs. arr. for one.

Asus2
A5
more. Oh, ho. I want to come o -
(Gtr. 5 cont. in slashes)

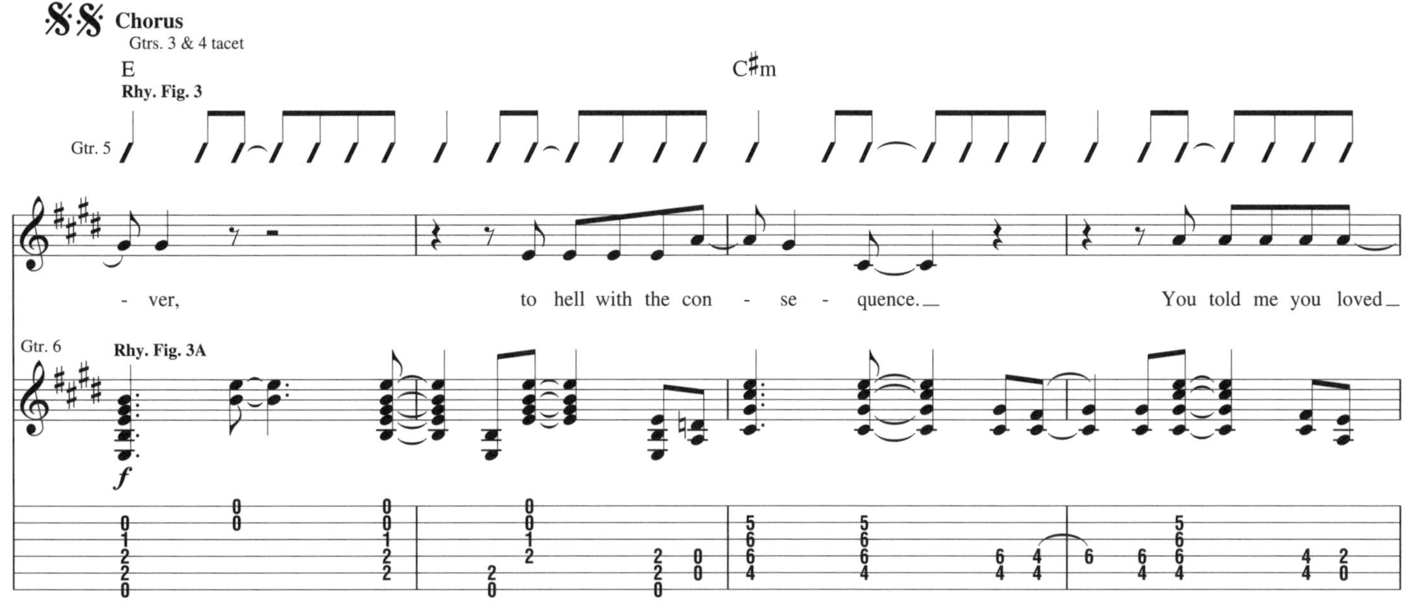
Chorus
Gtrs. 3 & 4 tacet
E
C#m
Rhy. Fig. 3
Gtr. 5
- ver, to hell with the con - se - quence. You told me you loved
Gtr. 6
Rhy. Fig. 3A

To Coda 2
Asus2
Dsus2
Asus2
End Rhy. Fig. 3
me, that's all I be-lieve. I want to come o-
End Rhy. Fig. 3A

E
G♯m
- ver. It's a need I can't ex - plain, to

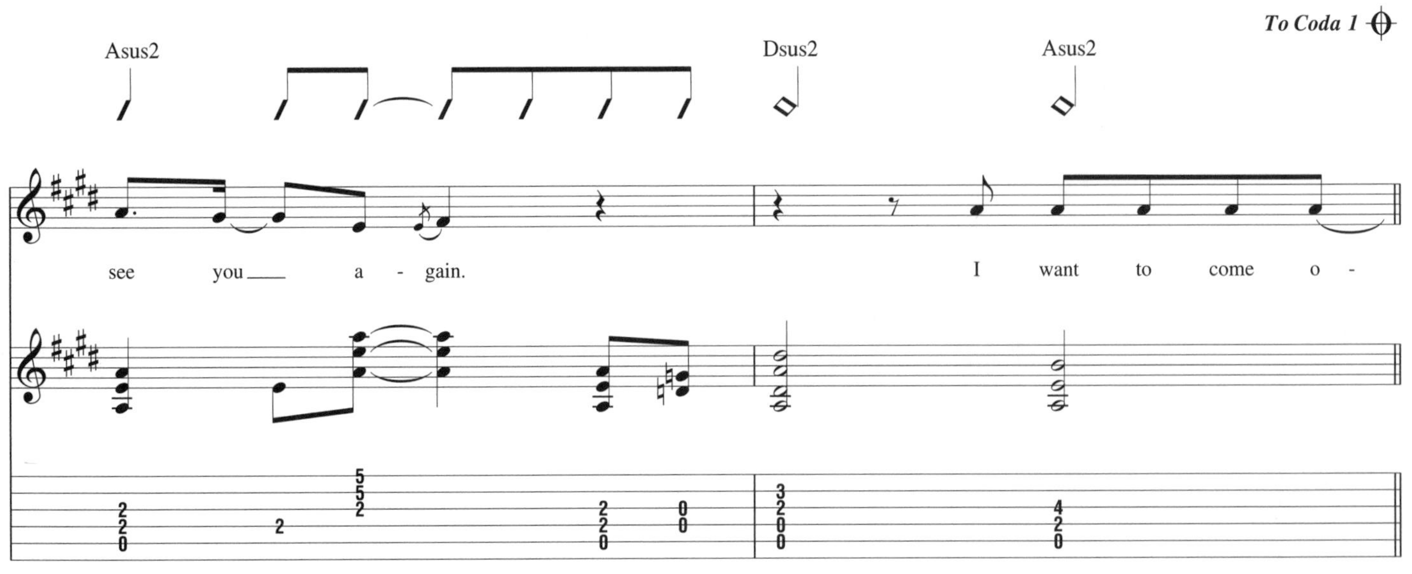
To Coda 1
Asus2
Dsus2
Asus2
see you a - gain. I want to come o -

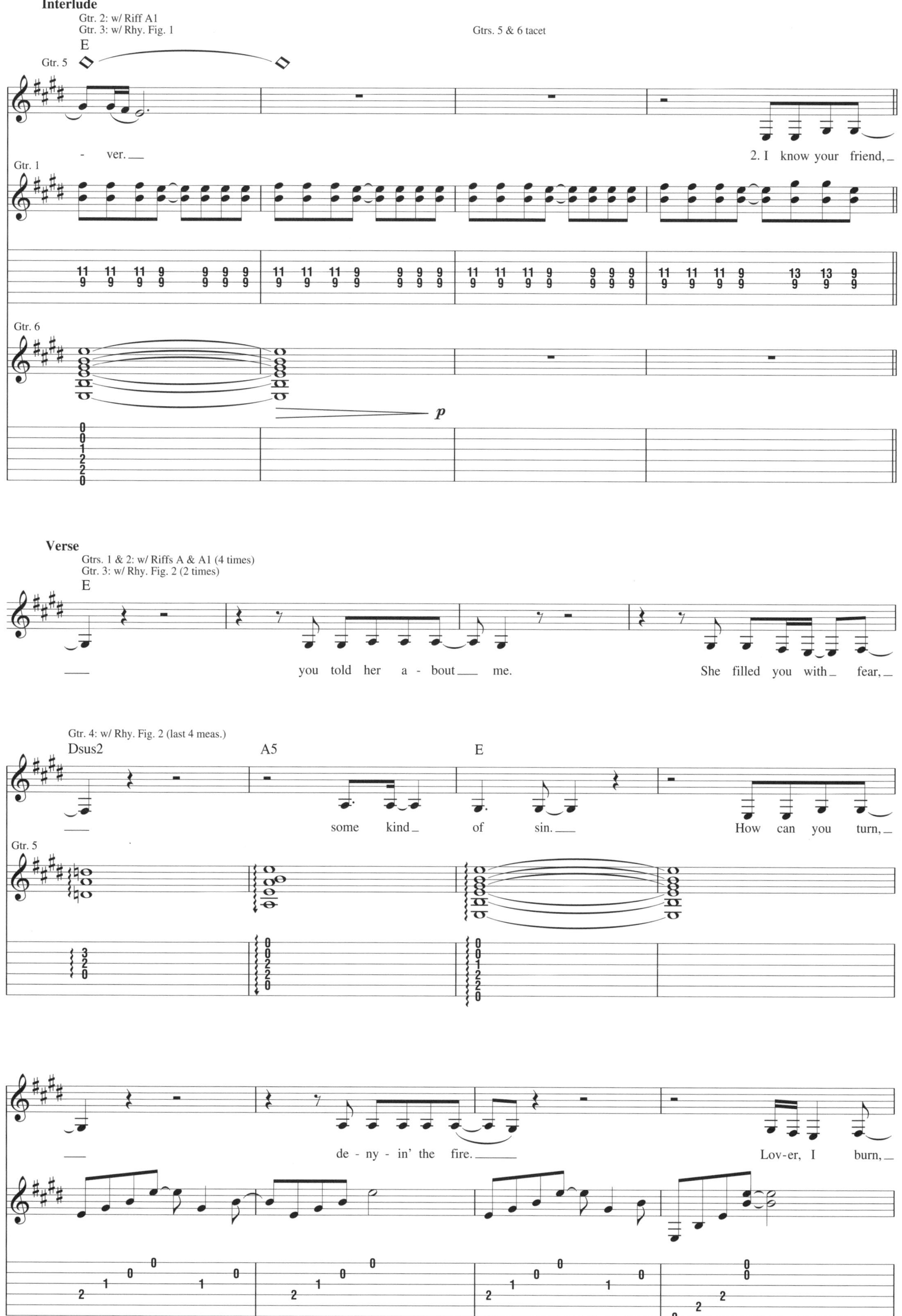

Interlude
Gtr. 2: w/ Riff A1
Gtr. 3: w/ Rhy. Fig. 1
Gtrs. 5 & 6 tacet
E
Gtr. 5
- ver.
2. I know your friend,
Gtr. 1
Gtr. 6
p
Verse
Gtrs. 1 & 2: w/ Riffs A & A1 (4 times)
Gtr. 3: w/ Rhy. Fig. 2 (2 times)
E
you told her a - bout me.
She filled you with fear,
Gtr. 4: w/ Rhy. Fig. 2 (last 4 meas.)
Dsus2
A5
E
some kind of sin.
How can you turn,
Gtr. 5
de - ny - in' the fire.
Lov-er, I burn,

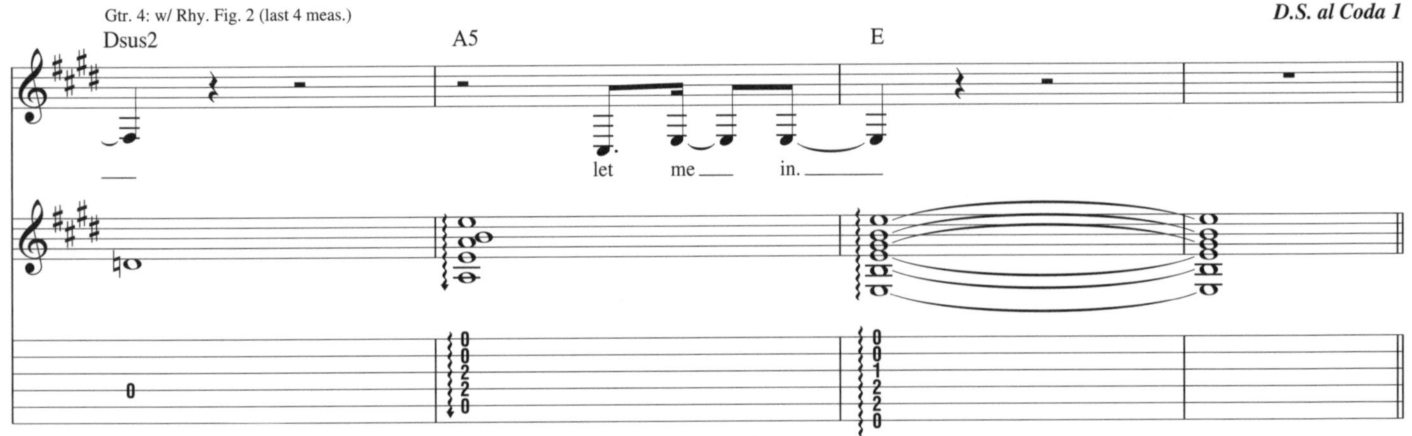
Gtr. 4: w/ Rhy. Fig. 2 (last 4 meas.)
D.S. al Coda 1
Dsus2
A5
E
let me in.

Coda 1
E
- ver.

Bridge
Gtr. 6 tacet
F♯m
Asus2
1.
Gtr. 5
Oh.
Gtr. 1
Gtr. 4

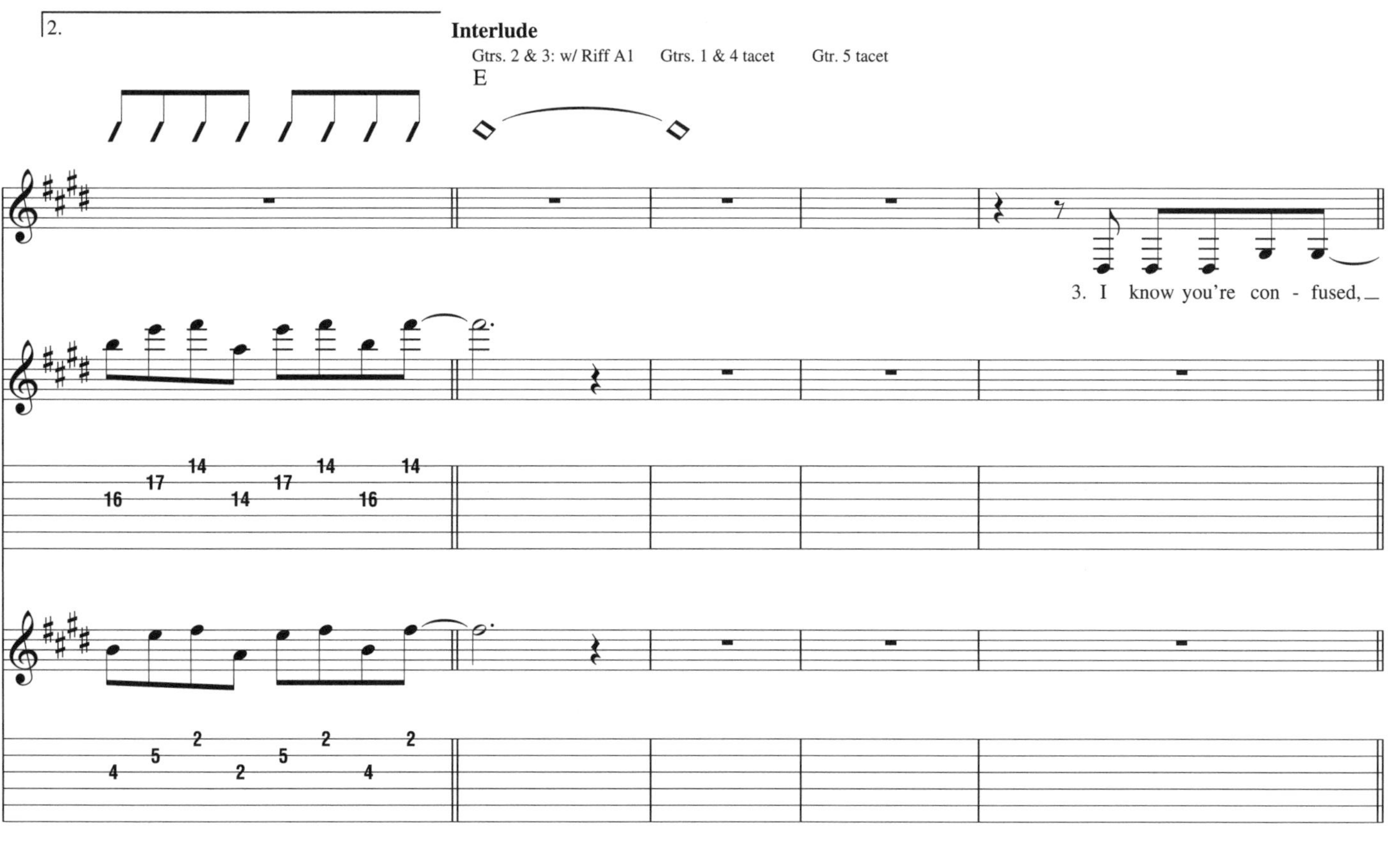
2.
Interlude
Gtrs. 2 & 3: w/ Riff A1
Gtrs. 1 & 4 tacet
Gtr. 5 tacet
E
3. I know you're con - fused,
16
17
14
14
17
14
16
14
4
5
2
2
5
2
4
2

Verse

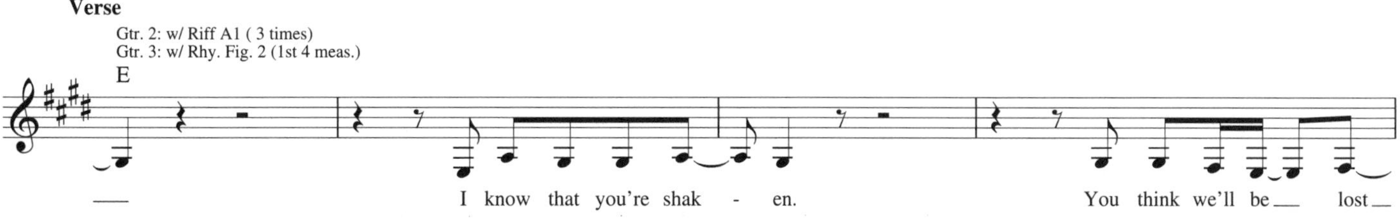
Gtr. 2: w/ Riff A1 (3 times)
Gtr. 3: w/ Rhy. Fig. 2 (1st 4 meas.)
E
I know that you're shak - en.
You think we'll be lost

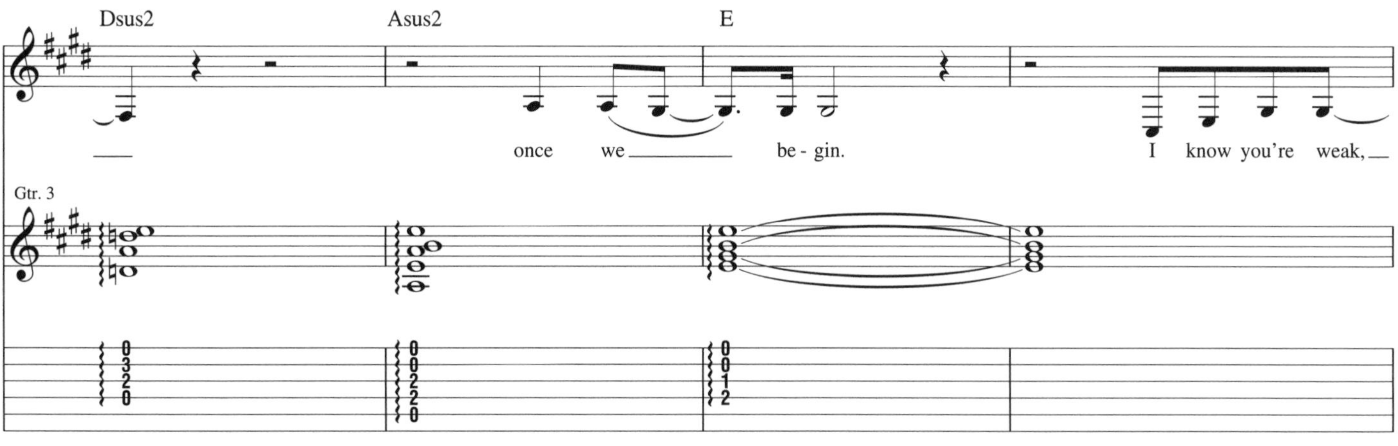
Dsus2
Asus2
E
once we be - gin.
I know you're weak,
Gtr. 3

Gtr. 1: w/ Riff A
Gtr. 3: w/ Rhy. Fig. 2 (1st 4 meas.)
I know that you want me.
Lov - er, don't

Dsus2 A5 N.C.

Gtrs. 1, 2, 3, 4 & 5 tacet

— speak, let me in. I want to come o -

Gtrs. 3, 4 & 5

Gtr. 1

delay off

Gtr. 2

delay off

P.M.

Asus2
Dsus2
Asus2
End Rhy. Fig. 4
- ver
to see you,
to see you a -
End Rhy. Fig. 4A

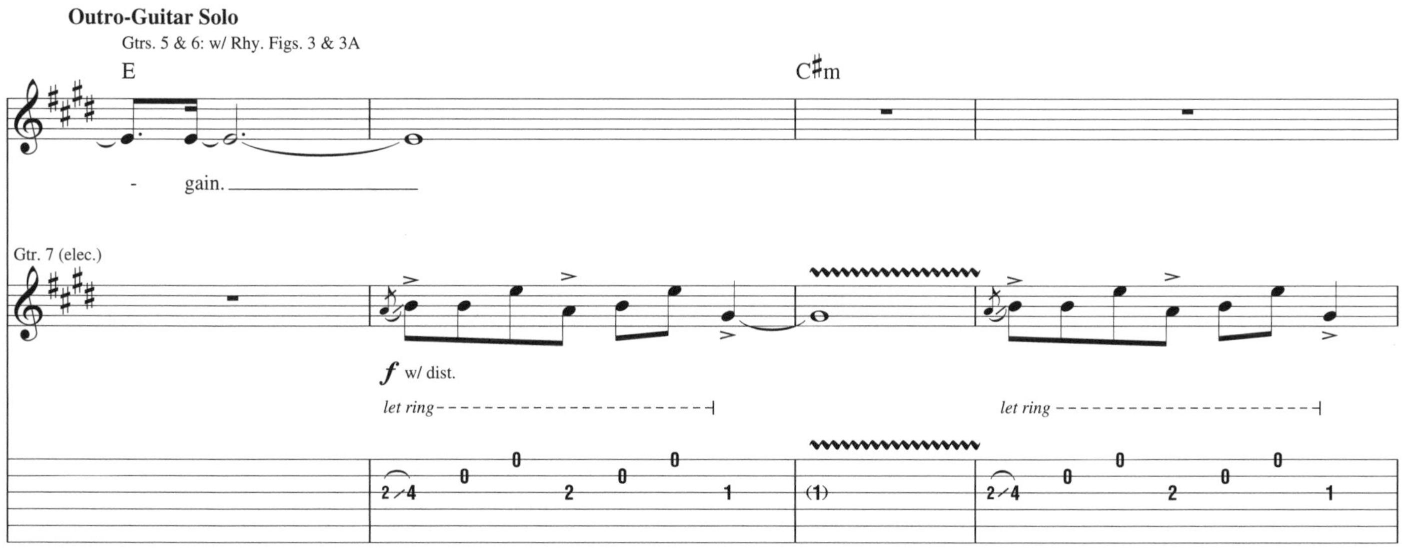
Outro-Guitar Solo
Gtrs. 5 & 6: w/ Rhy. Figs. 3 & 3A
E
C♯m
- gain.
Gtr. 7 (elec.)
f w/ dist.
let ring
let ring

Asus2
Dsus2
Asus2
let ring
1/2

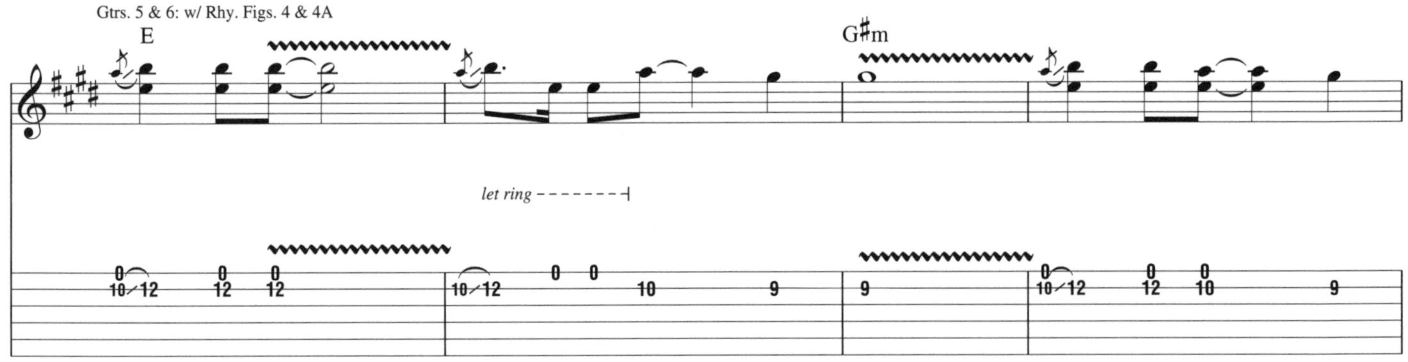
Gtrs. 5 & 6: w/ Rhy. Figs. 4 & 4A
E
G♯m
let ring

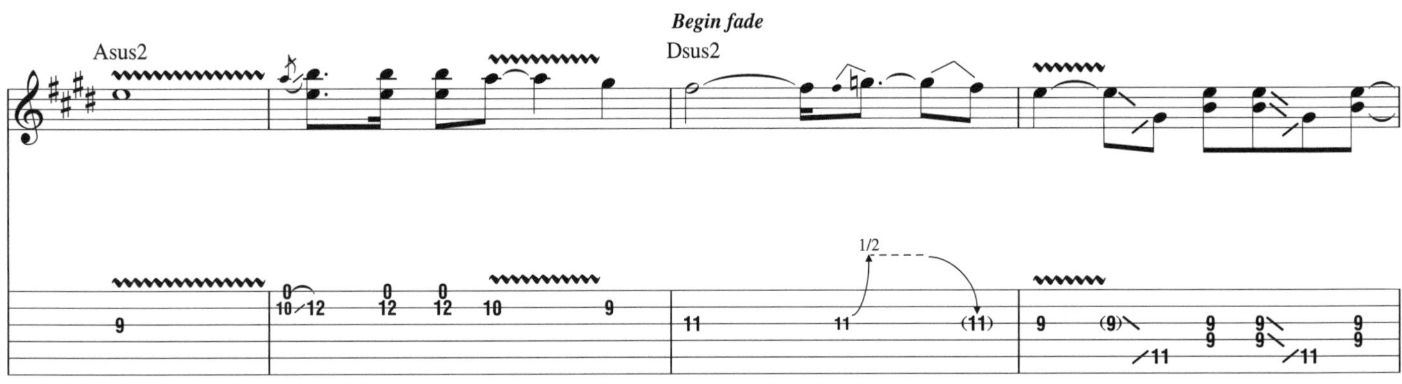
Begin fade
Asus2
Dsus2
1/2

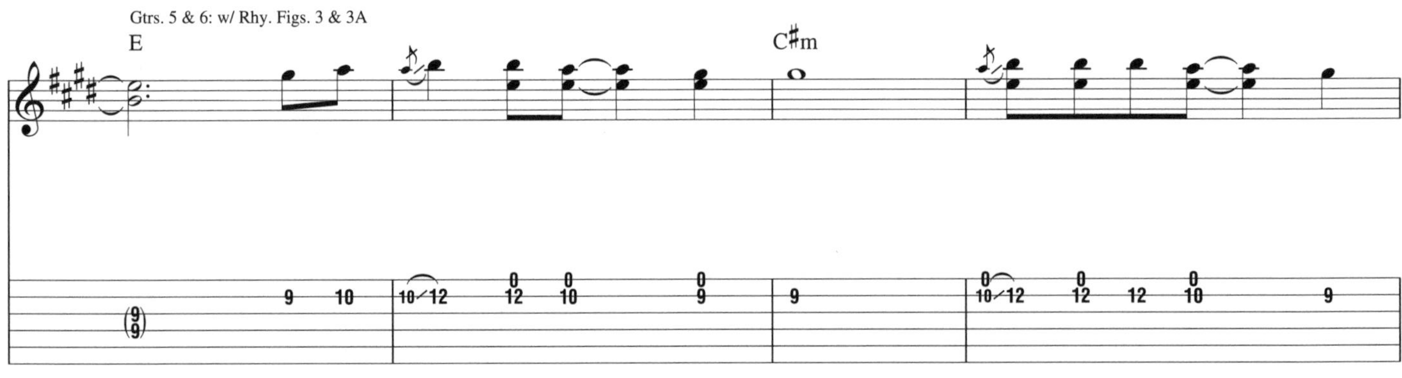
Gtrs. 5 & 6: w/ Rhy. Figs. 3 & 3A
E
C♯m

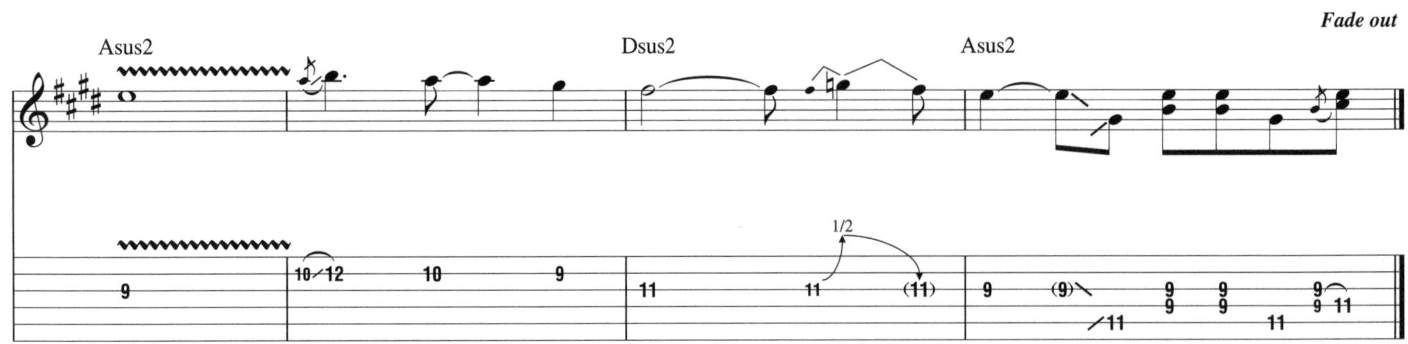
Fade out
Asus2
Dsus2
Asus2
1/2

from *Yes I Am*

I'm the Only One

Words and Music by Melissa Etheridge

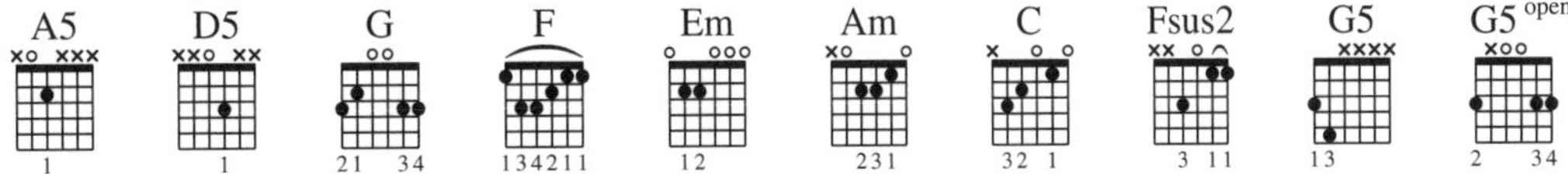

Intro

Moderately slow ♩ = 85

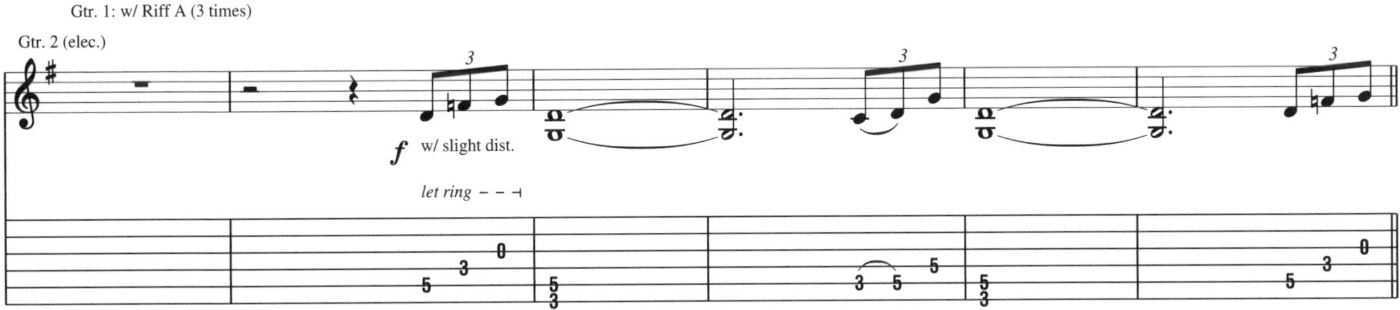

Verse

heart a - part as well.
To - night you told _ me that you
ache for some-thin' new, _ and
Rhy. Fig. 1
P.M.
let ring
some oth - er wom - an is look-in' like some-thin' that might be good _ for you.
Pre-Chorus
A5
Rhy. Fig. 2B
Gtr. 3 (elec.)
mf w/ slight dist.
Go on and hold her 'til the
End Rhy. Fig. 1
Rhy. Fig. 2
Gtr. 1
Rhy. Fig. 2A
Gtr. 2
D5
A5
D5
scream-in' is gone. _
Go on, be - lieve her when she tells you noth-in's wrong. _
End Rhy. Fig. 2B
(cont. in notation)
End Rhy. Fig. 2
(cont. in slashes)
End Rhy. Fig. 2A

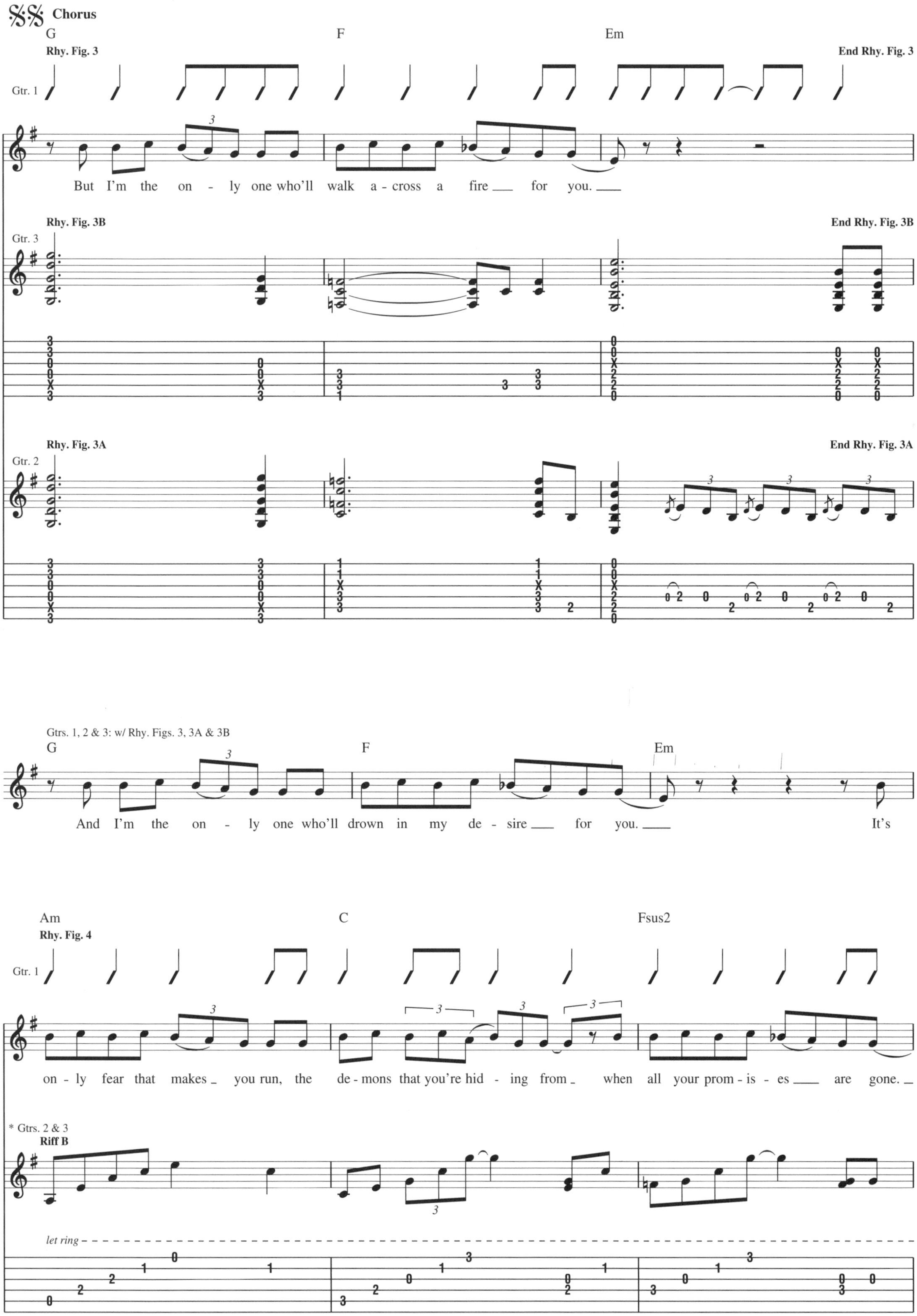

Chorus

G F Em

Rhy. Fig. 3 ... End Rhy. Fig. 3

Gtr. 1

But I'm the on - ly one who'll walk a - cross a fire ___ for you. ___

Rhy. Fig. 3B ... End Rhy. Fig. 3B

Gtr. 3

Rhy. Fig. 3A ... End Rhy. Fig. 3A

Gtr. 2

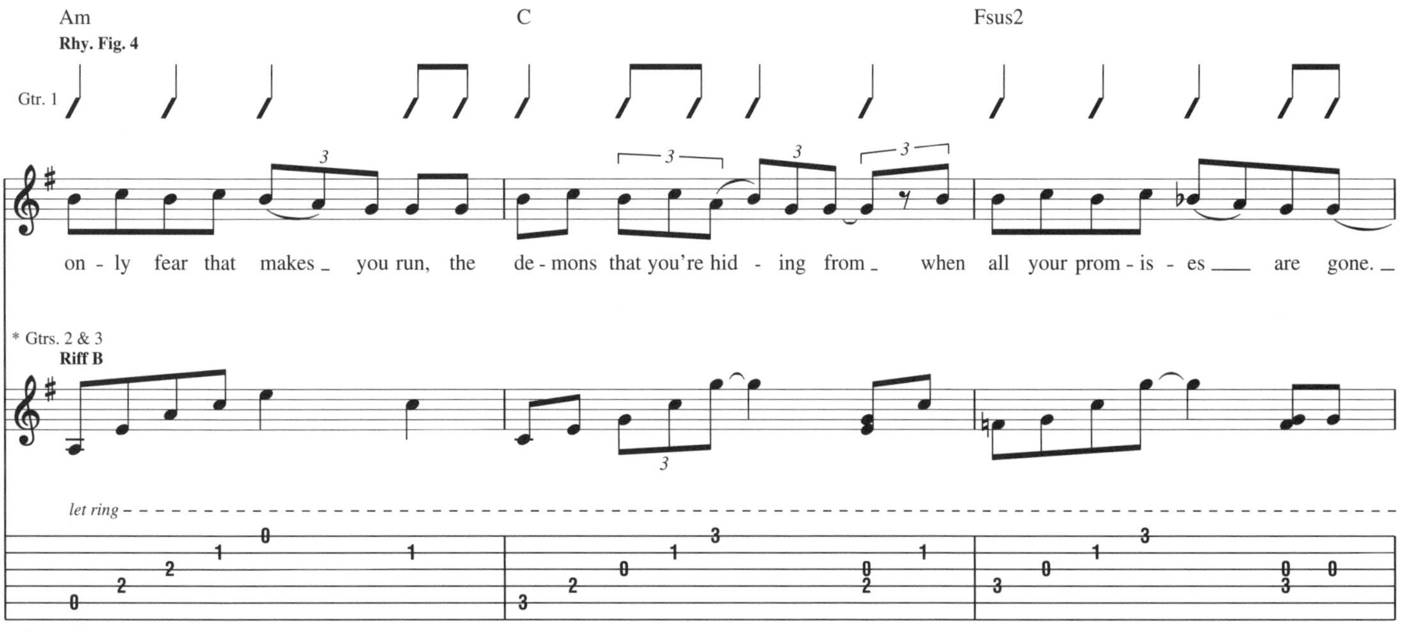

*Composite arrangement.

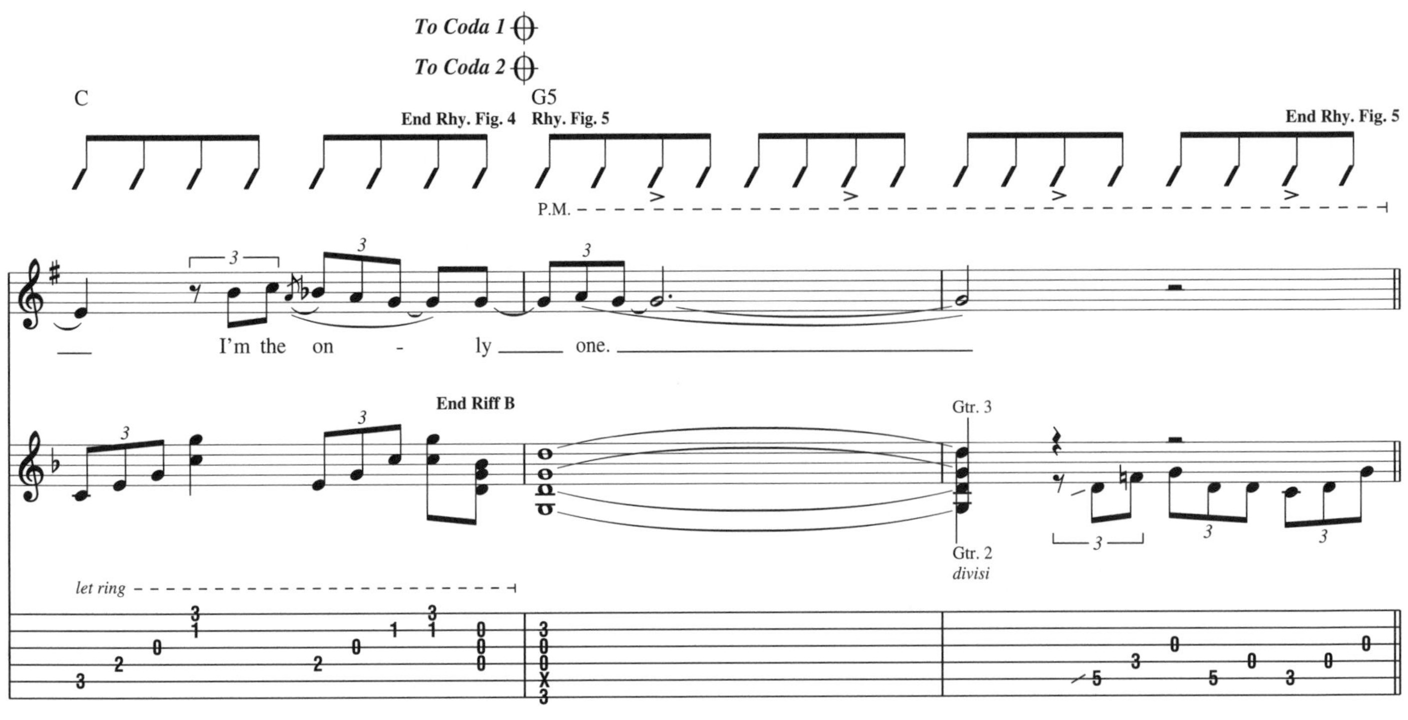

To Coda 1
To Coda 2
C
G5
End Rhy. Fig. 4
Rhy. Fig. 5
End Rhy. Fig. 5
P.M.
I'm the on - ly one.
End Riff B
Gtr. 3
Gtr. 2
divisi
let ring

Verse

Gtr. 3 tacet
Gtr. 1: w/ Rhy. Fig. 1 (1st 2 meas. only, 2 times)
G5
2. Please, ba - by, can't you see I'm try - ing to ex - plain I've been here be-fore and I'm lock-ing the door and I'm
Gtr. 2
P.M.
let ring

Gtr. 1: w/ Rhy. Fig. 1
not go - ing back a - gain. Her eyes and arms and skin won't make it go a - way. You'll
P.M.
let ring

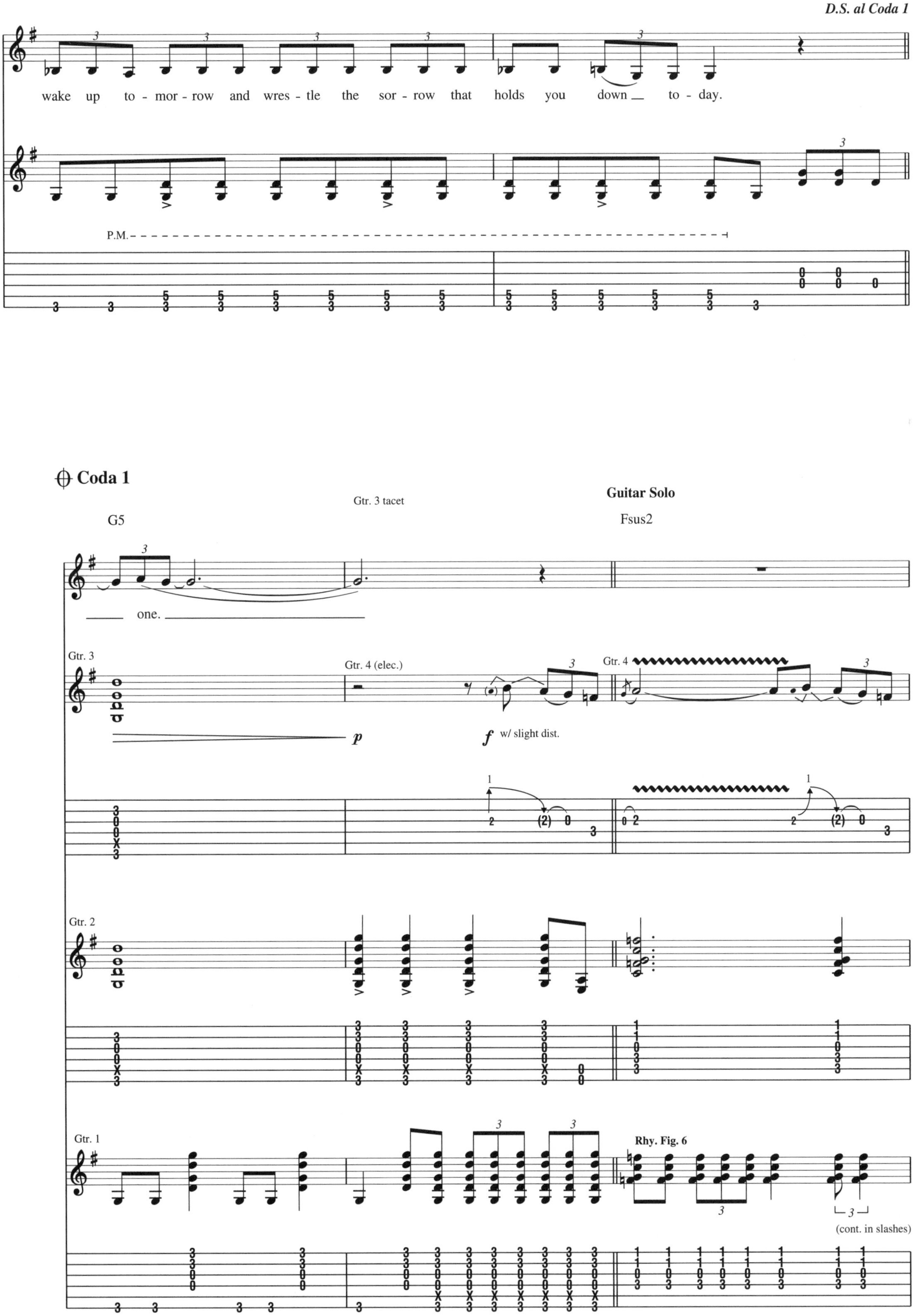

D.S. al Coda 1

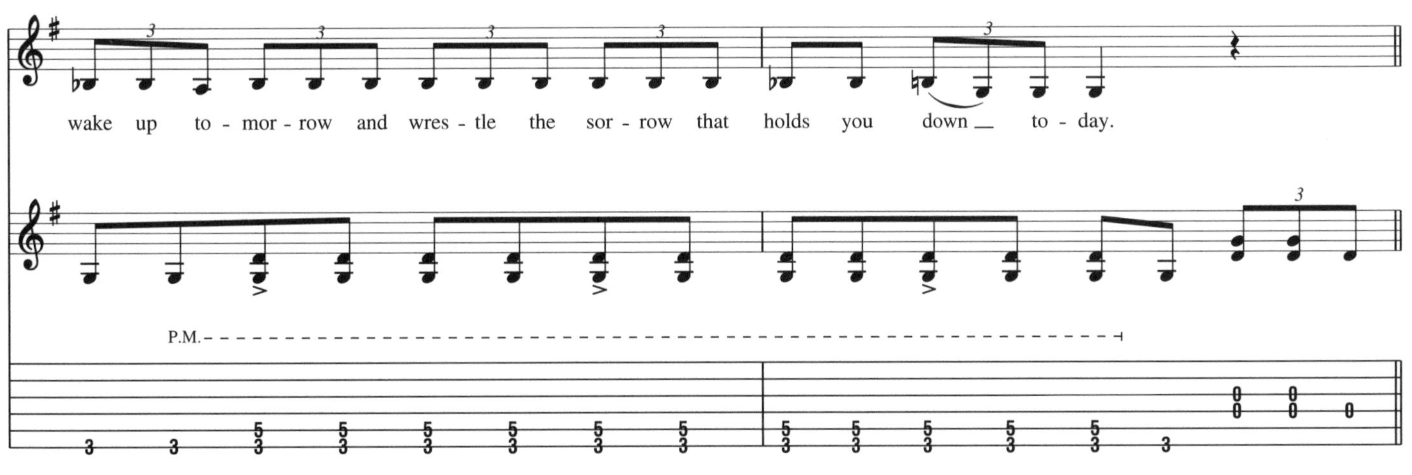

⊕ Coda 1

Gtr. 3 tacet

Guitar Solo

G5

Fsus2

one.

Gtr. 3

Gtr. 4 (elec.)

p

f w/ slight dist.

Gtr. 4

Gtr. 2

Gtr. 1

Rhy. Fig. 6

(cont. in slashes)

Gtr. 1
G5 open
Gtr. 4
let ring
hold bend
Gtr. 2
Gtr. 1: w/ Rhy. Fig. 6
Fsus2
End Rhy. Fig. 6
G5
Pre-Chorus
Gtrs. 1, 2 & 3: w/ Rhy. Figs. 2, 2A & 2B
A5
Go on and hold her 'til the

D.S.S. al Coda 2
D5
A5
D5
scream-ing is gone.
Go on be - lieve her when she tells you noth-ing's wrong.
Coda 2
Gtrs. 1, 2 & 3: w/ Rhy. Figs. 3, 3A & 3B (2 times)
G
F
Em
one, yeah, yeah.
And I'm the on - ly one who'll drown in my de - sire for you. It's
Gtr. 1: w/ Rhy. Fig. 4
Gtrs. 2 & 3: w/ Riff B
Am
C
on - ly fear that makes you run, the de - mons that you're hid - in' from when
Fsus2
C
all your prom - is - es are gone. I'm the on -
Outro
Gtr. 1: w/ Rhy. Fig. 5 (till fade)
G5
- ly one.
Gtr. 2
let ring
Gtr. 3
pp

I'm the on - ly one, babe.
I'm the on - ly one.
let ring
let ring
Riff C
End Riff C
mp

Begin fade
Gtr. 1: w/ Riff C (till fade)
Ain't no - bod - y else is gon - na love you,
ain't no - bod - y else is gon - na love
Gtr. 2
let ring

Fade out
you.
Hee, hee,
hee, hee, hee.
let ring
let ring

from *Yes I Am*

If I Wanted To

Words and Music by Melissa Etheridge

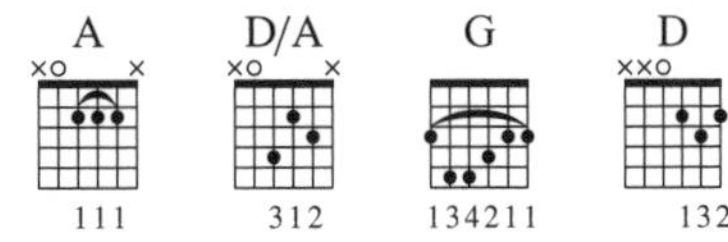

*Chord symbols reflect overall harmony.

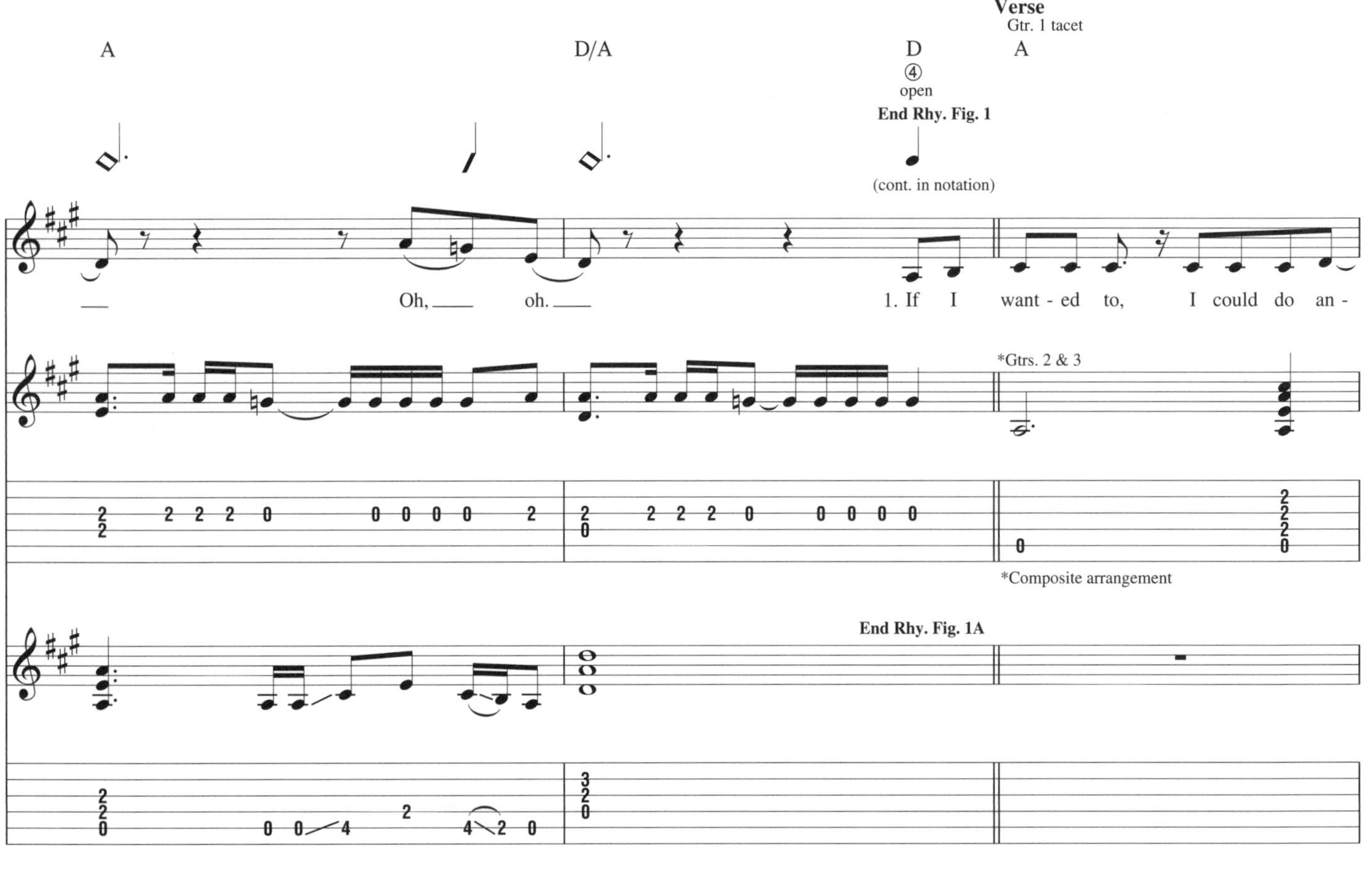
Verse
Gtr. 1 tacet
A
D/A
D
A
open
End Rhy. Fig. 1
(cont. in notation)
Oh, oh.
1. If I want - ed to, I could do an -
*Gtrs. 2 & 3
*Composite arrangement
End Rhy. Fig. 1A

D
A
D
- y - thing right. I could dance with the dev - il on a Sat - ur - day night. If I
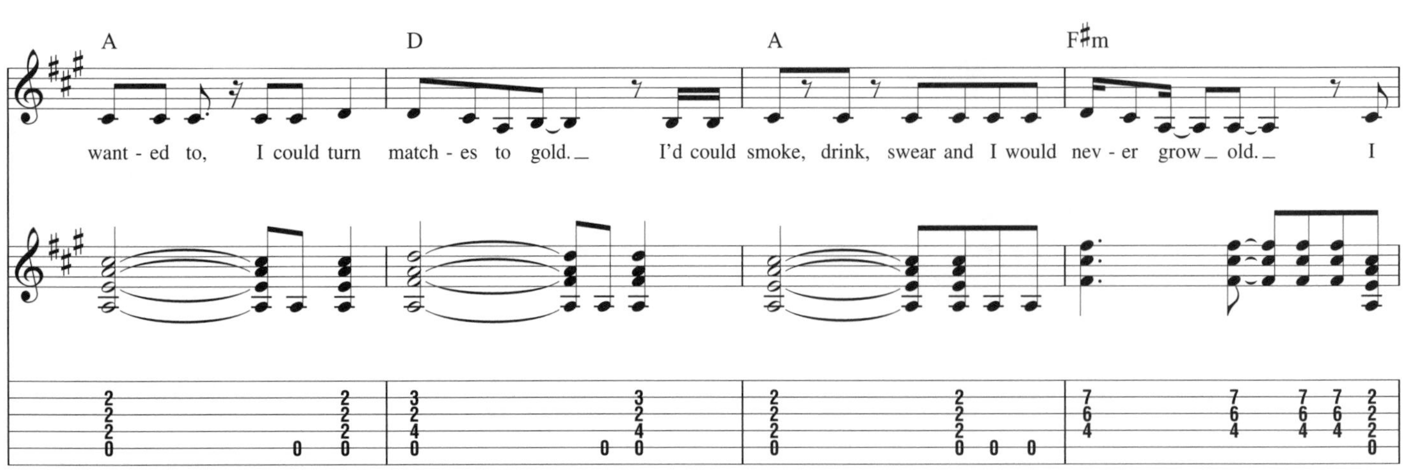
A
D
A
F♯m
want - ed to, I could turn match - es to gold. I'd could smoke, drink, swear and I would nev - er grow old. I

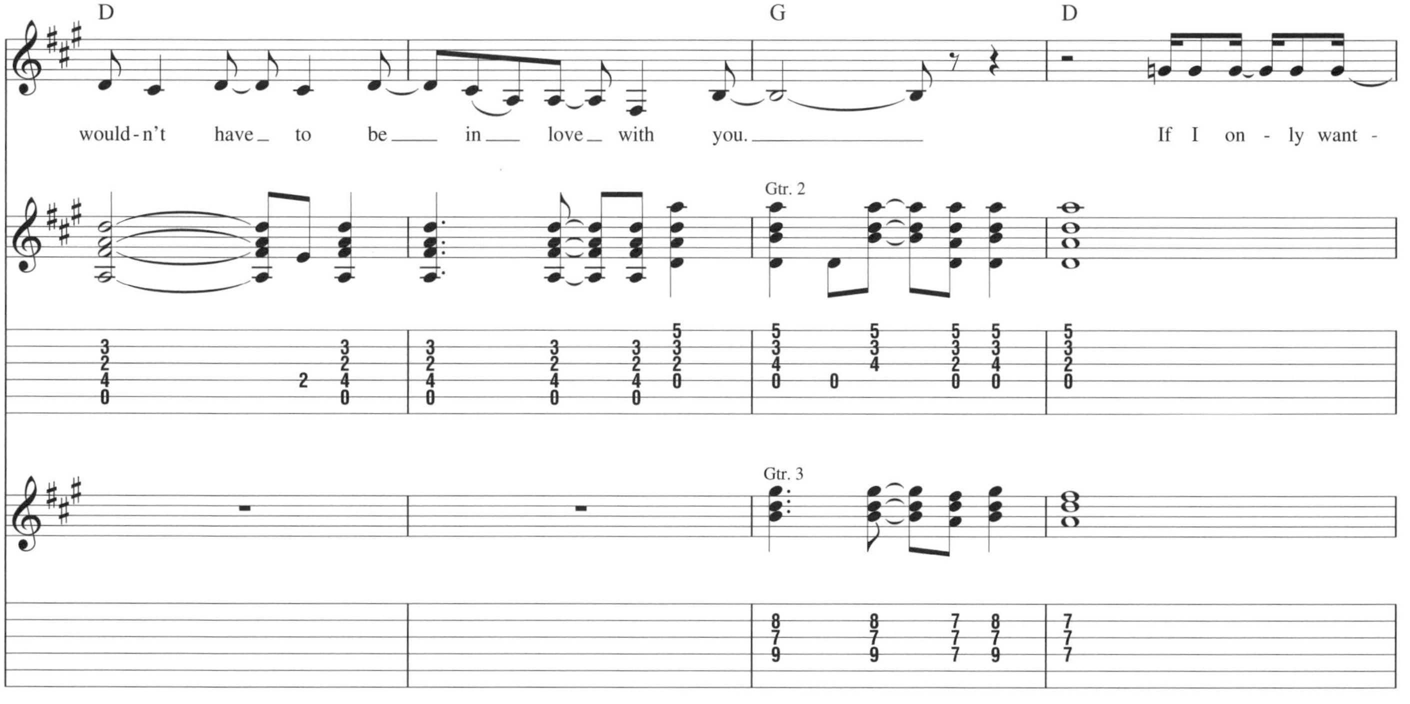
D
G
D
would-n't have to be in love with you.
If I on - ly want -
Gtr. 2
Gtr. 3

Gtrs. 2 & 3: w/ Rhy. Figs. 1 & 1A
A
D
A
D
- ed to.
Hey, if I on - ly want - ed to.
2. If I

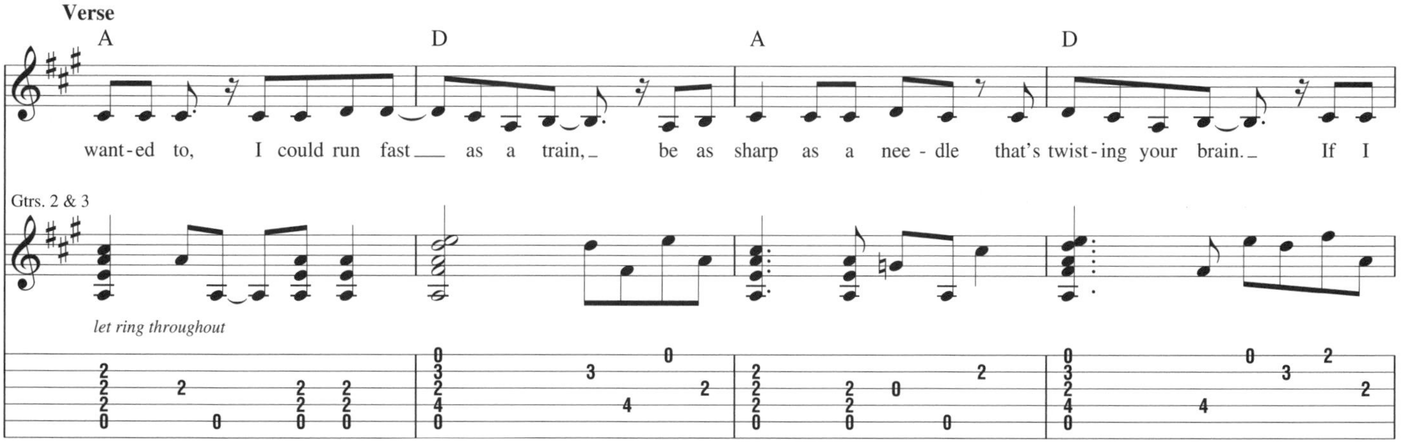
Verse
A
D
A
D
want-ed to, I could run fast as a train, be as sharp as a nee-dle that's twist-ing your brain. If I
Gtrs. 2 & 3
let ring throughout

A
D
A
F#m
want-ed to, I could turn moun-tains to sand, have po - lit - i - cal lead-ers in the palm of my hand. I

D
G
D
would - n't have to be in love with you.
If I on - ly want -

Gtrs. 2 & 3: w/ Rhy. Figs. 1 & 1A
A
D
A
D
- ed to.
Hey, if I on - ly want - ed to.

Bridge
F♯m
A
Bm
I could leave to - night
and I would be
Gtrs. 2 & 3

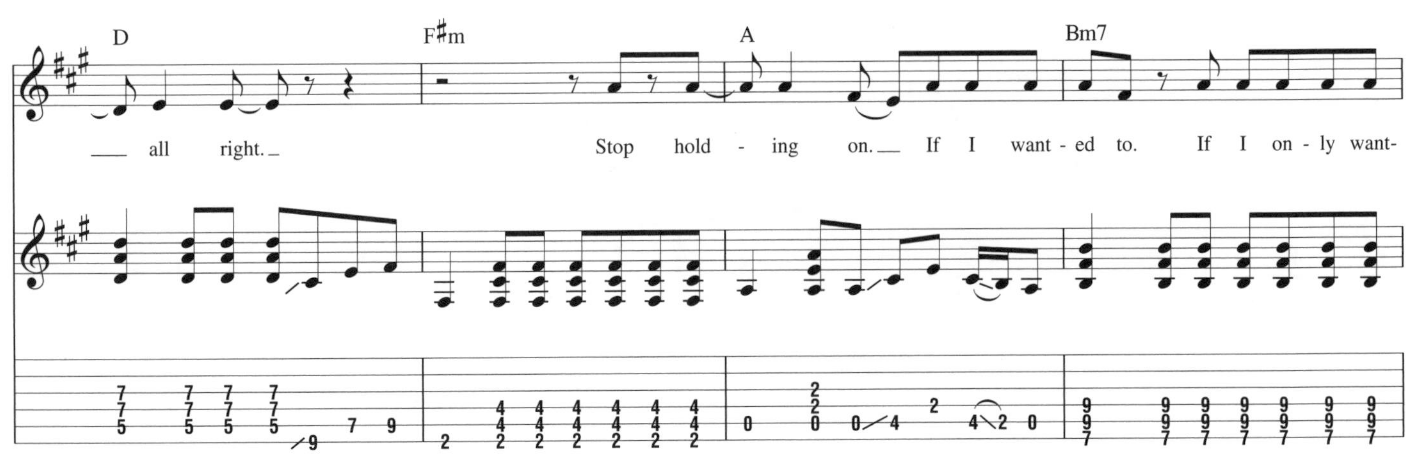
D
F♯m
A
Bm7
all right.
Stop hold - ing on. If I want - ed to. If I on - ly want-

Interlude
Gtr. 2: w/ Rhy. Fig. 1A (1 1/2 times)
Gtr. 3: w/ Rhy. Fig. 1 (1 1/2 times)
E7
A
D
ed to. Yeah, yeah. Oh, oh. Oh, oh.
Gtr. 1
Rhy. Fig. 2

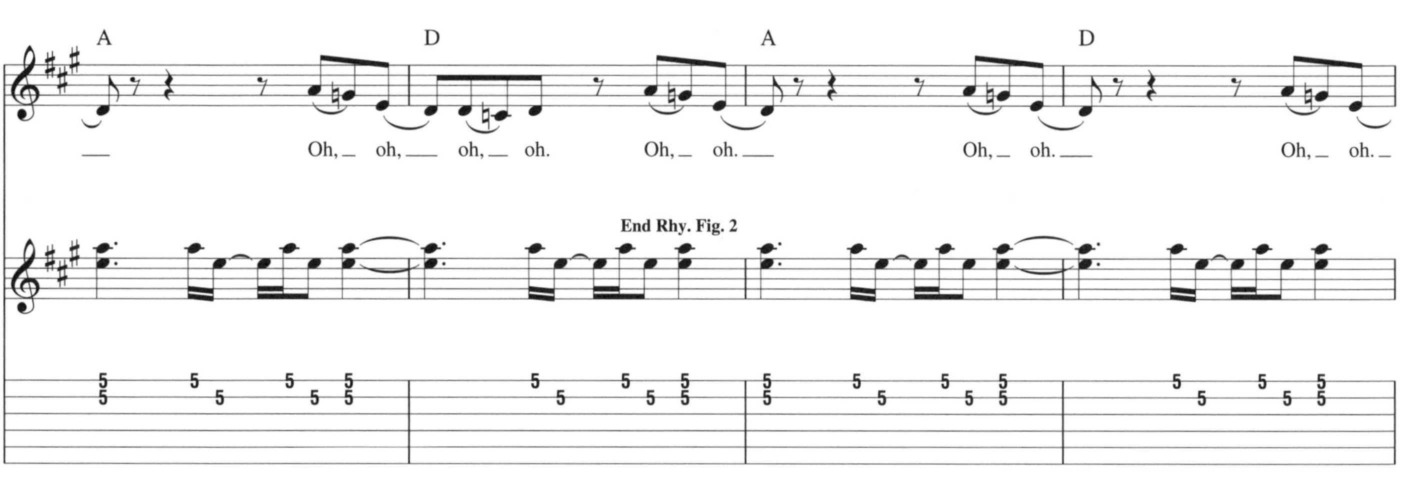
A
D
A
D
Oh, oh, oh, oh. Oh, oh. Oh, oh. Oh, oh.
End Rhy. Fig. 2

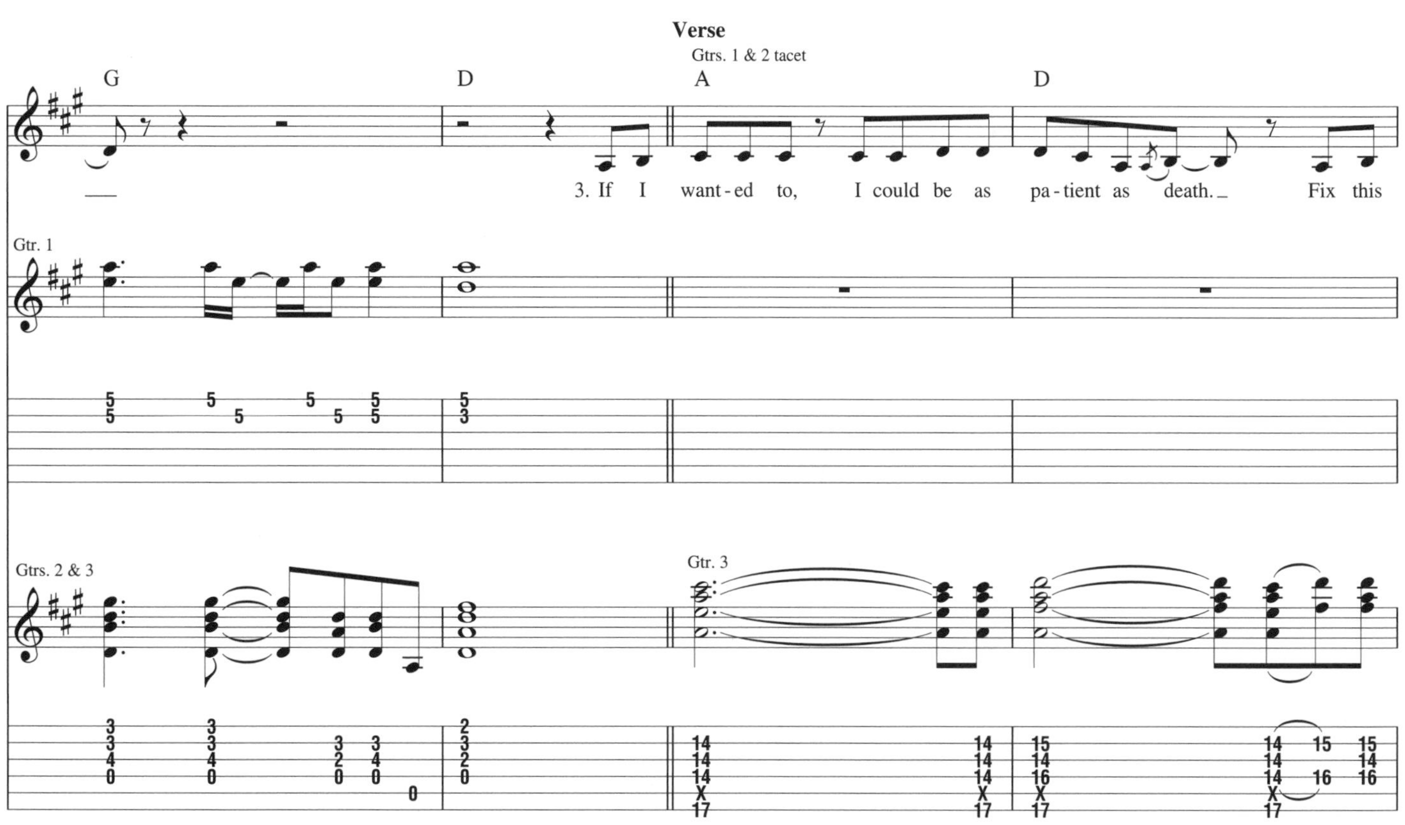
Verse
Gtrs. 1 & 2 tacet
G
D
A
D
3. If I want-ed to, I could be as pa-tient as death. Fix this
Gtr. 1
Gtrs. 2 & 3
Gtr. 3

A
D
F♯m
D
hole in my heart leak-ing in-to my flesh. If I want-ed to, I could turn sparks in-to ice. There'd nev-er
Gtrs. 2 & 3

A
F♯m
D
be an-oth - er wom - an who could make you think twice. I would-n't have to be

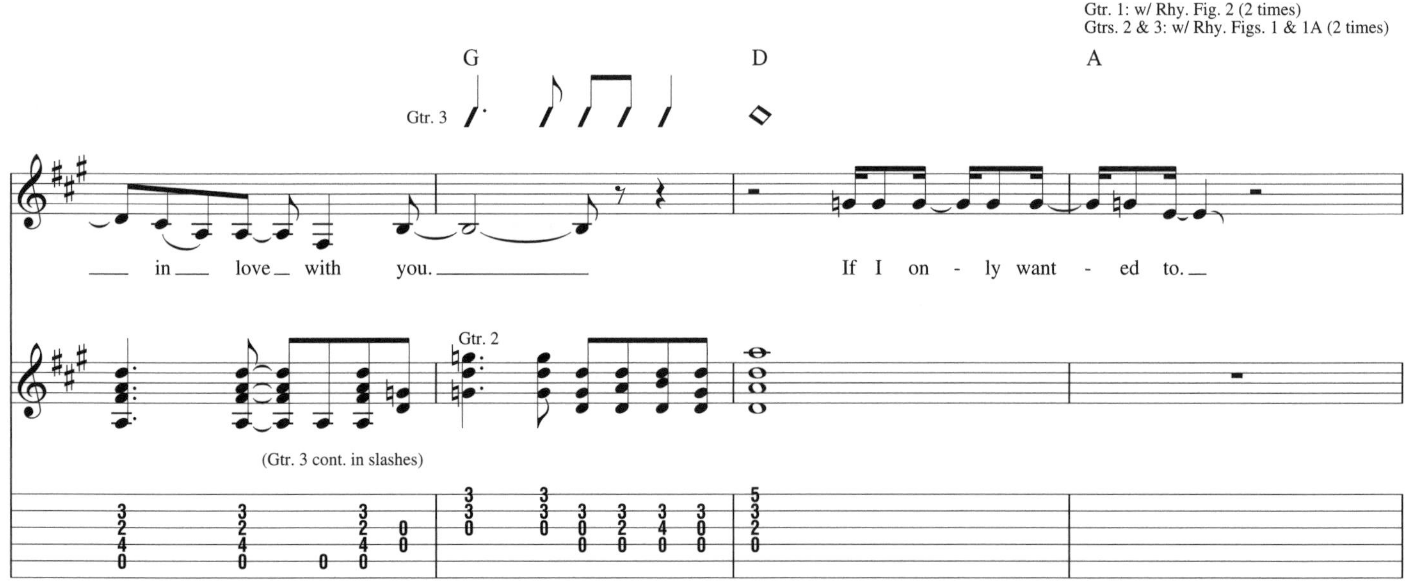
Gtr. 1: w/ Rhy. Fig. 2 (2 times)
Gtrs. 2 & 3: w/ Rhy. Figs. 1 & 1A (2 times)
G
D
A
Gtr. 3
in love with you. If I on - ly want - ed to.
Gtr. 2
(Gtr. 3 cont. in slashes)

D
A
D
Yeah, if I on - ly want - ed to. Hey, if I on - ly want -

A D A
- ed to. Hey, if I on - ly want - ed to. Oh, oh.

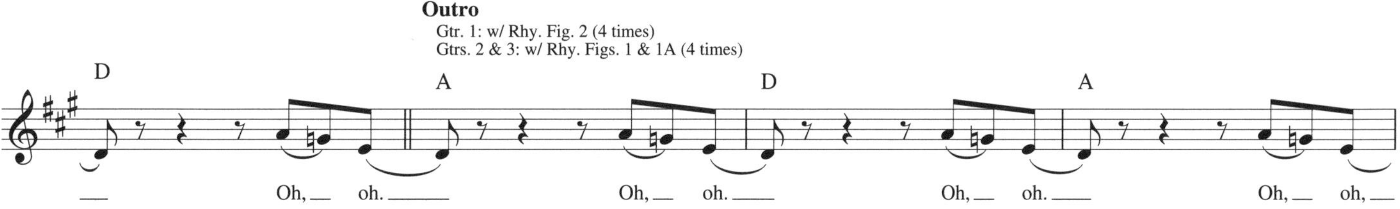
Outro
Gtr. 1: w/ Rhy. Fig. 2 (4 times)
Gtrs. 2 & 3: w/ Rhy. Figs. 1 & 1A (4 times)
D A D A
Oh, oh. Oh, oh. Oh, oh. Oh, oh,

D A D
oh, oh. Oh, oh. Oh, oh. Oh, oh.

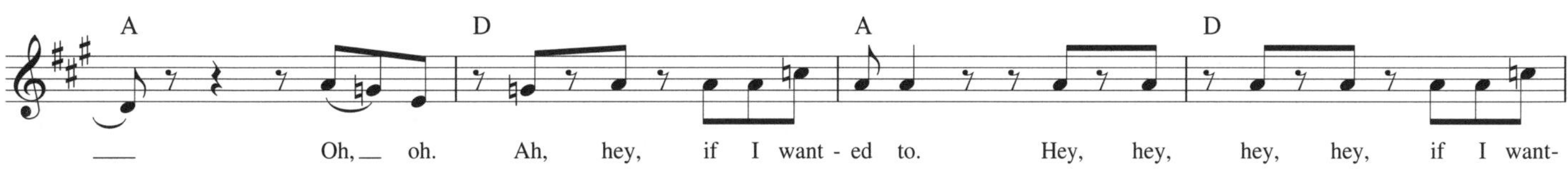
A D A D
Oh, oh. Ah, hey, if I want - ed to. Hey, hey, hey, hey, if I want-

A D A
ed to. Hey, hey, hey, hey, if I want - ed to. If I want -

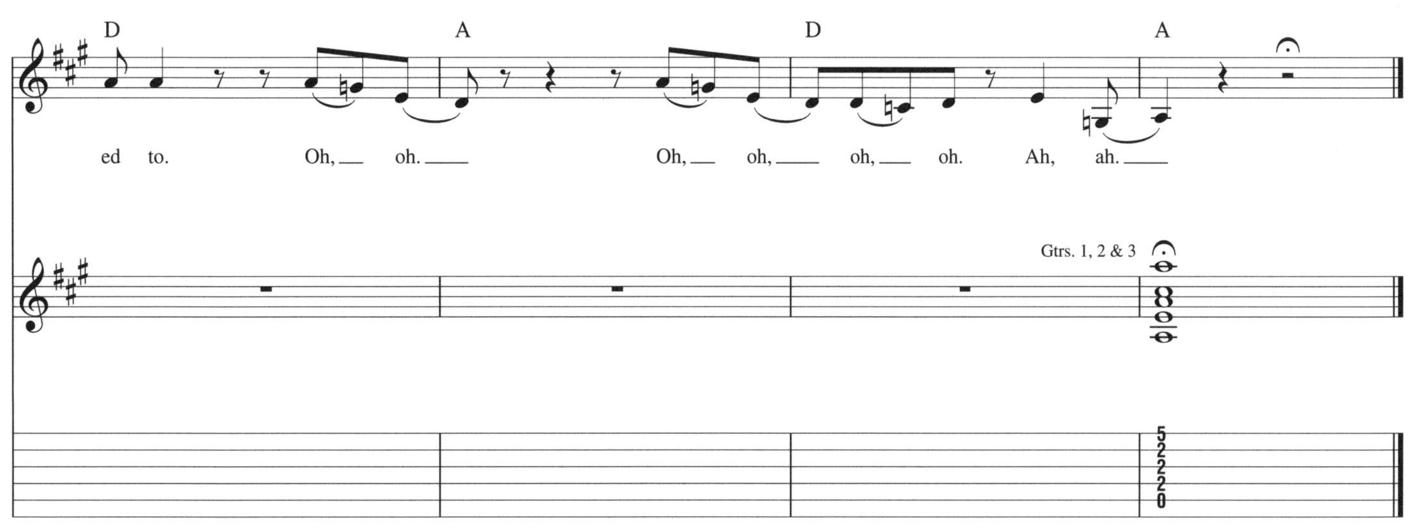
D A D A
ed to. Oh, oh. Oh, oh, oh, oh. Ah, ah.
Gtrs. 1, 2 & 3
5
2
2
2
0

from *Melissa Etheridge*

Like the Way I Do

Words and Music by Melissa Etheridge

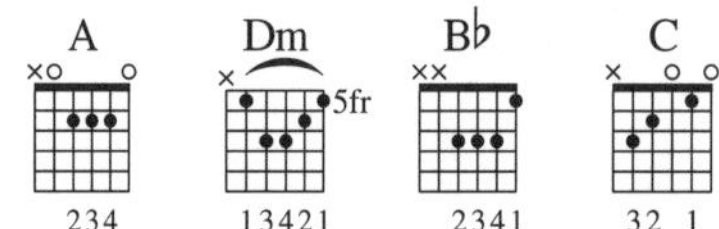

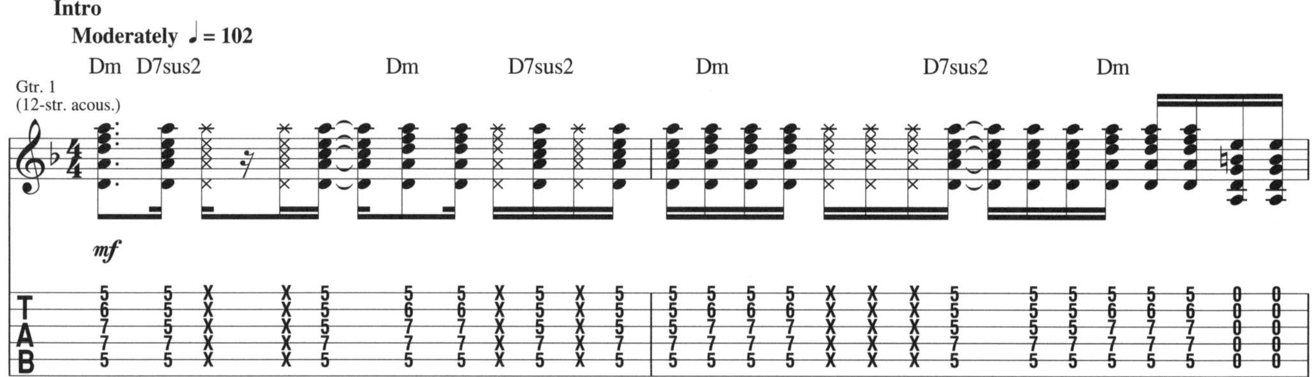

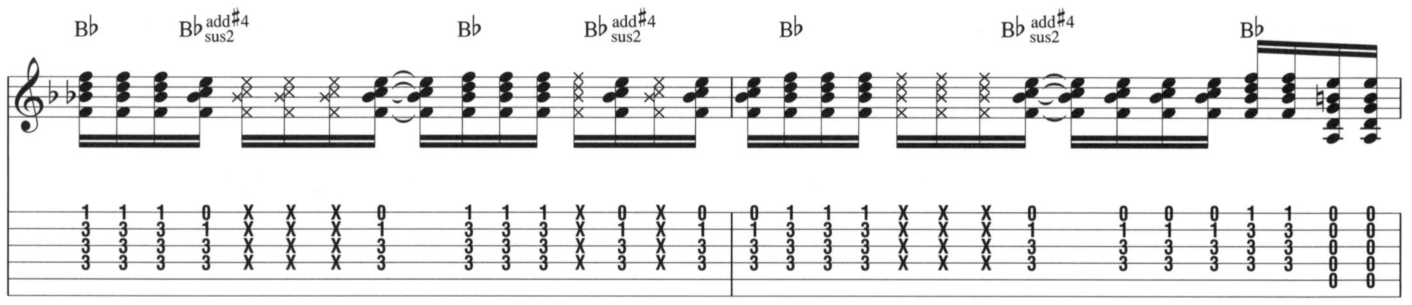

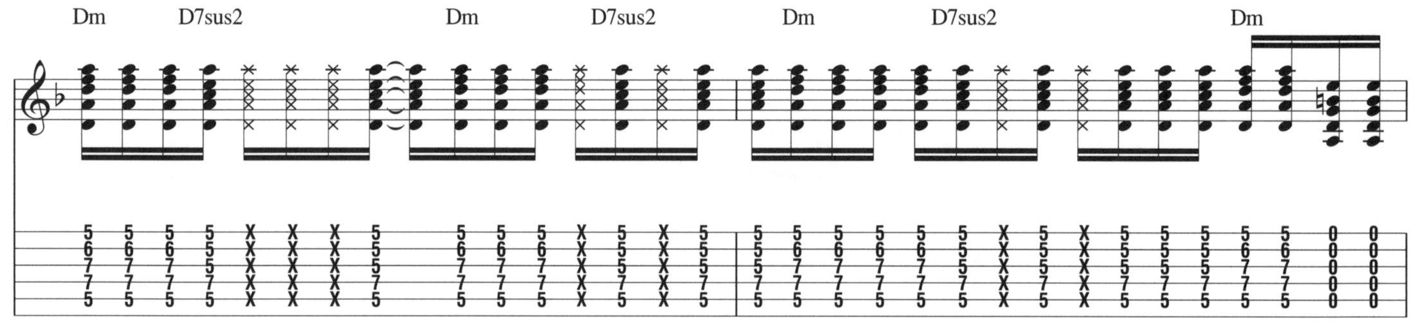

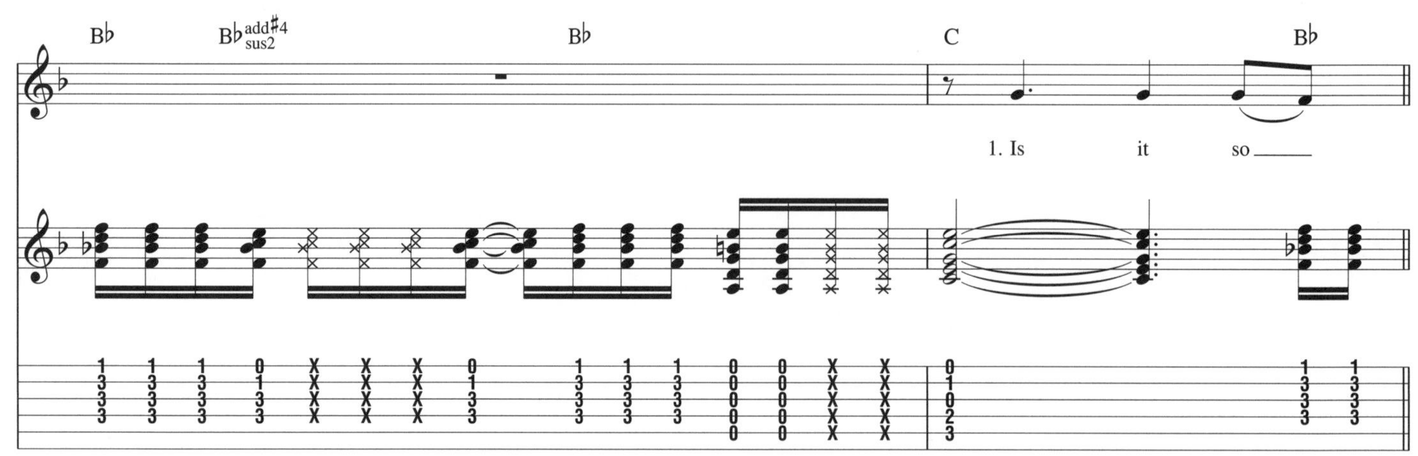

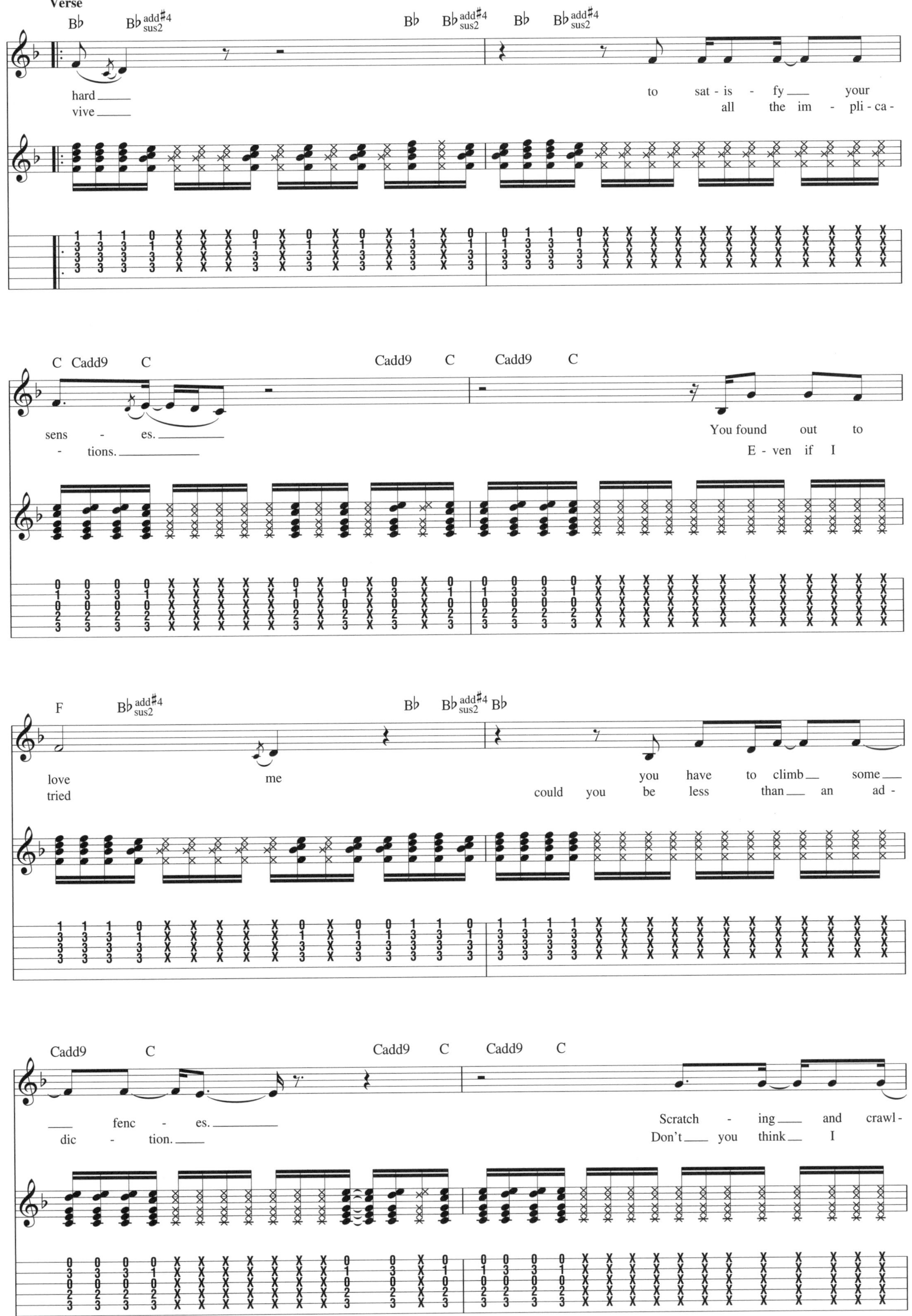
Verse
B♭ B♭sus2 add♯4 B♭ B♭sus2 add♯4 B♭ B♭sus2 add♯4
hard ___ to sat - is - fy ___ your
vive ___ all the im - pli - ca -
C Cadd9 C Cadd9 C Cadd9 C
sens - es. ___ You found out to
- tions. ___ E - ven if I
F B♭sus2 add♯4 B♭ B♭sus2 add♯4 B♭
love me you have to climb ___ some ___
tried could you be less than ___ an ad -
Cadd9 C Cadd9 C Cadd9 C
___ fenc - es. ___ Scratch - ing ___ and crawl -
dic - tion. ___ Don't ___ you think ___ I

B♭
B♭add♯4 sus2
- ing
know
a - long the floor to
there's so man - y oth-
Cadd9
C
touch you.
ers
who would beg, steal and
And just when it
feels right,
lie and fight, kill, and die,
you say you found some - one to
just to
A
hold you.
hold you,
Does she
hold you

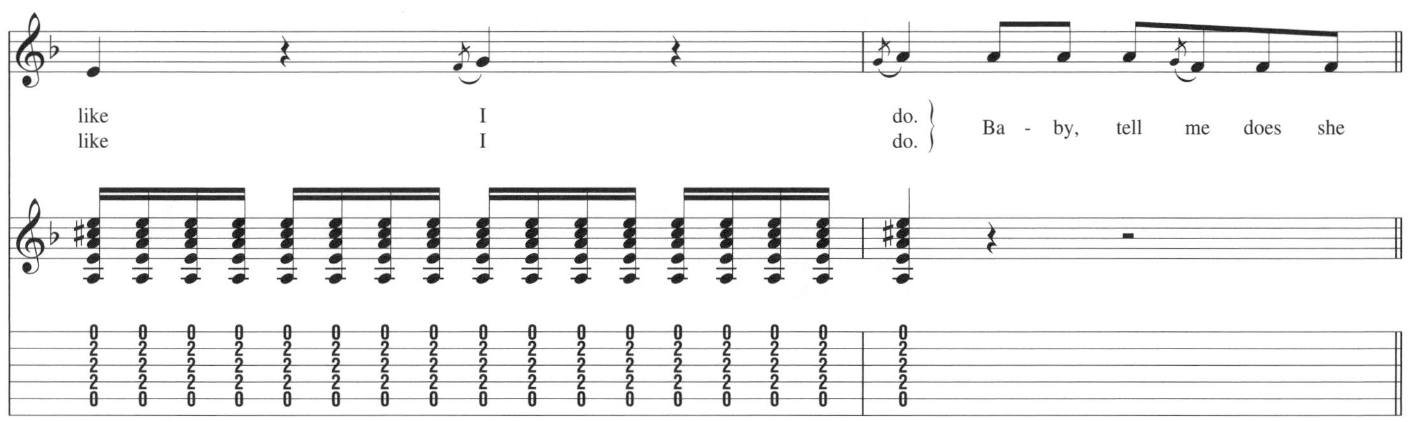
like I do.
like I do.
Ba - by, tell me does she

Chorus
Dm D7sus2 Dm D7sus2 Dm D7sus2 Dm
love you like the way I love you. Does she stim - u - late
Gtr. 1
Rhy. Fig. 1

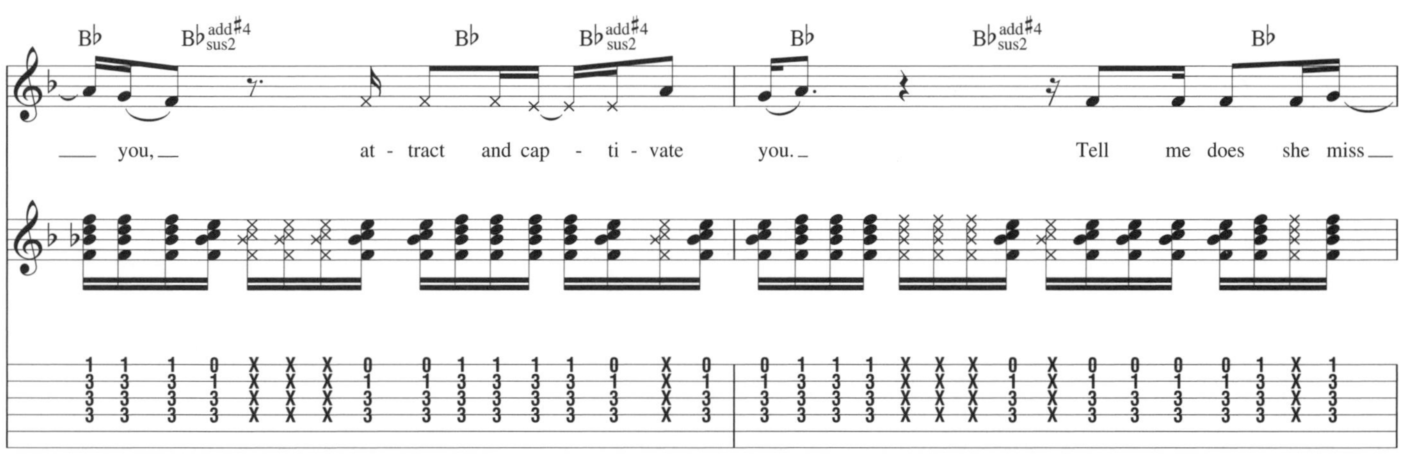
B♭ B♭sus2 add♯4 B♭ B♭sus2 add♯4 B♭ B♭sus2 add♯4 B♭
you, at - tract and cap - ti - vate you. Tell me does she miss

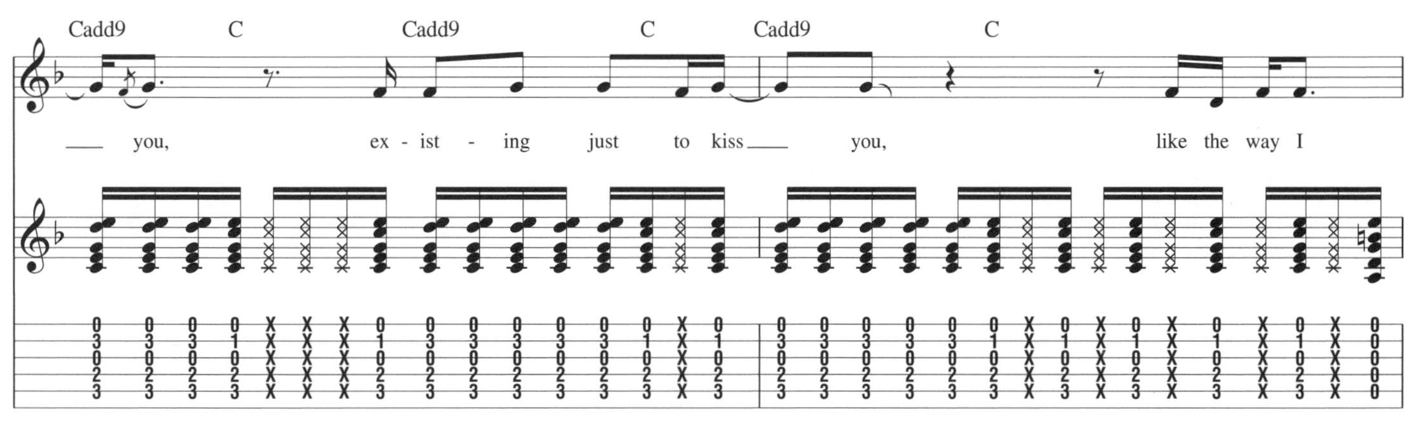
Cadd9 C Cadd9 C Cadd9 C
you, ex - ist - ing just to kiss you, like the way I

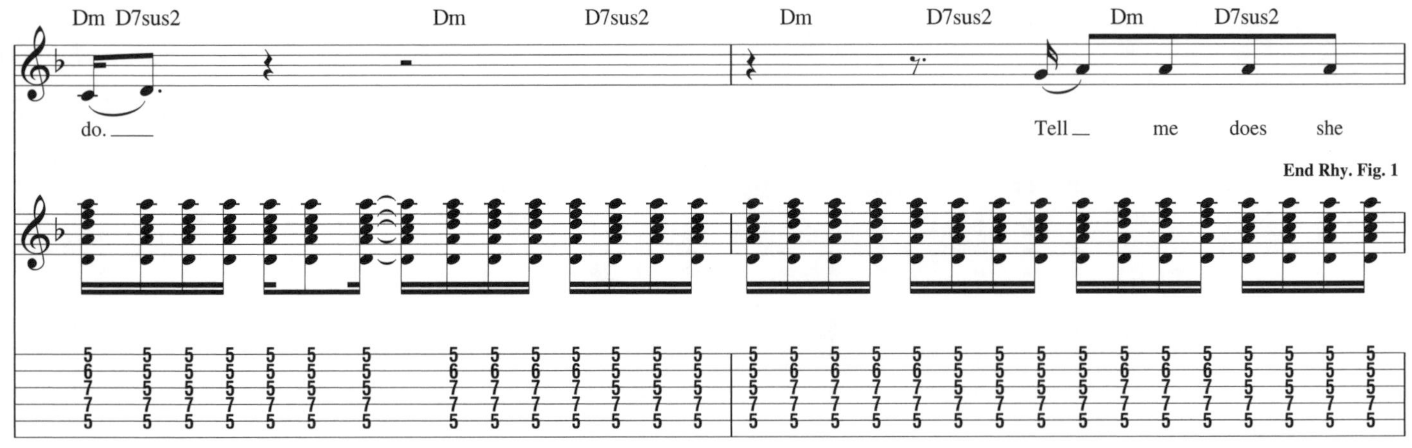
Dm D7sus2
Dm
D7sus2
Dm
D7sus2
Dm
D7sus2
do.
Tell me does she
End Rhy. Fig. 1

Gtr. 1: w/ Rhy. Fig. 1 (1st 6 meas.)
Dm D7sus2
Dm
D7sus2
Dm
D7sus2
Dm
want you, in - fat - u - ate and haunt you. Does she know just how to shock

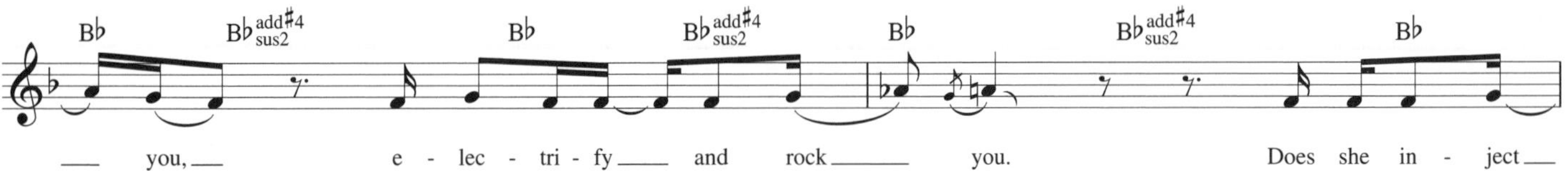
B♭
B♭add♯4sus2
B♭
B♭add♯4sus2
B♭
B♭add♯4sus2
B♭
you, e - lec - tri - fy and rock you. Does she in - ject

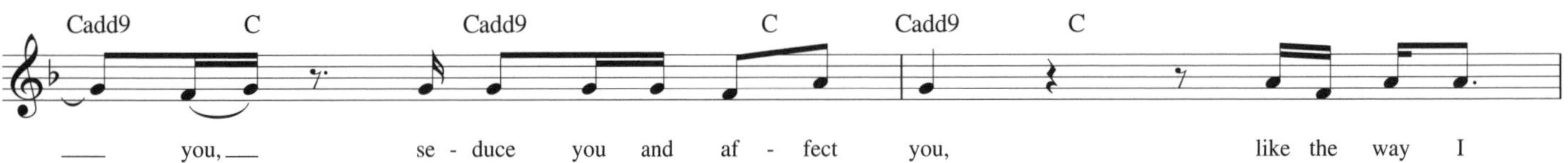
Cadd9
C
Cadd9
C
Cadd9
C
you, se - duce you and af - fect you, like the way I

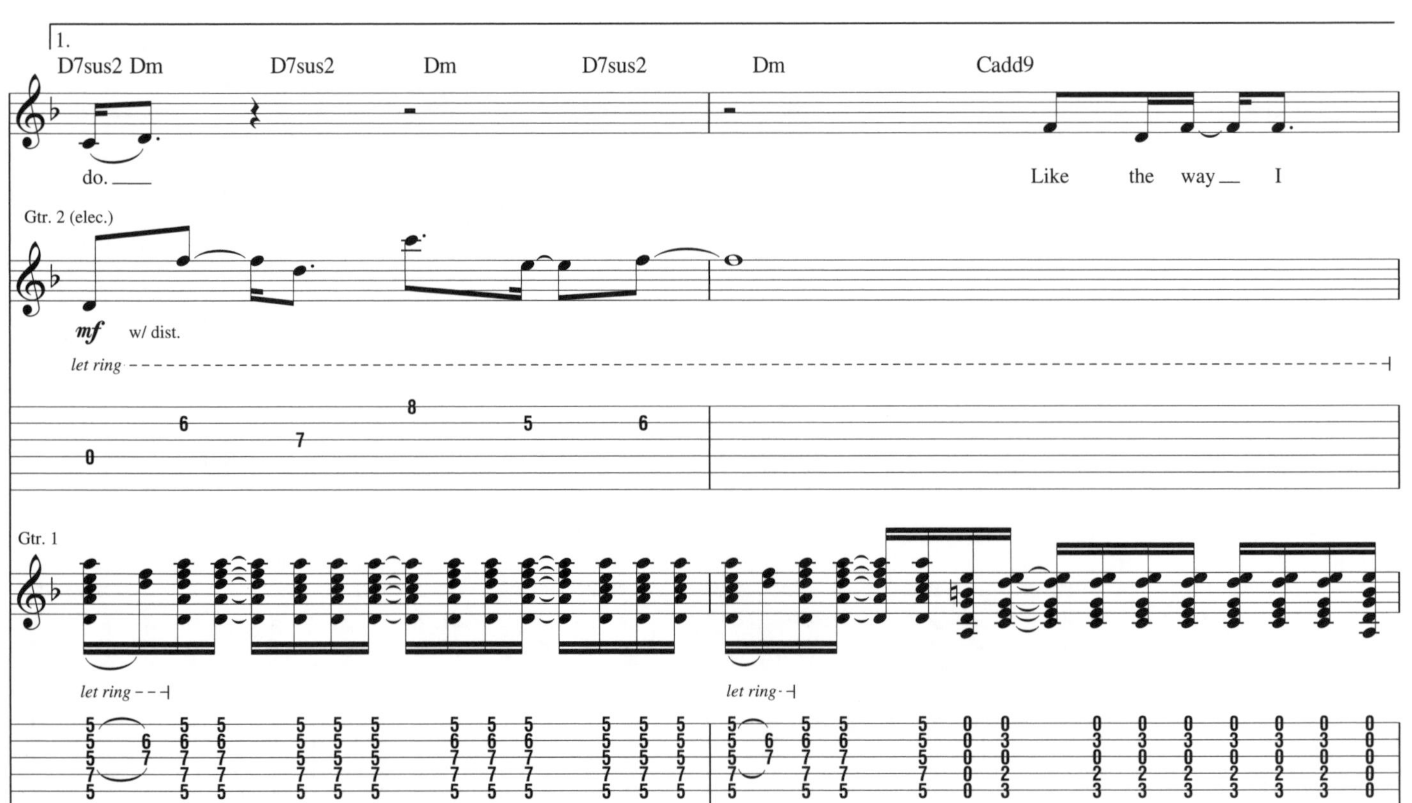
1.
D7sus2 Dm
D7sus2
Dm
D7sus2
Dm
Cadd9
do. Like the way I
Gtr. 2 (elec.)
mf
w/ dist.
let ring
Gtr. 1
let ring
let ring

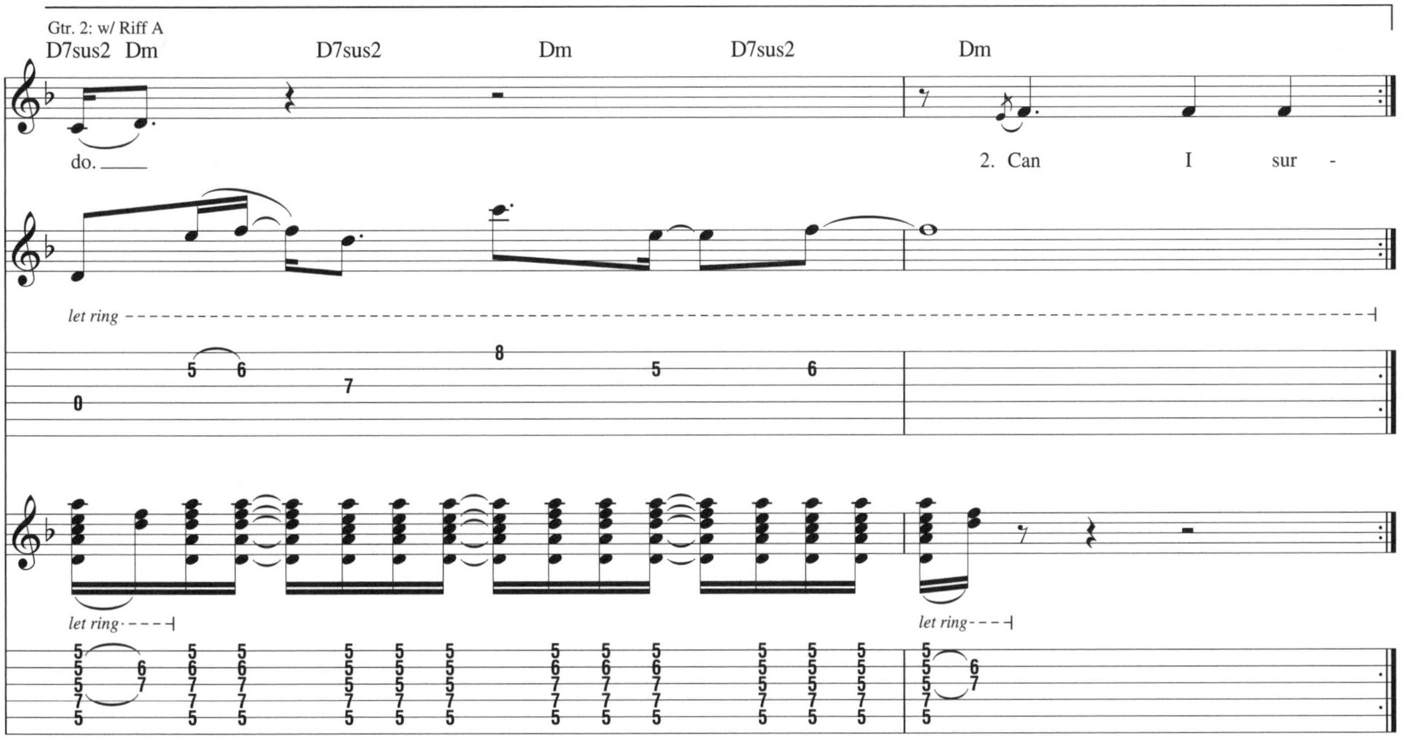
Gtr. 2: w/ Riff A
D7sus2 Dm
D7sus2
Dm
D7sus2
Dm
do.
2. Can I sur -
let ring
let ring
let ring

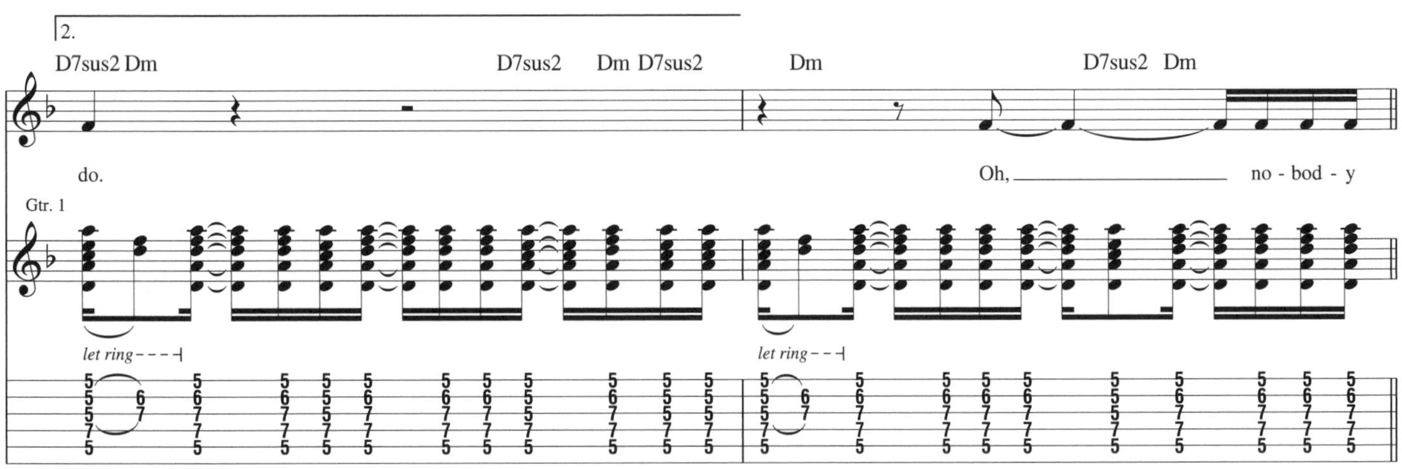
2.
D7sus2 Dm
D7sus2
Dm D7sus2
Dm
D7sus2 Dm
do.
Oh,
no - bod - y
Gtr. 1
let ring
let ring

Bridge

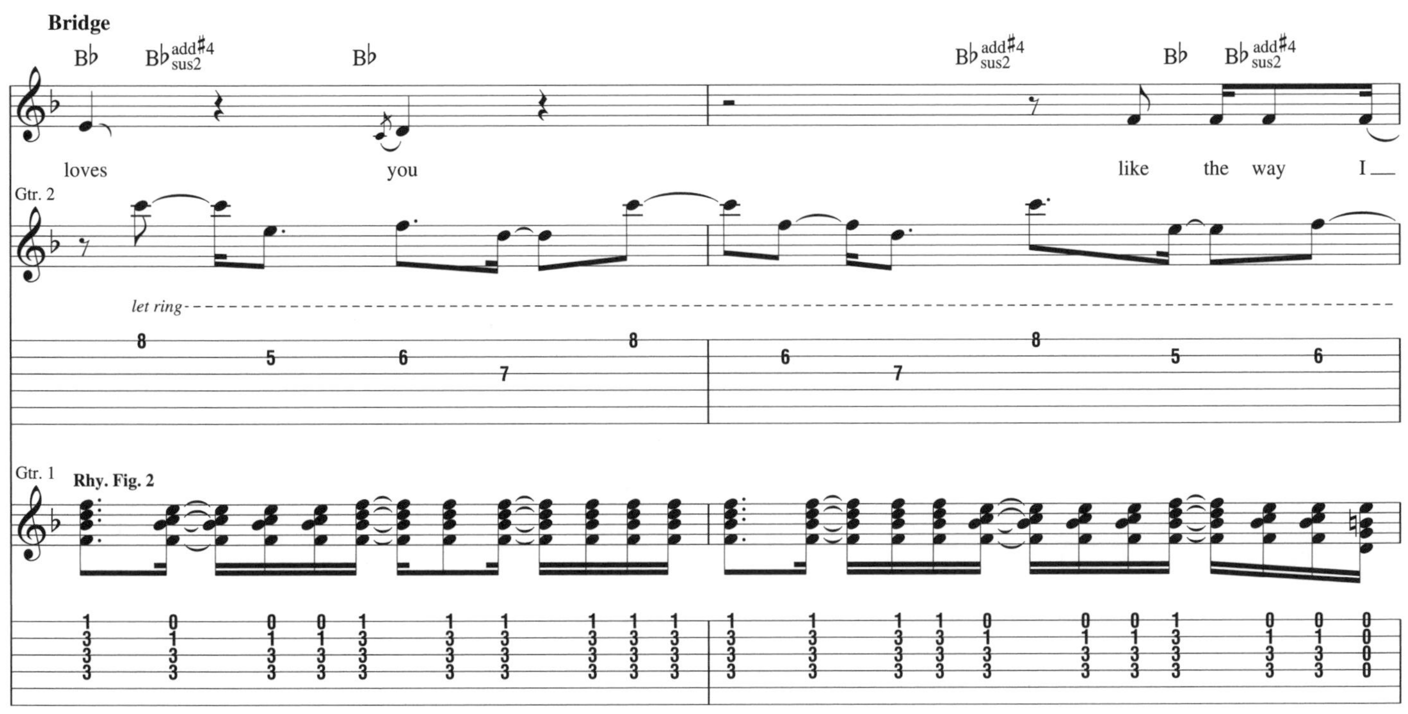
B♭
B♭add♯4 sus2
B♭
loves
you
like the way I
Gtr. 2
let ring
Gtr. 1
Rhy. Fig. 2

Gtr. 1: w/ Rhy. Fig. 2 (2½ times)
D7sus2 Dm D7sus2 Dm D7sus2 Dm D7sus2 Dm B♭ B♭add♯4sus2 B♭
do. No - bod-y wants you
let ring
End Rhy. Fig. 2
B♭add♯4sus2 B♭ B♭add♯4sus2 D7sus2 Dm D7sus2 Dm D7sus2 Dm D7sus2 Dm
like the way I do. No - bod - y
B♭ B♭add♯4sus2 B♭ B♭add♯4sus2 B♭ B♭add♯4sus2 D7sus2 Dm D7sus2 Dm D7sus2
needs you like the way I do. No - bod - y
Dm D7sus2 Dm B♭ B♭add♯4sus2 B♭ B♭add♯4sus2 B♭ B♭add♯4sus2
aches, no - bod - y aches just to hold you like the way I

A
Gtr. 1
do. No, no, no.
Gtr. 2
let ring
Tell me does she
Chorus
Gtr. 1: w/ Rhy. Fig. 1 (2 times)
Dm D7sus2 Dm D7sus2 Dm D7sus2 Dm
love you like the way I love you. Does she stim - u - late
Rhy. Fig. 3
P.M.
B♭ B♭add♯4sus2 B♭ B♭add♯4sus2 B♭ B♭add♯4sus2 B♭
you, at - tract and cap - ti - vate you. Ba - by, ba - by, tell me does she miss
P.M.

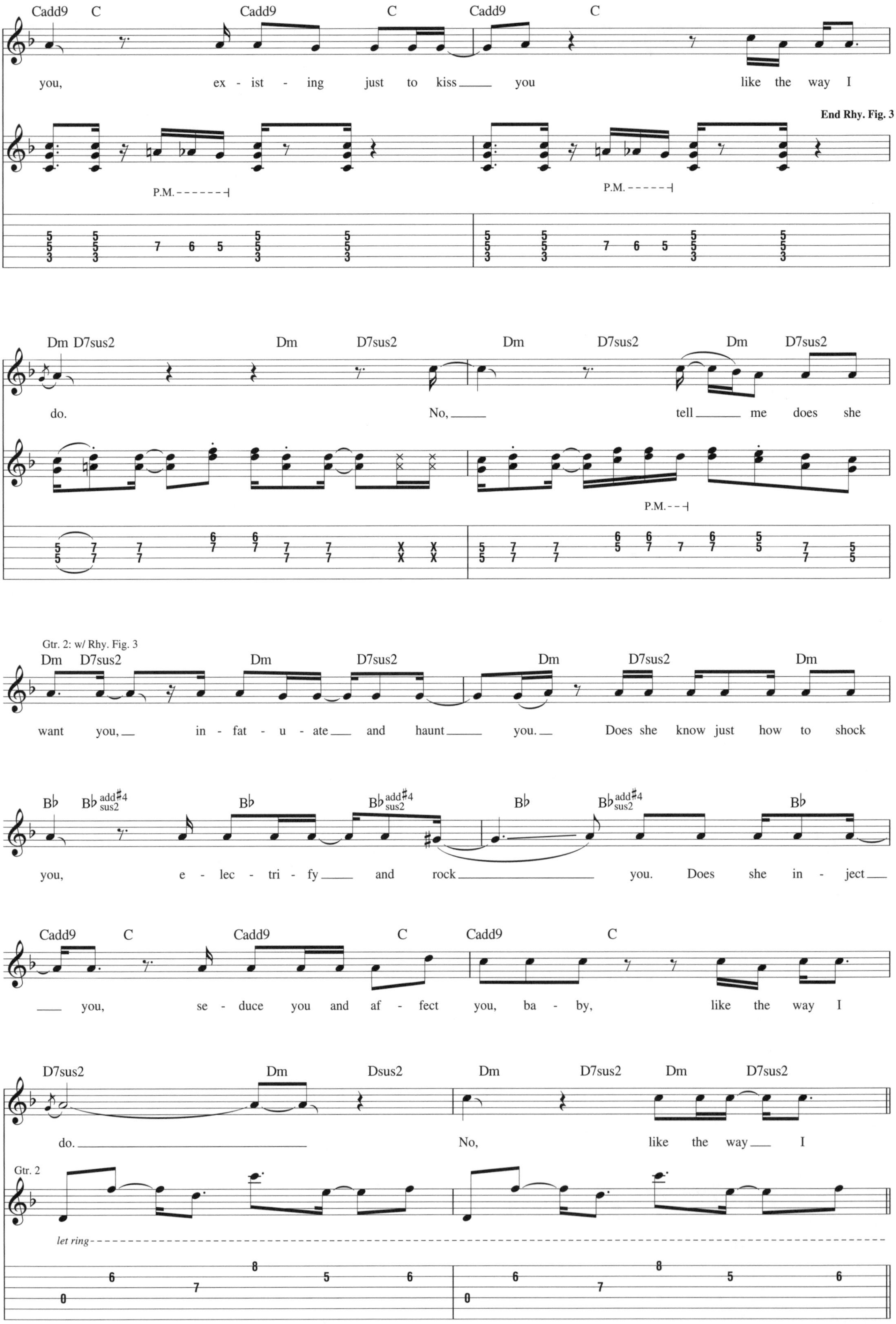

Cadd9 C Cadd9 C Cadd9 C

you, ex - ist - ing just to kiss ___ you like the way I

End Rhy. Fig. 3

P.M. P.M.

Dm D7sus2 Dm D7sus2 Dm D7sus2 Dm D7sus2

do. No, ___ tell ___ me does she

P.M.

Gtr. 2: w/ Rhy. Fig. 3

Dm D7sus2 Dm D7sus2 Dm D7sus2 Dm

want you, ___ in - fat - u - ate ___ and haunt ___ you. ___ Does she know just how to shock

B♭ B♭ add♯4 sus2 B♭ B♭ add♯4 sus2 B♭ B♭ add♯4 sus2 B♭

you, e - lec - tri - fy ___ and rock ___ you. Does she in - ject ___

Cadd9 C Cadd9 C Cadd9 C

___ you, se - duce you and af - fect you, ba - by, like the way I

Outro-Guitar Solo
Dm
Rhy. Fig. 4
Gtr. 1
B♭
do.
(Oh.)
Oh,
yeah.
Gtr. 2
let ring
C
let ring
Dm
End Rhy. Fig. 4
Gtr. 1: w/ Rhy. Fig. 4 (2 times)
let ring
let ring
1/4
let ring
B♭
let ring

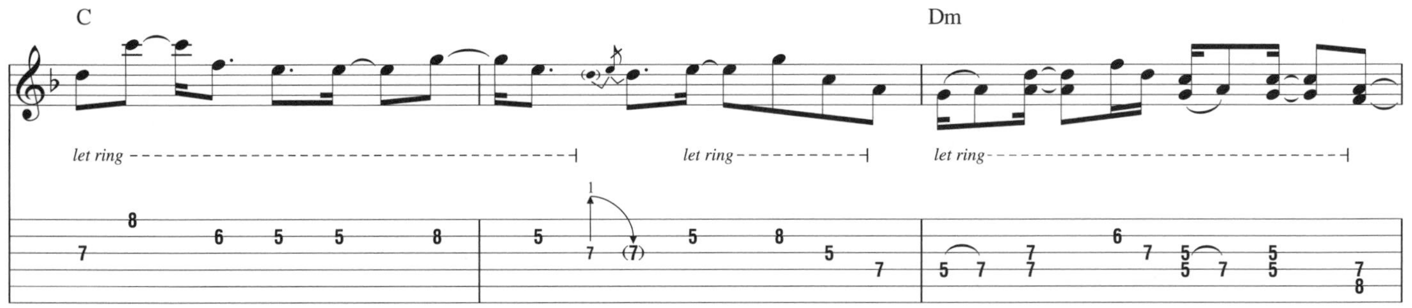
C
Dm
let ring
let ring
let ring

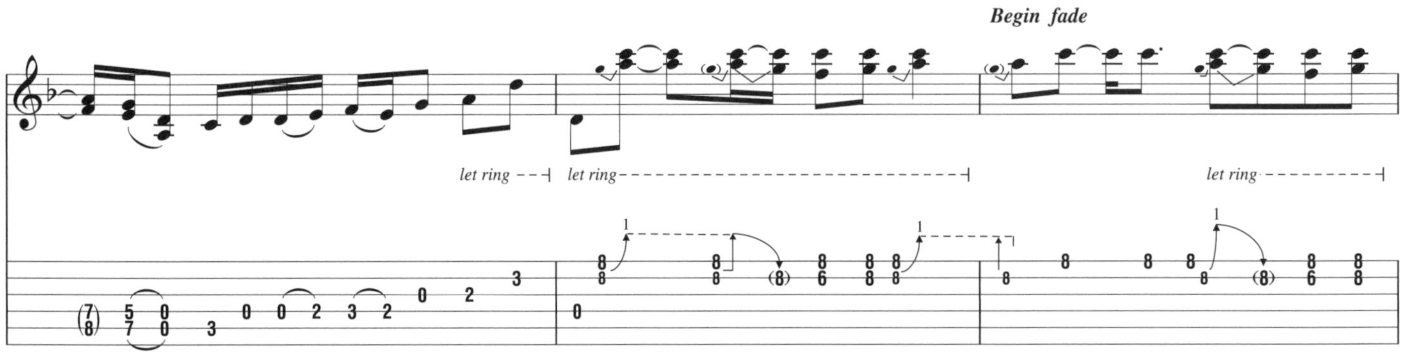
Begin fade
let ring
let ring
let ring

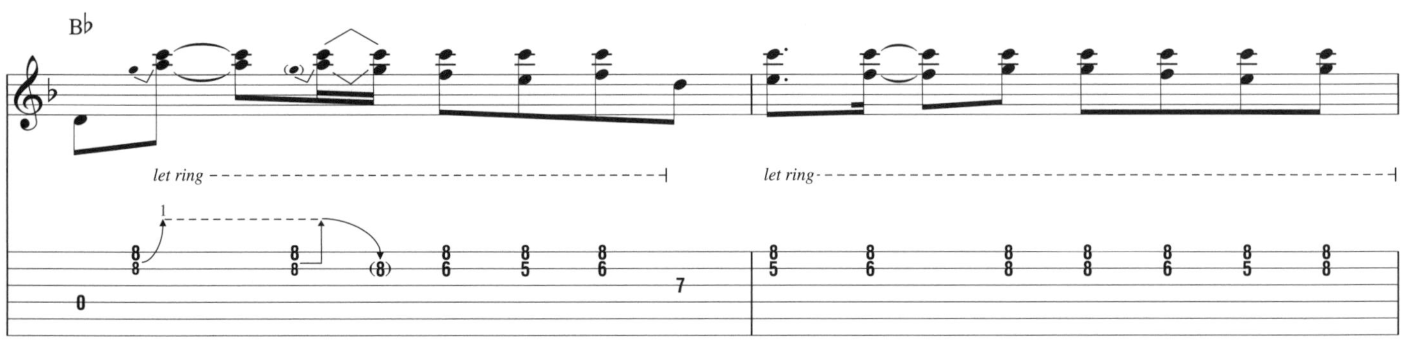
B♭
let ring
let ring

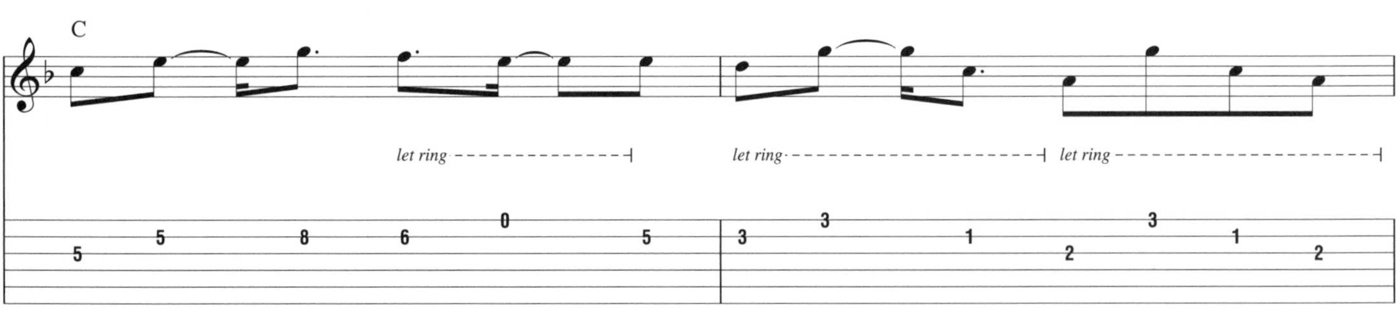
C
let ring
let ring
let ring

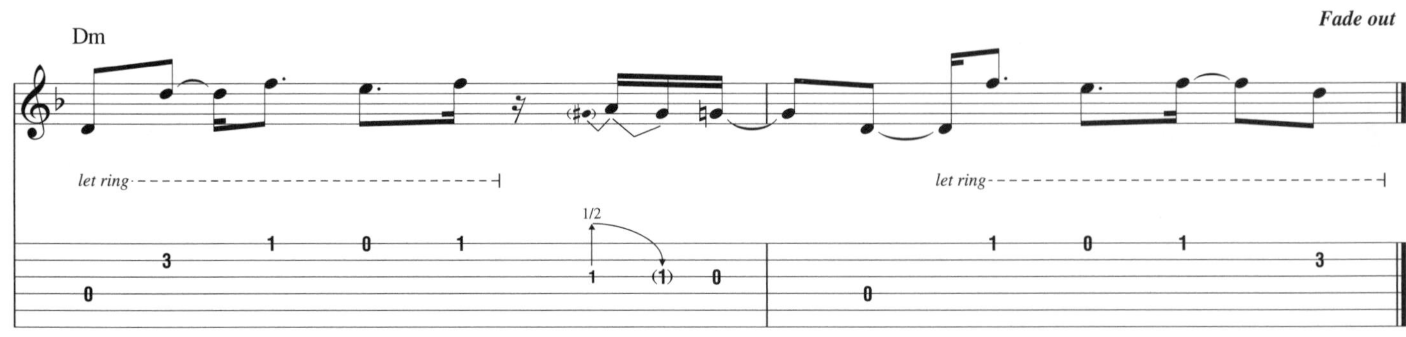
Dm
Fade out
let ring
let ring

from *Skin*

Lover Please

Words and Music by Melissa Etheridge

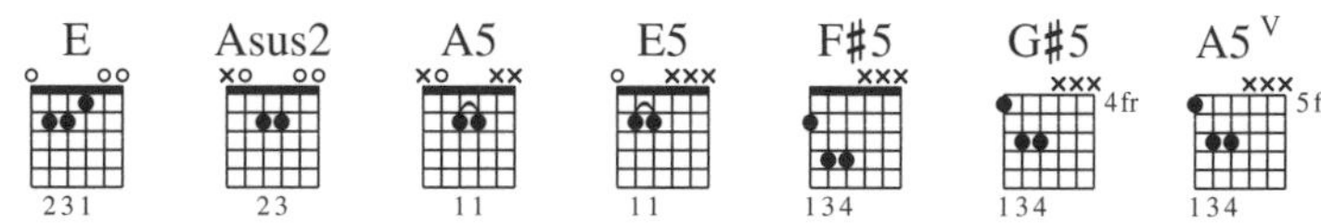

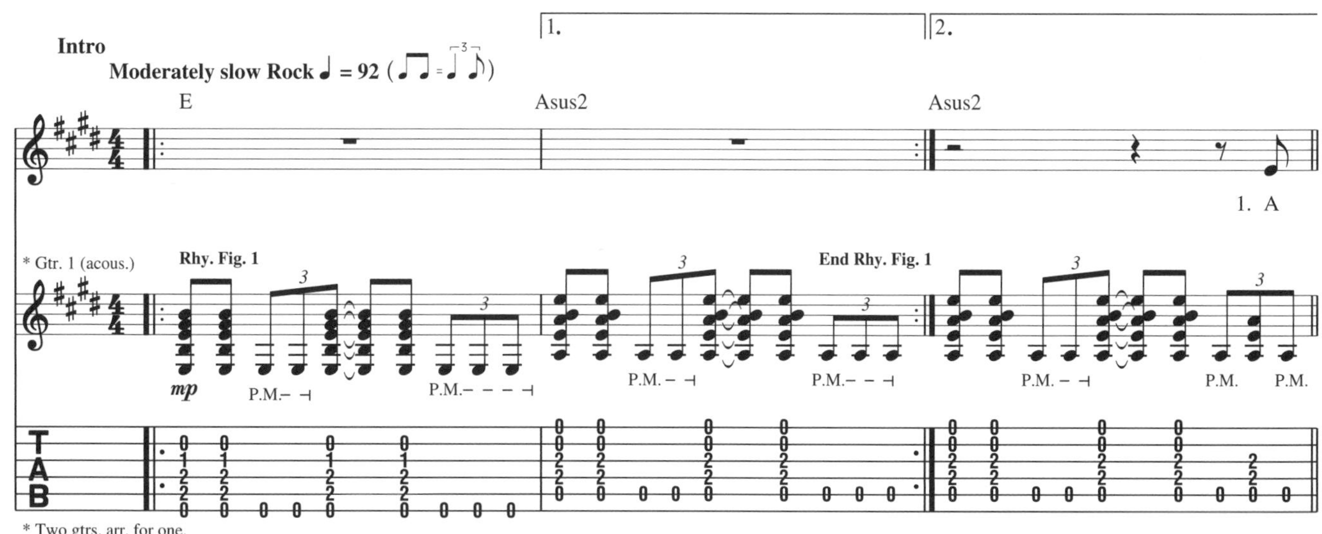

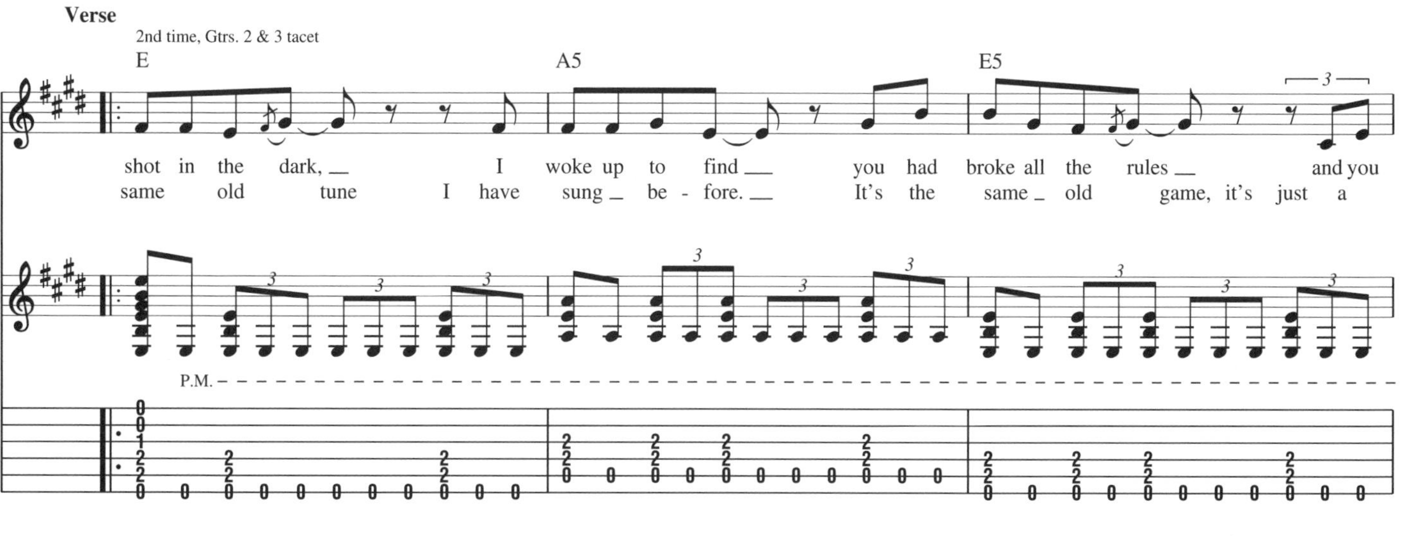

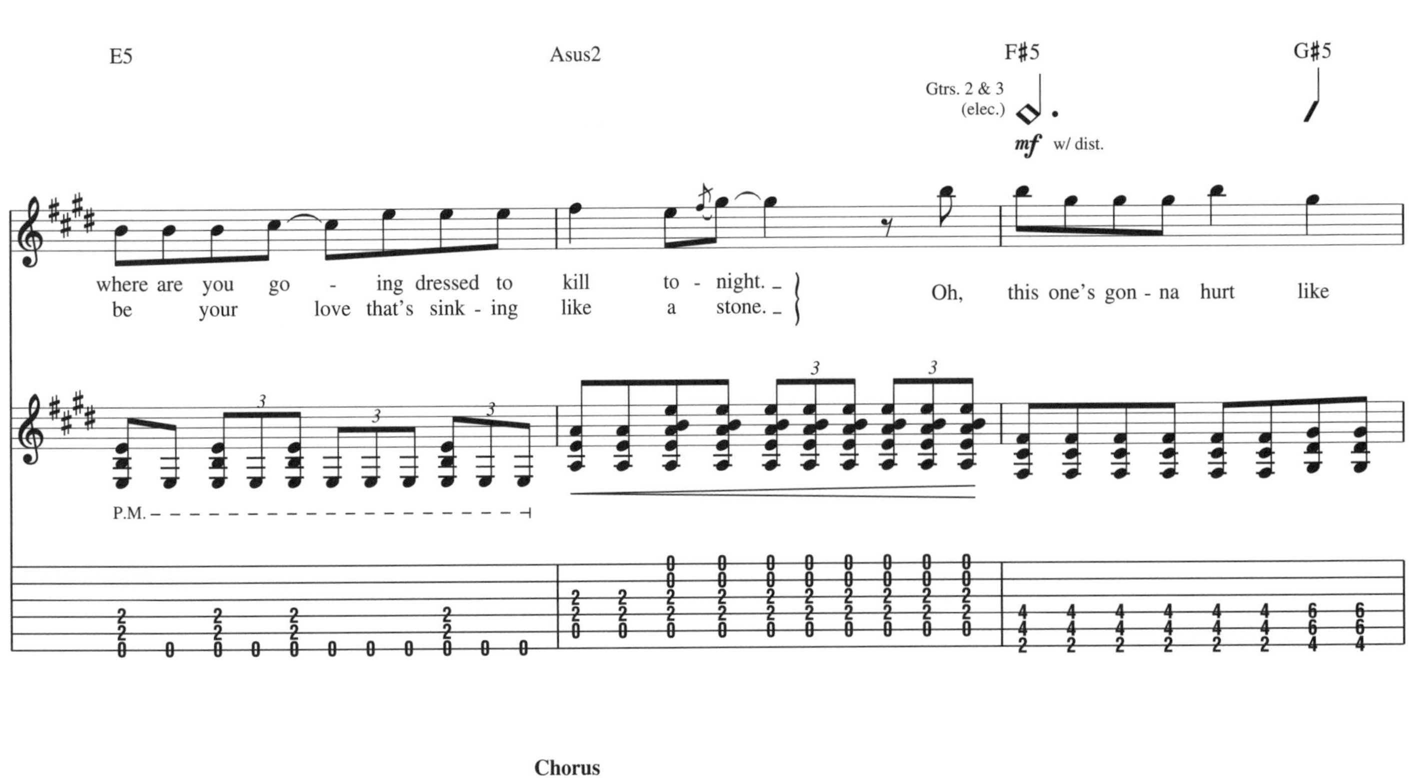
E5
Asus2
F#5
G#5
Gtrs. 2 & 3 (elec.)
mf w/ dist.
where are you go - ing dressed to kill to - night.
be your love that's sink - ing like a stone.
Oh, this one's gon - na hurt like
P.M.

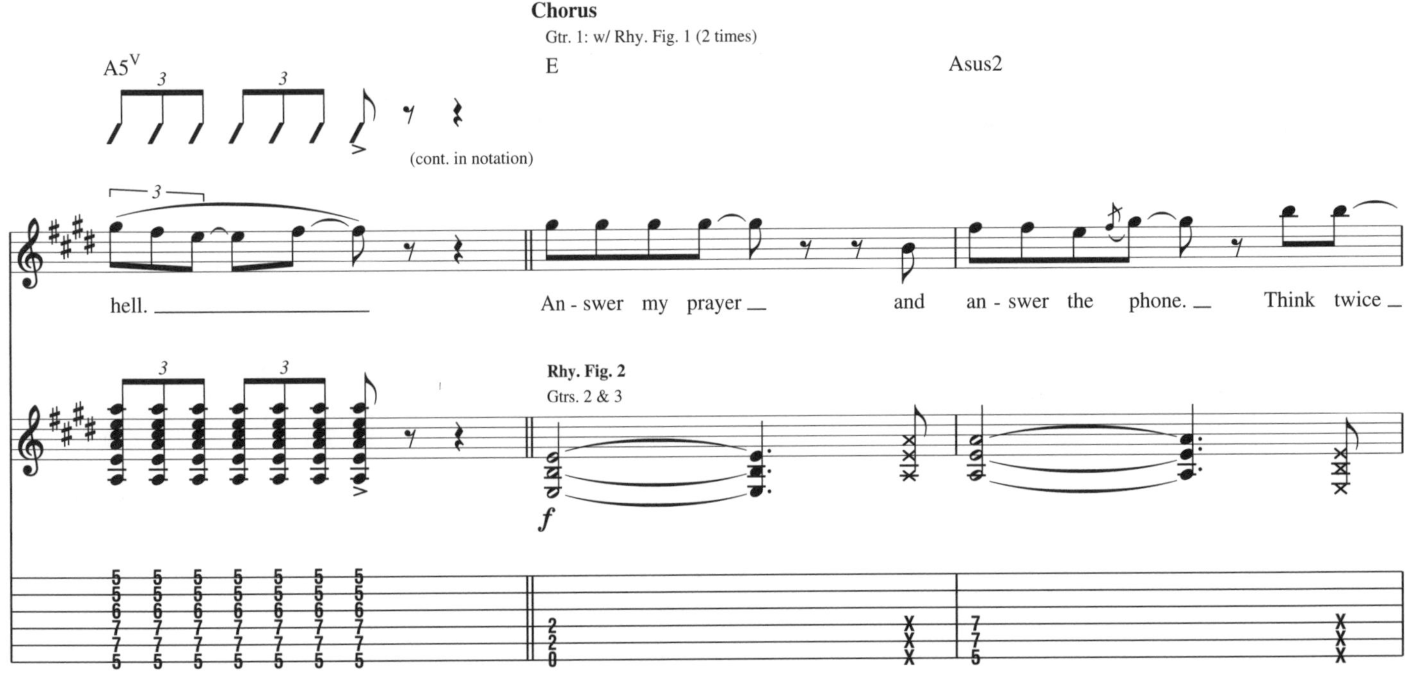
Chorus
Gtr. 1: w/ Rhy. Fig. 1 (2 times)
A5V
E
Asus2
(cont. in notation)
hell.
An - swer my prayer and an - swer the phone. Think twice
Rhy. Fig. 2
Gtrs. 2 & 3
f

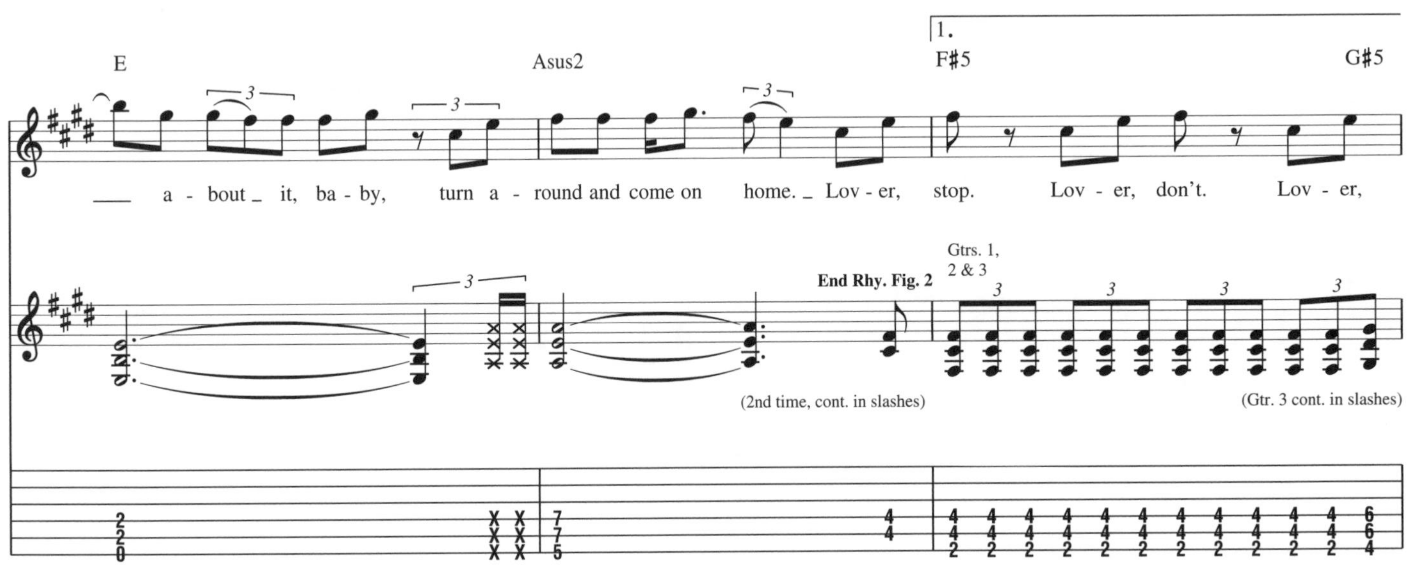
1.
E
Asus2
F#5
G#5
a - bout it, ba - by, turn a - round and come on home. Lov - er, stop. Lov - er, don't. Lov - er,
End Rhy. Fig. 2
Gtrs. 1, 2 & 3
(2nd time, cont. in slashes)
(Gtr. 3 cont. in slashes)

A5V E5

Gtr. 3

Rhy. Fill 1A End Rhy. Fill 1A

stop. Lov - er, lov - er, please. 2. It's the

Gtr. 2

Rhy. Fill 1 End Rhy. Fill 1

Gtr. 1

Rhy. Fig. 3 End Rhy. Fig. 3

P.M. P.M. P.M. *let ring*

2.

Gtr. 1: w/ Rhy. Fig. 3

F#5 G#5 A5V E5

Gtrs. 2 & 3

stop. Lov - er, don't. Lov - er, stop. Lov - er, lov - er, please.

Gtr. 1

Rhy. Fig. 4 End Rhy. Fig. 4

Gtr. 4 (elec.)

f

w/ dist. & talk box

Guitar Solo

Gtr. 1: w/ Rhy. Fig. 1 (2 times)
Gtrs. 2 & 3: w/ Rhy. Fig. 2
E
Asus2
Yeah.
Gtr. 5 (elec.)
f
w/ dist. & talk box
1/2

Gtr. 4
semi-harm.
1/2

Gtr. 1: w/ Rhy. Fig. 4
Gtr. 5 tacet
E
Asus2
F♯5
Rhy. Fig. 5
Gtrs 2 & 3
1/2
w/ talk box: This one's gon - na hurt like
1/2

Bridge
Gtrs. 2 & 3: w/ Rhy. Fills 1 & 1A
Gtr. 4 tacet
A5
End Rhy. Fig. 5
E
And they hold you like I want to. And they give you what I
Gtr. 4
Gtr. 1
hell.
want to. And they take it like I want to. And they
E5
P.M.
make it and they break it. Why must you re-
N.C.
P.M.
ject me. Why can't you pro-tect me. An-swer my prayer and
Chorus
Gtr. 1: w/ Rhy. Fig. 1 (2 times)
Gtrs. 2 & 3: w/ Rhy. Fig. 2
E

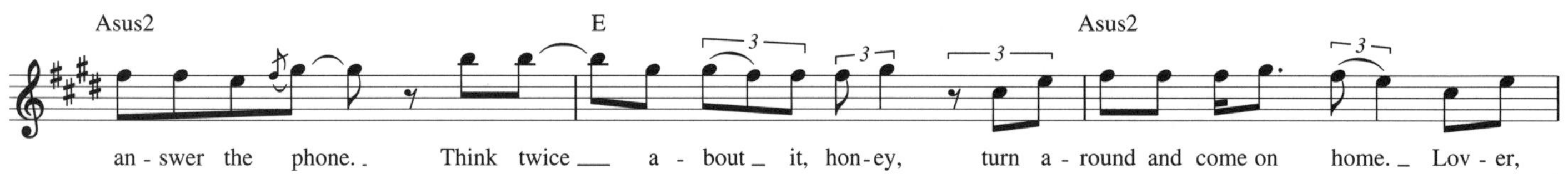

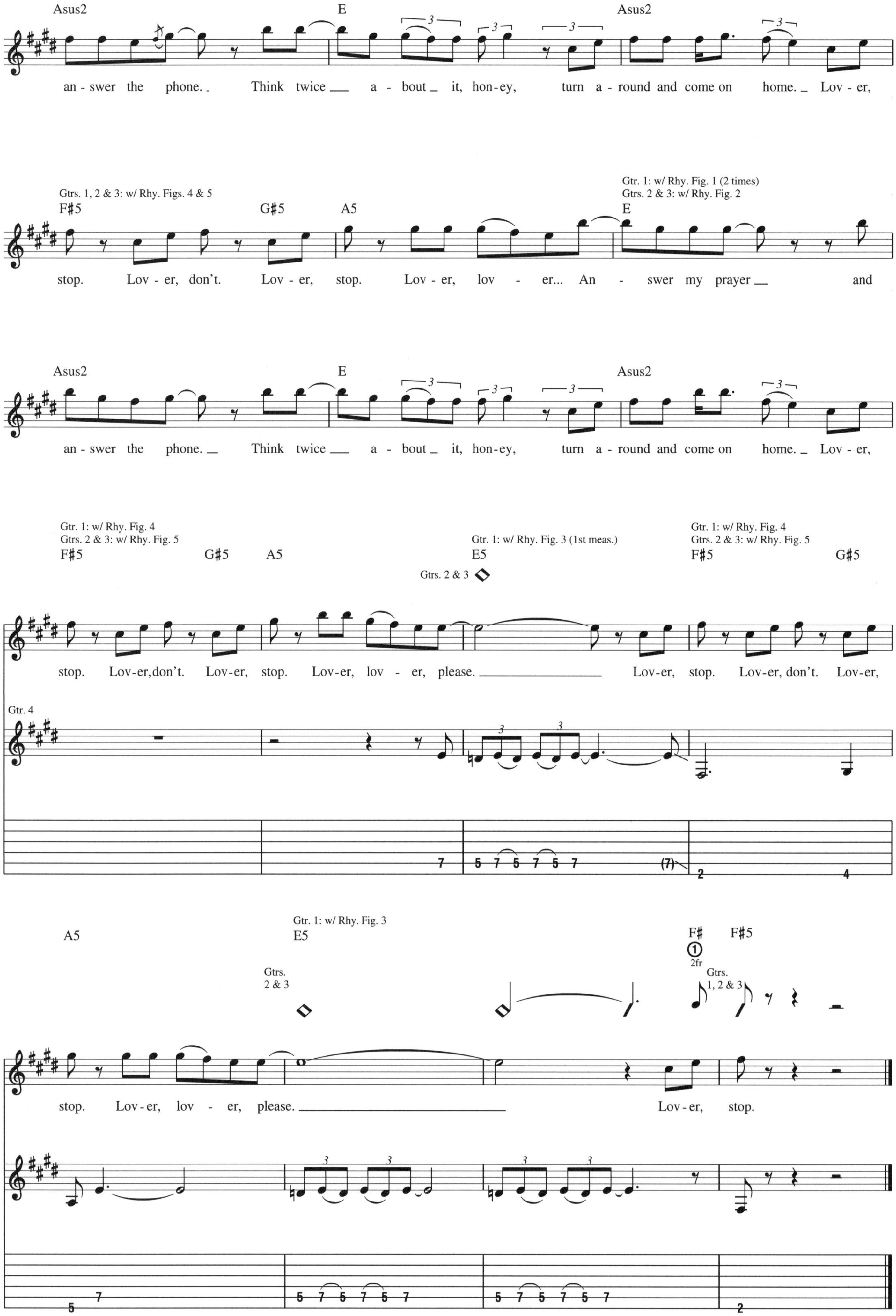

Gtr. 1: w/ Rhy. Fig. 4
Gtrs. 2 & 3: w/ Rhy. Fig. 5
F#5 G#5 A5
Gtr. 1: w/ Rhy. Fig. 3 (1st meas.)
E5
Gtrs. 2 & 3
Gtr. 1: w/ Rhy. Fig. 4
Gtrs. 2 & 3: w/ Rhy. Fig. 5
F#5 G#5

stop. Lov-er,don't. Lov-er, stop. Lov-er, lov - er, please. __________ Lov-er, stop. Lov-er, don't. Lov-er,

Gtr. 4

7 | 5 7 5 7 5 7 (7) | 2 4

A5
Gtr. 1: w/ Rhy. Fig. 3
E5
F# F#5
①
2fr
Gtrs. 2 & 3
Gtrs. 1, 2 & 3

stop. Lov-er, lov - er, please. __________ Lov-er, stop.

5 7 | 5 7 5 7 5 7 | 5 7 5 7 5 7 | 2

from *Brave and Crazy*

No Souvenirs

Words and Music by Melissa Etheridge

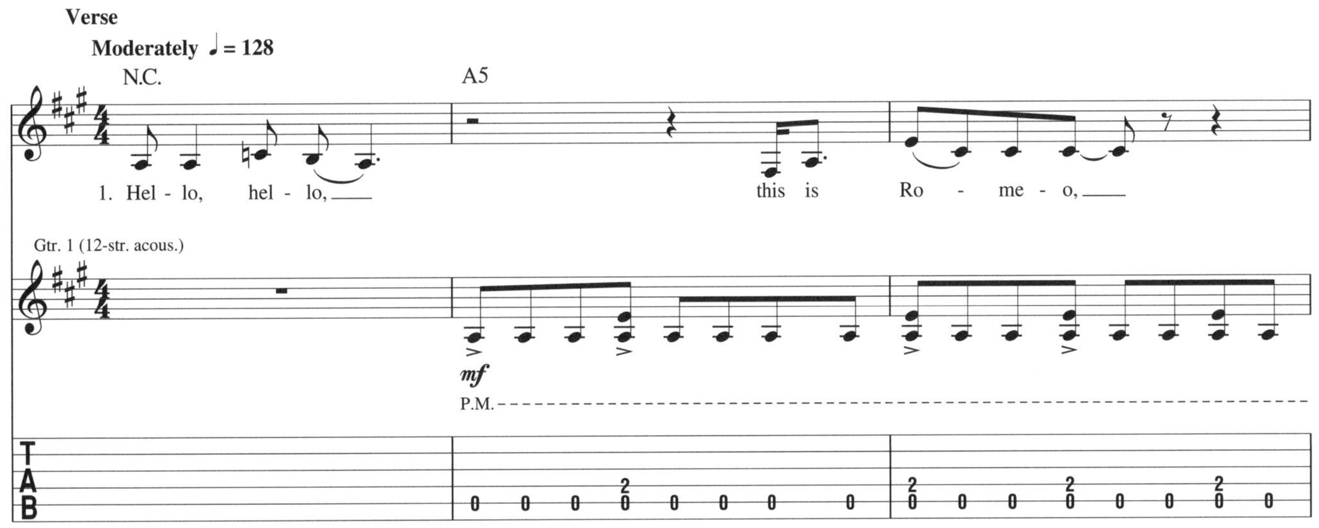

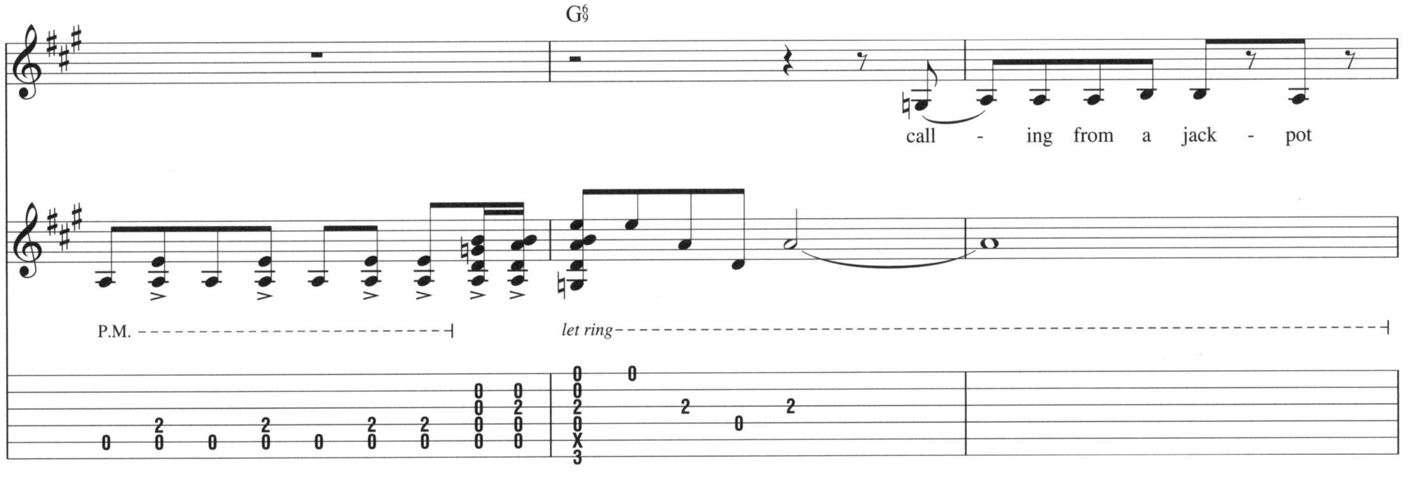

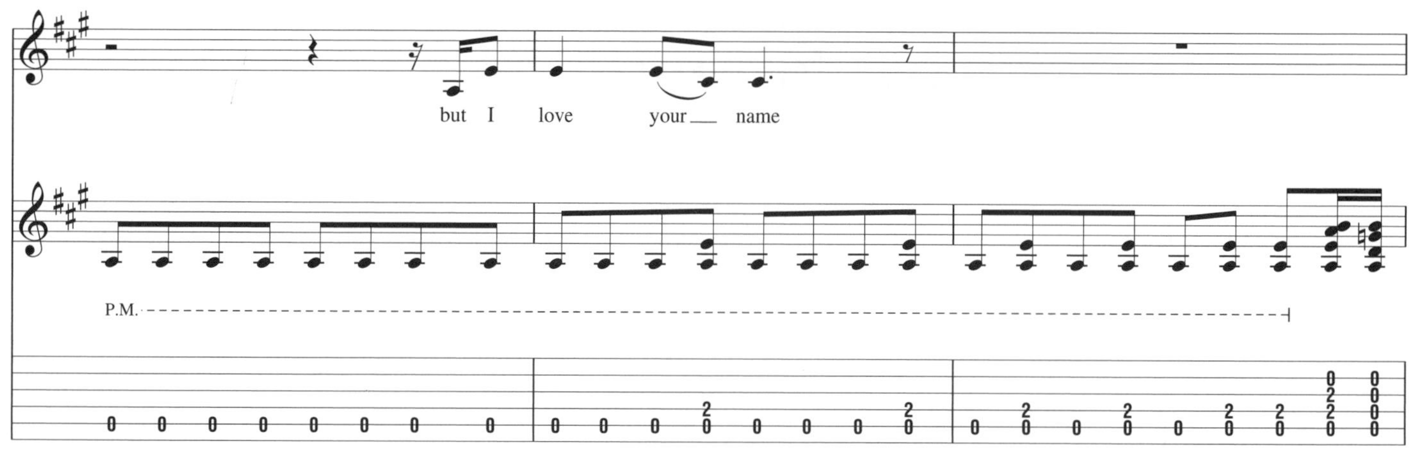
but I love your name
P.M.

G6/9
A5
and the way you make the buf - fa - lo roam.
let ring
P.M.

Bridge

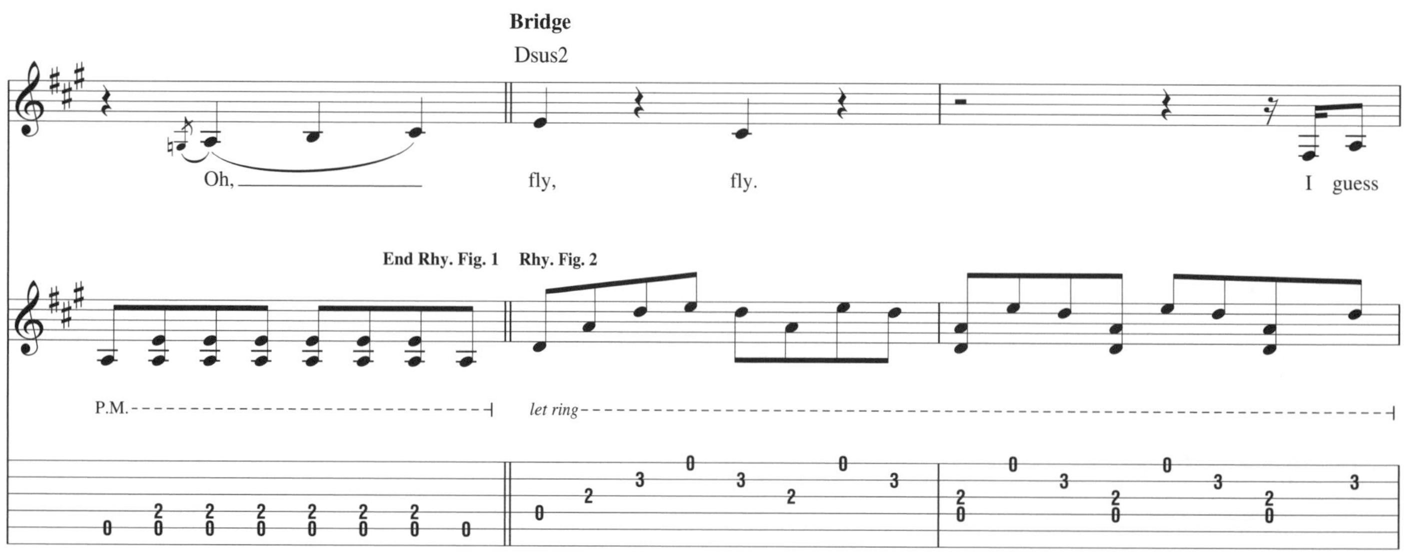
Dsus2
Oh, fly, fly. I guess
End Rhy. Fig. 1
Rhy. Fig. 2
P.M.
let ring

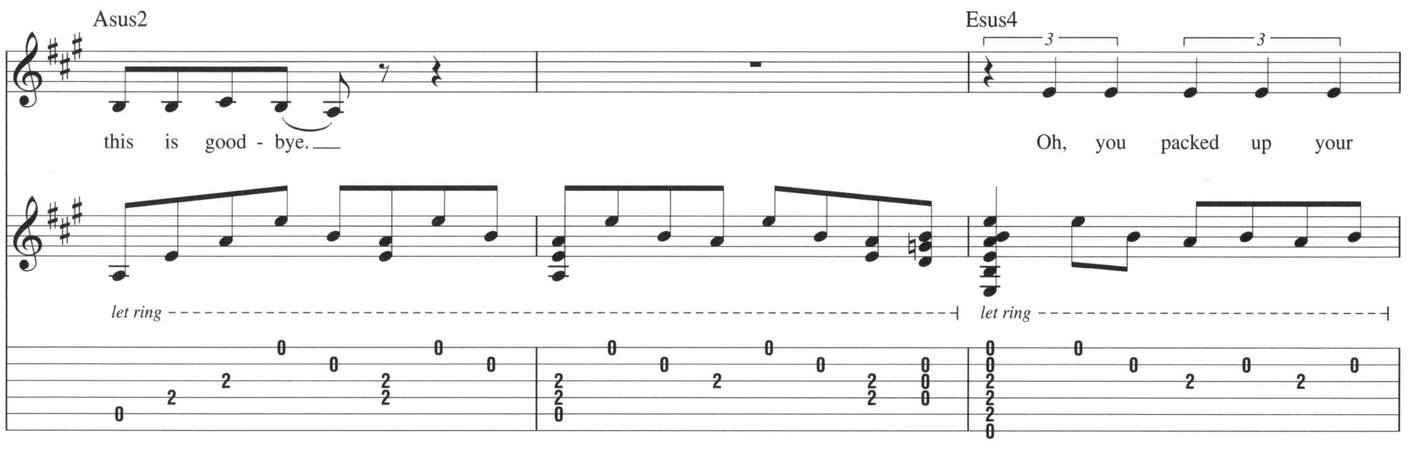
Asus2
Esus4
this is good - bye.
Oh, you packed up your
let ring
let ring

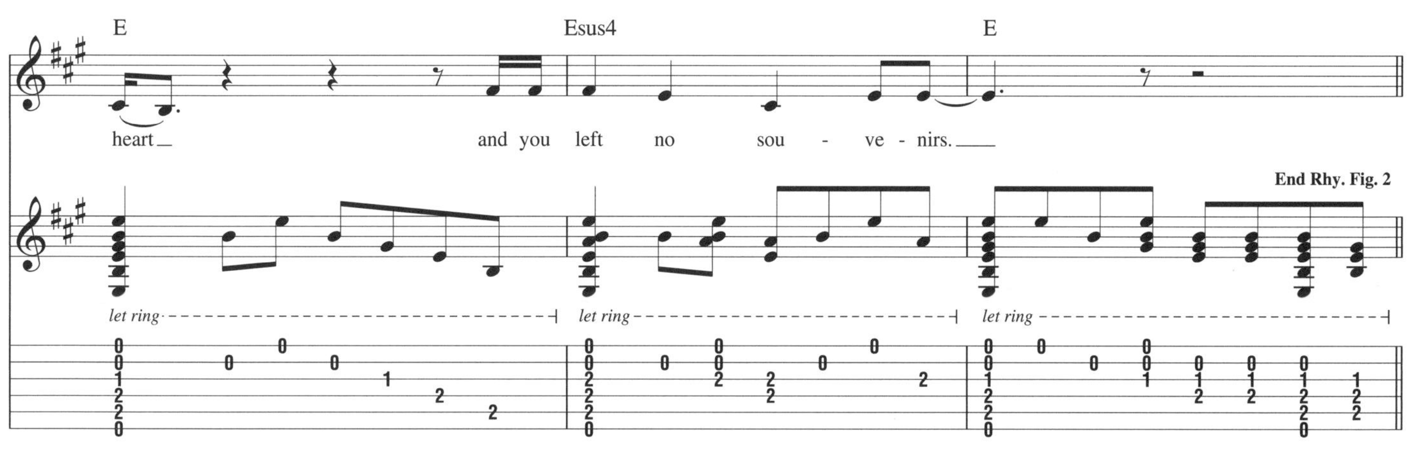
E
Esus4
E
heart
and you left no sou - ve - nirs.
End Rhy. Fig. 2
let ring
let ring
let ring

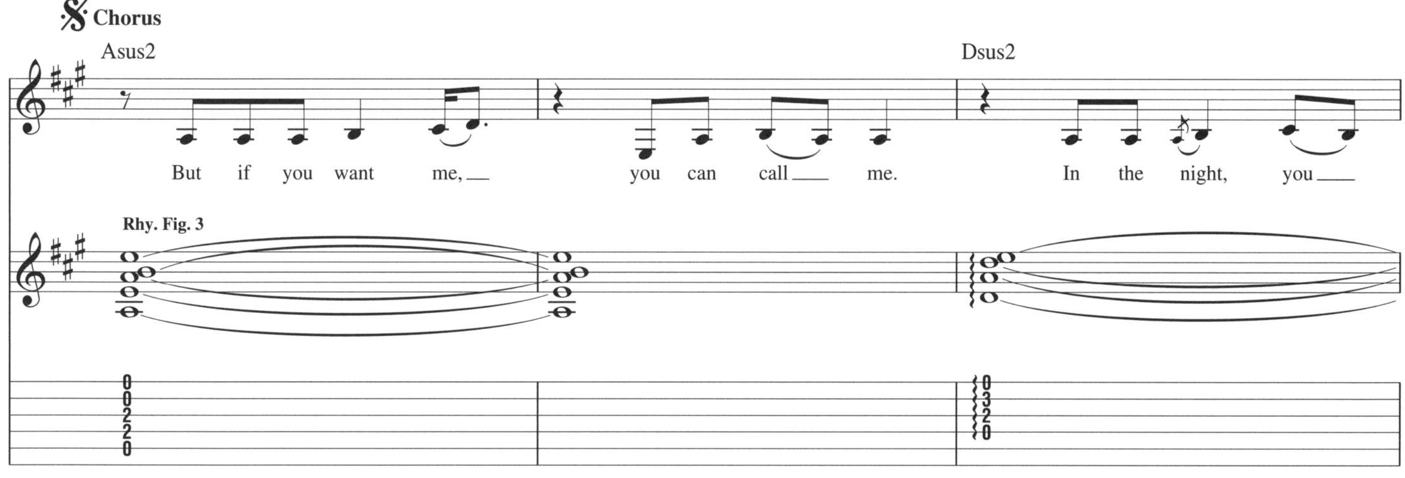
Chorus
Asus2
Dsus2
But if you want me,
you can call me.
In the night, you
Rhy. Fig. 3

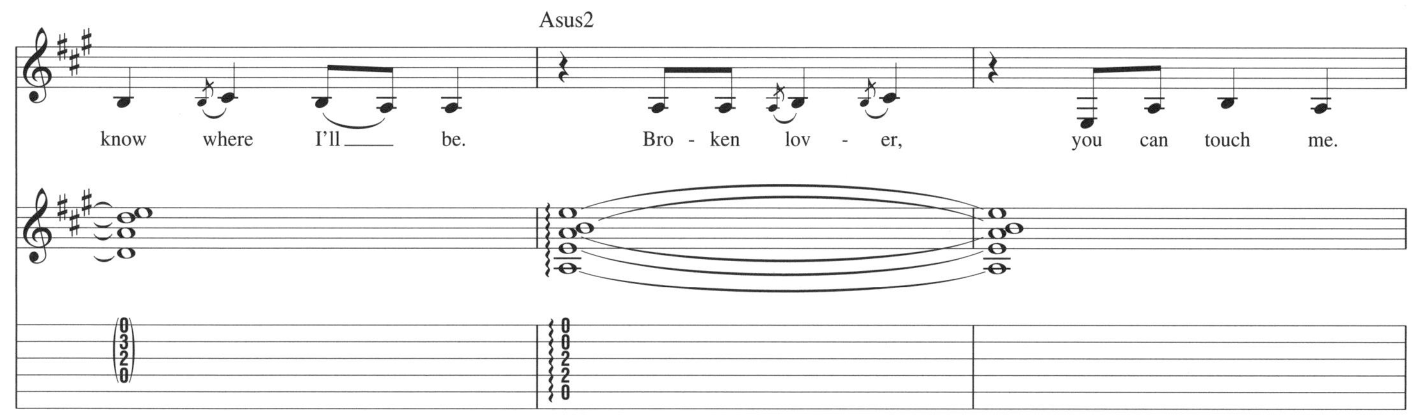
Asus2
know where I'll be.
Bro - ken lov - er,
you can touch me.

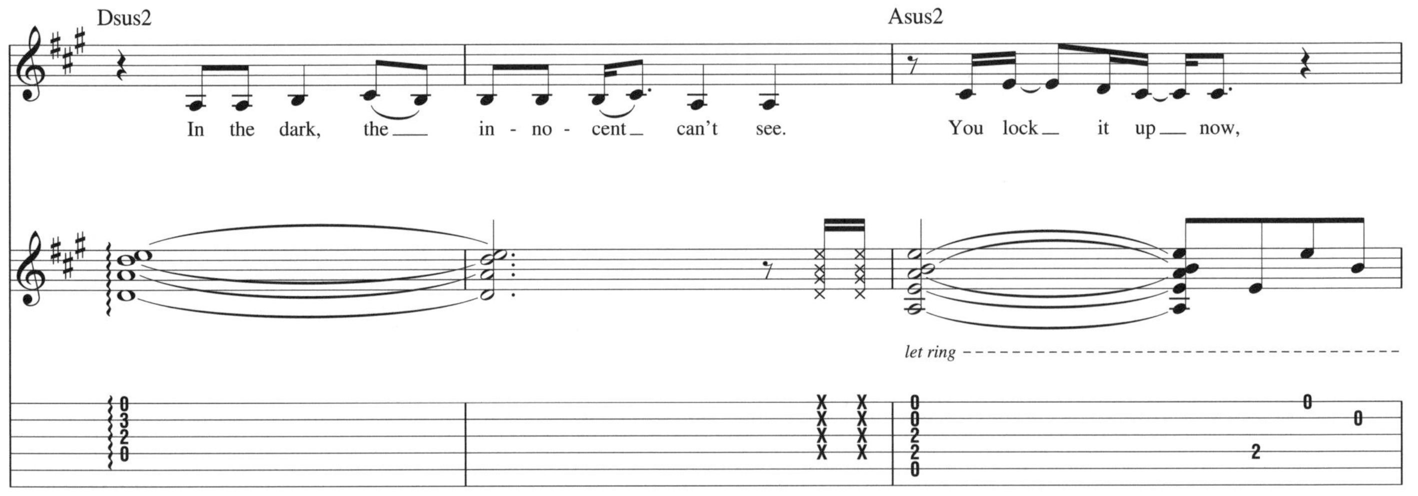
Dsus2
Asus2
In the dark, the innocent can't see. You lock it up now,
let ring

Dsus2
hide the key. It would mean surrender to let me see. Oh,
let ring
sim.

Asus2
D
brave, brave soldier, keep it under cover. You fell alone, like

A
no oth - er lov - er.
Burn the pic - tures,
break the rec - ords.

D
A
Run far a - way to a north - ern town.
Sell your fear and leave

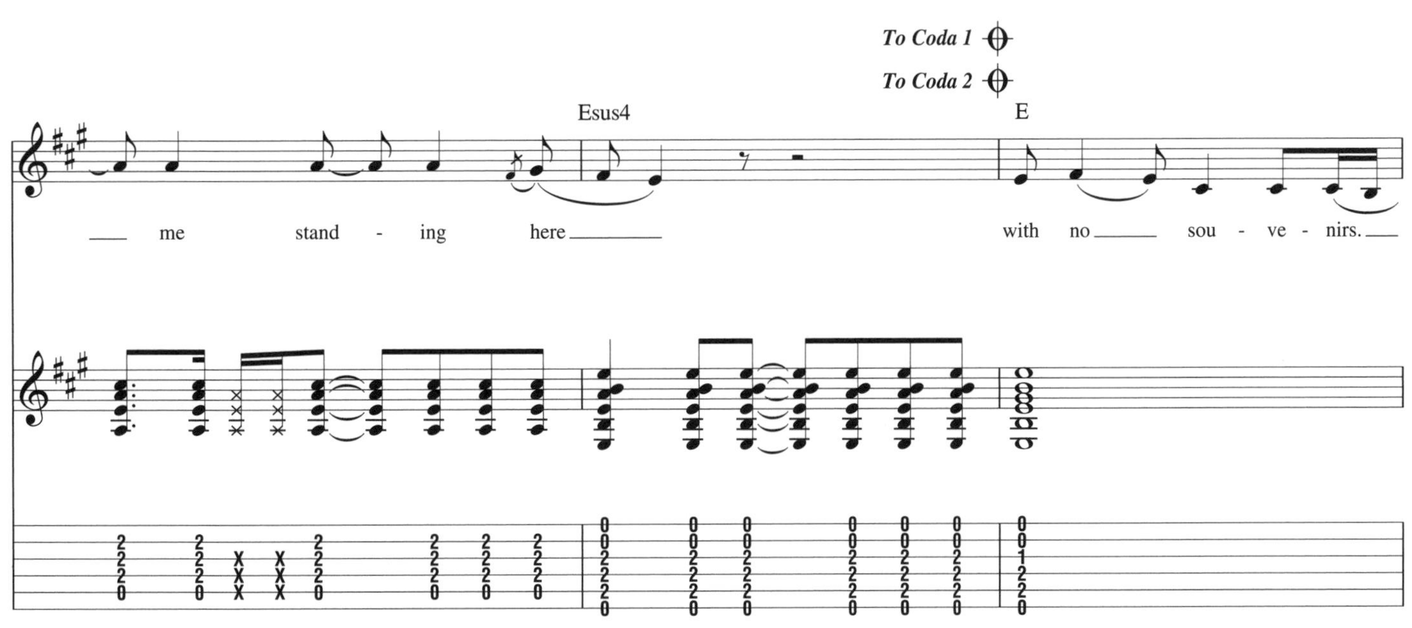
To Coda 1
To Coda 2
Esus4
E
me stand - ing here
with no sou - ve - nirs.

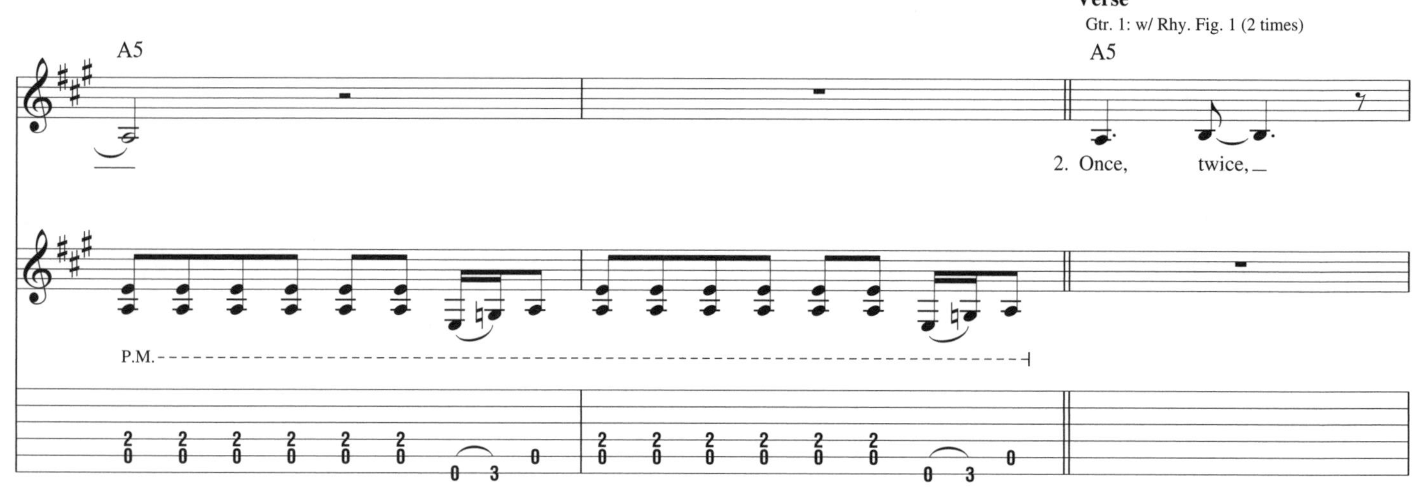
Verse
Gtr. 1: w/ Rhy. Fig. 1 (2 times)
A5
A5
2. Once, twice,
P.M.

G6/9
I thought it might be nice to

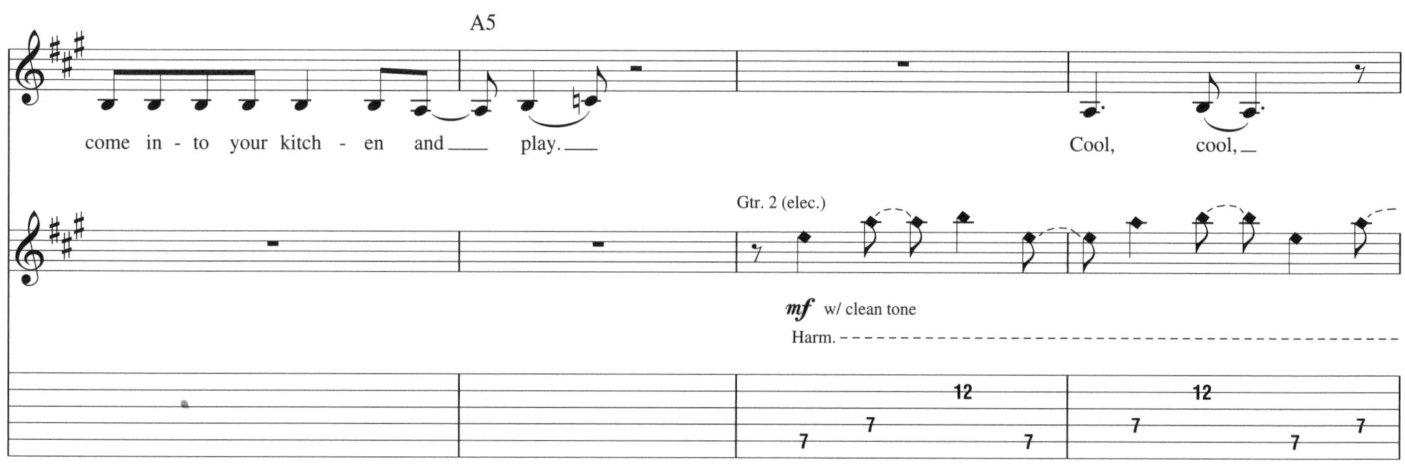
A5
come in - to your kitch - en and play.
Cool, cool,
Gtr. 2 (elec.)
mf w/ clean tone
Harm.

just a cra - zy fool.
Harm.

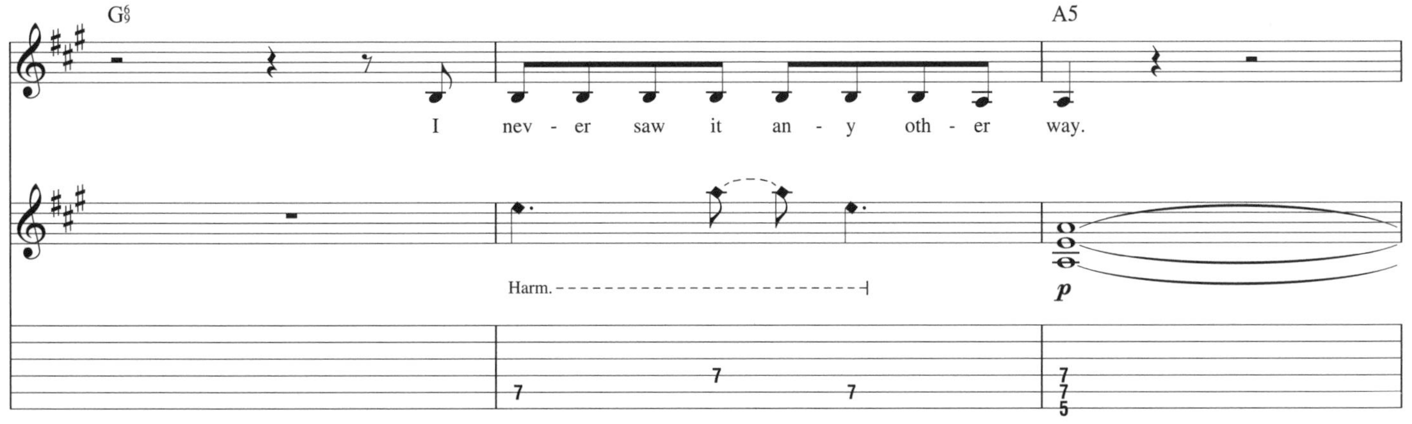

Bridge

Gtr. 1: w/ Rhy. Fig. 2
Gtr. 2 tacet

D.S. al Coda 1

Coda 1

Interlude

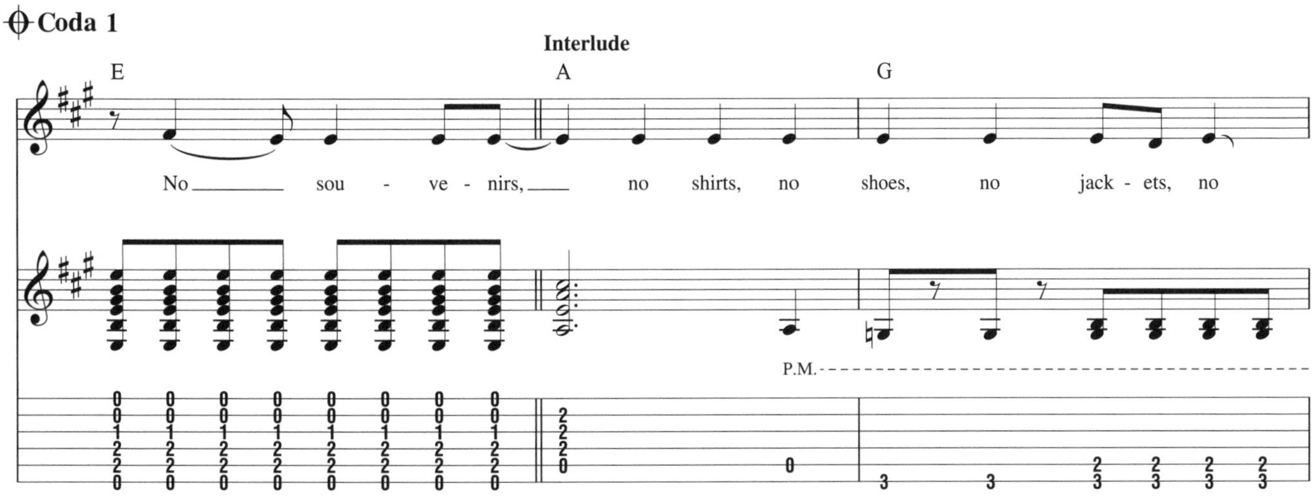

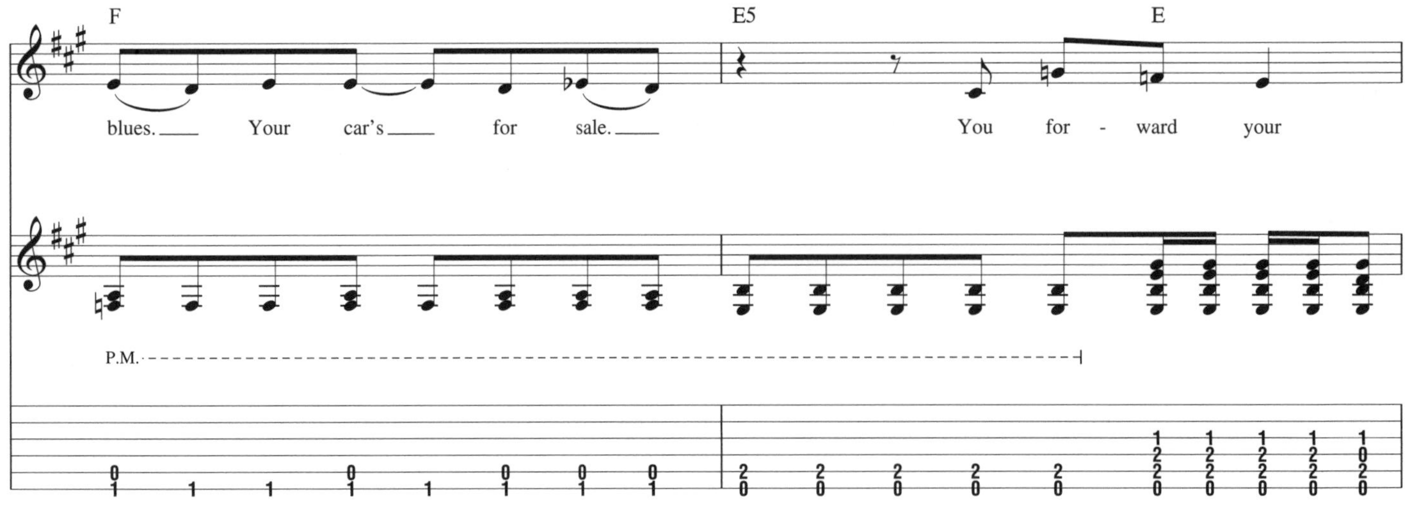
F
E5
E
blues. Your car's for sale.
You for - ward your
P.M.

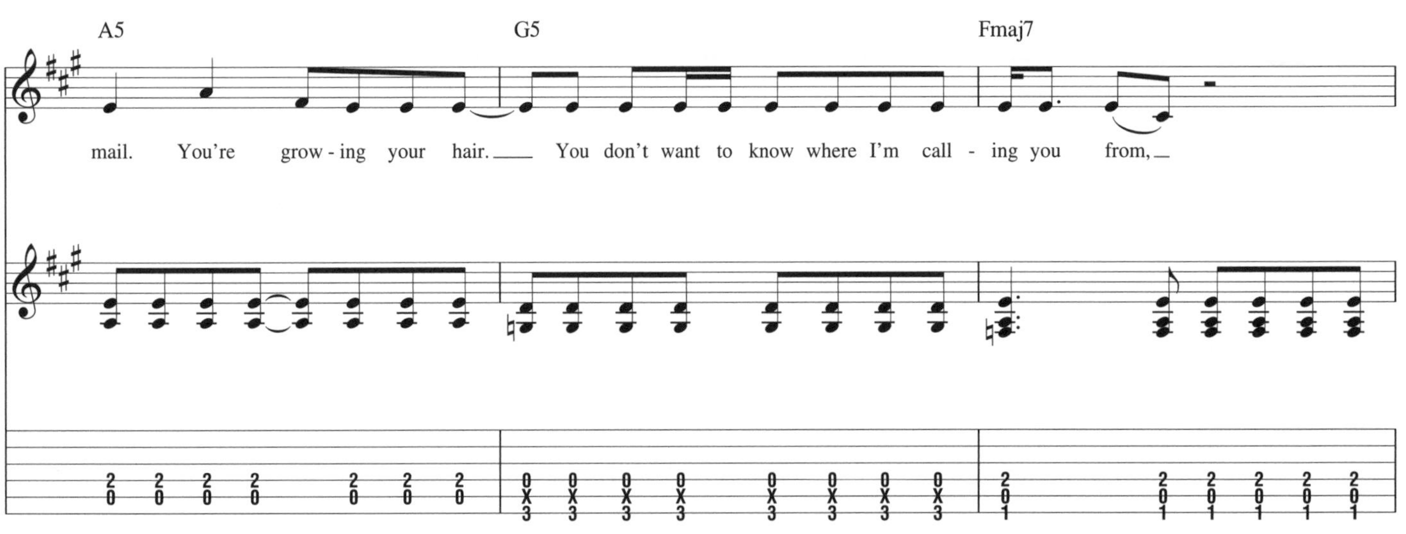
A5
G5
Fmaj7
mail. You're grow - ing your hair. You don't want to know where I'm call - ing you from,

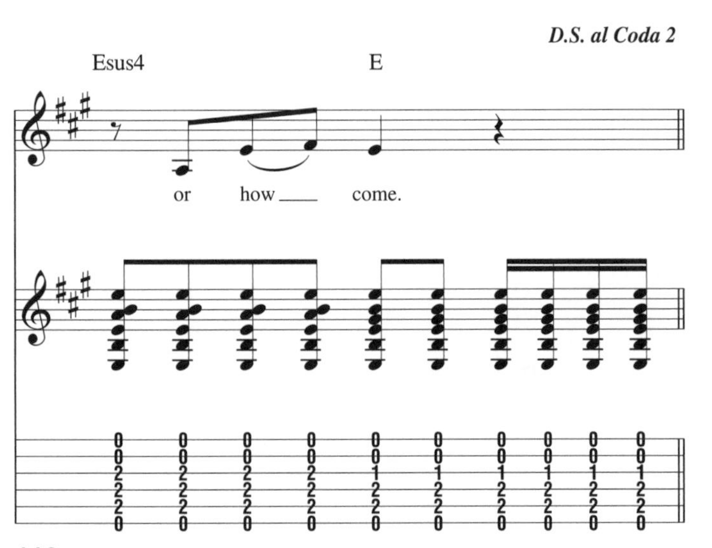
D.S. al Coda 2
Esus4
E
or how come.

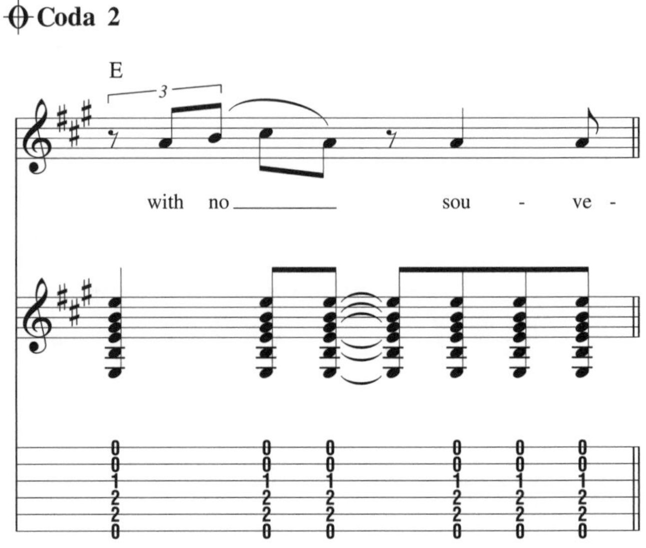
Coda 2
E
with no sou - ve -

Outro

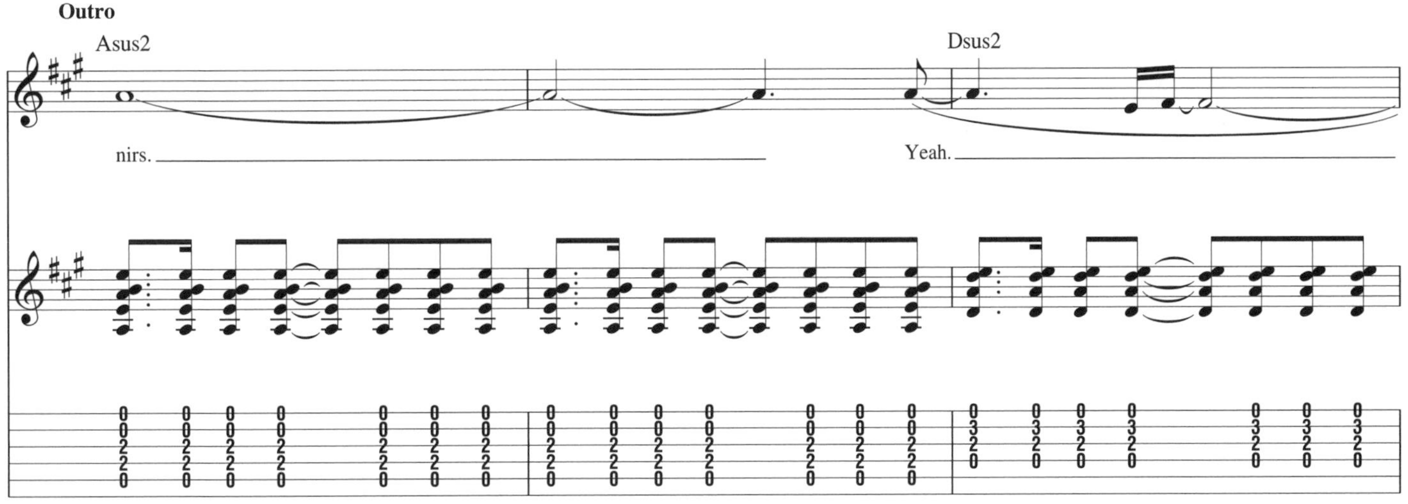

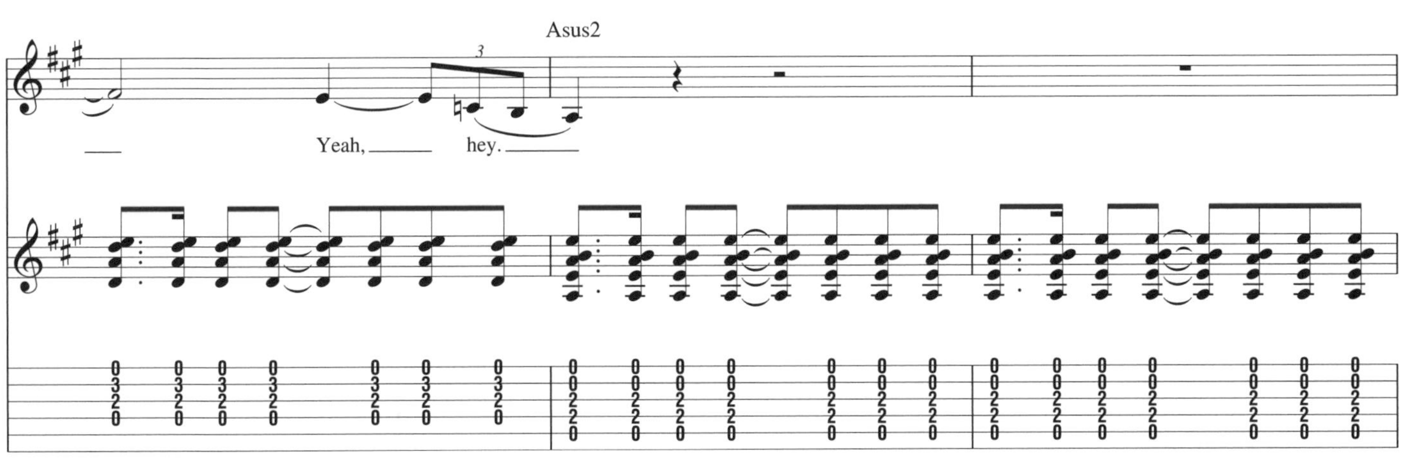

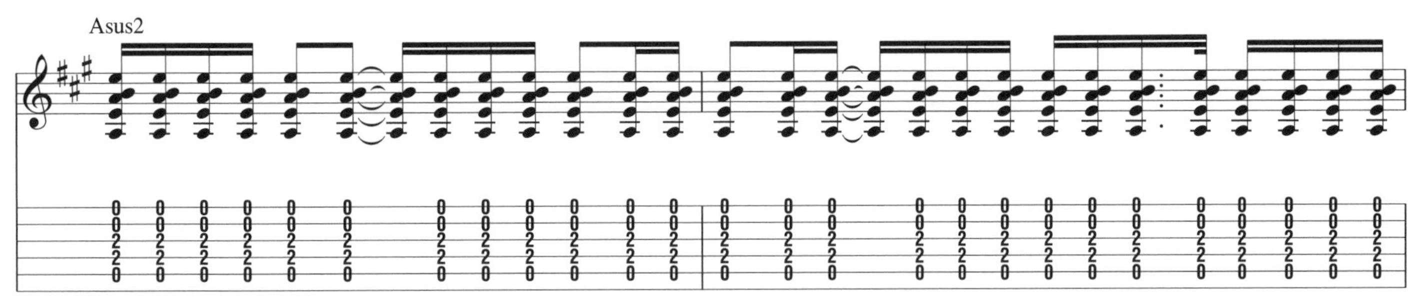

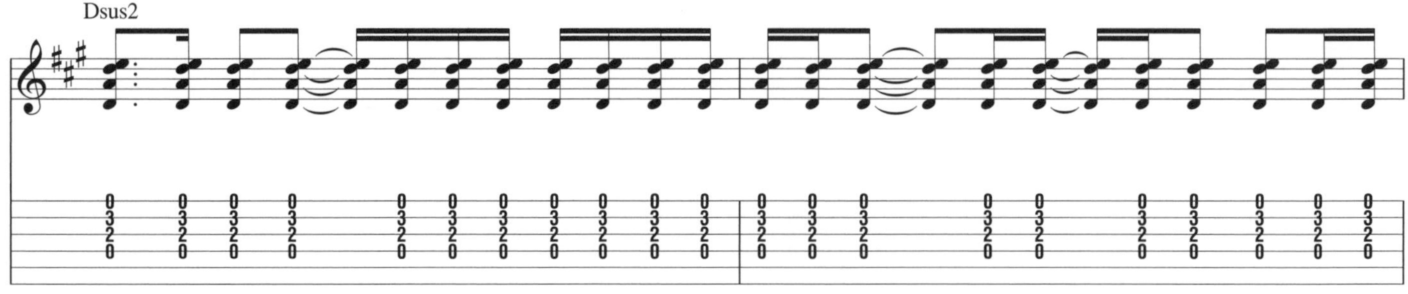
Dsus2

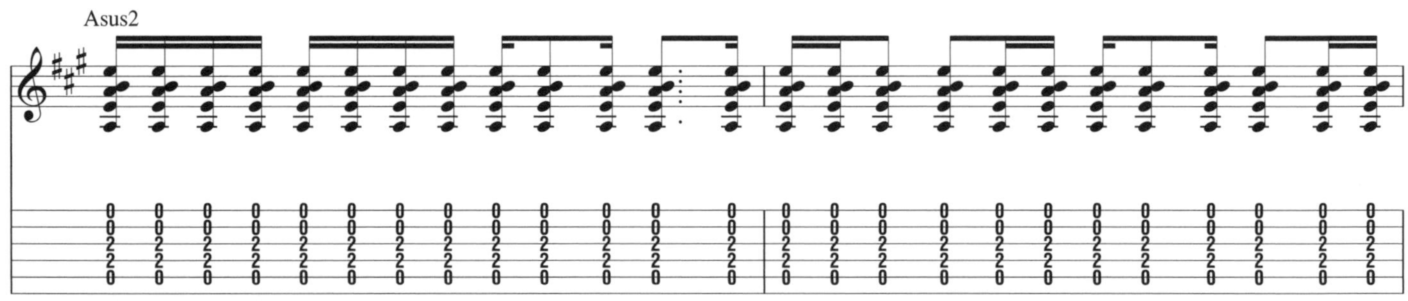
Asus2

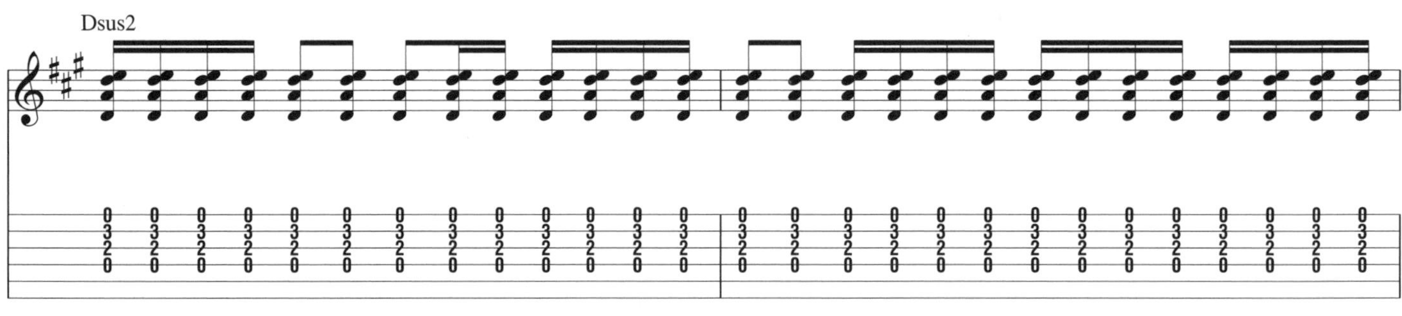
Dsus2

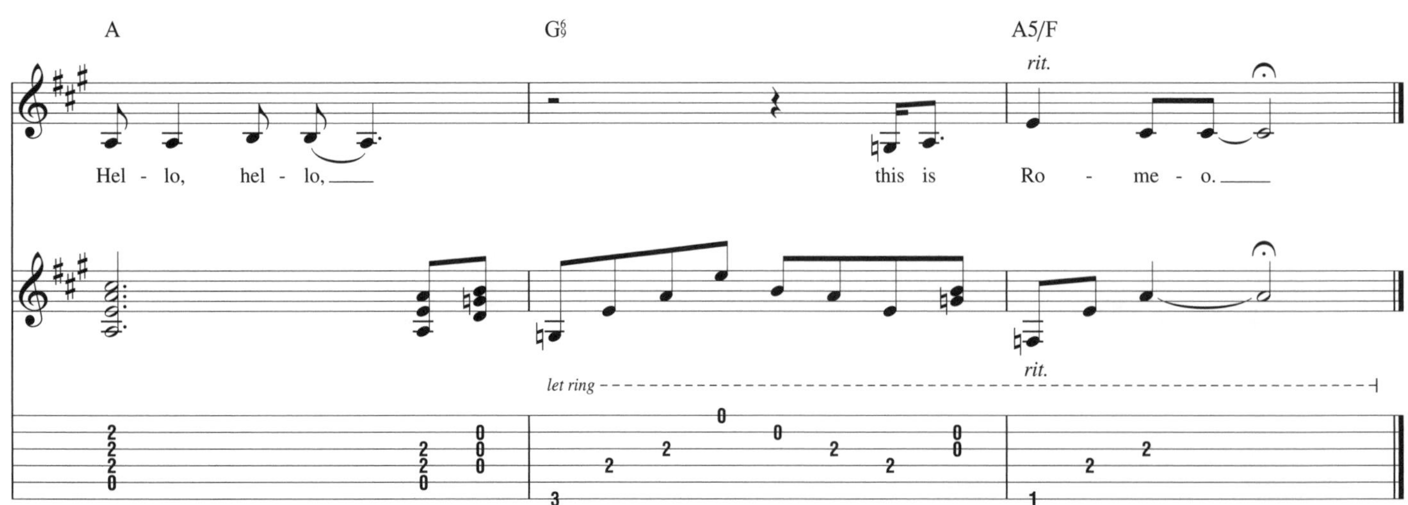
A
G6/9
A5/F
rit.
Hel - lo, hel - lo,
this is
Ro - me - o.
let ring
rit.

from *Your Little Secret*

Nowhere to Go

Words and Music by Melissa Etheridge

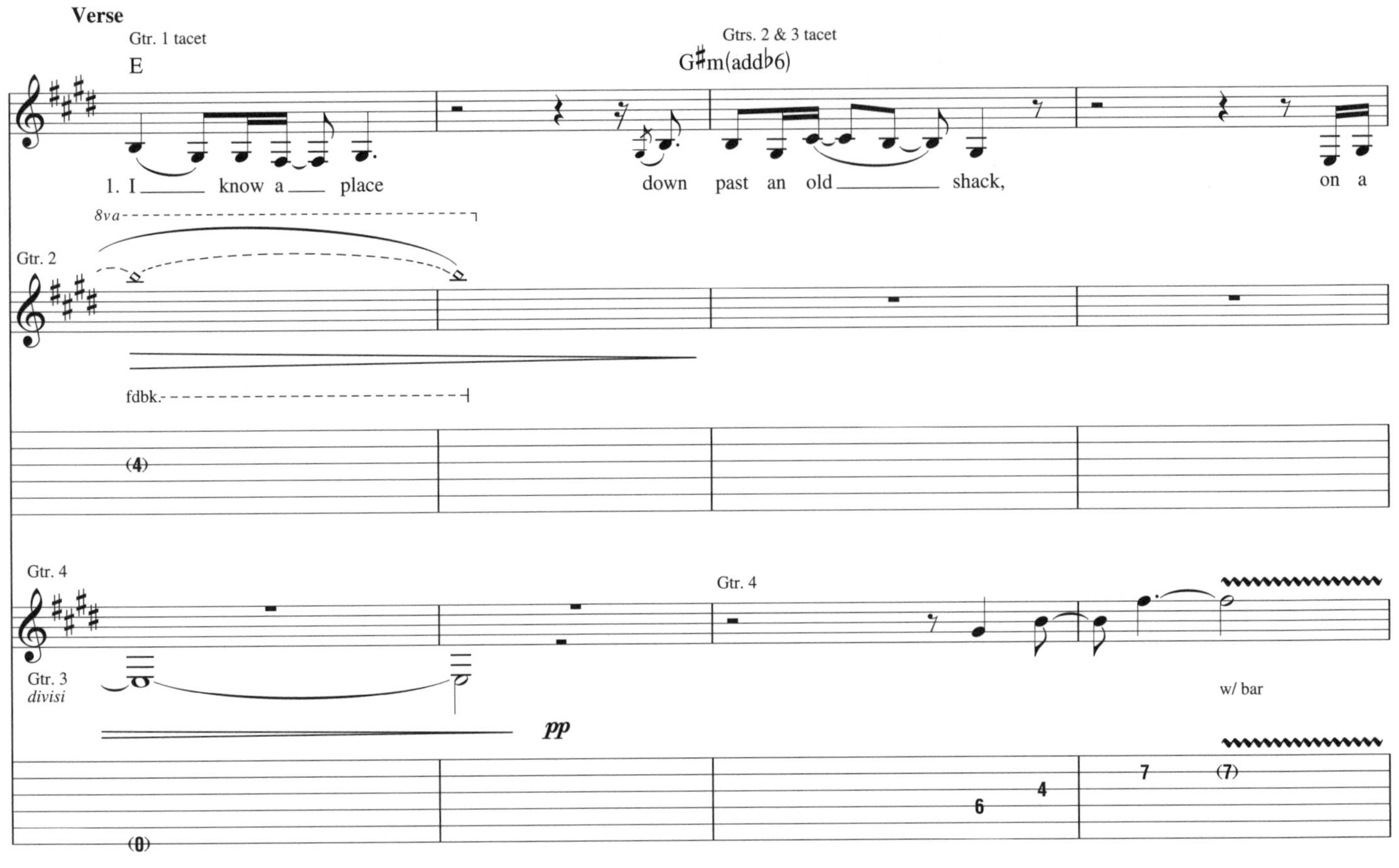
Verse
Gtr. 1 tacet
E
Gtrs. 2 & 3 tacet
G♯m(add♭6)
1. I know a place down past an old shack, on a
8va
Gtr. 2
fdbk.
Gtr. 4
Gtr. 3
divisi
pp
w/ bar

F♯m7
A
road that goes to no - where; ain't no - bod - y com - ing back. We can
Gtr. 4

E
G♯m(add♭6)
go there to-night, we can talk un - til dawn or may - be

F#m7 Asus2 Bsus4

___ some - thin' ___ else. ________ I'll leave the ___ ra - di - o ___ on, ________ the

Gtr. 2

8va

*pp fdbk.

*Vol. swell

Gtr. 4

Riff A

Gtr. 5 (clean)

Riff A1

mp

P.M.

Asus2 B Bsus4 B5

ra - di - o ___ on. ________ There's

8va

p

End Riff A

End Riff A1

P.M.

(cont. in slashes)

Chorus
Gtr. 2 tacet
E
E
2 fr
Asus2
Rhy. Fig. 1A
Gtr. 5
no one to hear.
You might as well scream.
They
Gtr. 4
Rhy. Fig. 1
E
Eadd9
Asus2
nev - er woke up
from the A - mer - i - can dream.
End Rhy. Fig. 1A
E
Rhy. Fig. 2
F♯m11
And they don't un - der - stand
what they don't see
and they
Gtr. 6 (clean)
Rhy. Fig. 2A
Gtr. 4
End Rhy. Fig. 1
Riff B

E/D# F#m11 End Rhy. Fig. 2 E

look through you and they look past me. Oh,

End Rhy. Fig. 2A

End Riff B Rhy. Fig. 3

G#m F#m Asus2 (cont. in notation)

you and I danc - ing slow, we got no - where to go.

End Rhy. Fig. 3

Interlude
Gtr. 6 tacet
E
Riff C
8va
Gtr. 2
*pp
mp
*Vol. swell
Gtr. 4
mp
w/ bar
Gtr. 5
mp
P.M.
Verse
E
Gtr. 2 tacet
2. Past the Wal - Mart and the pris - on, down
8va
End Riff C
w/ bar
Riff D
P.M.

G♯m(add♭6)
F♯m7
by the old V. A.,
just my jeans and my T - shirt,
Gtr. 4
Gtr. 5
P.M.

A
and my blue Chev - ro - let.
Well, it's
w/ bar
−1/4
End Riff D
P.M.

Gtr. 5: w/ Riff D (1st 6 meas.)
E
G♯m(add♭6)
Sat - ur - day night,
it feels like ev - 'ry - thing's wrong.
Gtr. 4

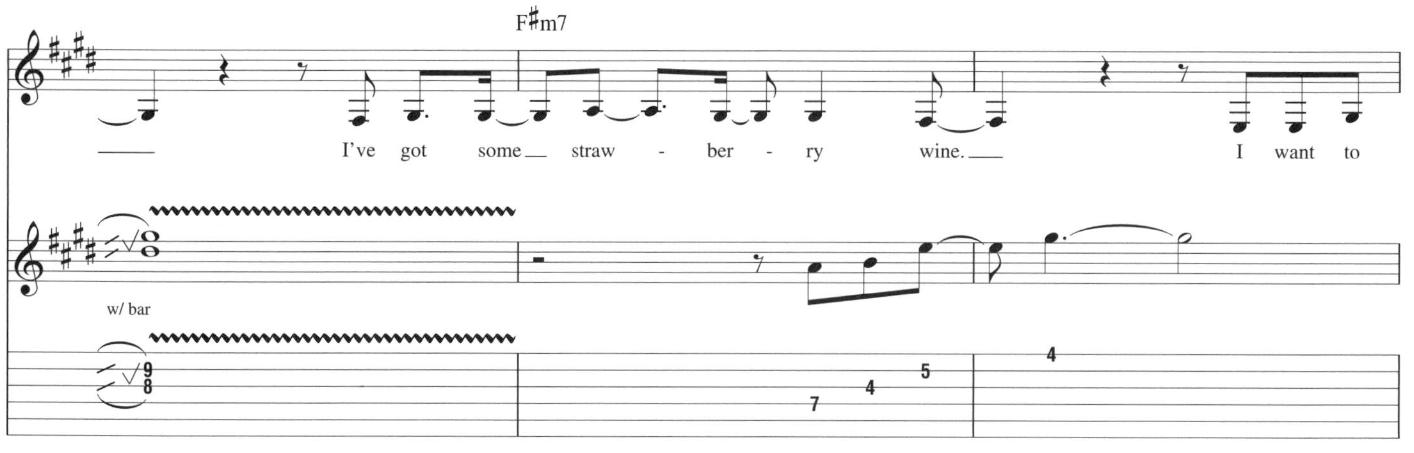
F#m7
I've got some straw - ber - ry wine.
I want to
w/ bar
9
8
7 4 5
4

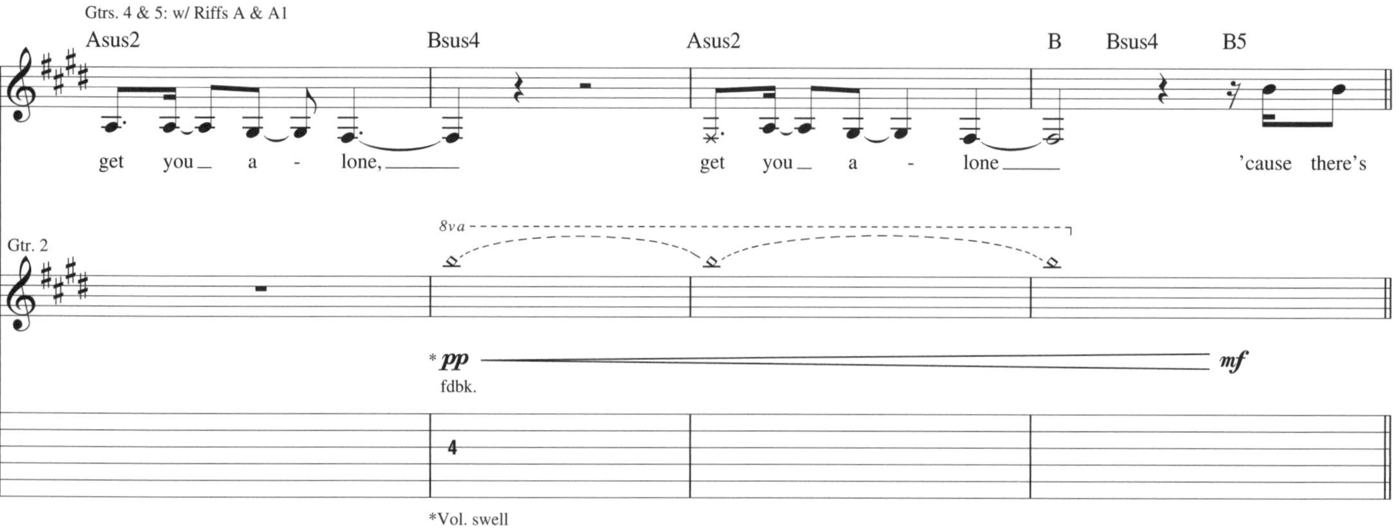
Gtrs. 4 & 5: w/ Riffs A & A1
Asus2 Bsus4 Asus2 B Bsus4 B5
get you a - lone,
get you a - lone
'cause there's
Gtr. 2
8va
*pp
fdbk.
mf
4
*Vol. swell

Chorus

Gtr. 2 tacet
Gtrs. 4 & 5: w/ Rhy. Figs. 1 & 1A
E Asus2
no one to hear.
You might as well scream.
They

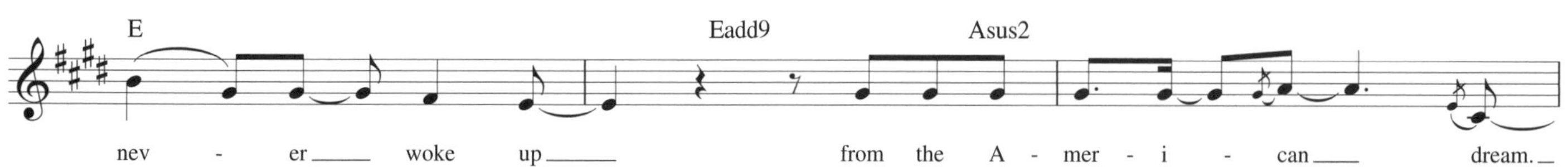
E Eadd9 Asus2
nev - er woke up
from the A - mer - i - can dream.

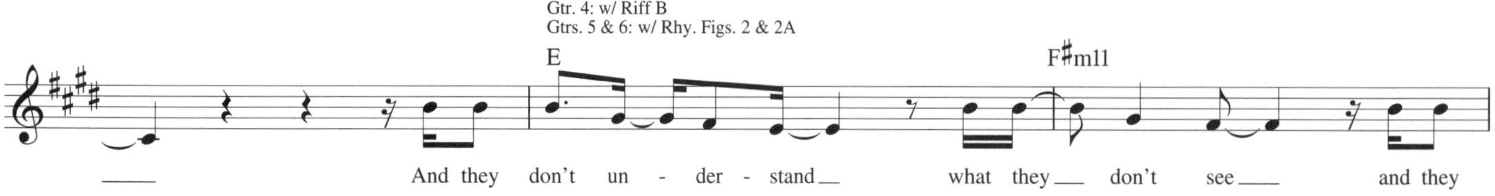
Gtr. 4: w/ Riff B
Gtrs. 5 & 6: w/ Rhy. Figs. 2 & 2A
E F#m11
And they don't un - der - stand
what they don't see
and they

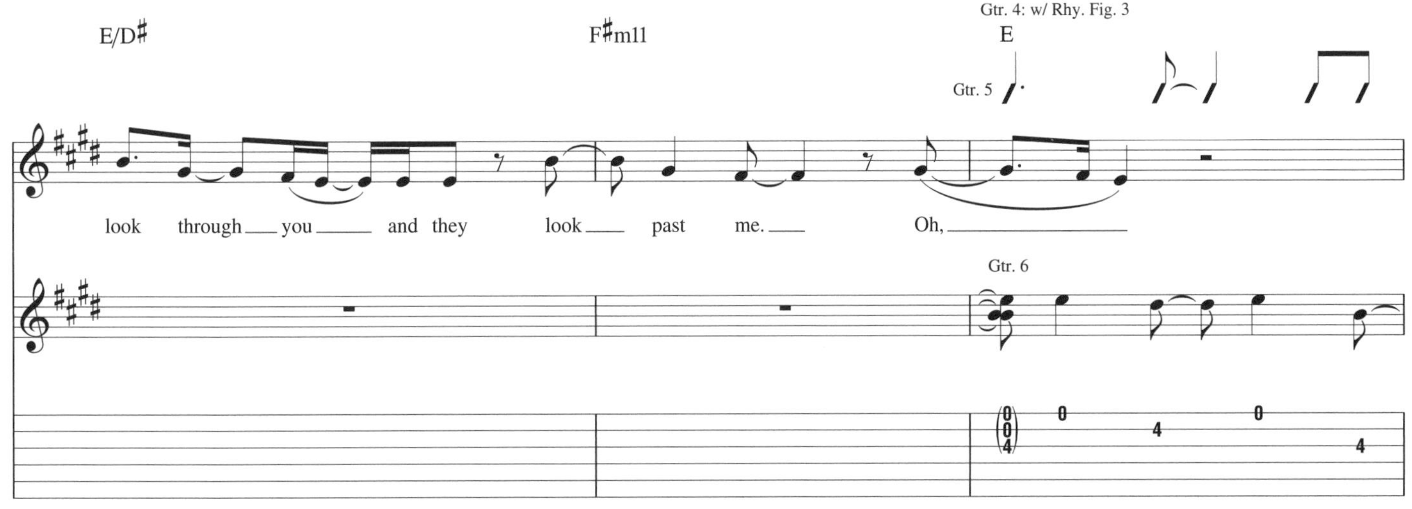
E/D♯
F♯m11
Gtr. 4: w/ Rhy. Fig. 3
E
Gtr. 5
look through you and they look past me. Oh,
Gtr. 6

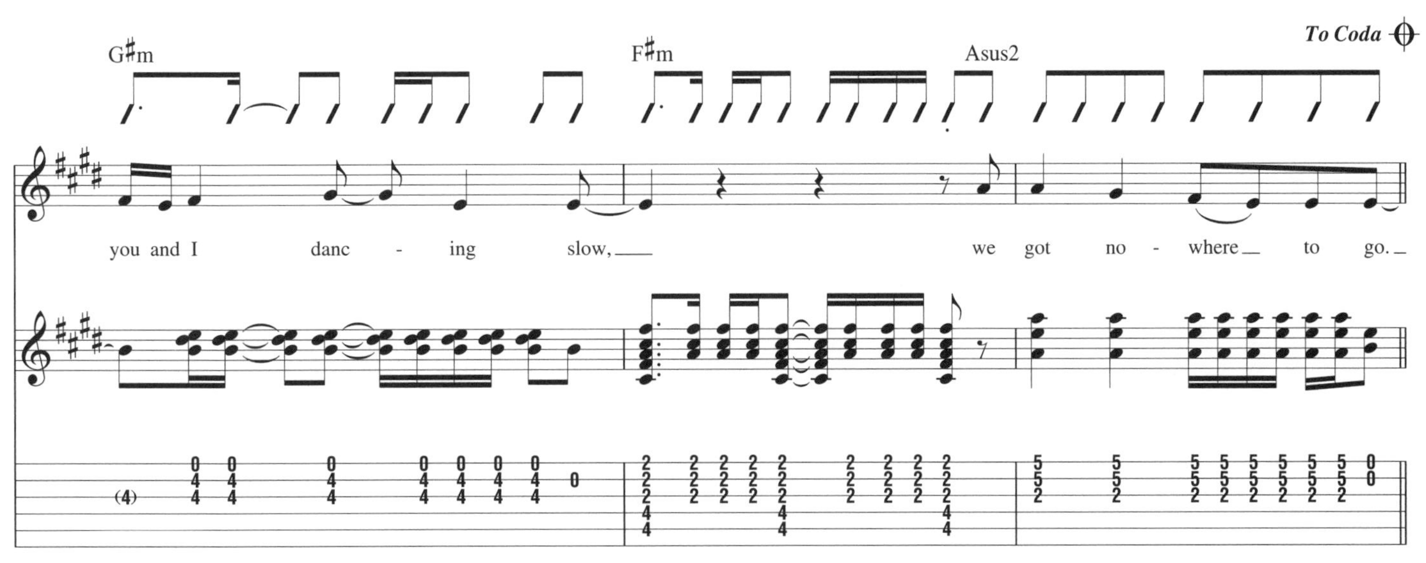
To Coda
G♯m
F♯m
Asus2
you and I danc - ing slow, we got no - where to go.

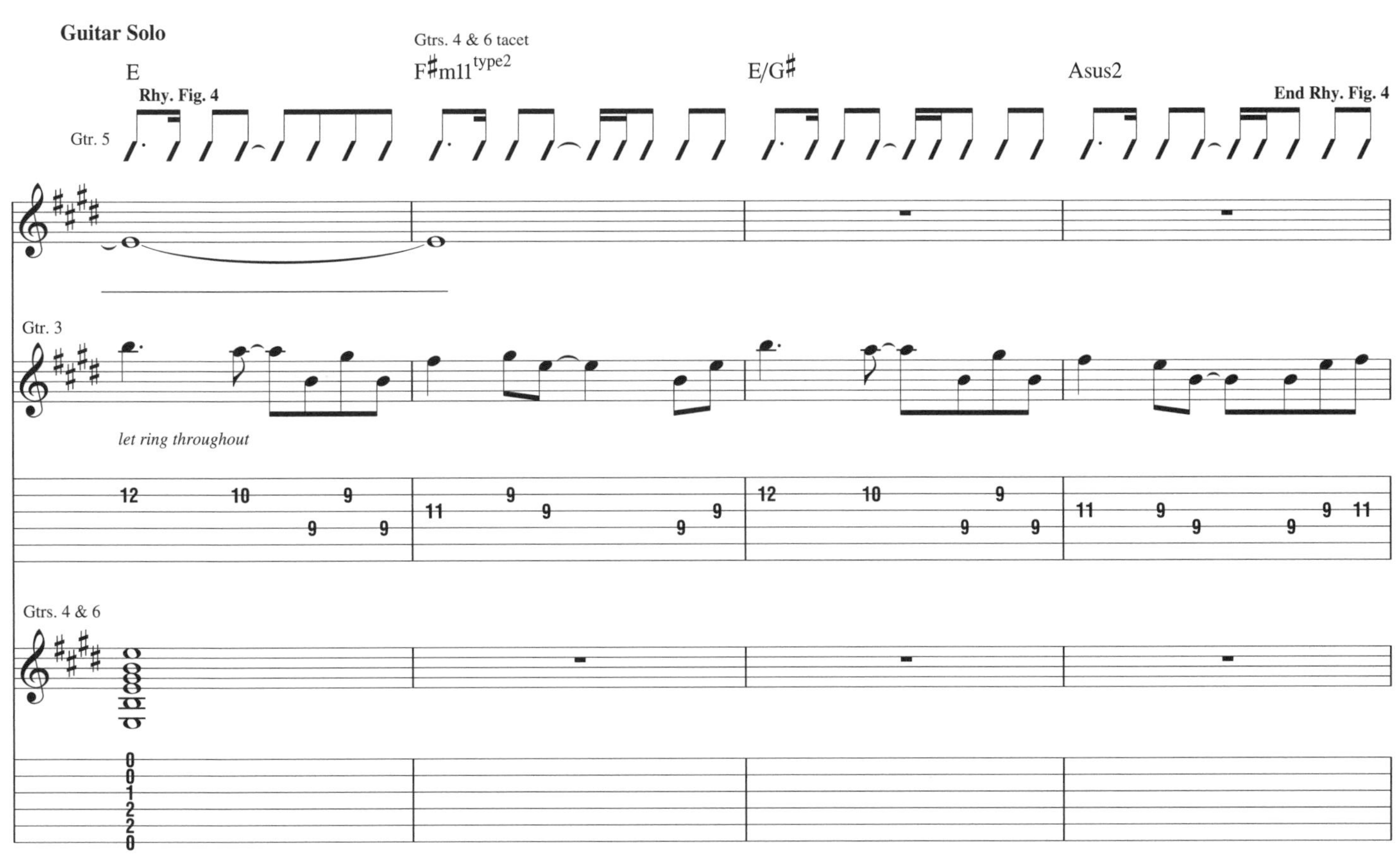
Guitar Solo
E
Rhy. Fig. 4
Gtr. 5
Gtrs. 4 & 6 tacet
F♯m11type2
E/G♯
Asus2
End Rhy. Fig. 4
Gtr. 3
let ring throughout
Gtrs. 4 & 6

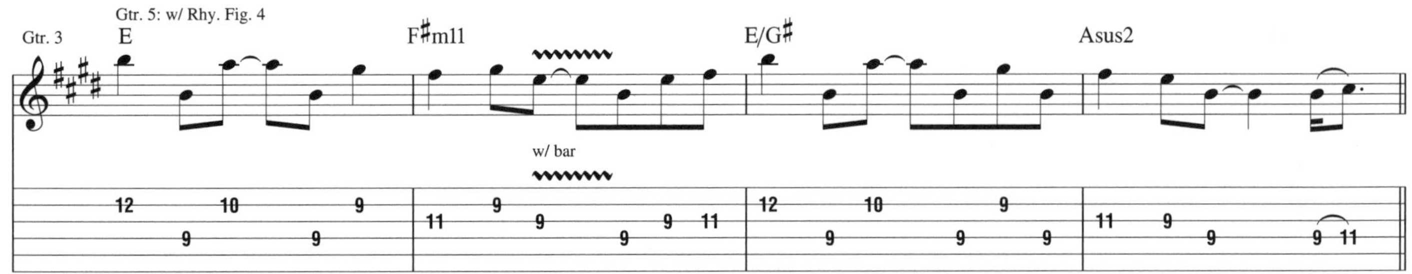

Interlude

Gtr. 2: w/ Riff C

E

3. Down

Gtr. 4

mp

Gtr. 5

mf

P.M.

Gtr. 3

pp

Verse

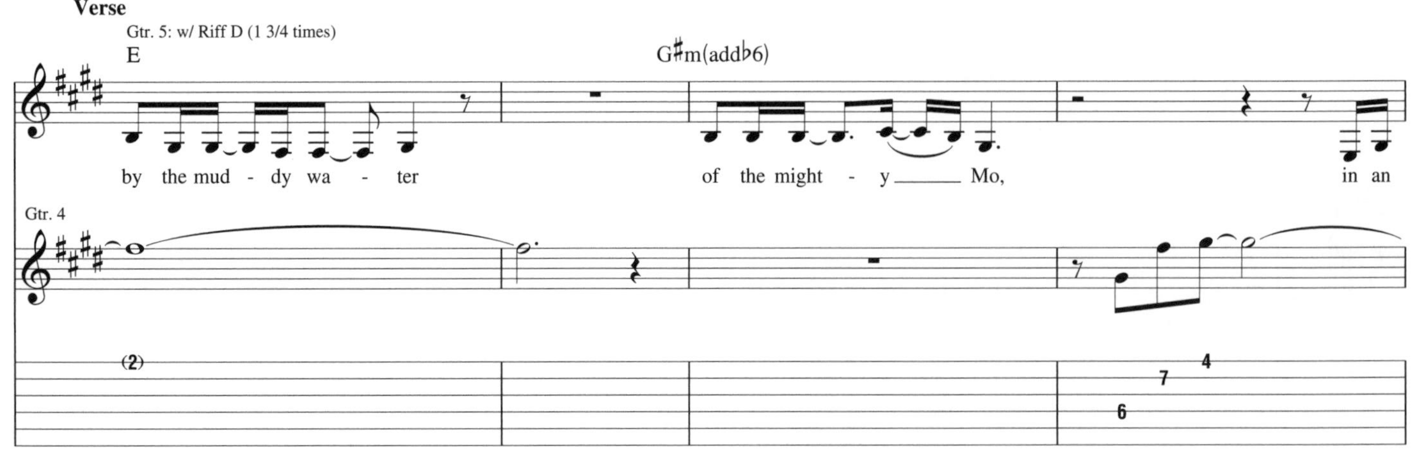

F♯m7
A
old a-ban - doned box car.
Will I ev-er know.
w/ bar

E
G♯m(add♭6)
Dance with me for - ev - er,
this mo-ment is di - vine.

F♯m7
I'm so close to heav - en,
this

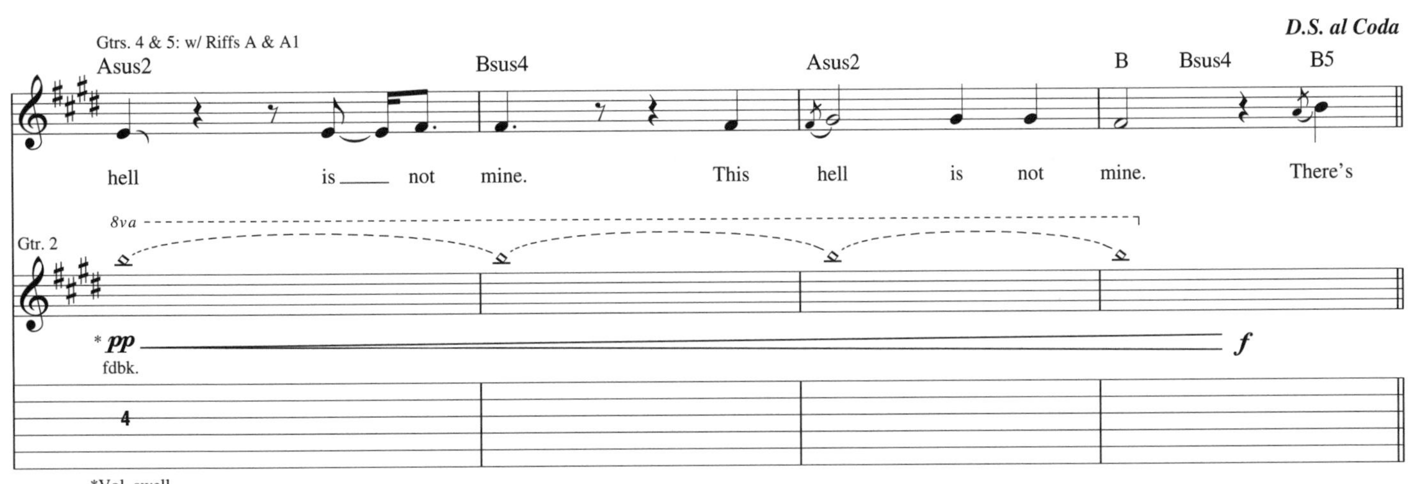
D.S. al Coda
Gtrs. 4 & 5: w/ Riffs A & A1
Asus2
Bsus4
Asus2
B
Bsus4
B5
hell is not mine.
This hell is not mine.
There's
8va
Gtr. 2
*pp
fdbk.
f
*Vol. swell

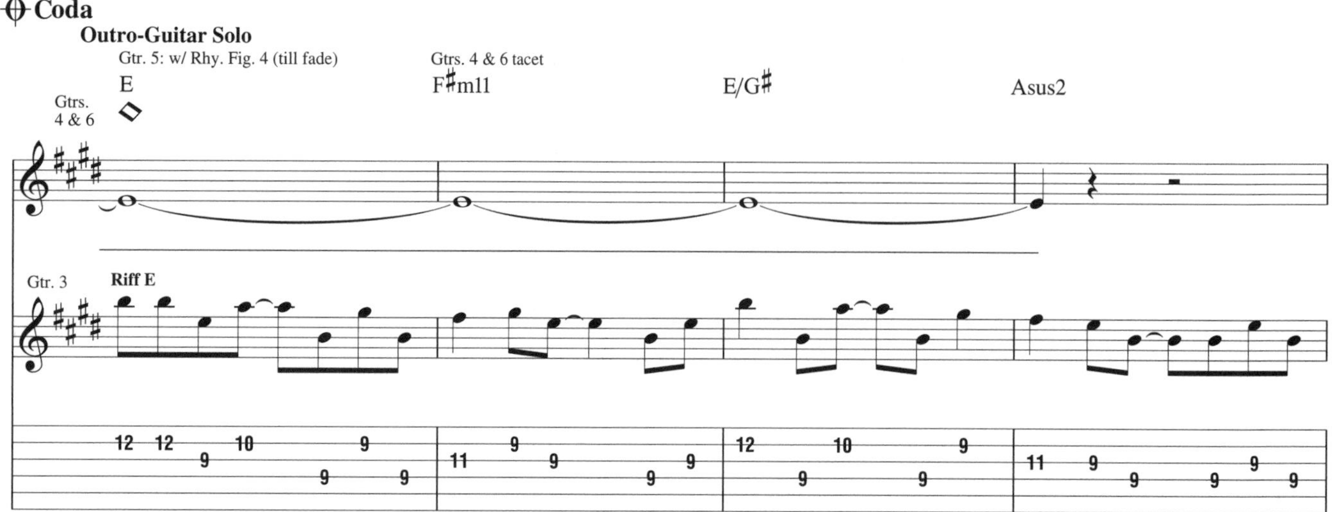
Coda
Outro-Guitar Solo
Gtr. 5: w/ Rhy. Fig. 4 (till fade)
Gtrs. 4 & 6 tacet
E
F#m11
E/G#
Asus2
Gtrs. 4 & 6
Gtr. 3
Riff E
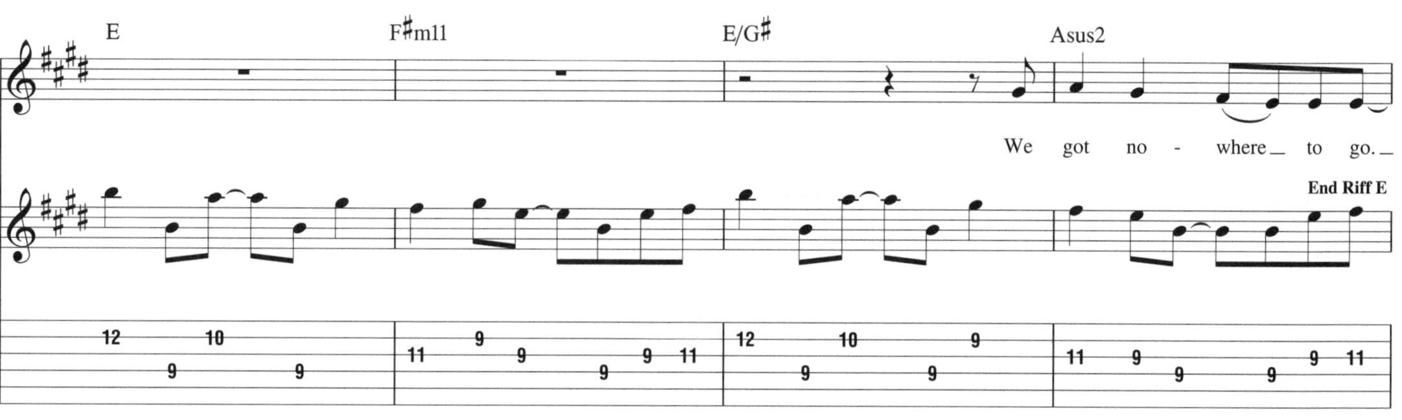
E
F#m11
E/G#
Asus2
We got no - where to go.
End Riff E

Gtr. 2: w/ Riff C (1st 4 meas.) (till fade)
Gtr. 3: w/ Riff E (till fade)
E
F#m11
E/G#
Asus2
E
F#m11
We got no - where to go.
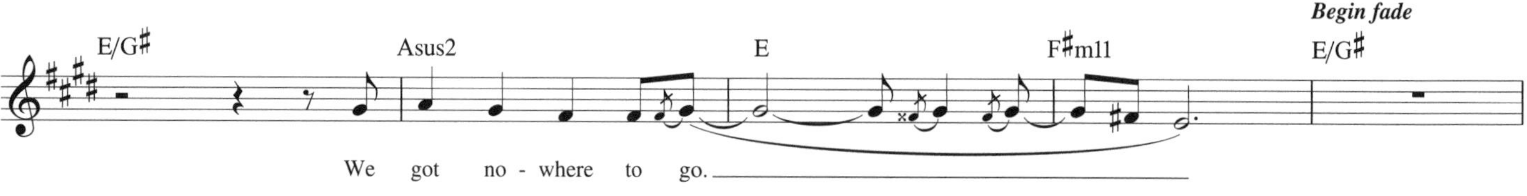
Begin fade
E/G#
Asus2
E
F#m11
E/G#
We got no - where to go.

Asus2
E
F#m11
E/G#
You and me,
you and me,
you and me
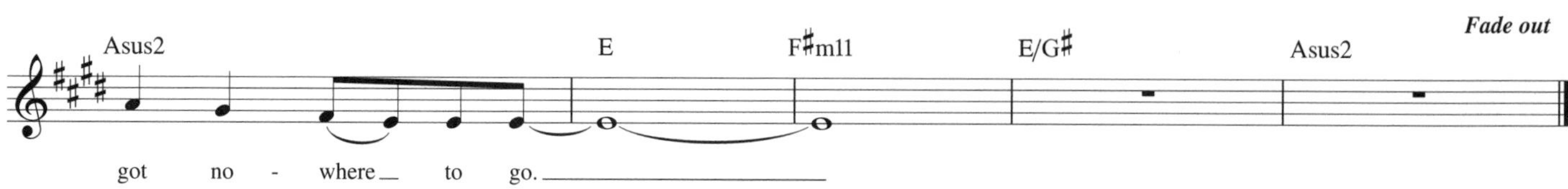
Fade out
Asus2
E
F#m11
E/G#
Asus2
got no - where to go.

from *Melissa Etheridge*

Similar Features

Words and Music by Melissa Etheridge

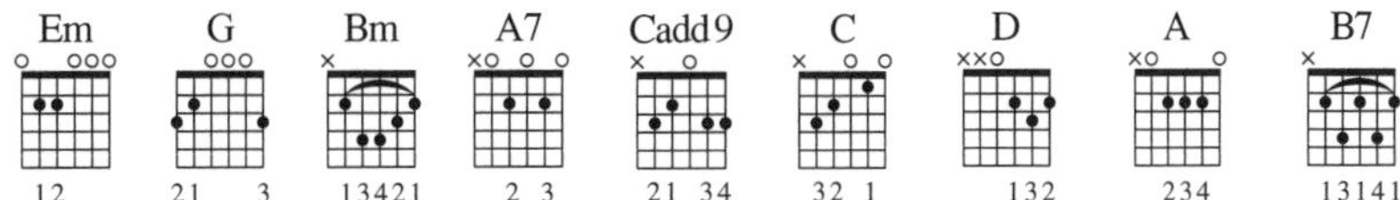

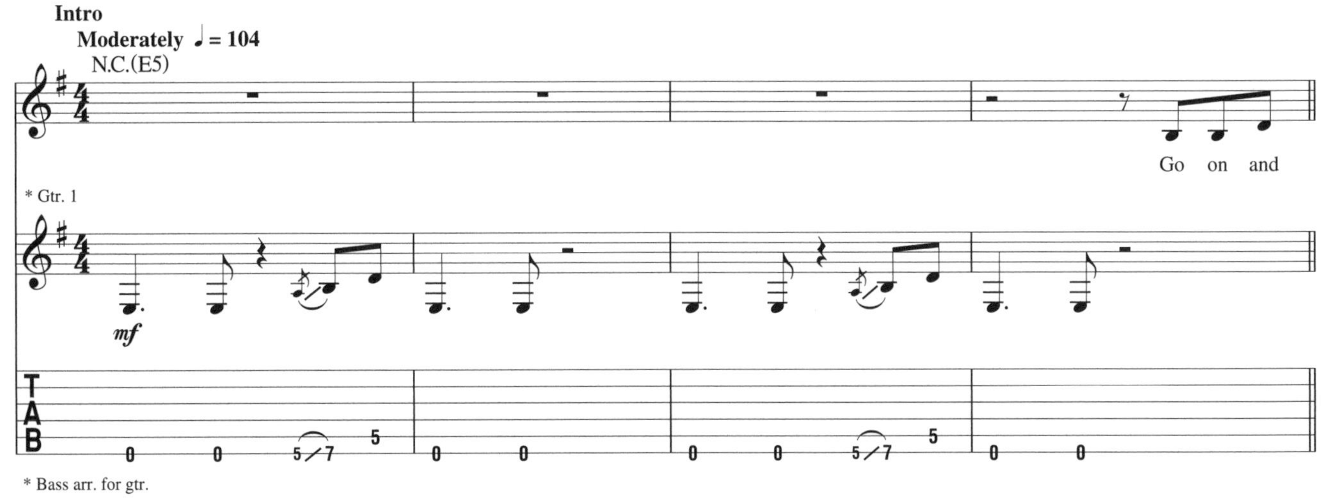

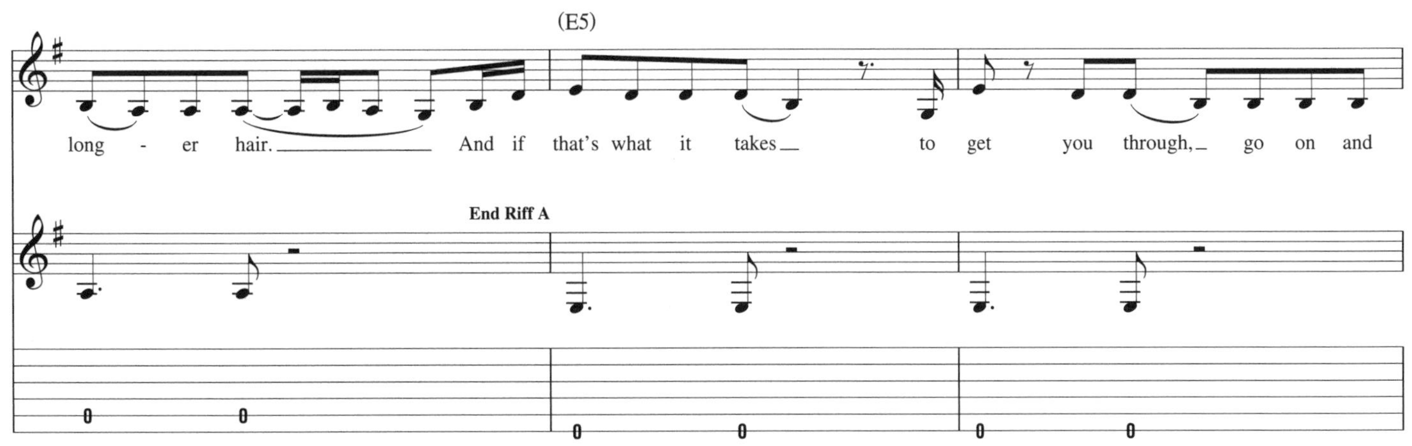

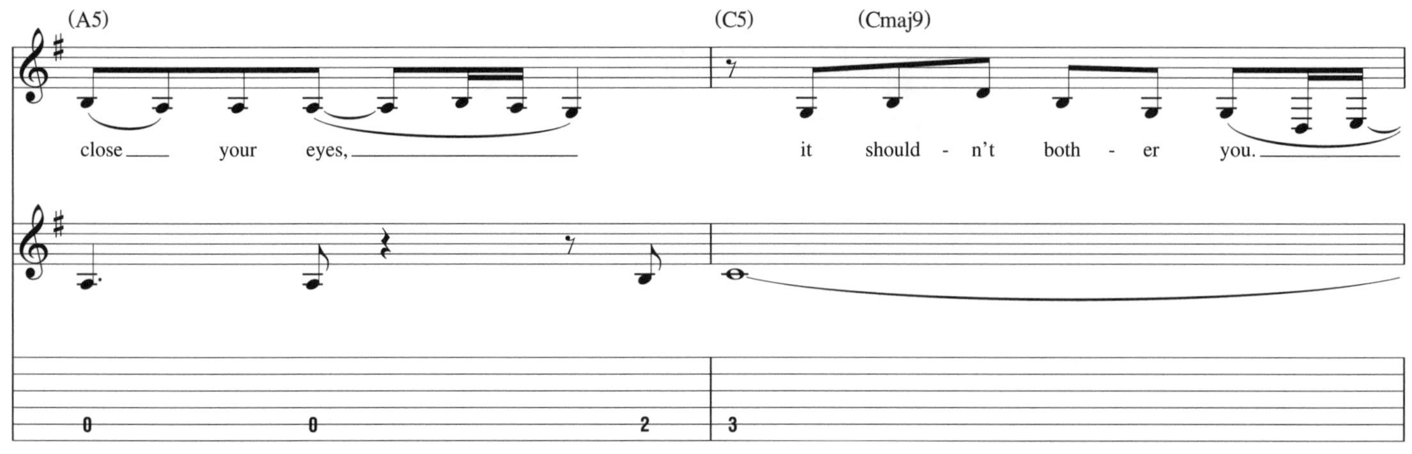
(A5)
(C5)
(Cmaj9)
close your eyes,
it should - n't both - er you.

Gtr. 2 (acous.)
Gtr. 1 tacet
Em
mf
Riff B
* Gtr. 3
End Riff B
f
* Synth. arr. for gtr.

Verse
Gtr. 3 tacet
G
Rhy. Fig. 1
Gtr. 2
1. You nev - er had to wait for noth - ing in your life. I guess
2. Danc - ing with the wall made you bit - ter sweet. There ain't
Gtr. 4 (elec.)
Rhy. Fig. 1A
mf
w/ clean tone & chorus
P.M.

Bm
End Rhy. Fig. 1
want - ing me must have been a steel blue knife. And when
much you can do when they just lay it at your feet. But could you
End Rhy. Fig. 1A
P.M.

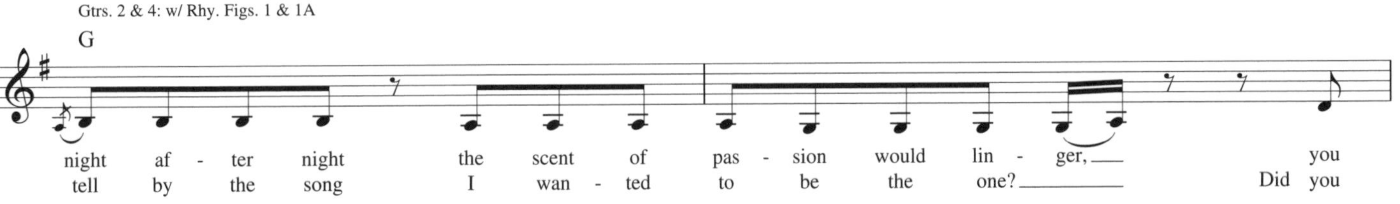
Gtrs. 2 & 4: w/ Rhy. Figs. 1 & 1A
G
night af - ter night the scent of pas - sion would lin - ger, you
tell by the song I wan - ted to be the one? Did you

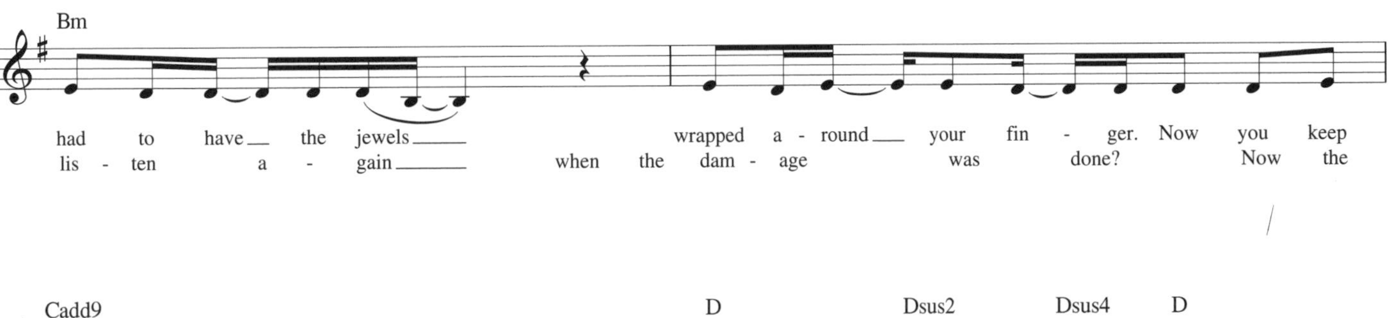
Bm
had to have the jewels wrapped a - round your fin - ger. Now you keep
lis - ten a - gain when the dam - age was done? Now the

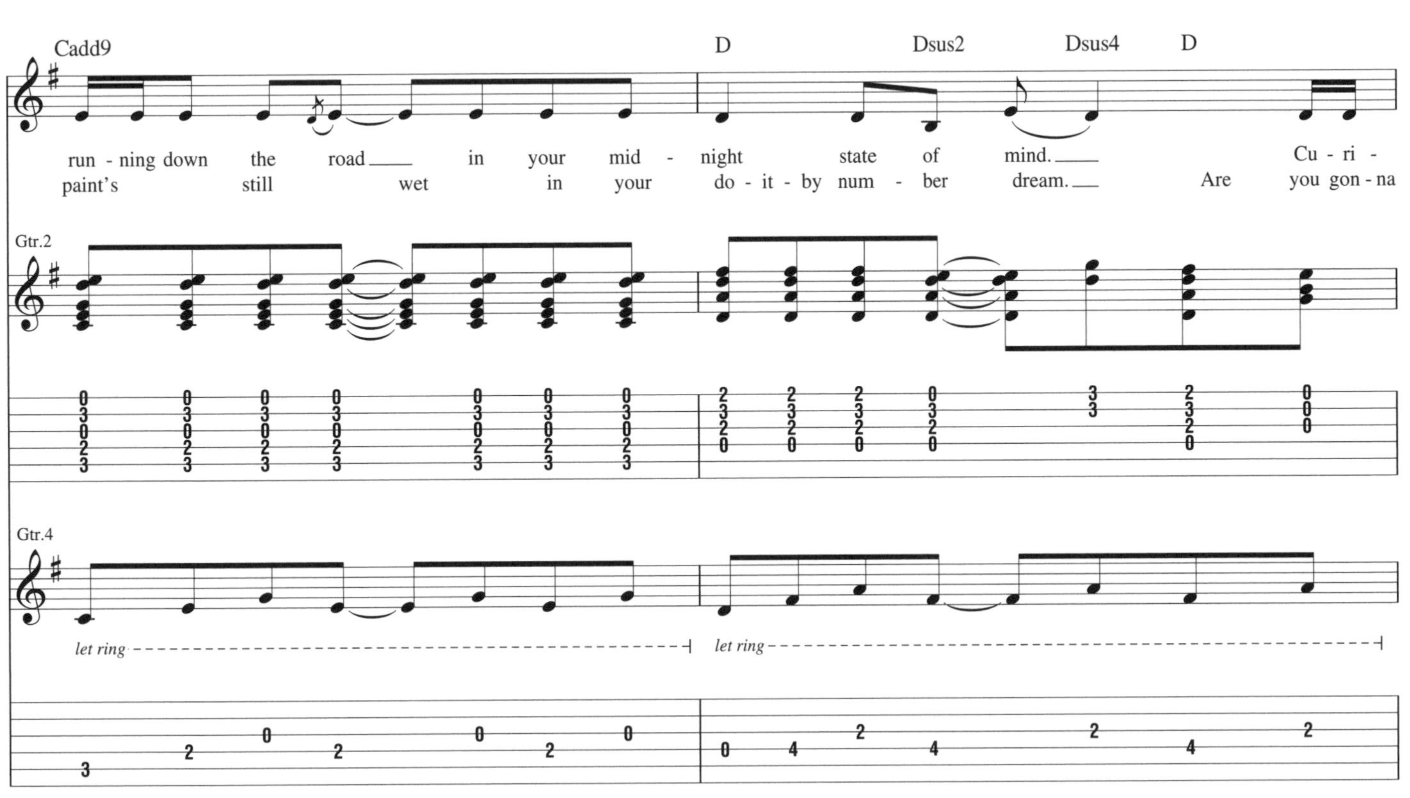
Cadd9
D
Dsus2
Dsus4
D
run - ning down the road in your mid - night state of mind. Cu - ri -
paint's still wet in your do - it - by num - ber dream. Are you gon - na
Gtr.2
Gtr.4
let ring
let ring

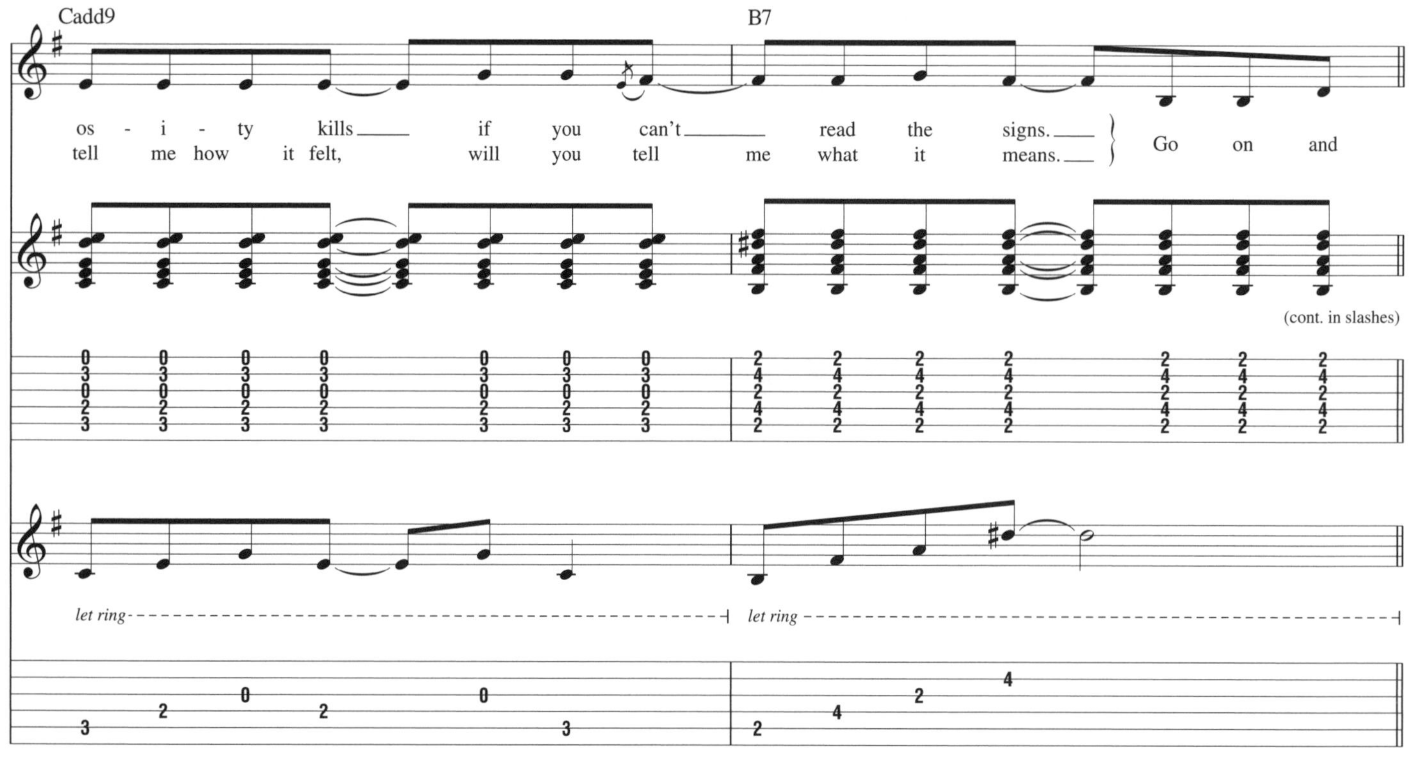
Cadd9
B7
os - i - ty kills if you can't read the signs.
tell me how it felt, will you tell me what it means.
Go on and
(cont. in slashes)
let ring
let ring

Chorus
Em
Rhy. Fig. 2
Gtr. 2
A7
close your eyes, i - mag - ine me there. She's got sim - i - lar fea - tures, with
Gtr. 4
Rhy. Fig. 2A
let ring
let ring

End Rhy. Fig. 2
Em
long - er hair. And if that's what it takes to get you through, go on and
End Rhy. Fig. 2A
let ring

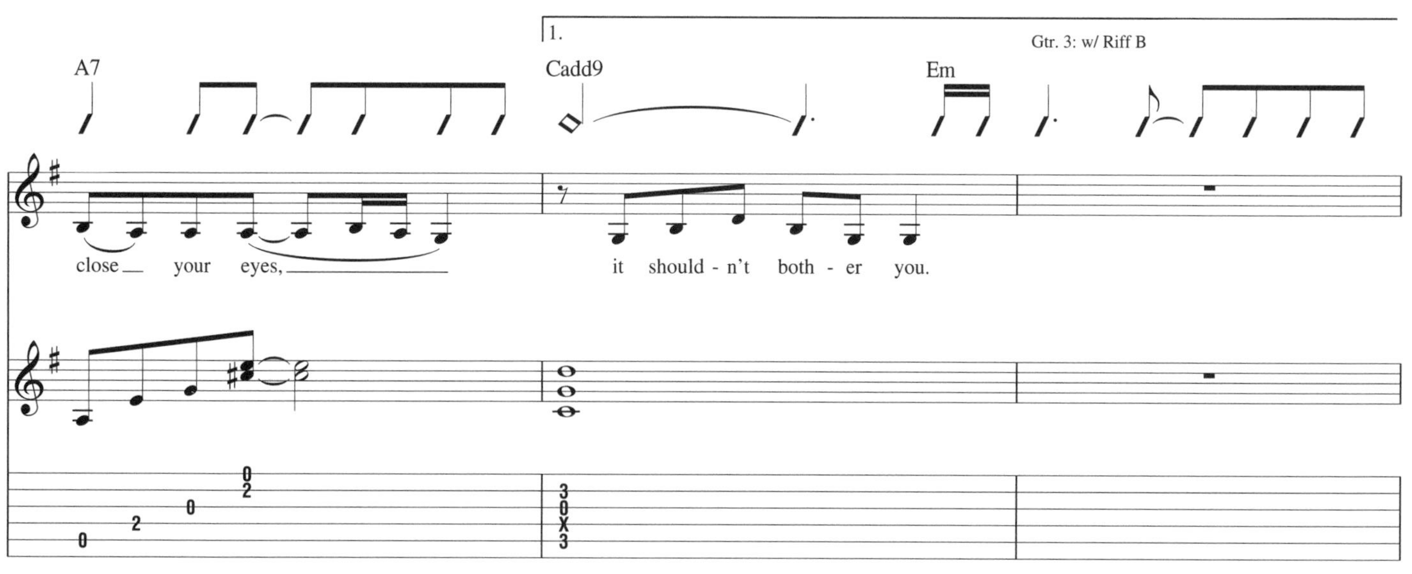

1.
Gtr. 3: w/ Riff B
A7
Cadd9
Em
close your eyes,
it should - n't both - er you.

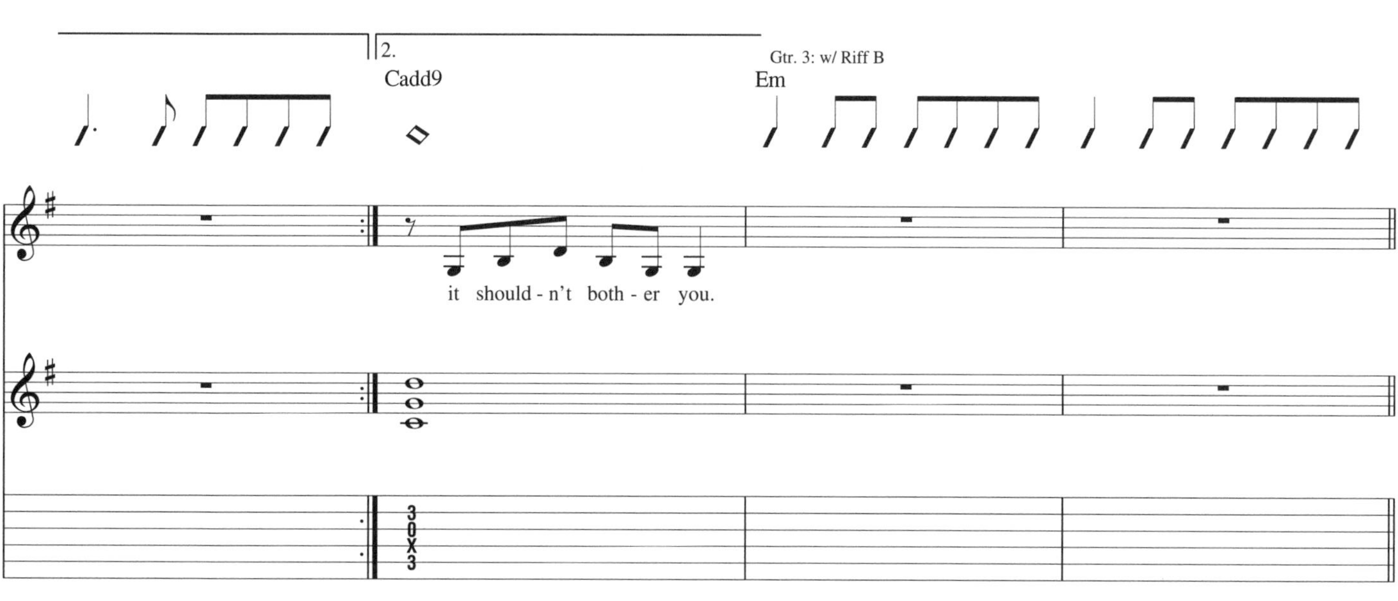

2.
Gtr. 3: w/ Riff B
Cadd9
Em
it should - n't both - er you.

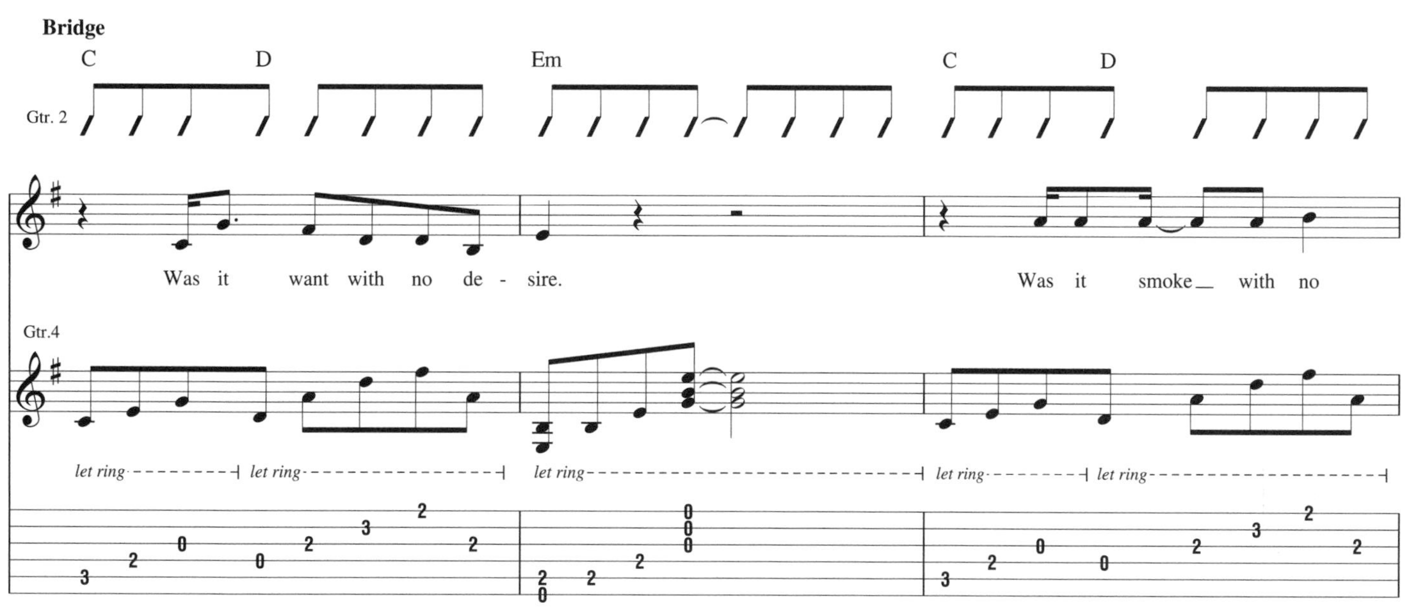

Bridge
C
D
Em
C
D
Gtr. 2
Was it want with no de - sire.
Was it smoke with no
Gtr.4
let ring

Em
A
fire.
Did I say it does-n't rip me a-part.
I lied.
let ring

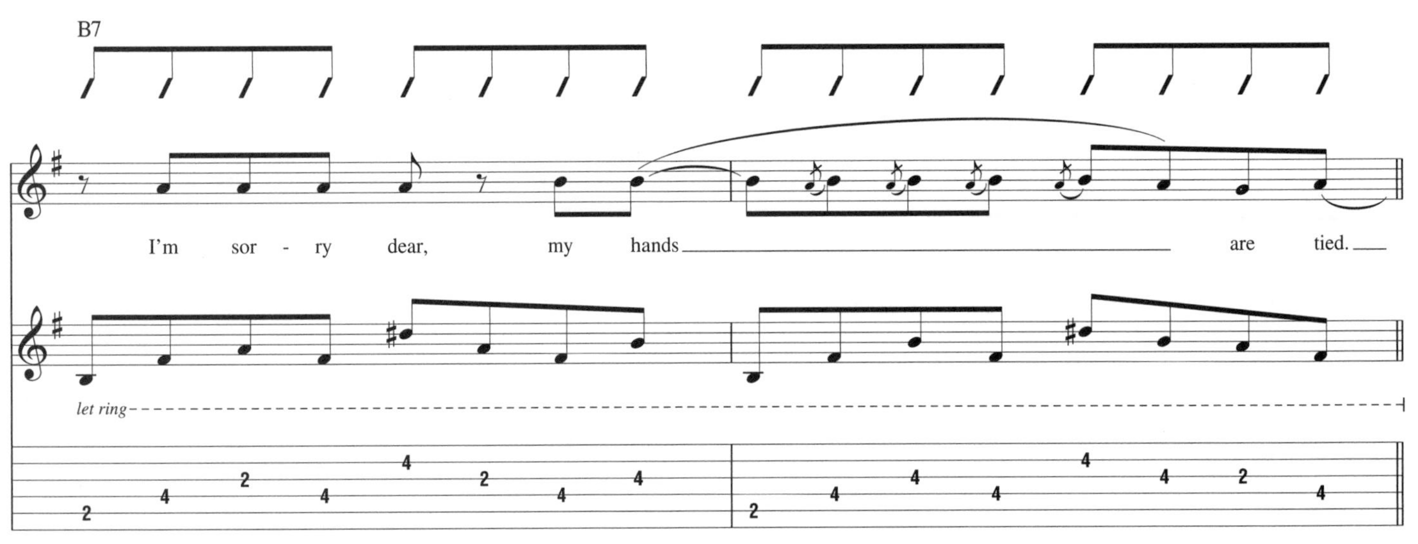
B7
I'm sor-ry dear, my hands are tied.
let ring

Interlude

Gtr. 2: w/ Rhy. Fig. 2
Em
A7
Gtr. 3
Riff C
End Riff C
Gtr. 4
let ring
let ring

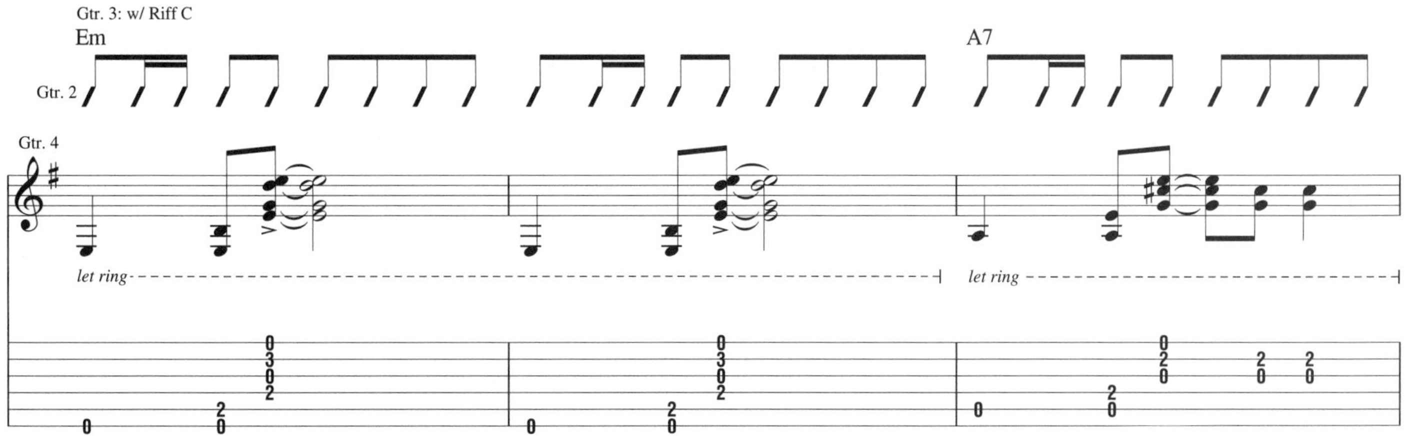
Gtr. 3: w/ Riff C
Em
A7
Gtr. 2
Gtr. 4
let ring
let ring

Chorus
Gtrs. 2 & 4 tacet
Gtr. 1: w/ Riff A
N.C.
N.C.(E5)
Go on and close your eyes, go on i - mag - ine me there. She's got
let ring

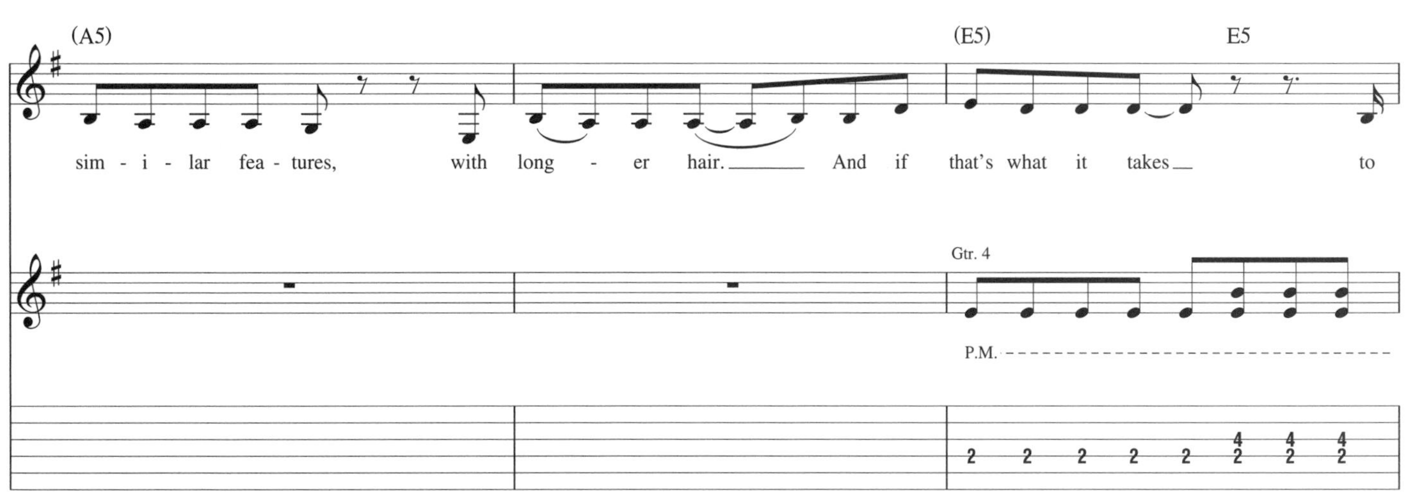
(A5)
(E5)
E5
sim - i - lar fea - tures, with long - er hair. And if that's what it takes to
Gtr. 4
P.M.

A5
C5
get you through, go on and close your eyes, it should - n't both - er you.
P.M.
P.M.
P.M.
Gtrs. 2 & 4: w/ Rhy. Figs. 2 & 2A
Em
Close your eyes, i - mag - ine me there. She's got
A7
sim - i - lar fea - tures, with long - er hair. And if that's what
Em
A7
Gtr. 2
it takes to get you through, close your eyes,
Gtr. 4
let ring
let ring
Outro
Gtr. 2: w/ Rhy. Fig. 2 (7 times)
Gtr. 3: w/ Riff B
Cadd9
Em
it should - n't both - er you.
Gtr. 4
let ring

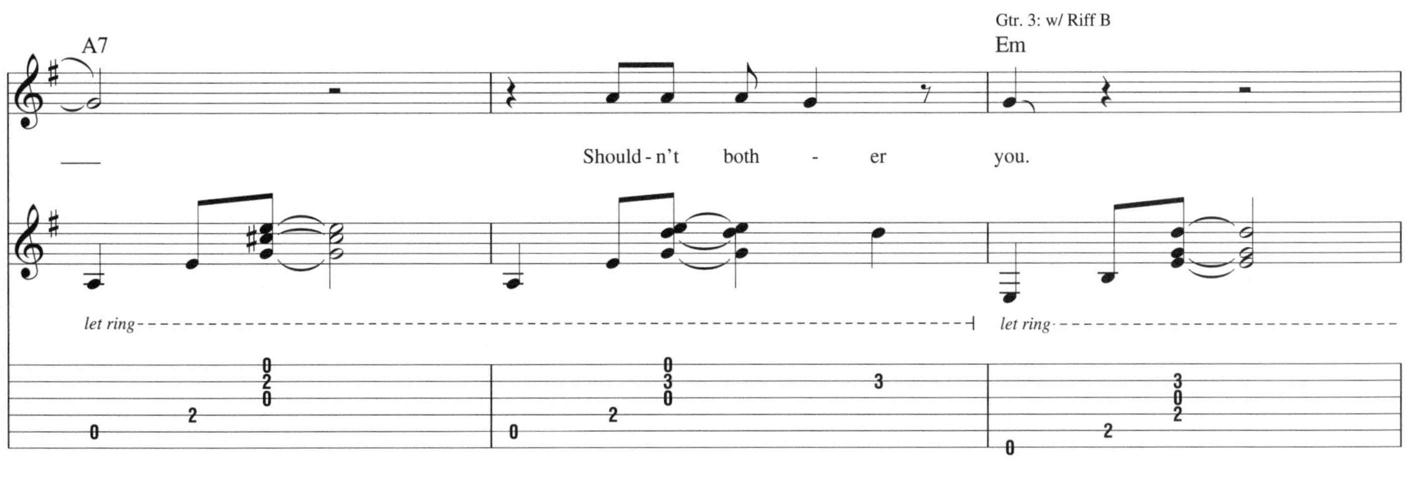
Gtr. 3: w/ Riff B
A7
Em
Should - n't both - er you.
let ring
let ring

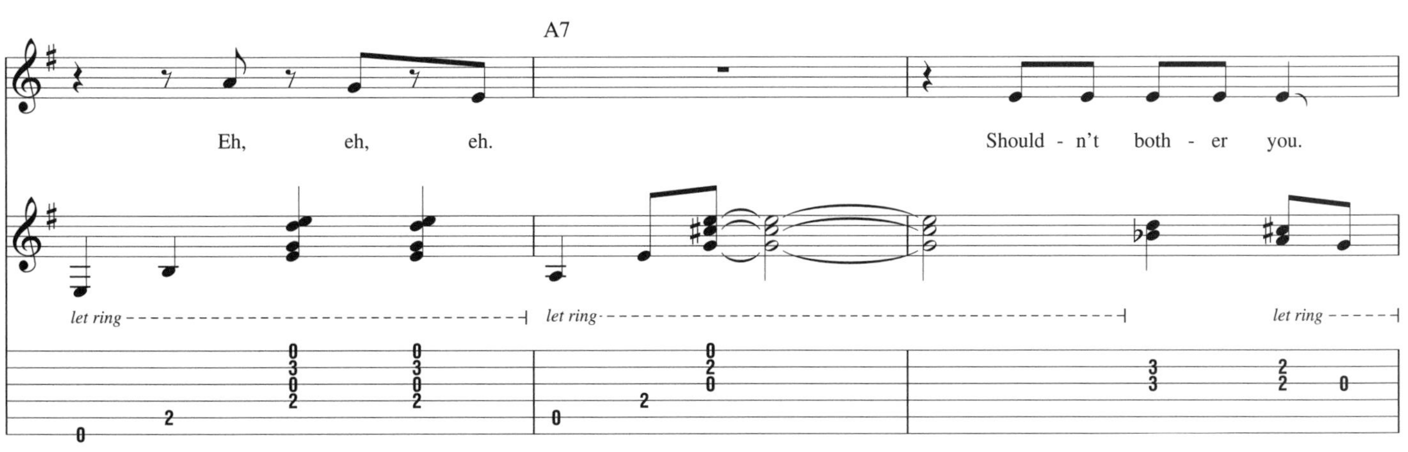
A7
Eh, eh, eh.
Should - n't both - er you.
let ring
let ring
let ring

Gtr. 3: w/ Riff B
Em
A7
Yeah, yeah, yeah.
let ring
let ring

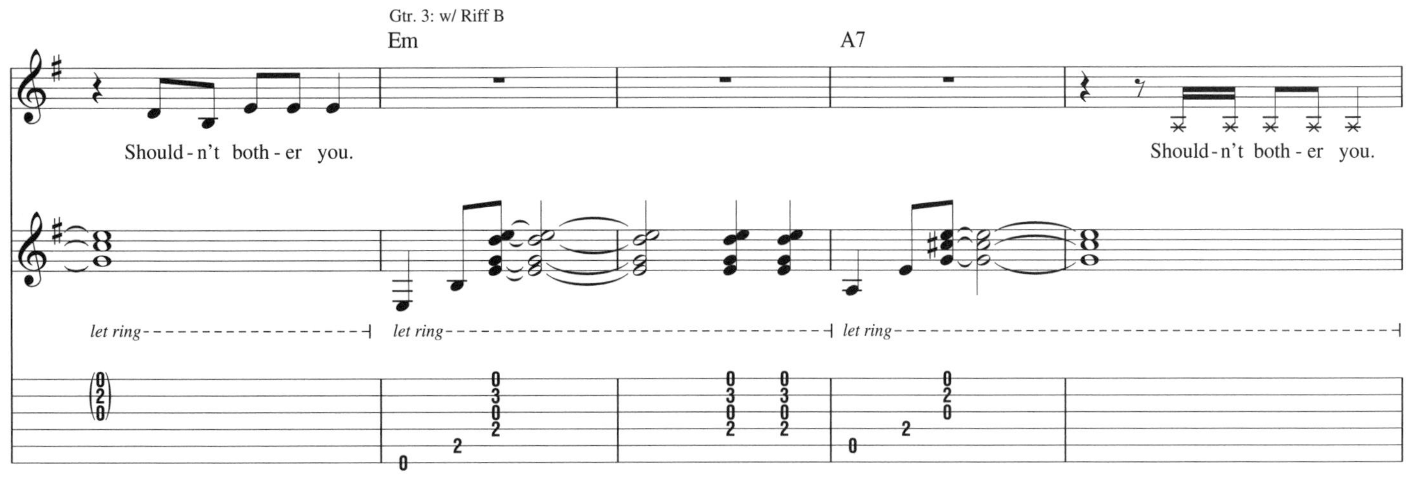
Gtr. 3: w/ Riff B
Em
A7
Should - n't both - er you.
Should - n't both - er you.
let ring
let ring
let ring

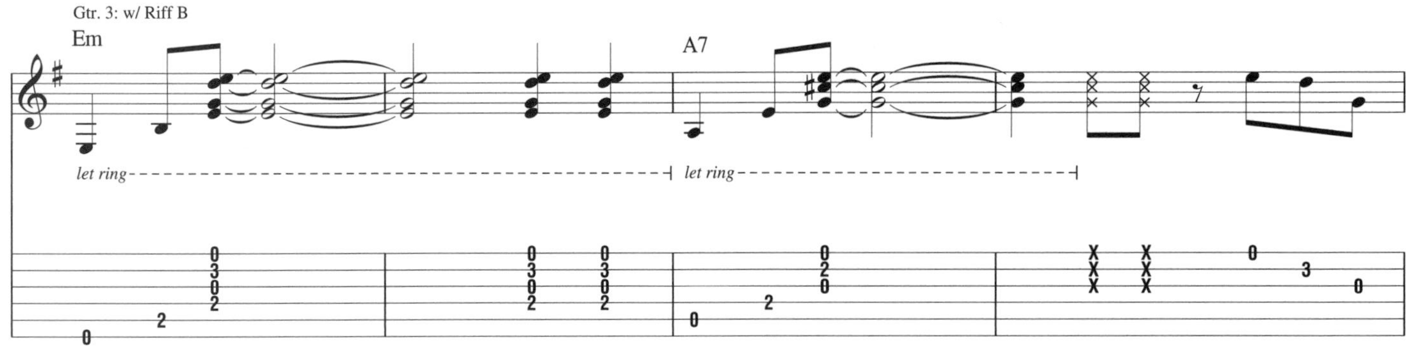
Gr. 3: w/ Riff B
Em
A7
let ring
let ring

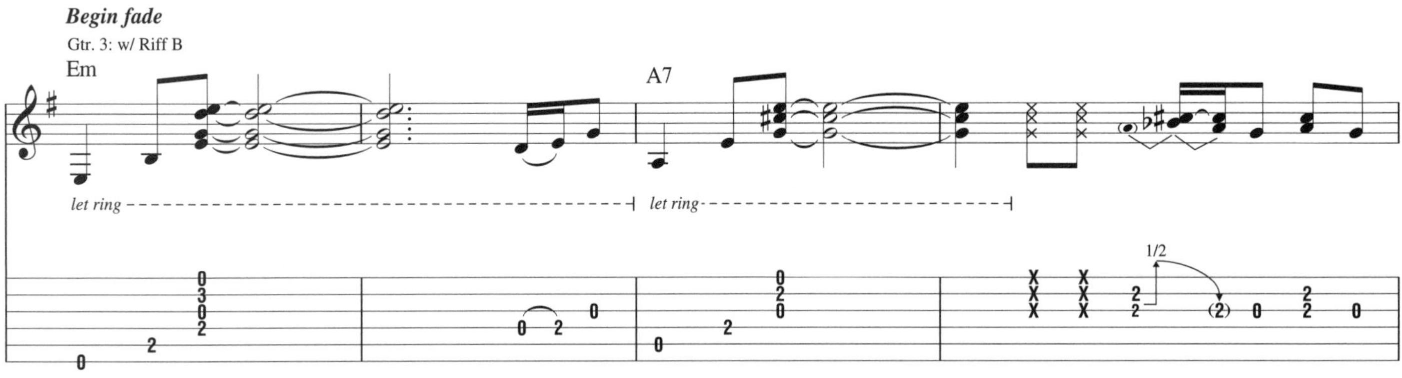
Begin fade
Gr. 3: w/ Riff B
Em
A7
let ring
let ring
1/2

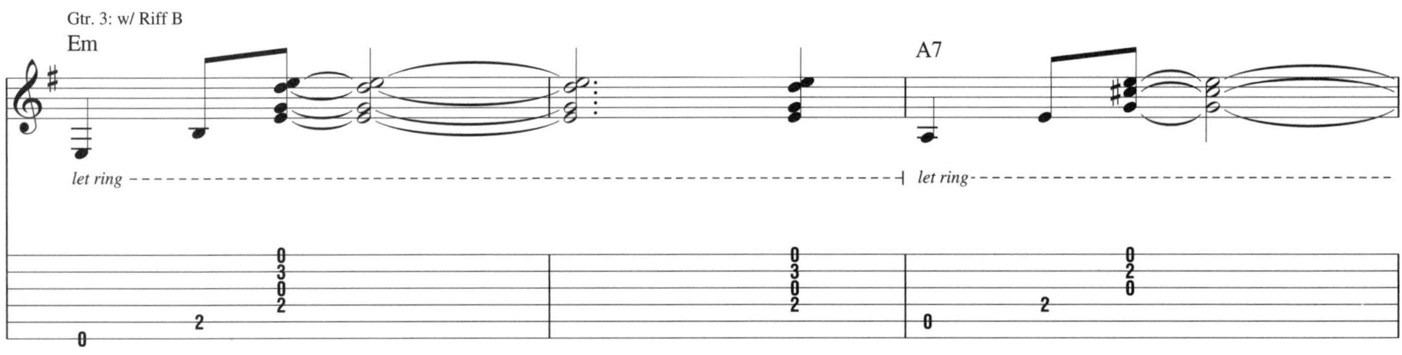
Gr. 3: w/ Riff B
Em
A7
let ring
let ring

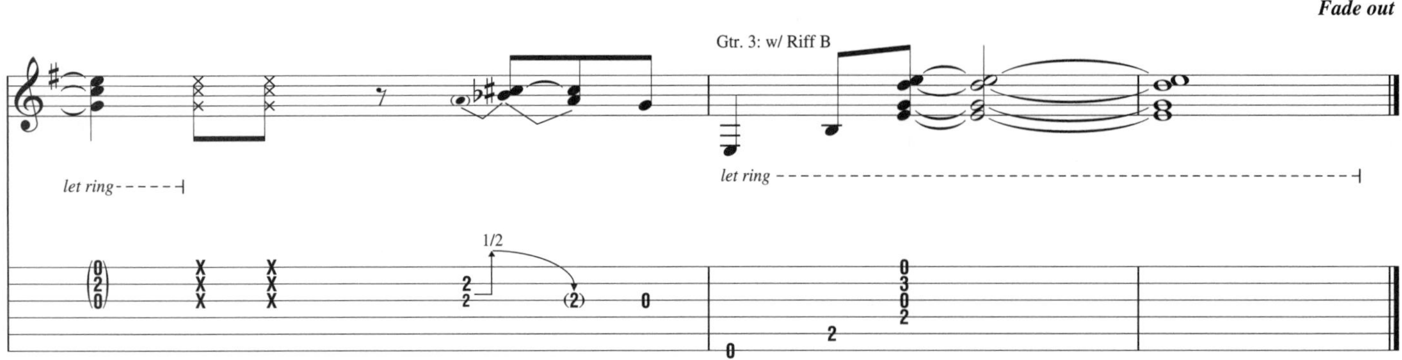
Fade out
Gr. 3: w/ Riff B
let ring
let ring
1/2

from *Never Enough*

2001

Words and Music by Melissa Etheridge

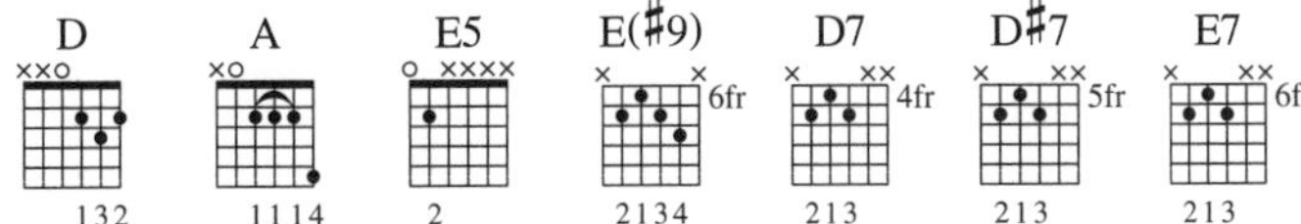

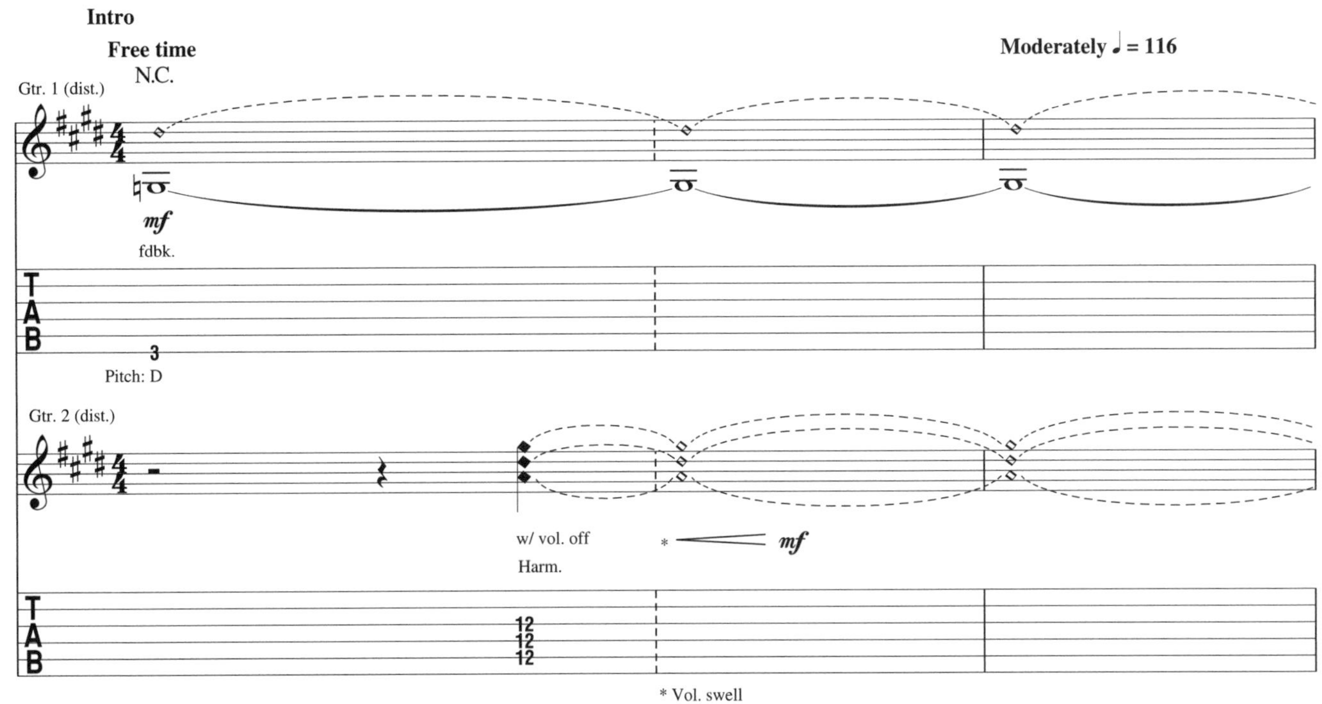

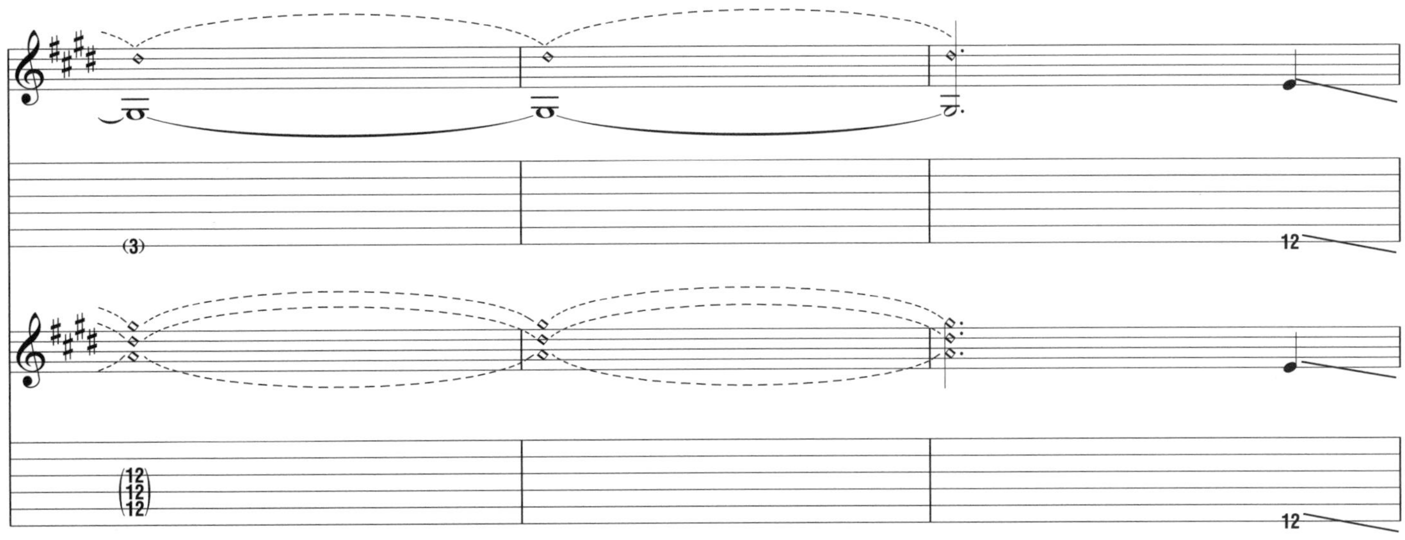

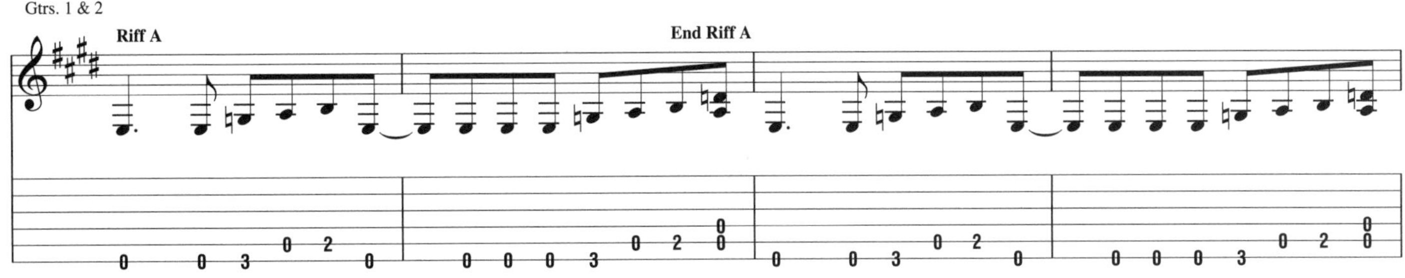

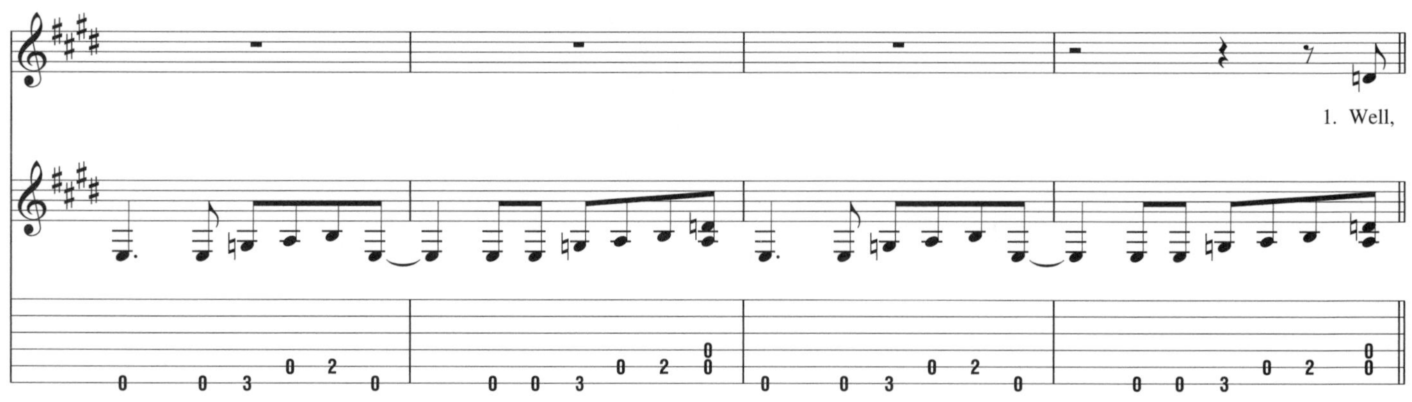

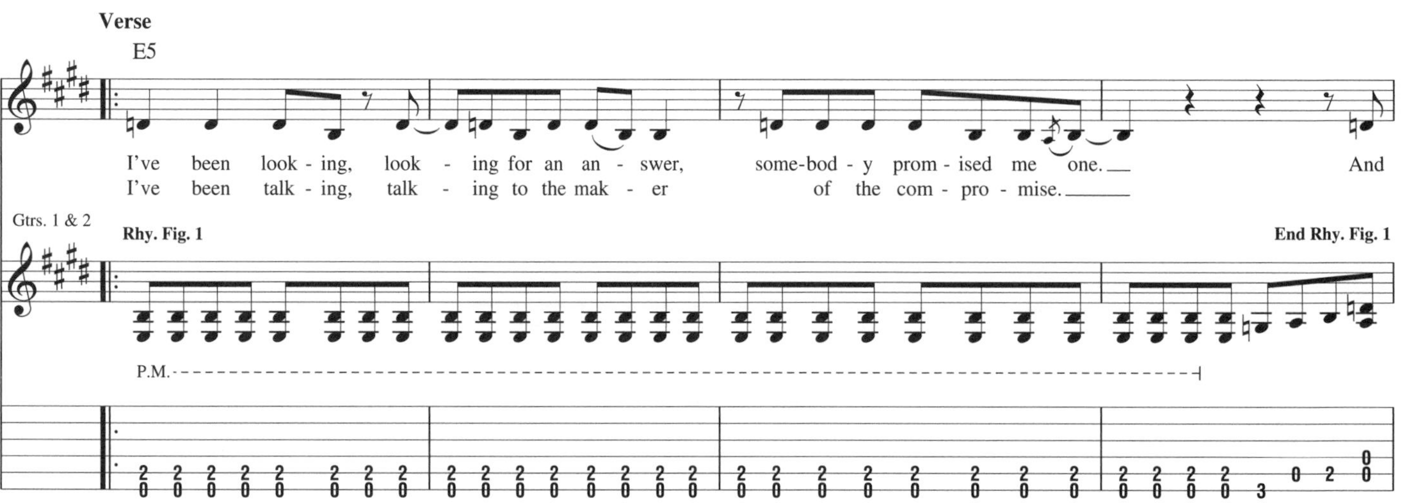

*Sing 1st time only.

Gtr. 3 tacet
D
A N.C.
(E5)
Rhy. Fig. 3A
End Rhy. Fig. 3A
Gtr. 3
Wake me up when we hit two - thou - sand one.
Oh, it's
Gtrs. 1 & 2
Rhy. Fig. 3
End Rhy. Fig. 3

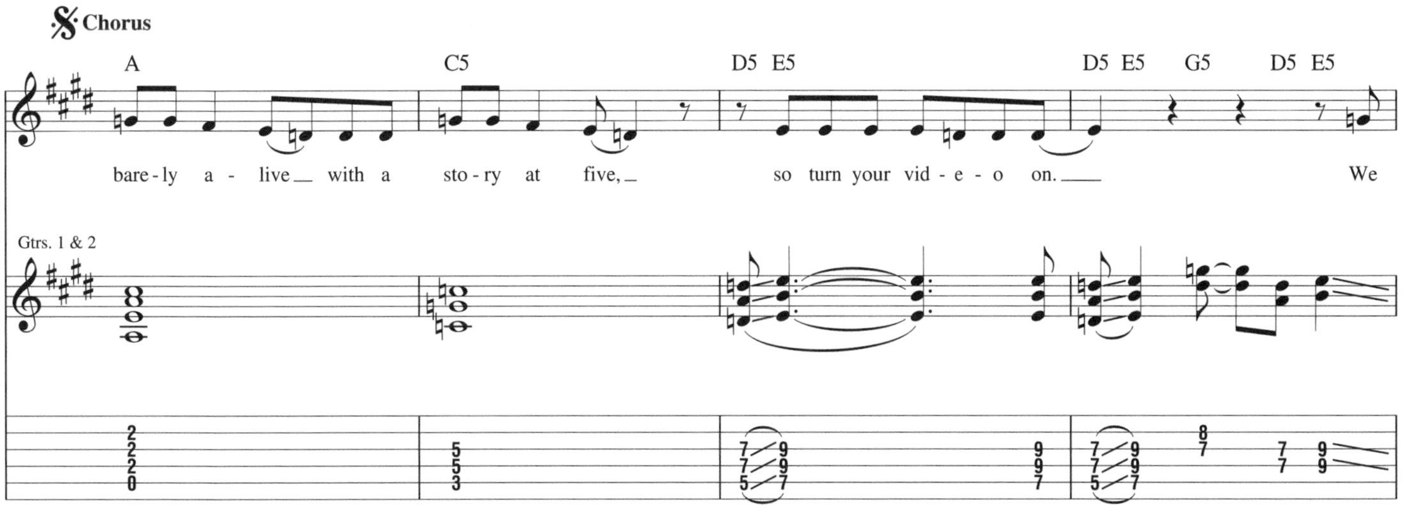
Chorus
A
C5
D5 E5
D5 E5 G5 D5 E5
bare - ly a - live with a sto - ry at five,
so turn your vid - e - o on.
We
Gtrs. 1 & 2

To Coda
A
C5
B5
N.C.
live in these years, dark age of fear.
Meet me in two - thou - sand one.
P.M.
1/4

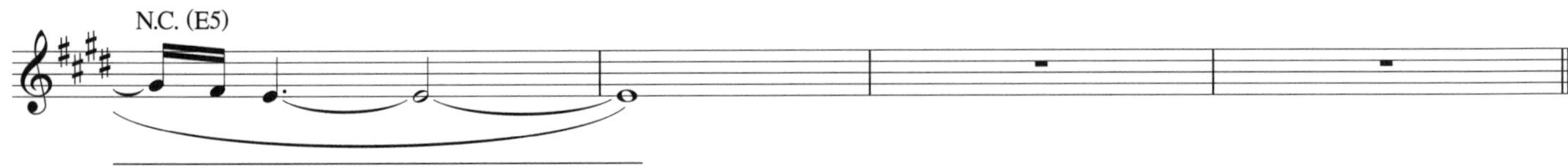

Verse

* Composite arrangement.

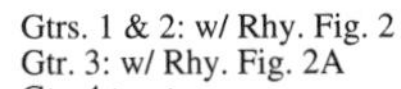
Gtrs. 1 & 2: w/ Rhy. Fig. 2
Gtr. 3: w/ Rhy. Fig. 2A
Gtr. 4 tacet

Gtrs. 1 & 2: w/ Riff B
D
A
N.C.(E5)
Wake me up when we hit two - thou - sand one.

Gtrs. 1 & 2: w/ Rhy. Fig. 3
Gtr. 3: w/ Rhy. Fig. 3A
Gtrs. 1 & 2: w/ Riff B
D.S. al Coda
D
A N.C.
(E5)
Wake me up when we hit two - thou - sand one.
Oh, it's

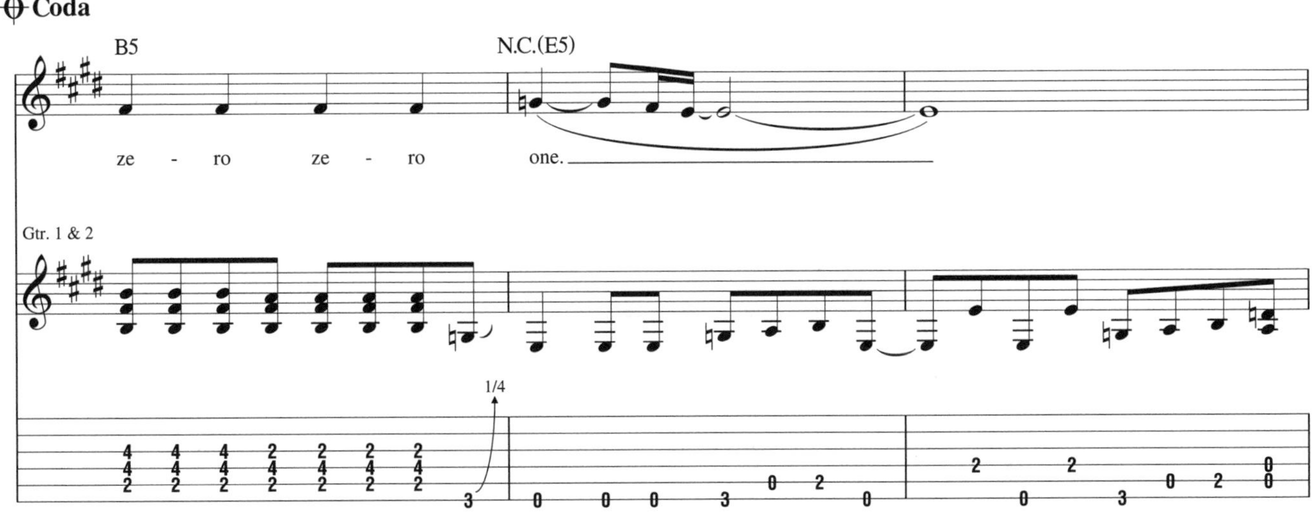
Coda
B5
N.C.(E5)
ze - ro ze - ro one.
Gtr. 1 & 2
1/4

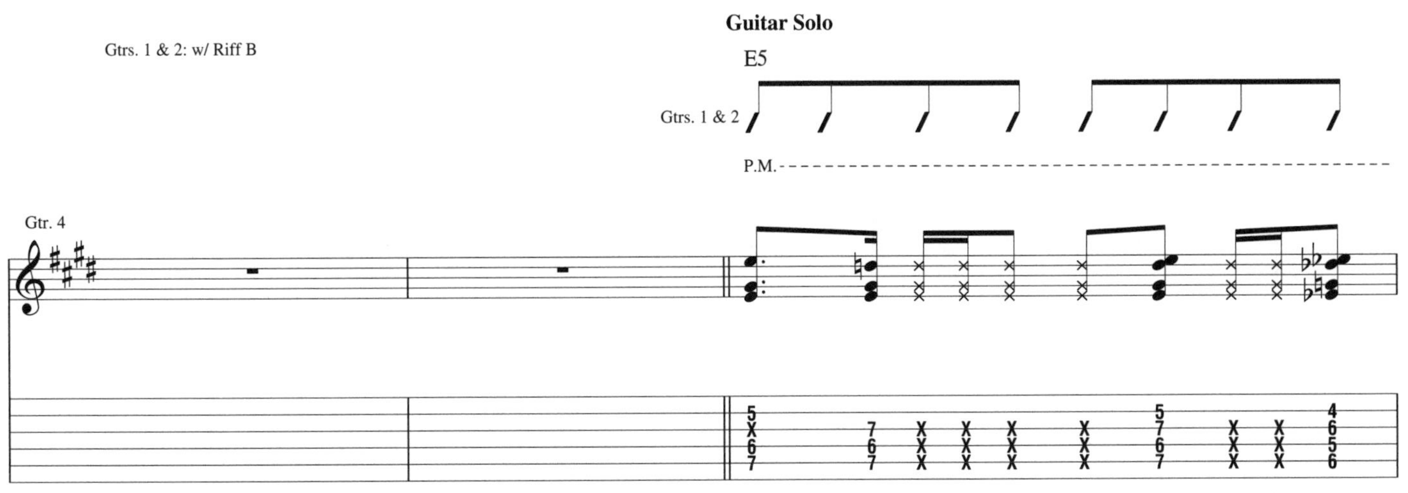
Gtrs. 1 & 2: w/ Riff B
Guitar Solo
E5
Gtrs. 1 & 2
P.M.
Gtr. 4

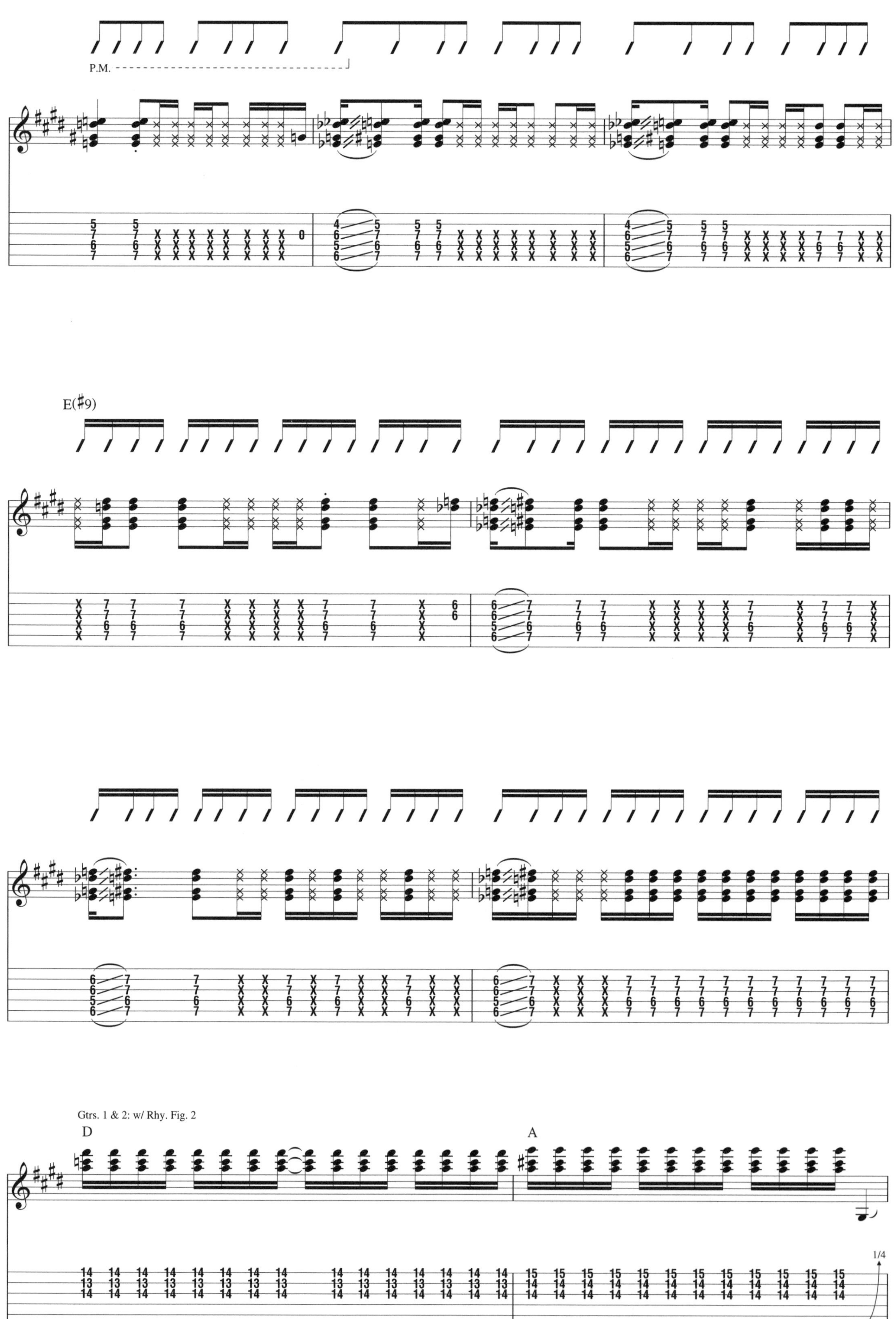
P.M.
E(#9)
Gtrs. 1 & 2: w/ Rhy. Fig. 2
D
A
1/4

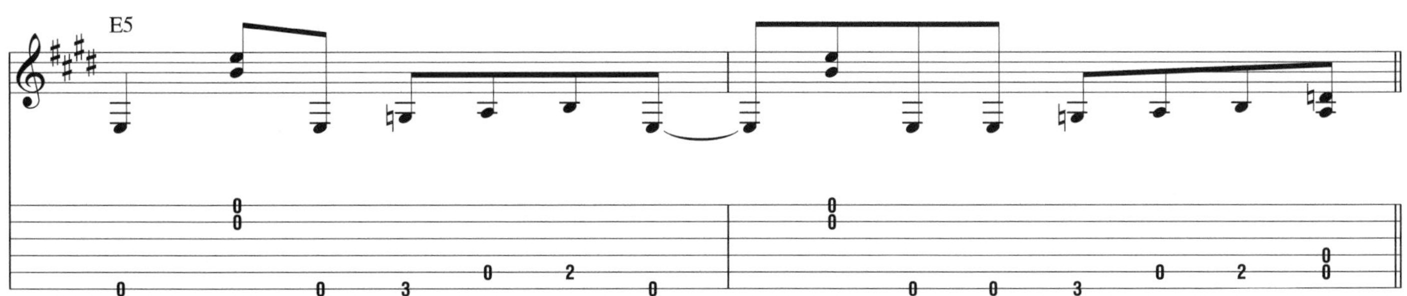

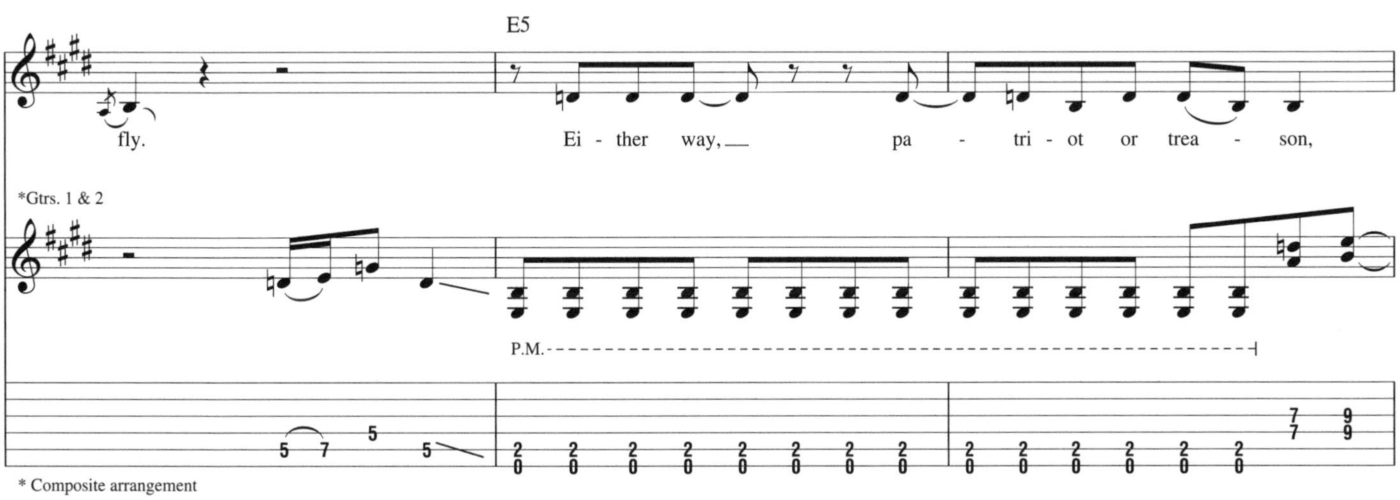

* Composite arrangement

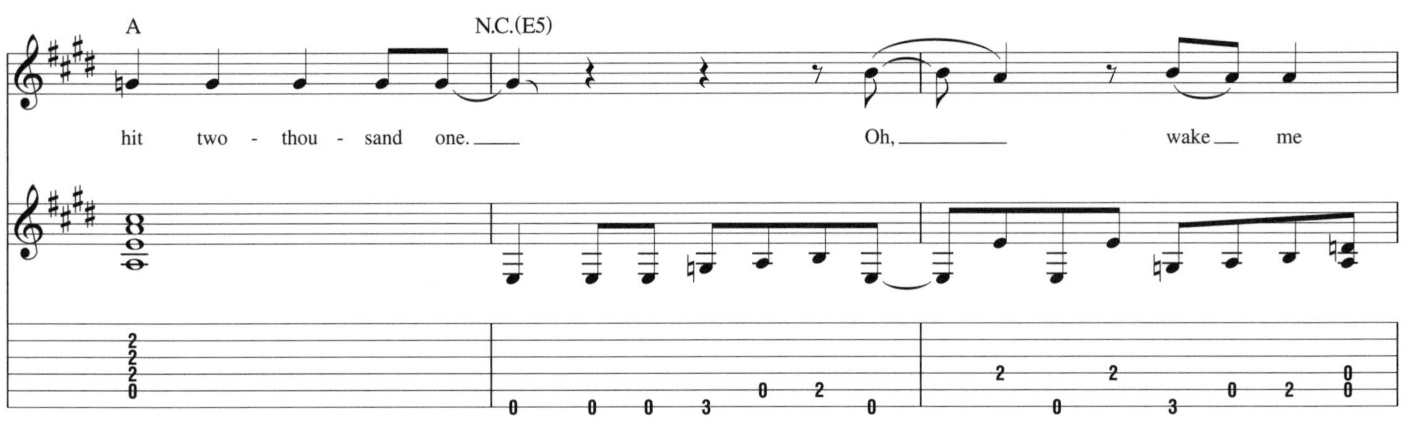
A
N.C.(E5)
hit two - thou - sand one.
Oh,
wake me

Gtr. 3: w/ Rhy. Fig. 2A
D
A
N.C.(E5)
up when we hit two - thou - sand one.
No,
1/4

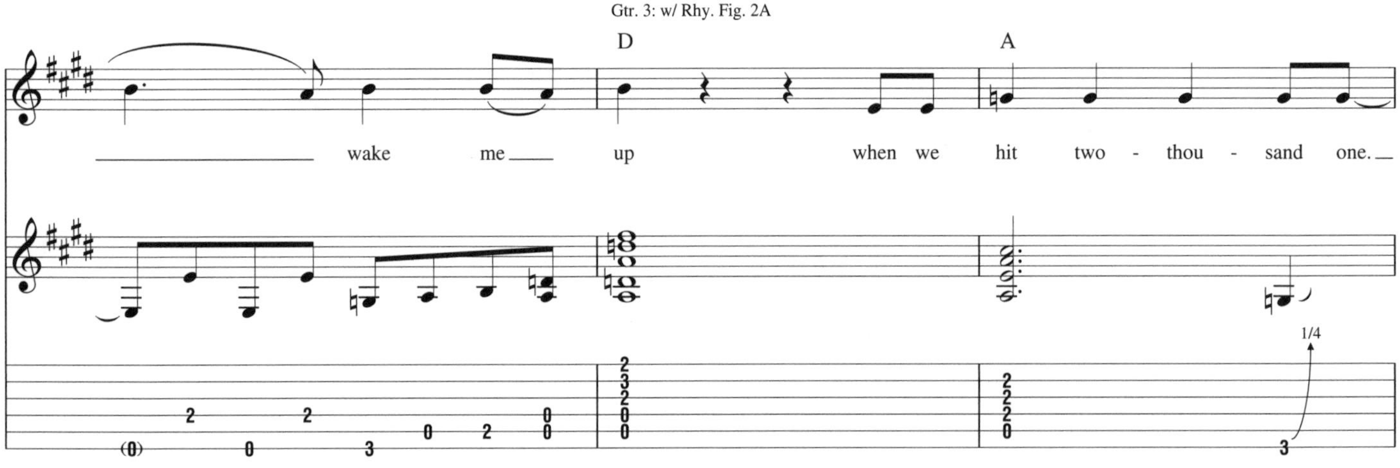
Gtr. 3: w/ Rhy. Fig. 2A
D
A
wake me up when we hit two - thou - sand one.
1/4

N.C.(E5)
Gtr. 3: w/ Rhy. Fig. 3A
D
Oh, wake me up when we

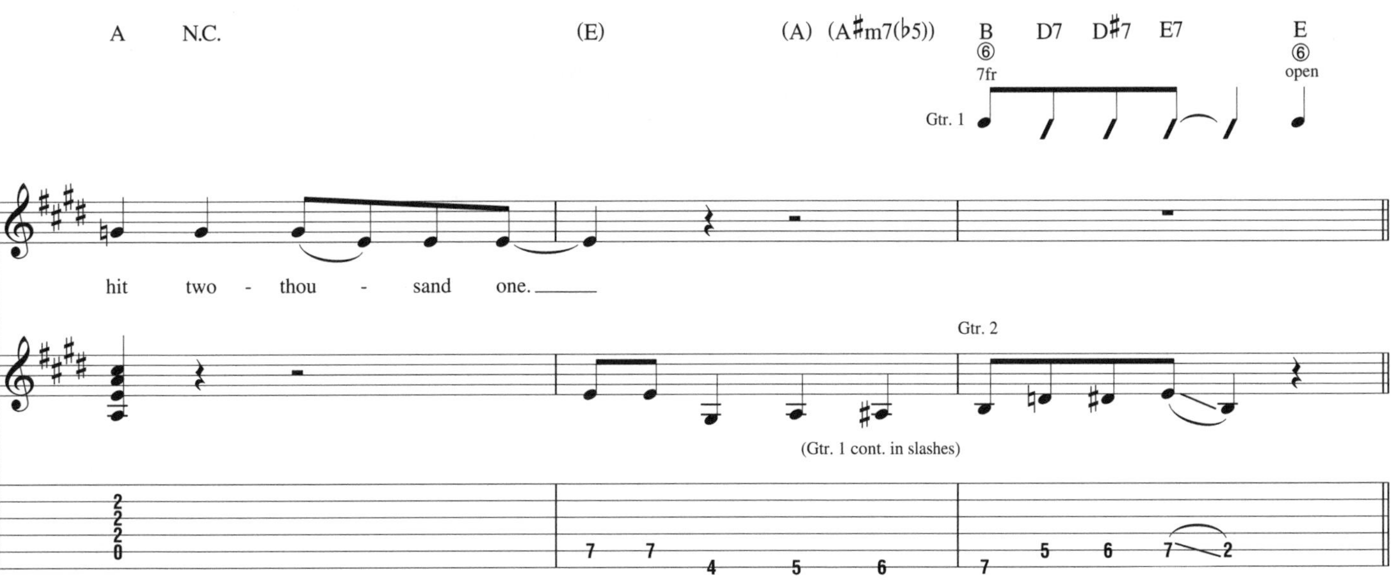
A
N.C.
(E)
(A) (A♯m7(♭5))
B
D7
D♯7
E7
E
7fr
open
Gtr. 1
hit two - thou - sand one.
Gtr. 2
(Gtr. 1 cont. in slashes)

Outro

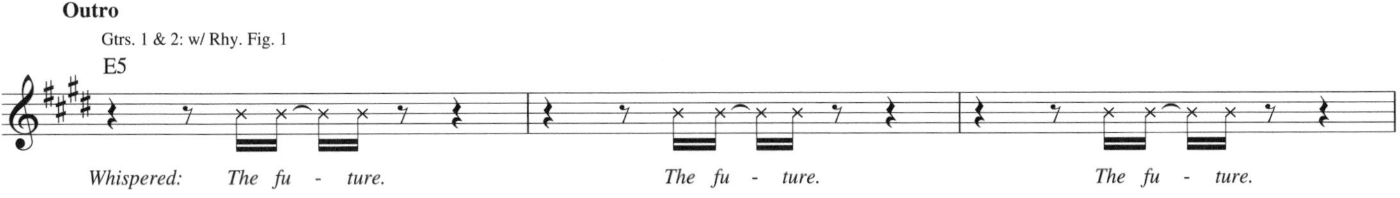
Gtrs. 1 & 2: w/ Rhy. Fig. 1
E5
Whispered: The fu - ture.
The fu - ture.
The fu - ture.

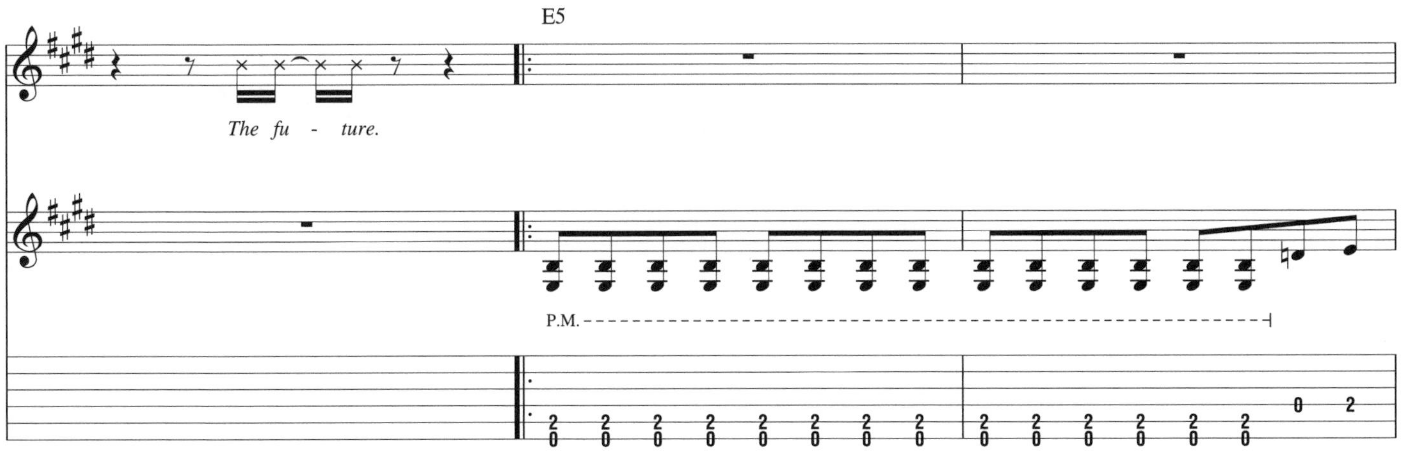
E5
The fu - ture.
P.M.

Play 3 times and fade
The fu - ture.
The fu - ture.
P.M.

from *Yes I Am*

Yes I Am

Words and Music by Melissa Etheridge

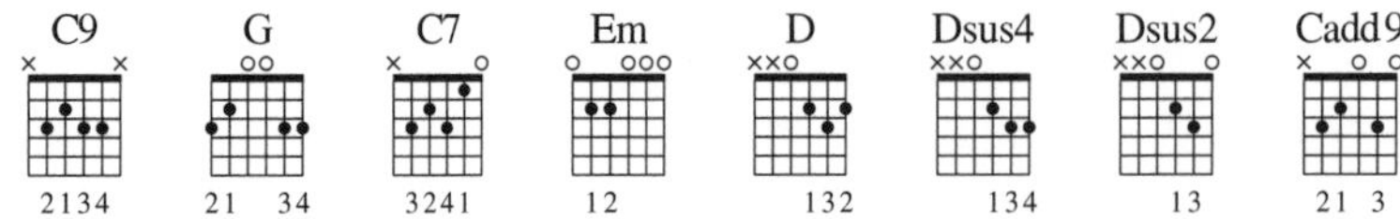

Intro

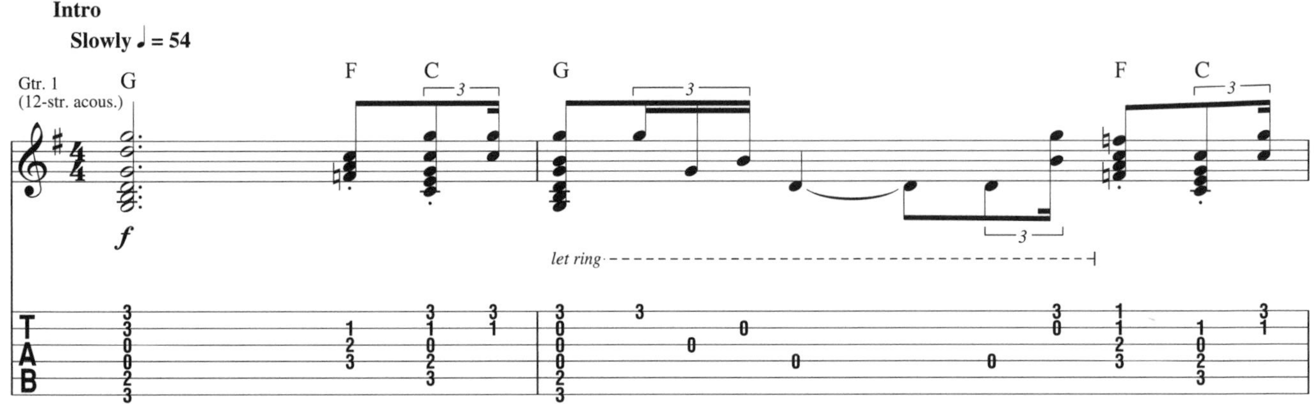

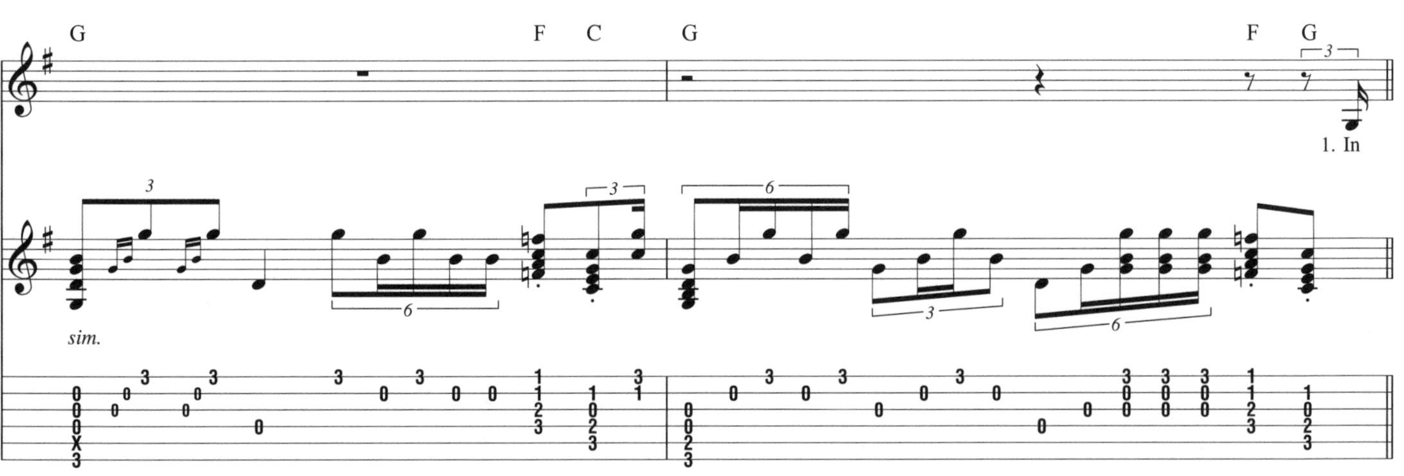

Verse

G
Fadd9
C
lov - ers come and check out in a hur - ry,
shal - low and hol-low a-gain.

C7
Come lay your bod - y be-side me,
to dream,
to sleep with the lamb.
To the

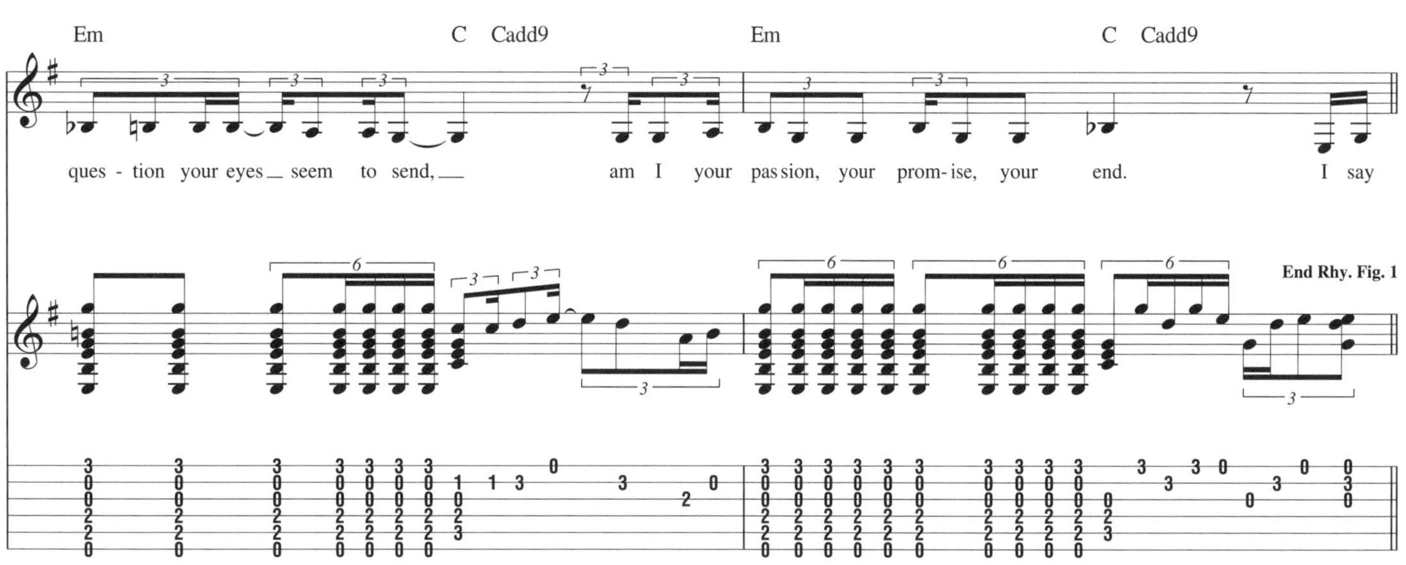
Em
C
Cadd9
ques - tion your eyes seem to send,
am I your pas sion, your prom - ise, your end.
I say
End Rhy. Fig. 1

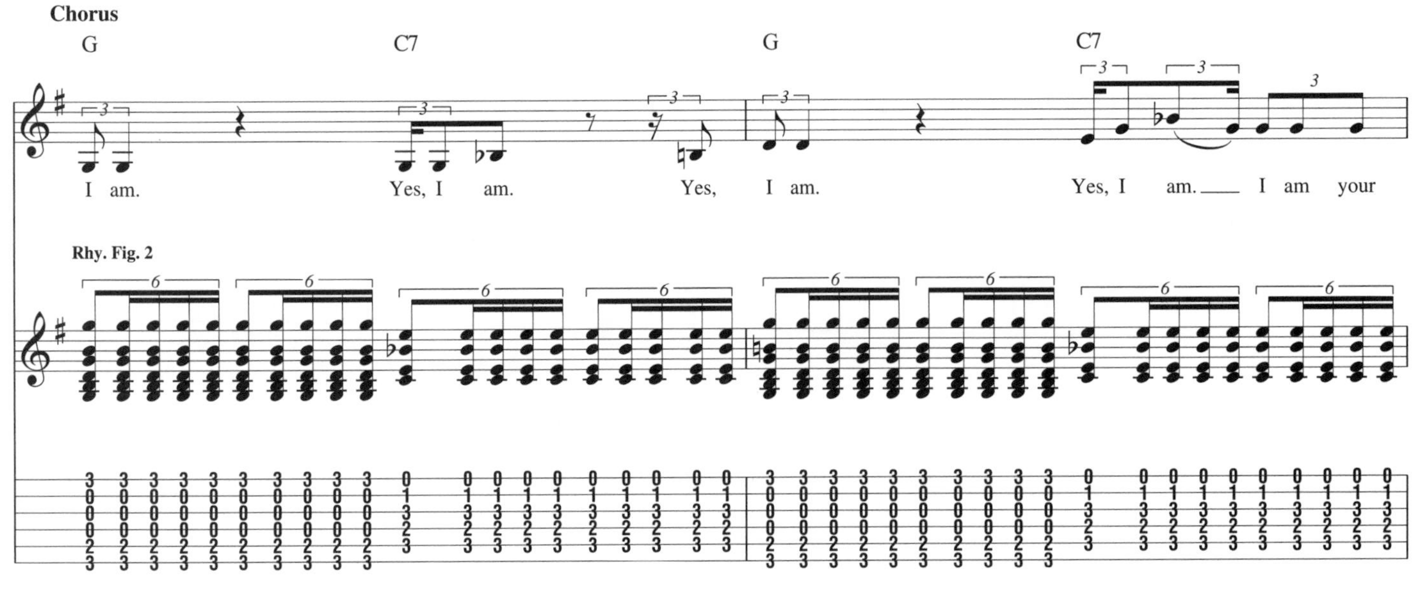
Chorus
G
C7
G
C7
I am. Yes, I am. Yes, I am. Yes, I am. I am your
Rhy. Fig. 2

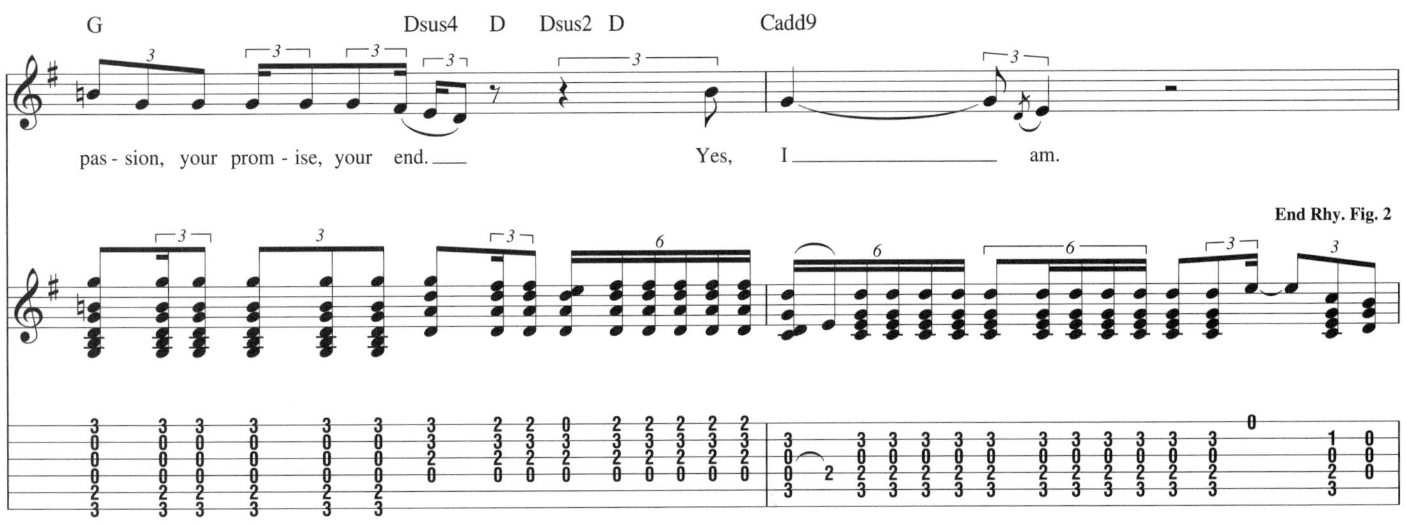
G
Dsus4 D Dsus2 D
Cadd9
pas - sion, your prom - ise, your end. Yes, I am.
End Rhy. Fig. 2

G
Fadd9 C
G
Fadd9 C

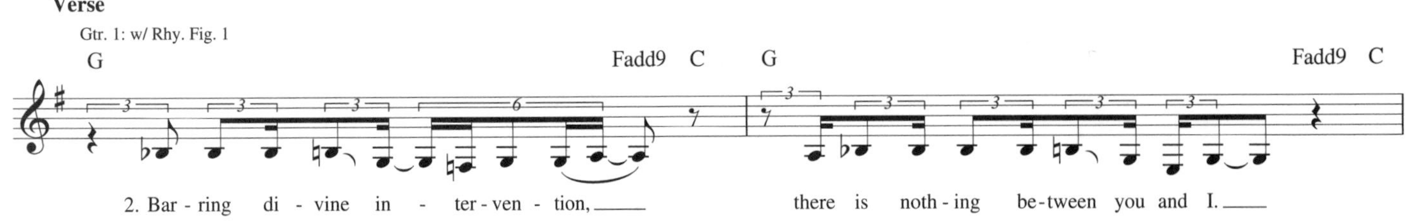
Verse
Gtr. 1: w/ Rhy. Fig. 1
G
Fadd9 C
G
Fadd9 C
2. Bar - ring di - vine in - ter - ven - tion, there is noth - ing be - tween you and I.

G
Fadd9 C
G
Fadd9 C
And if I care - less - ly for - got to men - tion
your bod - y, your pow - er can sanc - ti - fy.

C7
Come feed the hun - ger, the thirst.
Lay it down, the beast will die.
You can

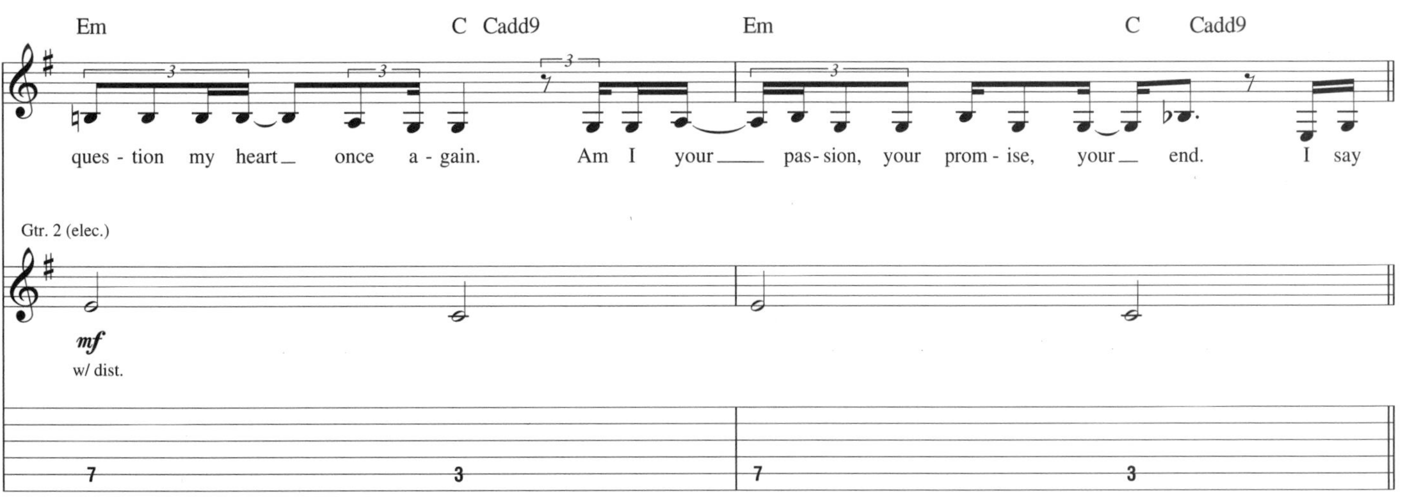
Em
C Cadd9
Em
C Cadd9
ques - tion my heart once a - gain.
Am I your pas - sion, your prom - ise, your end.
I say
Gtr. 2 (elec.)
mf
w/ dist.
7
3
7
3

Chorus

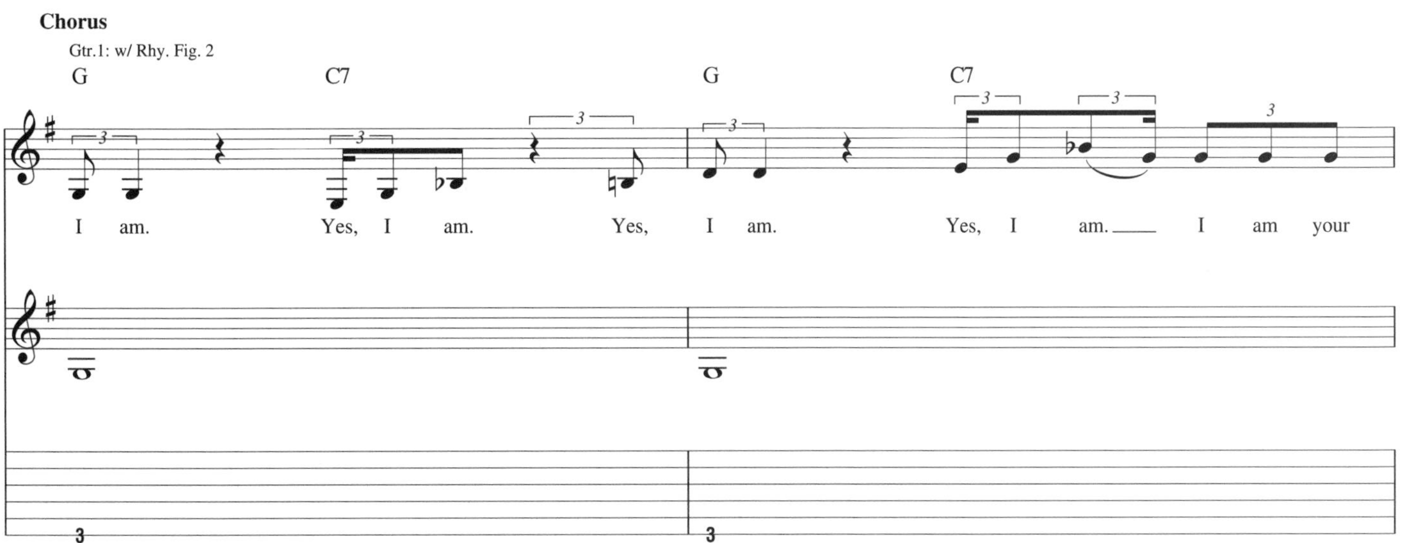
Gtr.1: w/ Rhy. Fig. 2
G
C7
G
C7
I am.
Yes, I am.
Yes, I am.
Yes, I am.
I am your
3
3

G
D
Dsus4
Cadd9
C9
Gtr. 3 (dist.)
mf
pas - sion, your prom - ise, your end.
Yes, I am.
Gtr. 2 tacet
G
Gtr. 3
Interlude
C7
Oh.
Em
C9

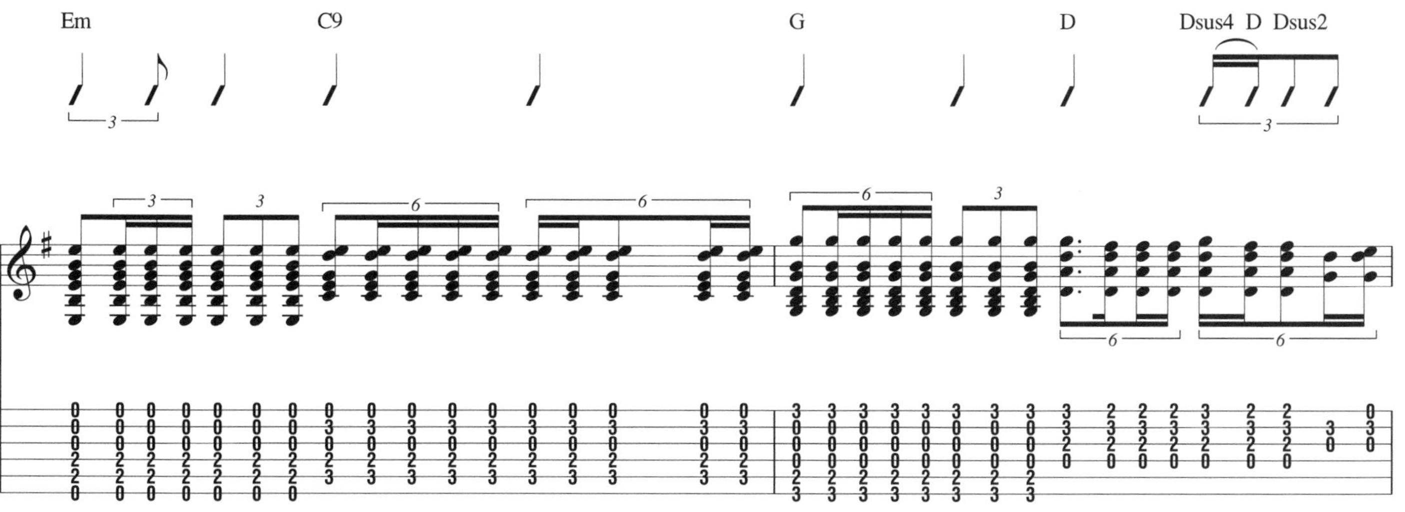
Em
C9
G
D
Dsus4 D Dsus2

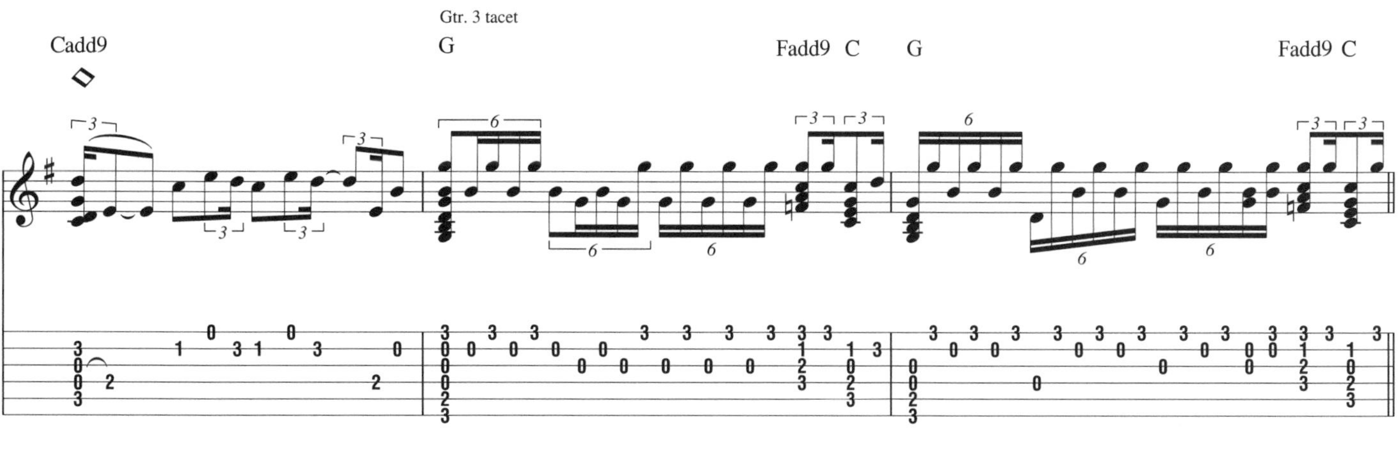
Cadd9
Gtr. 3 tacet
G
Fadd9 C
G
Fadd9 C

Verse

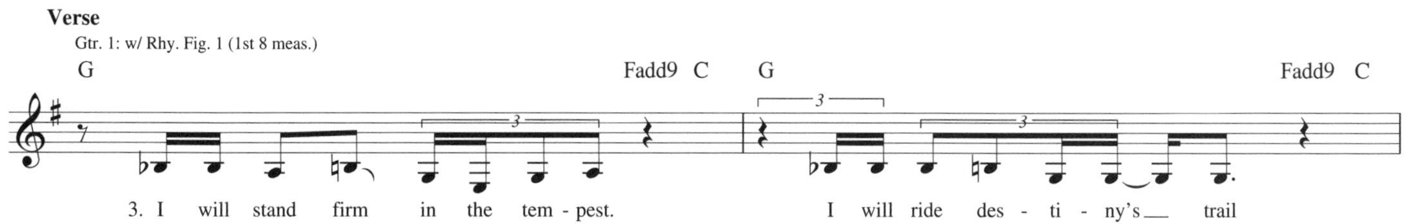
Gtr. 1: w/ Rhy. Fig. 1 (1st 8 meas.)
G
Fadd9 C
G
Fadd9 C
3. I will stand firm in the tem - pest.
I will ride des - ti - ny's trail

G
Fadd9 C
G
Fadd9 C
to be - lieve when the truth comes up emp - ty,
to hold and re - spect with - out fail.

C7
Come and be one in the mo-tion. A de-sire they can not com-pre-hend.

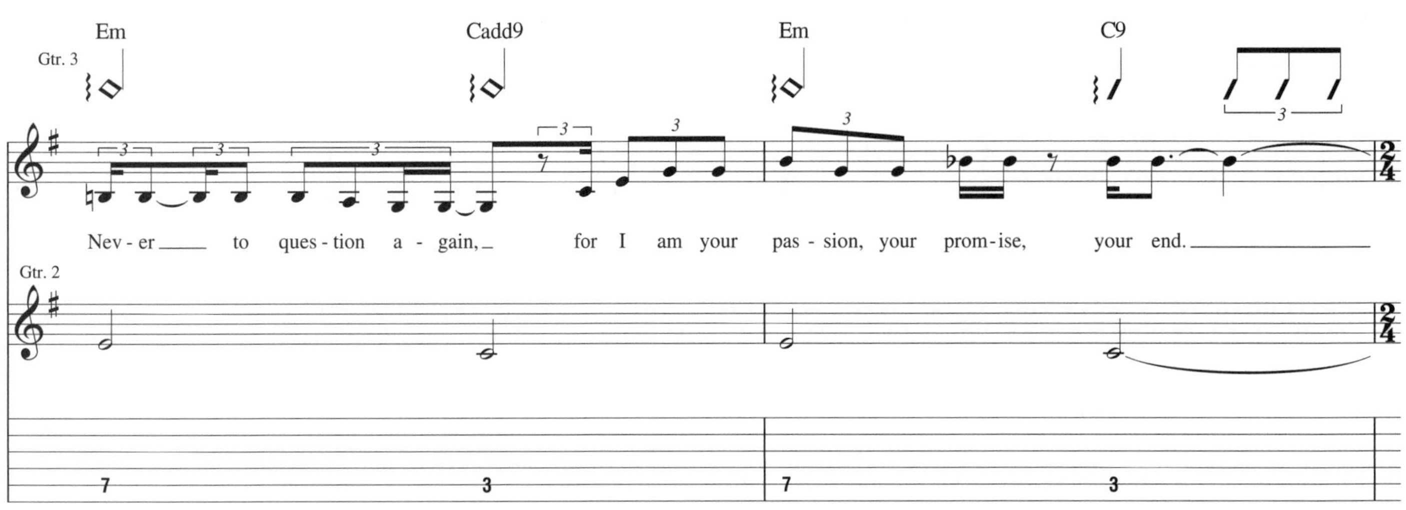
Em
Cadd9
Em
C9
Gtr. 3
Never to ques-tion a-gain, for I am your pas-sion, your prom-ise, your end.
Gtr. 2

Chorus

*C7
** Gtrs. 1 & 3
Gtr. 1: w/ Rhy. Fig. 2 (1st 2 meas.) (4 times)
G
C7
Rhy. Fig. 3A
Gtr. 3
Yes, I am. Oh, yes, I am. Oh,
Rhy. Fig. 3
* Gtr. 3 plays C9.
** Composite arrangement

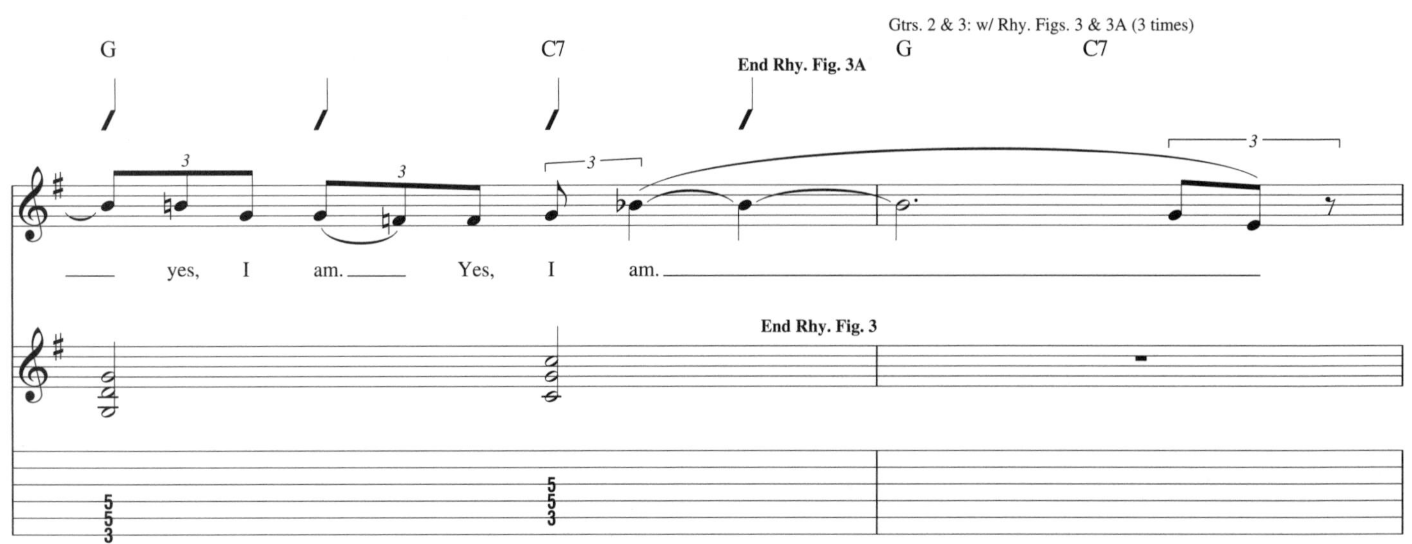
G
C7
End Rhy. Fig. 3A
Gtrs. 2 & 3: w/ Rhy. Figs. 3 & 3A (3 times)
G
C7
yes, I am. Yes, I am.
End Rhy. Fig. 3

G
C7
Yeah, yeah, yeah. Oh, yes, I am. Oh, yes, I am.
Yeah, yeah, yes, I am. Yes, I am. Yes, I am. Yes, I am.
Gtr. 3 tacet
Gtr. 3
D
Yes, I am.
Gtr. 1
Gtr. 2
Gtr. 4 (acous.)
divisi
let ring throughout
Begin Fade
Fade out

from *Your Little Secret*

Your Little Secret

Words and Music by Melissa Etheridge

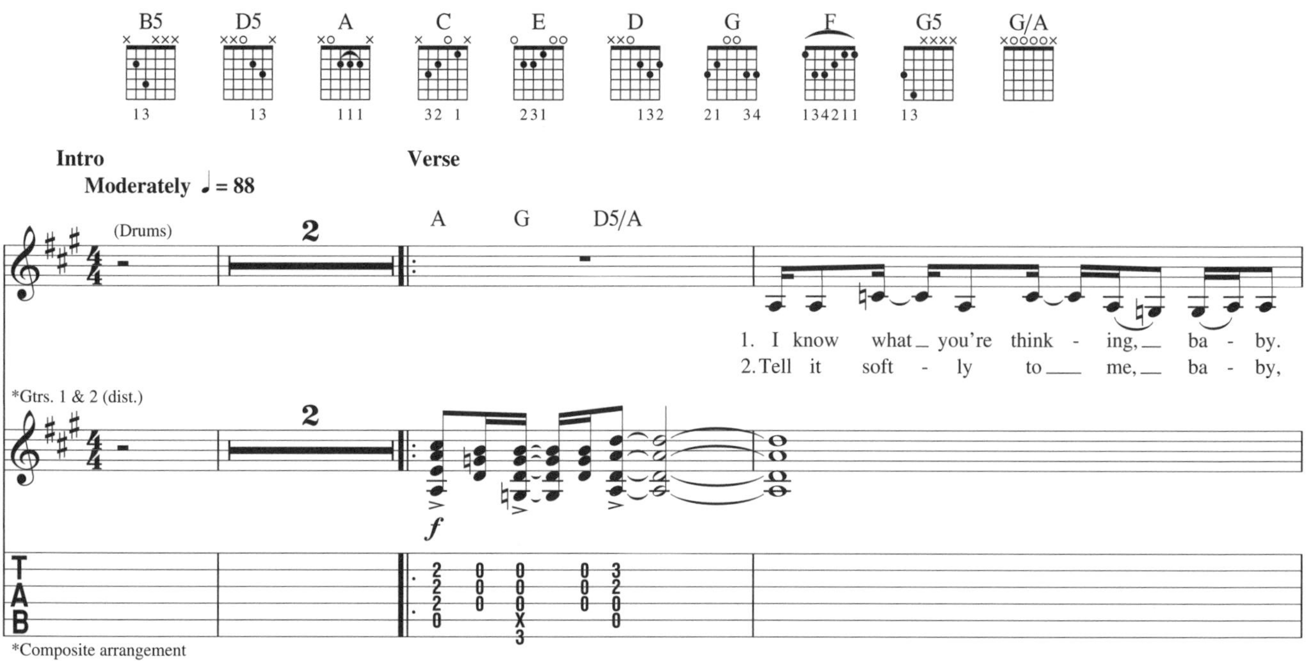

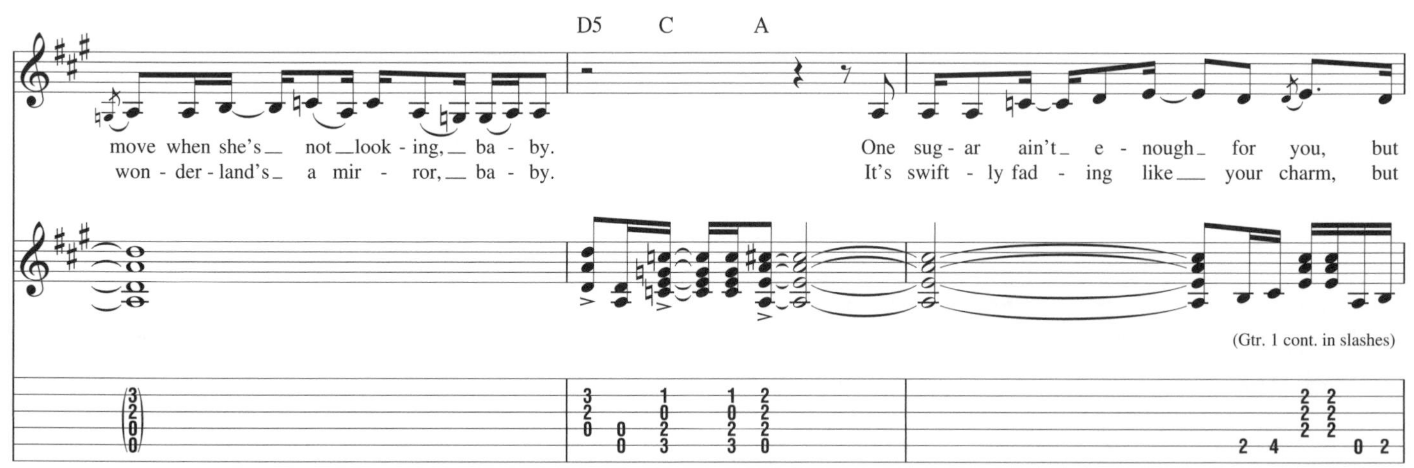

B5 D5 A

Gtr 1

you, you're tak - ing out your loans. You're bur - y - ing your bones be-fore your cov - er's blown.
you, you're step - ping out of line. You're spill - ing all the wine. Leave it on the vine,

Gtr. 3 (clean)

mp

let ring throughout

Gtr. 2

C E

You bet - ter take it home.
'cause I can't give you mine.

I

Chorus

Gtr. 3 tacet
A
D
G
D
Rhy. Fig. 1
End Rhy. Fig. 1
Gtr. 1
like the way you look. I know you like me, but
Gtr. 2
Rhy. Fig. 1A
End Rhy. Fig. 1A

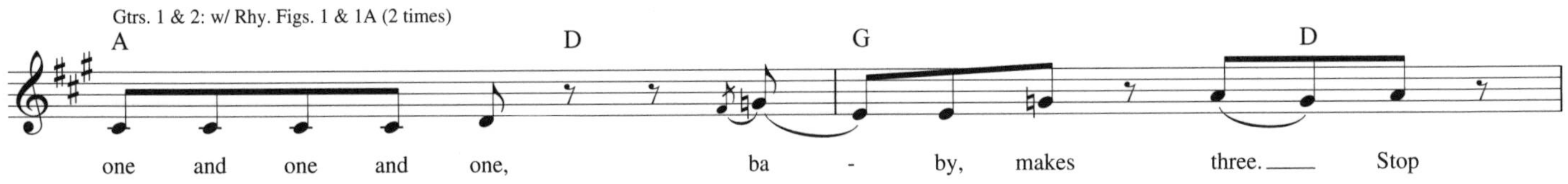

Gtrs. 1 & 2: w/ Rhy. Figs. 1 & 1A (2 times)
A
D
G
D
one and one and one, ba - by, makes three. Stop

A
D
G
D
play - ing those eyes if you want me to keep your lit - tle se -

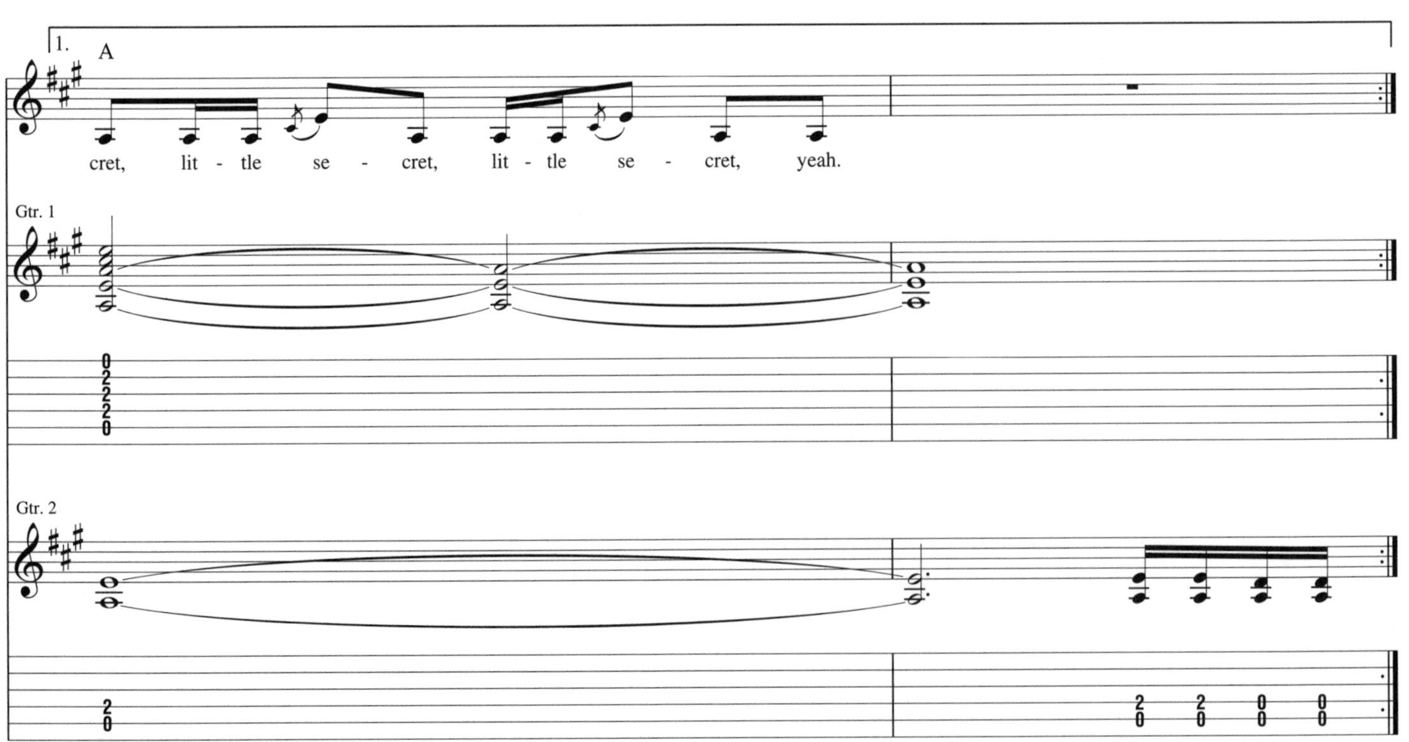

1.
A
cret, lit - tle se - cret, lit - tle se - cret, yeah.
Gtr. 1
Gtr. 2

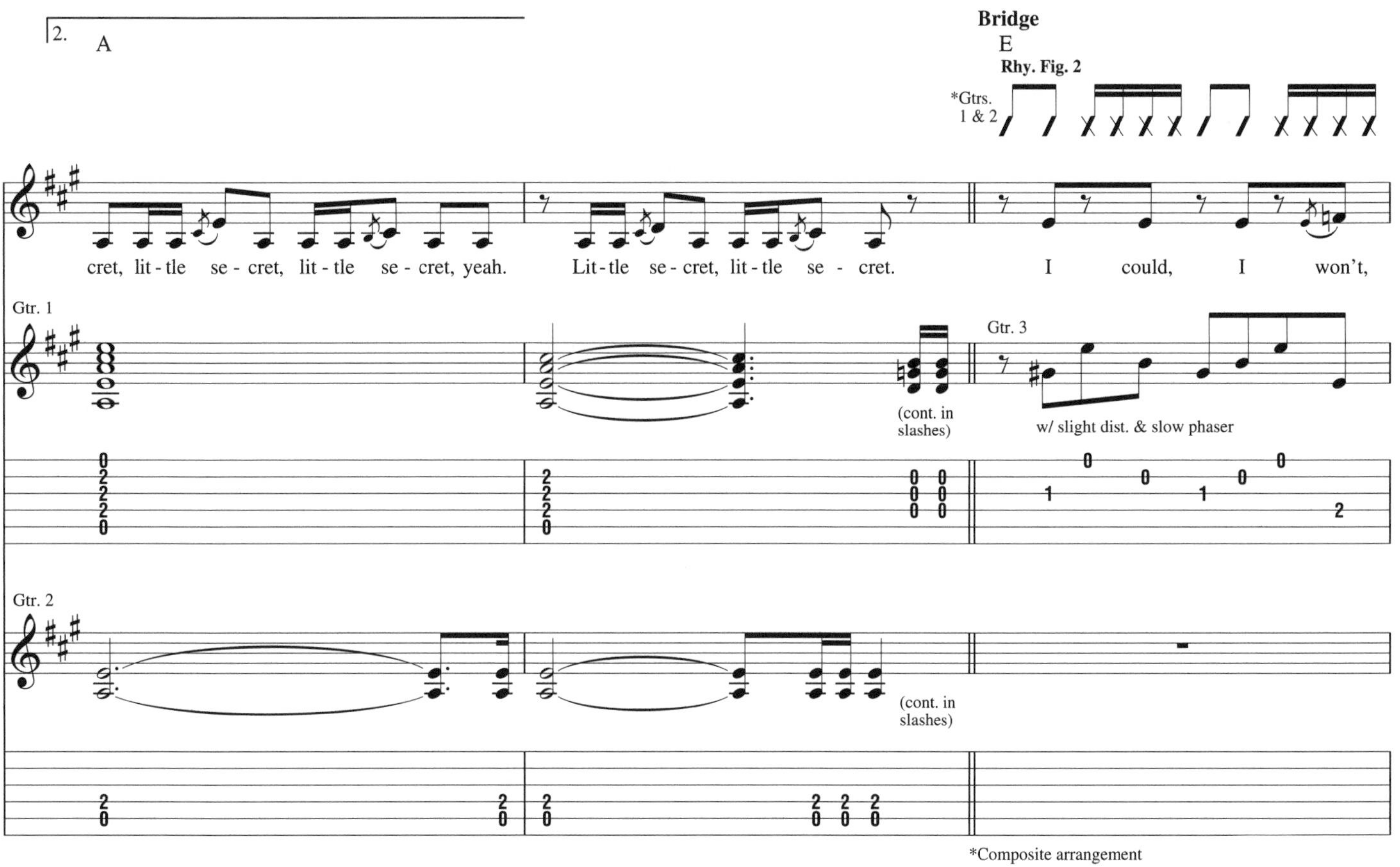
2.
A
Bridge
E
Rhy. Fig. 2
*Gtrs. 1 & 2
cret, lit-tle se-cret, lit-tle se-cret, yeah. Lit-tle se-cret, lit-tle se-cret. I could, I won't,
Gtr. 1
Gtr. 3
(cont. in slashes)
w/ slight dist. & slow phaser
Gtr. 2
(cont. in slashes)
*Composite arrangement

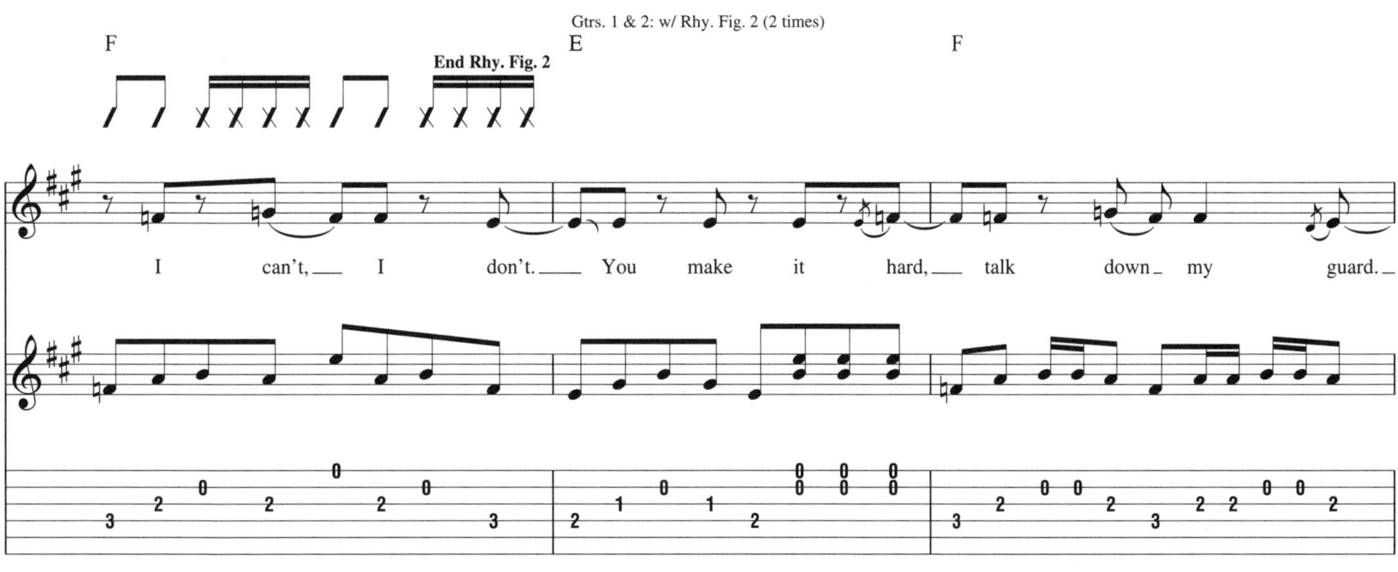
Gtrs. 1 & 2: w/ Rhy. Fig. 2 (2 times)
F
End Rhy. Fig. 2
E
F
I can't, I don't. You make it hard, talk down my guard.

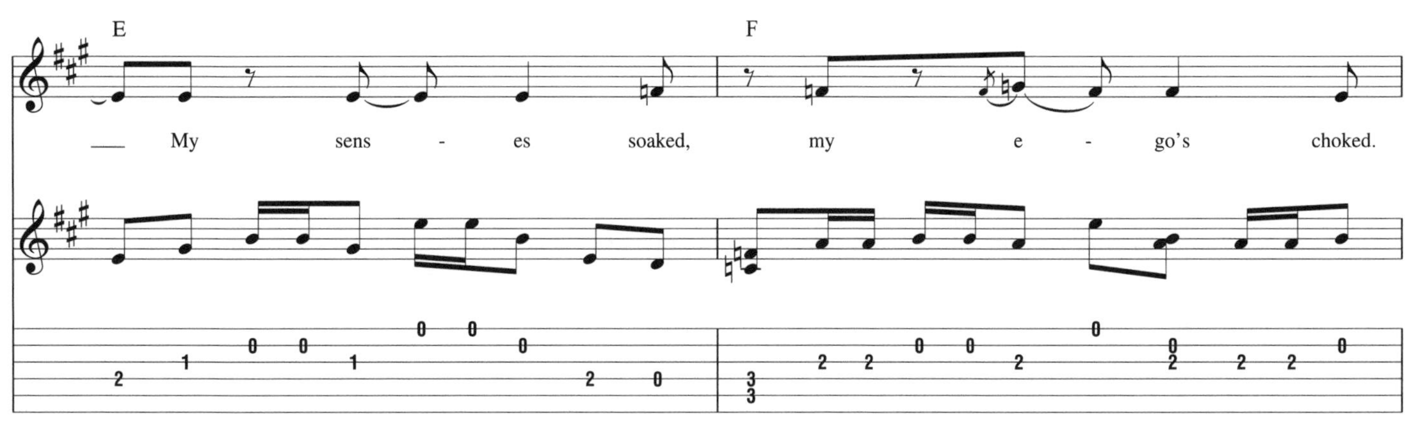
E
F
My sens - es soaked, my e - go's choked.

E
F
G5
Gtrs. 1 & 2
Gtr. 1
(Gtr. 2 cont. in notation)
I will not lie, I will not lie. I, I, I, ho.
Gtr. 3
Gtr. 2
Guitar Solo
Gtr. 1: w/ Rhy. Fig. 1 (4 times)
Gtr. 3 tacet
A
D
G
D
A
D
Gtr. 2
w/ bar
G
D
A
D
G
D
let ring
A
D
G
D
8va
loco

Chorus

Gtr. 1: w/ Rhy. Fig. 1 (2 times)
A D G D A D
like the way you look. I know you like me, but one and one and one, ba -

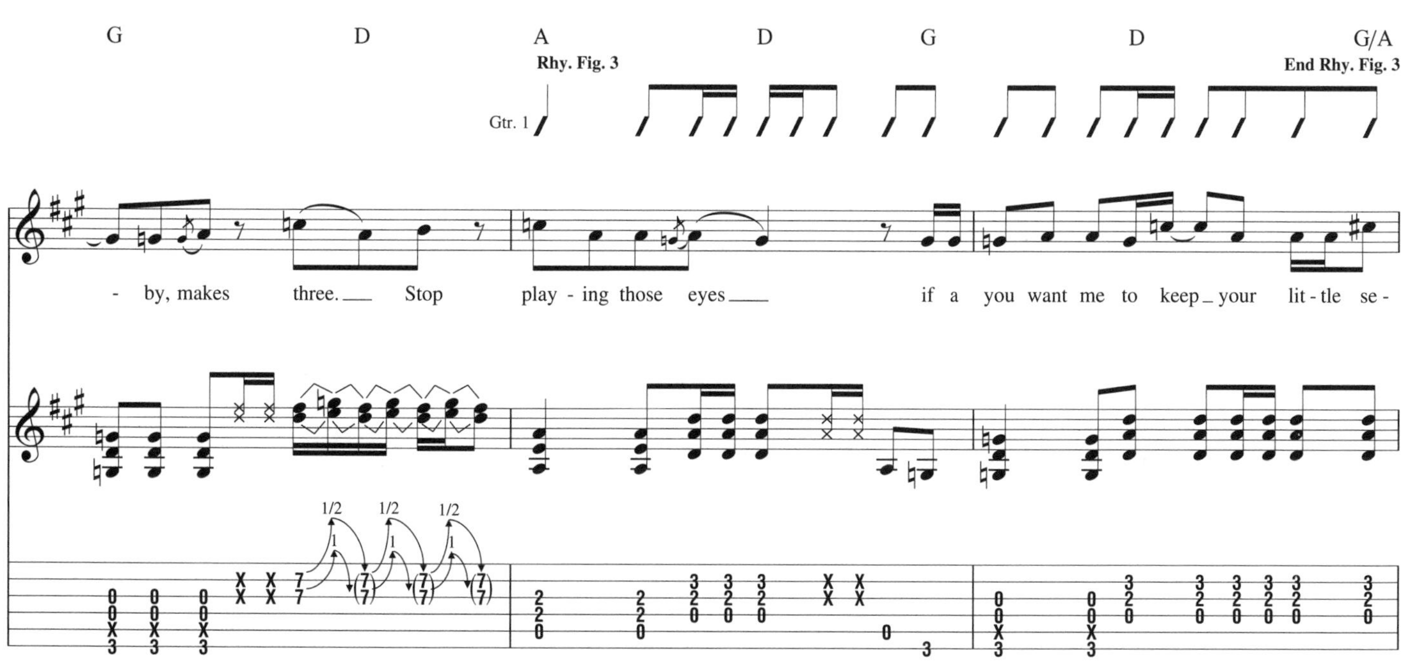

G D A D G D G/A
Rhy. Fig. 3
End Rhy. Fig. 3
Gtr. 1
- by, makes three. Stop play - ing those eyes if a you want me to keep your lit - tle se -

Gtr. 1: w/ Rhy. Fig. 3
A D G D G/A
cret, lit - tle se - cret, lit - tle se - cret, yeah. Lit - tle se - cret, lit - tle se - cret, yeah.
Rhy. Fig. 4
End Rhy. Fig. 4

Outro

Gtrs. 1 & 2: w/ Rhy. Figs. 3 & 4 (7 times)
A D G D G/A
Lit - tle se - cret, lit - tle se - cret, yeah. Lit - tle se - cret, lit - tle se - cret, yeah.
Rhy. Fig. 5
Gtr. 3
End Rhy. Fig. 5

Gtr. 3: w/ Rhy. Fig. 5 (6 times)
A D G D G/A A D G
Lit - tle se - cret, lit - tle se - cret, yeah. Lit - tle se - cret, lit - tle se - cret, now. Now, now, no, oh!

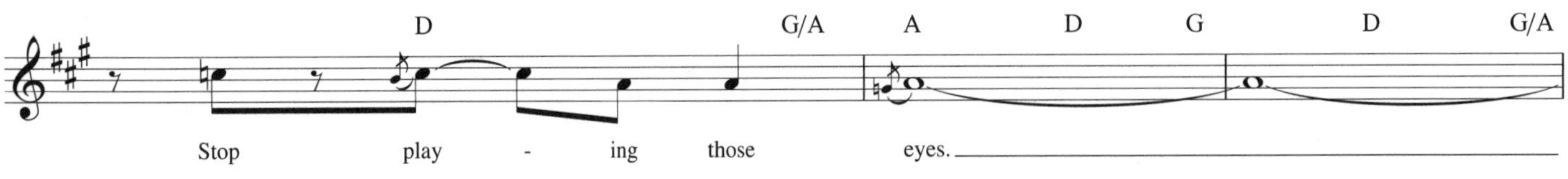
D G/A A D G D G/A
Stop play - ing those eyes.

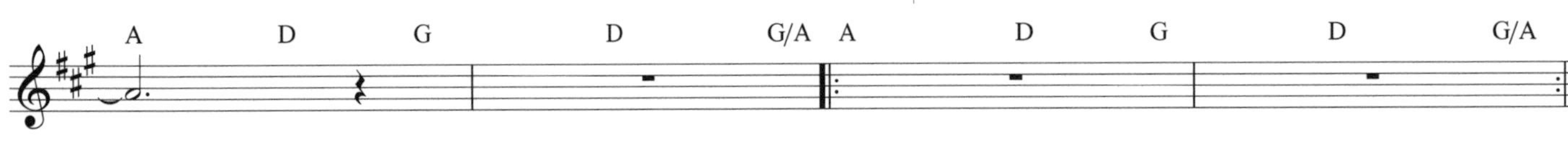
A D G D G/A A D G D G/A

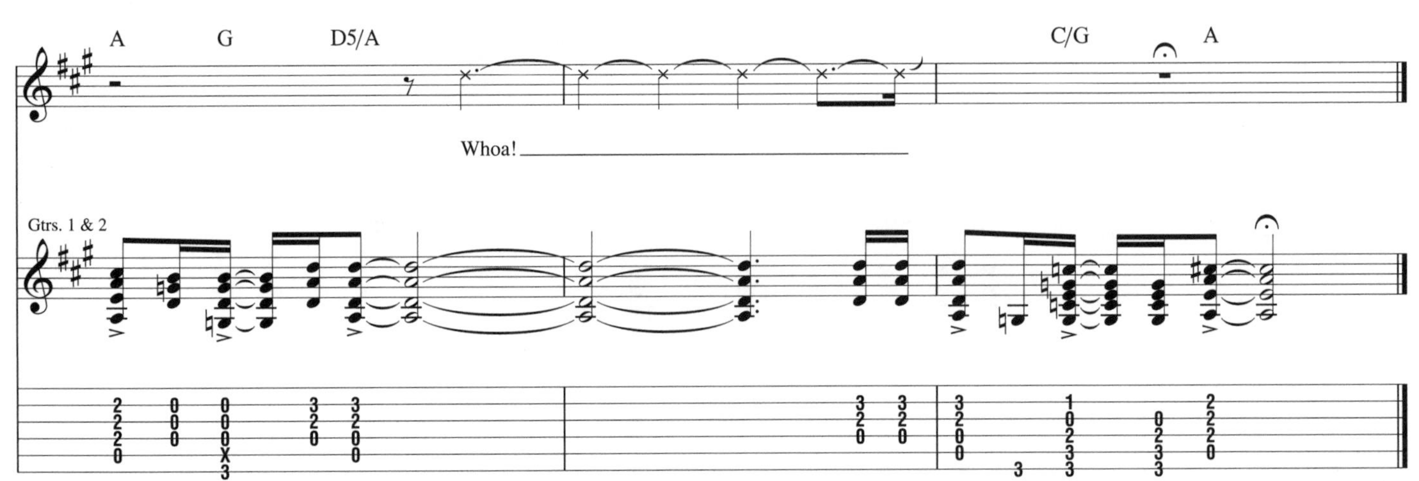
A G D5/A C/G A
Whoa!
Gtrs. 1 & 2

Guitar Notation Legend

Guitar Music can be notated three different ways: on a *musical staff*, in *tablature*, and in *rhythm slashes*.

RHYTHM SLASHES are written above the staff. Strum chords in the rhythm indicated. Use the chord diagrams found at the top of the first page of the transcription for the appropriate chord voicings. Round noteheads indicate single notes.

THE MUSICAL STAFF shows pitches and rhythms and is divided by bar lines into measures. Pitches are named after the first seven letters of the alphabet.

TABLATURE graphically represents the guitar fingerboard. Each horizontal line represents a string, and each number represents a fret.

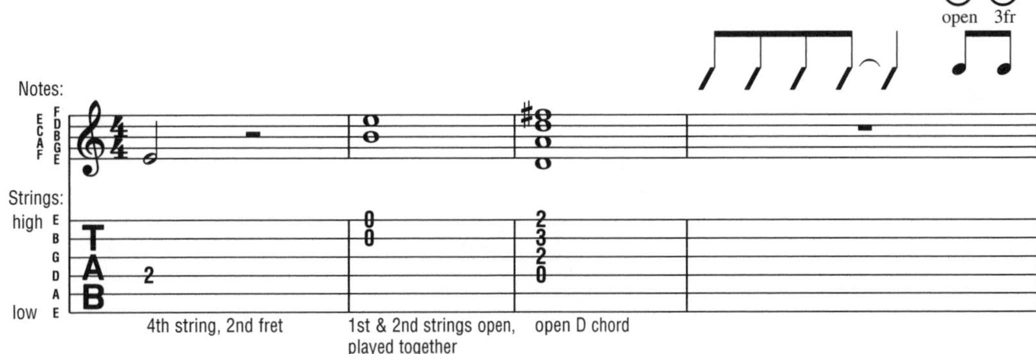

HALF-STEP BEND: Strike the note and bend up 1/2 step.

WHOLE-STEP BEND: Strike the note and bend up one step.

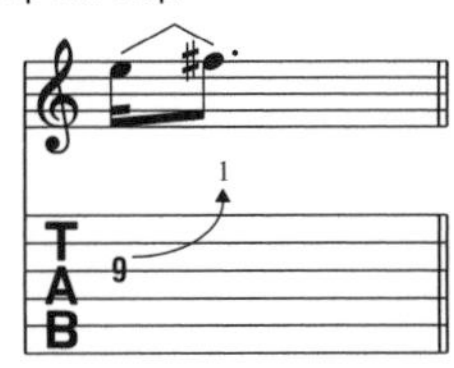

GRACE NOTE BEND: Strike the note and immediately bend up as indicated.

SLIGHT (MICROTONE) BEND: Strike the note and bend up 1/4 step.

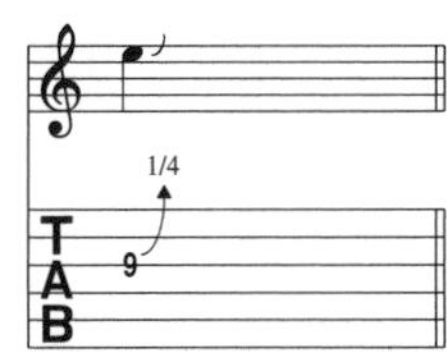

BEND AND RELEASE: Strike the note and bend up as indicated, then release back to the original note. Only the first note is struck.

PRE-BEND: Bend the note as indicated, then strike it.

VIBRATO: The string is vibrated by rapidly bending and releasing the note with the fretting hand.

WIDE VIBRATO: The pitch is varied to a greater degree by vibrating with the fretting hand.

HAMMER-ON: Strike the first (lower) note with one finger, then sound the higher note (on the same string) with another finger by fretting it without picking.

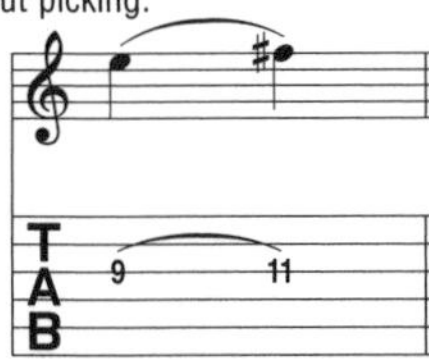

PULL-OFF: Place both fingers on the notes to be sounded. Strike the first note and without picking, pull the finger off to sound the second (lower) note.

LEGATO SLIDE: Strike the first note and then slide the same fret-hand finger up or down to the second note. The second note is not struck.

SHIFT SLIDE: Same as legato slide, except the second note is struck.

TRILL: Very rapidly alternate between the notes indicated by continuously hammering on and pulling off.

TAPPING: Hammer ("tap") the fret indicated with the pick-hand index or middle finger and pull off to the note fretted by the fret hand.

NATURAL HARMONIC: Strike the note while the fret-hand lightly touches the string directly over the fret indicated.

PINCH HARMONIC: The note is fretted normally and a harmonic is produced by adding the edge of the thumb or the tip of the index finger of the pick hand to the normal pick attack.

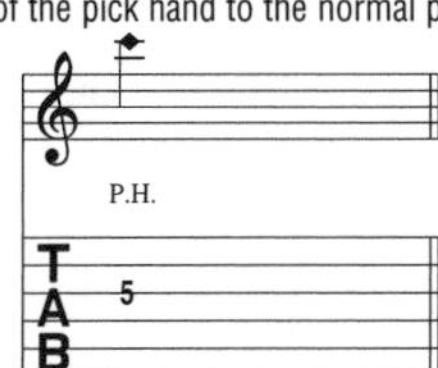

PICK SCRAPE: The edge of the pick is rubbed down (or up) the string, producing a scratchy sound.

MUFFLED STRINGS: A percussive sound is produced by laying the fret hand across the string(s) without depressing, and striking them with the pick hand.

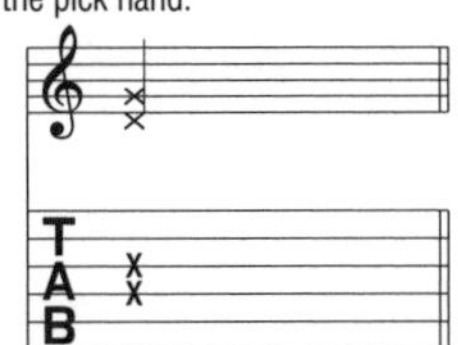

PALM MUTING: The note is partially muted by the pick hand lightly touching the string(s) just before the bridge.

RAKE: Drag the pick across the strings indicated with a single motion.

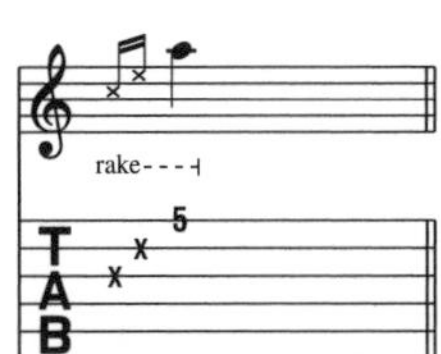

TREMOLO PICKING: The note is picked as rapidly and continuously as possible.

VIBRATO BAR DIVE AND RETURN: The pitch of the note or chord is dropped a specified number of steps (in rhythm) then returned to the original pitch.

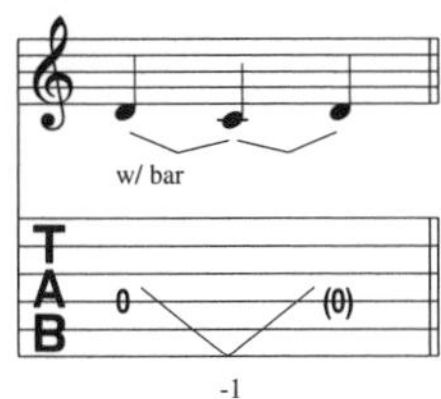

VIBRATO BAR SCOOP: Depress the bar just before striking the note, then quickly release the bar.

VIBRATO BAR DIP: Strike the note and then immediately drop a specified number of steps, then release back to the original pitch.

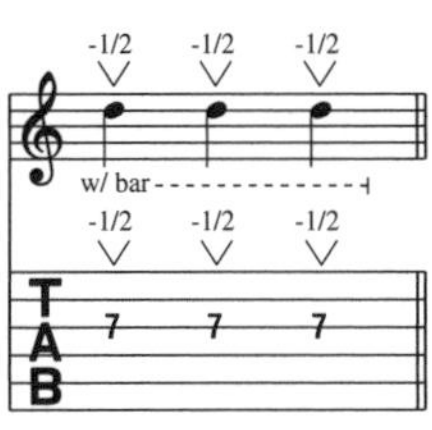

RECORDED VERSIONS GUITAR®

RECORDED VERSIONS

The Best Note-For-Note Transcriptions Available

ALL BOOKS INCLUDE TABLATURE

00690501 Adams, Bryan – Greatest Hits $19.95
00692015 Aerosmith – Greatest Hits $22.95
00690488 Aerosmith – Just Push Play $19.95
00690178 Alice in Chains – Acoustic $19.95
00694865 Alice in Chains – Dirt $19.95
00694925 Alice in Chains – Jar of Flies/Sap $19.95
00690387 Alice in Chains – Nothing Safe – The Best of the Box $19.95
00694932 Allman Brothers Band – Volume 1 .... $24.95
00694933 Allman Brothers Band – Volume 2 .... $24.95
00694934 Allman Brothers Band – Volume 3 .... $24.95
00690513 American Hi-Fi $19.95
00694878 Atkins, Chet – Vintage Fingerstyle $19.95
00690418 Audio Adrenaline, Best of $17.95
00690366 Bad Company Original Anthology - Bk 1 .... $19.95
00690367 Bad Company Original Anthology - Bk 2 .... $19.95
00694929 Beatles: 1962-1966 .... $24.95
00694930 Beatles: 1967-1970 .... $24.95
00694880 Beatles – Abbey Road $19.95
00690110 Beatles – Book 1 (White Album) $19.95
00694832 Beatles – For Acoustic Guitar $19.95
00660140 Beatles – Guitar Book $19.95
00694863 Beatles – Sgt. Pepper's Lonely Hearts Club Band $19.95
00690397 Beck – Midnite Vultures $19.95
00694884 Benson, George – Best of $19.95
00692385 Berry, Chuck $19.95
00692200 Black Sabbath – We Sold Our Soul for Rock 'N' Roll $19.95
00690305 Blink 182 – Dude Ranch $19.95
00690389 Blink 182 – Enema of the State $19.95
00690523 Blink 182 – Take Off Your Pants & Jacket $19.95
00690028 Blue Oyster Cult – Cult Classics $19.95
00690168 Buchanan, Roy – Collection $19.95
00690491 Bowie, David – Best of $19.95
00690451 Buckley, Jeff – Collection $24.95
00690364 Cake – Songbook $19.95
00690293 Chapman, Steven Curtis – Best of $19.95
00690043 Cheap Trick – Best of $19.95
00690171 Chicago – Definitive Guitar Collection $22.95
00690415 Clapton Chronicles – Best of Eric Clapton $18.95
00690393 Clapton, Eric – Selections from Blues $19.95
00690074 Clapton, Eric – The Cream of Clapton $24.95
00690010 Clapton, Eric – From the Cradle $19.95
00660139 Clapton, Eric – Journeyman $19.95
00694869 Clapton, Eric – Unplugged $22.95
00694896 Clapton, Eric/John Mayall – Bluesbreakers $19.95
00690162 Clash, Best of $19.95
00690494 Coldplay – Parachutes $19.95
00694940 Counting Crows – August & Everything After $19.95
00694840 Cream – Disraeli Gears $19.95
00690401 Creed – Human Clay $19.95
00690352 Creed – My Own Prison $19.95
00690484 dc Talk – Intermission: The Greatest Hits $19.95
00690289 Deep Purple, Best of $17.95
00690384 Di Franco, Ani – Best of $19.95
00690322 Di Franco, Ani – Little Plastic Castle $19.95
00690380 Di Franco, Ani – Up Up Up Up Up Up $19.95
00695382 Dire Straits – Sultans of Swing $19.95
00690347 Doors, The – Anthology $22.95
00690348 Doors, The – Essential Guitar Collection $16.95
00690524 Etheridge, Melissa – Skin $19.95
00690349 Eve 6 .... $19.95
00690496 Everclear, Best of $19.95
00690515 Extreme II – Pornograffitti $19.95
00690323 Fastball – All the Pain Money Can Buy $19.95
00690235 Foo Fighters – The Colour and the Shape $19.95
00690394 Foo Fighters – There Is Nothing Left to Lose $19.95
00690222 G3 Live – Satriani, Vai, Johnson $22.95
00690536 Garbage – Beautiful Garbage $19.95
00690438 Genesis Guitar Anthology $19.95
00690338 Goo Goo Dolls – Dizzy Up the Girl $19.95
00690114 Guy, Buddy – Collection Vol. A-J $22.95
00690193 Guy, Buddy – Collection Vol. L-Y $22.95
00694798 Harrison, George – Anthology $19.95
00692930 Hendrix, Jimi – Are You Experienced? $24.95
00692931 Hendrix, Jimi – Axis: Bold As Love $22.95
00694944 Hendrix, Jimi – Blues $24.95
00692932 Hendrix, Jimi – Electric Ladyland $24.95
00690218 Hendrix, Jimi – First Rays of the New Rising Sun $27.95
00690017 Hendrix, Jimi – Woodstock $24.95
00660029 Holly, Buddy $19.95
00690054 Hootie & The Blowfish – Cracked Rear View $19.95
00690457 Incubus – Make Yourself $19.95
00690544 Incubus – Morningview $19.95
00690136 Indigo Girls – 1200 Curfews $22.95
00694833 Joel, Billy – For Guitar $19.95
00694912 Johnson, Eric – Ah Via Musicom $19.95
00694799 Johnson, Robert – At the Crossroads $19.95
00690271 Johnson, Robert – The New Transcriptions $24.95
00699131 Joplin, Janis – Best of $19.95
00693185 Judas Priest – Vintage Hits $19.95
00690444 King, B.B. and Eric Clapton – Riding with the King $19.95
00690339 Kinks, The – Best of $19.95
00690279 Liebert, Ottmar + Luna Negra – Opium Highlights $19.95
00694755 Malmsteen, Yngwie – Rising Force $19.95
00694956 Marley, Bob – Legend $19.95
00694945 Marley, Bob – Songs of Freedom $24.95
00690283 McLachlan, Sarah – Best of $19.95
00690382 McLachlan, Sarah – Mirrorball $19.95
00690442 Matchbox 20 – Mad Season $19.95
00690239 Matchbox 20 – Yourself or Someone Like You $19.95
00694952 Megadeth – Countdown to Extinction $19.95
00690391 Megadeth – Risk $19.95
00694951 Megadeth – Rust in Peace $22.95
00690495 Megadeth – The World Needs a Hero $19.95
00690040 Miller, Steve, Band – Greatest Hits $19.95
00690448 MxPx – The Ever Passing Moment $19.95
00690189 Nirvana – From the Muddy Banks of the Wishkah $19.95
00694913 Nirvana – In Utero $19.95
00694883 Nirvana – Nevermind $19.95
00690026 Nirvana – Unplugged™ in New York $19.95
00690121 Oasis – (What's the Story) Morning Glory $19.95
00690358 Offspring, The – Americana $19.95
00690485 Offspring, The – Conspiracy of One $19.95
00690203 Offspring, The – Smash $18.95
00694847 Osbourne, Ozzy – Best of $22.95
00694830 Osbourne, Ozzy – No More Tears $19.95
00690538 Oysterhead – The Grand Pecking Order $19.95
00694855 Pearl Jam – Ten $19.95
00690439 Perfect Circle, A – Mer De Noms $19.95
00690176 Phish – Billy Breathes $22.95
00690424 Phish – Farmhouse $19.95
00690240 Phish – Hoist $19.95
00690331 Phish – Story of the Ghost $19.95
00690428 Pink Floyd – Dark Side of the Moon $19.95
00690456 P.O.D. – The Fundamental Elements of Southtown $19.95
00693864 Police, The – Best of $19.95
00690299 Presley, Elvis – Best of Elvis: The King of Rock 'n' Roll $19.95
00694975 Queen – Greatest Hits $24.95
00694910 Rage Against the Machine $19.95
00690395 Rage Against the Machine – The Battle of Los Angeles $19.95
00690145 Rage Against the Machine – Evil Empire $19.95
00690478 Rage Against the Machine – Renegades $19.95
00690426 Ratt – Best of $19.95
00690055 Red Hot Chili Peppers – Bloodsugarsexmagik $19.95
00690379 Red Hot Chili Peppers – Californication $19.95
00690090 Red Hot Chili Peppers – One Hot Minute $22.95
00694899 R.E.M. – Automatic for the People $19.95
00690014 Rolling Stones – Exile on Main Street $24.95
00690135 Rush, Otis – Collection $19.95
00690502 Saliva – Every Six Seconds $19.95
00690031 Santana's Greatest Hits $19.95
00120123 Shepherd, Kenny Wayne – Trouble Is $19.95
00690419 Slipknot $19.95
00690530 Slipknot – Iowa $19.95
00690330 Social Distortion – Live at the Roxy $19.95
00690385 Sonicflood $19.95
00694957 Stewart, Rod – Unplugged...And Seated $22.95
00690021 Sting – Fields of Gold $19.95
00690519 Sum 41 – All Killer No Filler $19.95
00690425 System of a Down $19.95
00690531 System of a Down – Toxicity $19.95
00694824 Taylor, James – Best of $16.95
00690238 Third Eye Blind $19.95
00690403 Third Eye Blind – Blue $19.95
00690295 Tool – Aenima $19.95
00690039 Vai, Steve – Alien Love Secrets $24.95
00690343 Vai, Steve – Flex-able Leftovers $19.95
00660137 Vai, Steve – Passion & Warfare $24.95
00690392 Vai, Steve – The Ultra Zone $19.95
00690370 Vaughan, Stevie Ray and Double Trouble – The Real Deal: Greatest Hits Volume 2 .... $22.95
00690455 Vaughan, Stevie Ray – Blues at Sunrise $19.95
00690116 Vaughan, Stevie Ray – Guitar Collection $24.95
00660136 Vaughan, Stevie Ray – In Step $19.95
00660058 Vaughan, Stevie Ray – Lightnin' Blues 1983-1987 .... $24.95
00690417 Vaughan, Stevie Ray – Live at Carnegie Hall $19.95
00694835 Vaughan, Stevie Ray – The Sky Is Crying $22.95
00690015 Vaughan, Stevie Ray – Texas Flood $19.95
00120026 Walsh, Joe – Look What I Did... .... $24.95
00694789 Waters, Muddy – Deep Blues $24.95
00690071 Weezer $19.95
00690516 Weezer (The Green Album) $19.95
00690286 Weezer – Pinkerton $19.95
00690447 Who, The – Best of $24.95
00690320 Williams, Dar – Best of $17.95
00690319 Wonder, Stevie – Some of the Best $17.95
00690443 Zappa, Frank – Hot Rats $19.95